A History of Icelandic Literature

A HISTORY

OF

ICELANDIC LITERATURE

BY

Stefán Einarsson

THE JOHNS HOPKINS PRESS
for
The American-Scandinavian Foundation

NEW YORK

1957

© 1957 by The Johns Hopkins Press, Baltimore 18, Md.
Distributed in Great Britain by Oxford University Press, London
Printed in the U. S. A. by J. H. Furst Co., Baltimore
Library of Congress Catalog Card Number 57–9519
Second printing, 1959

In Memory of my Wife

MARGARETHE E. SCHWARZENBERG

May 26, 1892–January 7, 1953

Preface

It was in the spring of 1945 that Dr. Henry Goddard Leach asked me to write this history for the American-Scandinavian Foundation. I agreed with some misgivings, for I thought that it might take five years; the misgivings were apparently well founded. In some cases (e. g. the Eddic poems) the materials were embarrassingly rich, in other cases (e. g., the late medieval sacred poetry) too meager.

As in the case of most of my work on Icelandic literature, I found my materials in the Icelandic Collection of the Cornell University Library. Indeed, most of this history has been written there during my summer vacations. The summer of 1951 was, however, spent in Iceland (with a grant from the American Philosophical Society at Philadelphia) to collect books and information about authors, especially of the period 1940–50, and to consult with professors of literature at the University of Iceland, especially Sigurður Nordal, Einar Ól. Sveinsson, and Steingrímur J. Þorsteinsson, about their special fields. I am sure that the book is the better for what I learned from them.

For the period 1800–1940 I leaned heavily on my own work and that of Professor Richard Beck, published in *Islandica* in 1948 and 1950 respectively. For this I want to thank him and the publishers (Cornell University Library and Press). Yet I hope on the one hand that I have been able to avoid too direct borrowing and on the other that I have succeeded in correcting some errors in the picture of modern literary development which I had tentatively drawn up in 1948. If so, it will be due to special studies in this period appearing later than my book, especially Steingrímur J. Þorsteinsson's *Einar Benediktsson* and Kristinn E. Andrésson's literary history of the period 1918–1948.

Thanks are due to Icelandic authors and publishers for generosity in providing me with books, likewise to the Rector, the Librarian, and many professors at the University of Iceland for hospitality and help.

I owe thanks, too, to the Head of the Cornell University Library and his staff, but especially to Professor Emeritus Halldór Hermannsson and to the Curator of the Icelandic Collection, Jóhann S. Hannesson, for reading and criticizing my manuscript. I am grateful to Dr. Henry

Goddard Leach for reading the manuscript and for much encouragement while the book was in the making.

I am indebted to my old friend and student John G. Allee for making the index.

But to no one do I owe as much as to my deceased wife, who was more than "my second hand" in all my scholarly work. Without her handwritten card-index of the Icelandic periodicals, it would have been hard for me, if not impossible, to do what work I have done on the literary history of Iceland. It is therefore only fitting that I should dedicate this work to her memory.

STEFÁN EINARSSON

The Johns Hopkins University
Baltimore, Md.
May, 1957.

Contents

[ix]

A History of Icelandic Literature

Introduction

Icelandic origins clear

In comparison with most other European national literatures that of Iceland is relatively clear in origin. Thanks also to its literature, the history of Iceland lacks those grey prehistoric mists of other nations whose gloom can be pierced only by the more or less feeble rays of archaeology. Among the Germanic nations only the English have a somewhat similar native tradition to refer to, though by comparison it has suffered too much from Christian influence.

Twelfth-century history

Though no Icelandic literature was written down earlier than the twelfth century, it has preserved clear, and in general dependable, accounts of the settlement of the country. We are told that Iceland was discovered by Norse Vikings sometime near the middle of the ninth century, that the first settler, Ingólfr Arnarson from Firðir in West Norway, settled in Reykjarvík (now Reykjavík) in the year 874. Within the next sixty years the country was almost completely settled by Norsemen who came in part directly from Norway, in part after having spent some time in the Norse settlements of the British Isles: Shetland, the Orkneys, the Hebrides, the western shores of England (Lancastershire) and Scotland, and the east coast of Ireland. We are told, furthermore, that the main reason for the exodus from Norway was political. In the last quarter of the ninth century, King Haraldr inn hárfagri (the Fairhaired) had been seized with the ambition to subjugate the many petty independent kings and chieftains, not to mention smaller free farmers in Norway, under his rule, as had already been done by kings in Sweden, Denmark, and England. King Haraldr succeeded in unifying Norway, but many of the chieftains and farmers preferred to leave the country rather than to submit to what they considered his tyranny. Some of them went directly to the recently discovered Iceland, while others went first to the older settlements in the British Isles, settling there as Vikings and venting their wrath for the tyrant by raiding the shores of Norway. King Haraldr's answer was an expedition to put down the troublemakers in the West, an event which resulted in a fresh stream of immigrants from these parts to Iceland. The nature of this emigration had one major effect upon the new population of Iceland: it produced a high percentage of men of noble birth, though these high-born people also imported slaves from Ireland.

These facts and opinions about the settlement of Iceland and the origin of the Icelandic nation are all derived from the historians of the twelfth and thirteenth centuries, especially Ari inn fróði and Snorri Sturluson. They have been submitted to considerable scrutiny by modern historians, but in spite of doubts and disagreements, they seem to have emerged unshaken from the discussion.

Viking literature

The settlers of Iceland took with them from Norway not only an old-fashioned family solidarity, but also a new typical Viking ideology. Both speak from all the native products of the Old Icelandic literature. They also brought two distinct, if related, types of poetry: the Eddic and the skaldic poetry. There is no doubt that both types were practised in Norway at the time of the emigration, hence a discussion of their origin might well be left to the history of Norwegian literature. Yet, since the Eddic poems were preserved only in Iceland, and since the skaldic poetry, preserved only in Iceland, too, soon became the monopoly of Icelanders, even in Norway, one cannot very well dismiss their origin here. Most of all we should like to know the reasons why this literature grew and was further cultivated in the colony of Iceland while it died out in the mother country, Norway.

Origin of Eddic poetry

The Eddic poetry falls into two or three classes, based upon their subject matter: mythical, gnomic, and heroic poems. Of these especially the last named clearly belong to the tradition of heroic poetry found or known to have existed in all Germanic tribes: The Old High German *Hildebrandslied*, the Old English *Beowulf*, *Widsíþ*, *Finnsburg*, *Waldere*, and *Deor* are specimens of the same tradition. The Eddic poems are related to these not only in subject matter but also in form: the Old Germanic alliterative line is common to all this poetry. This poetic tradition extends unbroken back to the Migration Period, perhaps back to the Gothic poetry of Ermanric's (Jörmunrekkr's) court, supposed to have been visited by the Old English legendary *scop* Wídsíþ. Though the mythical poems of the *Edda* have no parallel elsewhere, they, as well as the gnomic poems, which have parallels in Old English, all share the form of the heroic poetry.

Origin of skaldic poetry

The origin of the skaldic poetry presents a much more difficult problem. Though sharing in the alliterative pattern with the Eddic poetry, it differs radically in form by the introduction of a fixed number of syllables as well as of an intricate pattern of inrimes and assonances. If this type of poetry developed free from outside influences in Scandinavia, notably in Norway as tradition has it, it must have grown out of the Eddic type of verse—somewhat like the complex fugue, which grew out of the simple canon in medieval Europe.

Such radical spontaneous developments are, however, far from common in literature. Indeed, I believe this is the only case of an absolutely original new genre to be developed within the confines of Scandinavia. It is therefore natural that scholars should have looked in many directions for possible sources.

Western influence

The Icelander Guðbrandur Vigfússon and the Norwegian Sophus Bugge believed that the most important influences came from the British Isles, on the fringes of which the Norwegians had settled before 800.

The first Viking raids on England were made by Norwegians from Hörðaland (O. E. Hæredaland) in 787. The same tribe struck at Ireland in 795, and by 853 the Norsemen had established a kingdom in Dublin, ruling also the west coast of England and Scotland, as well as all the neighboring islands. Here a great deal of intermarriage took place, causing the racial mixture in Iceland testified to partly by the sagas— which state that several of the most noble settlers came " from the West "—and partly by modern anthropological research (Guðmundur Hannesson, Jón Steffensen).

Was the Irish blood the cause of the literary temperament of the Icelanders, differentiating them from their Norwegian ancestors? Or was it the Irish culture? The latter would seem more plausible if it could be proved, for Irish literary culture at this time possessed several traits, seemingly foreshadowing what was to arise in Iceland. Literary tradition was in the hands of a highly specialized class of poets who had to learn scores and scores of poems and tales before they were admitted to the poetical practice and duly supported by kings and chieftains.

Here Sophus Bugge thought he found the inspiration of skaldic poetry, as he also thought that many of the Old Norse myths had been inspired by Christianity.

But apart from the remarkable lack of Irish influence on the Old Icelandic language, there are two major obstacles to this theory. The oldest skaldic poetry (Bragi, Þjóðólfr of Hvinir), dating from 800–850, was older than any possible Irish influence, unless the tradition was in error. But it seems well supported not only by Swedish archaeology confirming Þjóðólfr's *Ynglingatal*, but also by the testimony of the Eggjum runic stone (*ca.* 700) in Sogn in Norway.

The second obstacle to the theory of Irish origins is the great difference in detail between Irish and skaldic poetry, though both have certain methods in common (counting syllables, inrime, assonance) and both produce the general impression of artificiality. Professor Kemp Malone, expert in Icelandic and Irish, looked for but did not discover the connection. Closer parallels to skaldic lines seem, as a matter of fact, to be found in Welsh poetry of the twelfth century, whatever the explanation.

As it is, one can at most assume, with Andreas Heusler, only a very general impact of Irish culture. The Vikings observed the Irish court poets and their enviable function in society. This certainly must have stimulated their already formed habit of reciting poems for princes and telling stories, but further influence can hardly be assumed.*

East Norse origins

Recently an attempt was made by the brilliant but erratic archivist Barði Guðmundsson to explain the early difference between Norwegians and Icelanders by claiming East Norse origin for the latter. According to this view, the chiefs in West Norway who were compelled to emigrate by Haraldr inn hárfagri were originally of East Norse origin, being Danish and Swedish Vikings who had settled there, perhaps in the seventh century, for the convenience of raiding the West.

The author of this theory marshals place names, personal names, cult

---

* The latest research, G. Turville-Petre, has marshalled new evidence for the theory of Irish origins in an article in *Skírnir* (1954). He still can show no close parallels except in method. With Guðbrandur Vigfússon he dates Bragi 835–900 and considers him the author of *dróttkvætt*. See also his *Origins of Icelandic Literature* (Oxford, 1953).

memories, scraps of skaldic poetry, archaeological remains, and, last but not least, genealogical material to prove his thesis.

He claims that literary tradition was best preserved in families practicing the fertility cult of Freyr and Freyja. These families settled in farmsteads called *Hof* and *Saurbœir*, kept swine, had matron priestesses (*hofgyðjur*), used matronymics, favored personal names in *-arr*, and practiced skaldship.

Now, the center of the Frey-cult was in Uppsala in Sweden and names in *-arr* are frequent in East Norse. Also, many of the best Icelandic families claimed kinship with such East Norse royalty as the Ynglingar (Swedish) and the Skjöldungar (Danish).

Snorri's claim that Óðinn brought poetic practice from the Black Sea regions to Sweden is, of course, grist to Barði Guðmundsson's mill, as would be any skaldic verse on runic stones in Sweden or Denmark. Unfortunately the Rök inscription (*ca.* 835) is hardly skaldic enough, while the skaldic stanza on the Karlevi-stone (*ca.* 1000) is too late and not Swedish.

Baltic theory

That the Baltic lands once must have been centers of heroic poetry is obvious from Old English poetry and Saxo. Yet the German scholars have as a rule assumed a northward course of heroic poetry from the Goths and the South Germanic tribes to Scandinavia, chiefly on the basis of the Sigurðr-Nibelungen cycle. During the war, the Swedish scholar Fritz Askeberg opposed this point of view arguing that a centrally located region, like the Baltic, would be more likely to produce such poetry than comparatively unimportant border regions.

Askeberg, too, believed that skaldic poetry developed gradually in Scandinavia rather than overnight in the West through Irish influence. The same point of view was taken by Hollander in his *Skalds*.

Norwegian origin

Sigurður Nordal believes that the skaldic meter (*dróttkvætt*) was invented by Bragi inn gamli in Norway who was later apotheosized for this feat. In *Maal og Minne* (1952), Hallvard Lie follows Nordal's lead, arguing that Bragi created the new form in analogy with the rich ornamental art of the Oseberg ship. He thinks Bragi devised his baroque shield poetry in imitation of the anaturalistic pictures of the shield—a tempting but probably fallacious theory.

The old Germanic alliterative line is found in Norway on two runic

stones, the Tune-stone, in Östfold, fifth century: *Ek Wiwar after /
Woduriðe / Witaðahalaiban / worahto runor* and the magic stone from
Eggjum, in Sogn (*ca. 700*). The latter contains enigmatic diction which
foreshadows skaldic poetry. It is an interesting coincidence, that this
stone should be found in the district from which, according to Nordal,
came the ruling clan of Iceland, the descendants of Grímr hersir of
Sogn. Here one could find corroboration for the magic origin of skaldic
poetry (Lindquist, Ohlmarks), but also the milieu of petty but rich
Viking kings, claimed by Moberg. How equivocal is the material for
decision is curiously illustrated by the fact that Barði Guðmundsson
claims Eastern origin for the clan of Grímr hersir, and Bugge could
point to their long sojourn in the West before they settled in Iceland.

Most scholars—among them the above mentioned—think that the
silence of the sources indicates that Norwegian court poetry died out in
the tenth century, except in the royal family itself. Jan de Vries alone
assumes a parallel flowering of skaldic poetry in Norway, whose loss he
attributes to Icelandic lack of interest in anything but their own court
poetry. But why did they then not also forget the early Norwegian
skaldic and Eddic poetry?

Viking heathendom

We shall now cast a glance at the Vikings in Iceland and try to understand in what way the new land affected their lives and their nascent
literature.

The settlers were heathen, and remained so for over a century (874–
1000). They worshipped several gods and goddesses, among which the
fertility god Freyr, the farmers' and seafarers' friend Þórr, and the poets'
and warriors' master Óðinn were most important. Doubtless the piety for
these numina differed according to personal temperaments, as illustrated
by the first settlers, Ingólfr and Hjörleifr, the former being pious, the latter not. To the Viking, Óðinn might embody the ideal of enterprising and
vigorous youth or the ruthless warlord as compared to the sluggish stay-
at-home Þórr. But Þórr was not to be sneered at when it came to
defending the world from hostile forces beyond the horizon, among them
the ever more ascending White-Christ (Hvíta-Kristr). In general the
conditions of the Viking age can hardly have contributed to conservative
piety, and we hear of several men believing in their own " might and
main," probably godless fellows. Besides, one could choose to worship
the deity which appealed specially to one's personal fancy, and a free

friendship often developed between god and man. This tolerance was also extended to White-Christ until his worshippers multiplied and began to threaten the pagan social order. Gods and men alike were subject to Weird (Urðr), all-powerful fate.

Viking ideals

One thing is certain: believing in gods was not a compelling factor in the ideology of the Vikings. What was it then? Over and over again we hear that the motive for their actions was " to gain fee and fame." On a Viking raid both could be gained, the first by victory, the second by bravery. At home, fame and loyalty alike were won by generous gifts to followers. Bravery and generosity were thus cardinal virtues, without which no fame was gained, however great a hoard a man might have amassed. But—and here we come to a cardinal point—a life without fame was not worth living, for it was fame alone in the kind judgment (dómr um dauðan hvern) of the survivors that lasted beyond death.

To win this everlasting fame one must lead a life of honor, in personal freedom, subject to no one, but closely hedged in by conventional morality or public opinion. When Rollo (Göngu-Hrólfr) arrived in France with his Vikings, he was asked: " Who is your king? " He answered: " We have no king; we are all equal." The heroic code demanded not only generosity toward kinsmen, friends, and guests, but also scrupulous watchfulness against all infringements on one's personal rights or those of one's kinsmen. If such offences were not avenged, one lost face and the honor was forever tarnished. Death was always preferable to a life of shame.

Aims of settlers

No doubt the chieftains who sought the security, the rich pastures, and the reserves of game of Iceland had high hopes of being able to lead heroic lives there, each shipowner at the head of his family, dependents, and slaves. And at first he could take extensive lands, settling down as a goði (priest-chieftain) in their midst and distributing the remainder to his followers, who owed him personal allegiance in return for his protection. The goði (pl. goðar) was normally of noble birth; his power was called goðorð and his retainers þingmenn. Often he built a temple (hof) at his home, his retainers paying a nominal tribute to it (hoftollr).

But in Iceland there were no aboriginal natives to be enslaved or exploited as in England and France, nor could the goðar expect their fellow-settlers to pay a tribute they had left Norway to avoid. The *goði* thus had to be content to be *primus inter pares* working or living off his own land like everyone else. The ambition of the smaller farmers must have been satisfied, if they were allowed to farm their land in peace and raise a new family, where the old family ties had been cut by the emigration. They may have hoped fervently to restore the old " peace-family " (OE *gesibb* " peace," Germ. *Gesippe* " family ") solidarity, which speaks so eloquently from law codes like *Vígslóði* (Code of Killing) and *Baugatal* (List of Rings, to be paid as wergild), but that was apparently out of the question. Instead they organized themselves into *hreppar* (sg. *hreppr*), roughly corresponding to American " townships," of twenty privately-owned farmsteads or more, which would have pastures and fishing rights in common, take care of the poor and infirm, and—to a certain degree—mutually insure their livestock or houses against loss or fire. It seems that it was more expensive to live on a big estate with many slaves than to turn the slaves into independent cotters.

Creation of the Commonwealth and the Althing (Alþingi)

After sixty years of settlement the chiefs (*goðar*) felt that some organization was needed to equalize their own powers and to curb lawlessness in the land. A certain number of *goðorðs* (thirty-six) was authorized by law and the incumbents were to meet every summer at Þingvellir to judge cases as they arose and lay down the law of the land. Thus in 930 was formed the unique institution of the Althing (*Alþingi*) which, while the Old Icelandic Commonwealth lasted (930–1262), was to act as a supreme lawgiver and court in the land—while each individual, supported by his *goði* and his friends, had to act as his own executive in carrying out the law. The land had, indeed, only one public official, the lawspeaker (*lögsögumaðr*) whose task it was to recite from memory the whole body of the law in three consecutive summers and to answer inquiries in legal matters.

Landmarks in law

No doubt the body of the law was to a great extent taken over from Norway: the author of the first code, Úlfljótr, is said to have patterned it on the law of Gulaþing in West Norway. Very ancient and of great importance was the Code of Killing (*Vígslóði*), legalizing the forms of vengeance and the payment of wergild, when feuds broke out between clans apparently of firmer family texture than ever existed in Iceland.

Typically Icelandic were, on the other hand, the mushrooming rules of procedure, obviously designed by crafty *goðar* as safeguards for the preservation of their individual powers. Real progress was scored in jurisdiction when a Fifth Court (*Fimmtardómur*) was established which could act as a supreme court when the judges of the previously founded Quarter Courts (*Fjórðungsdómar*) could not agree on a verdict.

Introduction of Christianity

Most important of all the acts of the Althing was the introduction of Christianity in the year 1000. The issue was a heated one; the two parties, heathen and Christian, almost had clashed in fight when the moderate leader of the Christians asked the heathen leader to decide the issue. After mature consideration, the latter ruled that all the people should become Christians and be baptized, but one could sacrifice to the heathen gods and eat horseflesh in secret.

With this compromise, Christianity proved to be a most beneficial influence on the subsequent fate of Icelandic literature. In adopting it the old *goðar* took care to exercise their old power over the new religion. This they did by building new churches—they were encouraged to do so—and providing priests for them, either by having their own sons prepared for the office, or by " beating " a poor but bright boy " to the book." In the latter case the priest was nothing more than a servant. However deplorable this condition must have seemed from the point of view of the Church, there is little doubt that the Icelanders owe the preservation and the composition of their native literature to that very condition. By teaching the *goðar* and their sons to read and write their own mother tongue, the weak Church gave them the needed impulse to start writing in the vernacular. Had the Church been stronger, as it was elsewhere, it might have produced Latin writers, but it would have killed off the native growth. In that case we should have had no Eddas, no skaldic poetry, and no sagas. The ancient history of Scandinavia and Iceland would have been archaeology only.

Noble families as carriers of literature

This brings us to inquire what role the noble families of *goðar* played as carriers of tradition and literature in Iceland. It must have been a decisive role. Being of noble birth, they cherished genealogy and family traditions, both in verse and in anecdote. These studies were greatly intensified by nostalgic memories of the old country. No single cause is likely to have been more important in turning the settlers into poets and historians than this uprooting from the old country. Significantly, most families cannot be traced farther than one or two generations back of the first settler. If the homes of the chieftains are likely to have been hearths of heroic poetry, they must also have cultivated the mythological poetry for religious purposes. And the skald's praise would always be welcomed by the chieftain.

Appetite for news and the role of the Althing

It is hard to overestimate the appetite developing on the isolated farm-steads for news from anywhere. The guests were so welcome that some people even built their houses across the road to catch the wayfarer. But nowhere could this hunger for news—from kinsmen in other dis-tricts, from relatives abroad, and from the great adventurous world—be as easily satisfied as at the Althing. Here hundreds of the best people from all over the island turned the lava plains and chasms of Þingvellir into a busy and gay capital during two weeks of the brightest and longest summer days. Here was ample audience for men who had something to tell, and men with intellectual curiosity had a chance to exchange views and learning. To mention two often-quoted instances only : here a young Icelandic story-teller learned the *Útferðar saga* of Haraldr harðráði, king of Norway, from the king's own follower, Halldór Snorrason. And here Bishop Magnús of Skálholt, just returned from abroad, brought the most recent news from Norway and the wide world.

Icelandic globe-trotters and court poets

In this connection it should be stressed that the Icelanders of the old Commonwealth were probably the greatest globe-trotters of their time in Scandinavia. They went everywhere : to Scandinavia and the British Isles, visiting Norwegian, Swedish, Danish, Irish, and English courts, to Russia (Garðaríki) and to Byzantium (Mikligarðr) where they served as Varangians (Væringjar) or bodyguards to the emperor. They settled Greenland (Grœnland) in the Western Hemisphere and made trips to the North American mainland. And wherever they went they stored their minds with impressions of great men and adventurous deeds. Their service as court poets all over the North made them especially fit to follow the official history of these countries ; indeed, the court poet was, in his limited way, the official historian of the time.

Ex boreale lux

And so it came to pass that the Old Icelandic literature became a great aurora borealis, throwing the only light available on the primordial darkness of Northern history and, still more important, holding up the only torch in existence for the ideals by which our old Northern and Germanic ancestors lived and died before the advent of Christianity.

Eddic Poetry

Codex Regius

In the summer of 1662 Bishop Brynjólfur Sveinsson of Skálholt sent King Frederik III of Denmark a book on old vellum. It was not a particularly impressive volume, neither in size, workmanship, nor state of preservation; a whole quire of eight leaves was missing from it. Yet, this inconspicuous book was one of the most important ever to come out of Iceland—in some respects, perhaps, the most important. For in it was to be found most of the mythological, didactic, and heroic poetry of Old Iceland. Without it our idea of this poetry would have been very scant, indeed, and that not only in Iceland and Scandinavia, but also in other Germanic countries, notably Germany. Of all Icelandic books it has been the most edited, translated, and commented on. Even now American scholars are preparing a Variorum Edition.

Edda Sæmundi Multiscii

Bishop Brynjólfur Sveinsson, who had got possession of the book in 1643, called it *Edda Sæmundi multiscii*, i. e., the *Edda* of Sæmund the Learned. He and Icelandic scholars of his time knew well the *Edda* of Snorri Sturluson, the so-called *Snorra Edda*, a textbook of poetry. Seeing that Snorri's mythology, as presented in that book, was based on old poetry, the scholars of the seventeenth century assumed that there had been an earlier *Edda*, made up of poems only, that had been Snorri's source. This manuscript seemed to confirm their assumption. It was attributed to Sæmundr inn fróði, who in the seventeenth century had become legendary for his alleged learning and magic. The name *Sæmundar Edda* has since then been used, though scholars have also used the descriptive terms, *The Elder Edda* or *The Poetic Edda*.

[14]

The name Edda

The meaning of the name *Edda* is obscure, and the problem, such as it is, is naturally not connected with our collection but with Snorri's textbook of poetics. Some scholars derive it from *óðr* " poem, poetry "; it would then mean " poetics." Others derive it from *Oddi*, the place where Snorri received his education. The meaning would then be " the book of Oddi." Otherwise the word occurs in the sense " grandmother " in *Rígspula*, surely not applicable here.

Age of the manuscript

As a matter of fact our manuscript is certainly younger than the *Snorra Edda*. The latter dates from *ca.* 1220–30, while the *Codex regius* of the *Sæmundar Edda* dates from the second half of that century, and, though a copy, may represent an original from about the middle of that century at the latest (Bugge: *ca.* 1240, Finnur Jónsson: before 1200). It is, indeed, not unlikely that Snorri's *Edda* itself inspired the collector to do this very important work. The collection, on the other hand, is older than the *Völsunga saga*, which to a considerable extent is but a paraphrase of it and renders us invaluable service in having also preserved the matter of the poems in the lost quire.

Sources of the manuscript

Nobody has ever doubted the Icelandic origin of our manuscript. But in *Maal og Minne* (1951) the distinguished Norwegian grammarian and palaeographist Didrik Arup Seip claimed that the manuscript bore unmistakable traces of having been copied from Norwegian originals. If this were true it would disturb most scholars' belief that the Eddic poems were preserved in Icelandic memories only. As a matter of fact Seip's arguments have been met chiefly by Hans Kuhn in *Acta Philologica Scandinavica* (1952). Kuhn claims that it would probably be possible to take any undoubtedly Icelandic manuscript and show up similar Norwegian features in it. This means that a real answer to the question must wait until the genuine Icelandic manuscripts have been treated to the same extent grammatically and palaeographically as Seip has his Norwegian manuscripts for his history of the Norwegian language. Until then it is probably safer to follow the old classification of manuscripts, though based on rougher data.

Sources of the collector

What were the sources of our collector? Did he write the whole from his own copious memory, did he listen to men or women reciting, or did he copy older collections? No one knows. We do know that Snorri in his *Edda* quotes several mythological and a few heroic poems in a form that sometimes differs from that of the *Codex Regius*. But there is always a possibility that there might have existed some smaller collections that might have contributed to the large collection. Snorri might have found some of that kind in the library at Oddi, where he grew up.

Eddic Poems in the Codex Regius and outside of it

The poems in the *Codex Regius* are arranged as follows. First come the mythological and didactic poems: *Völuspá* (The Sibyl's Vision or Prophesy), *Hávamál* (Sayings of the High One, i. e., Óðinn), *Vafþrúðnismál* (The Lay of Vafþrúðnir), *Grímnismál* (The Lay of Grímnir), *Skírnismál* (The Lay of Skírnir) or *För Skírnis* (Skírnir's Journey or Quest), *Hárbarðsljóð* (The Lay of Hárbarðr), *Hymiskviða* (The Lay of Hymir), *Lokasenna* (The Quarrel or Flyting of Loki), *Þrymskviða* (The Lay of Þrymr), *Völundarkviða* (The Lay of Völundr), and *Alvíssmál* (The Lay of Alvíss). With the exception of *Völundarkviða* these are all mythical and didactic poems. It looks as if the collector had already started to write down the heroic poems—which with *Völundarkviða* make up the remainder of the volume—and only then discovered that he had forgotten *Alvíssmál*, the last of the mythical poems.

The heroic poems are: *Helgakviða Hundingsbana* I (The First Lay of Helgi Hundingsbani, i. e., Slayer of Hundingr), *Helgakviða Hjörvarðssonar* (The Lay of Helgi Hjörvarðsson), *Helgakviða Hundingsbana* II (The Second Lay of Helgi Hundingsbani), also called *Frá Völsungum* (About the Völsungar), *Frá dauða Sinfjötla* (About the Death of Sinfjötli, in prose), *Grípisspá* (The Prophesy of Grípir), *Reginsmál* (The Lay of Reginn), *Fáfnismál* (The Lay of Fáfnir), and *Sigrdrífumál* (The Lay of Sigrdrífa), whose conclusion, falling in the great gap of the *Codex Regius,* is supplied from late paper manuscripts. After the break follows *Brot af Sigurðarkviðu* (Fragment of a Lay of Sigurðr), then *Guðrúnarkviða* I (The First Lay of Guðrún), *Sigurðarkviða in skamma* (The Short Lay of Sigurðr), *Helreið Brynhildar* (Brynhildr's Ride to Hel), *Guðrúnarkviða* II (The Second Lay of Guðrún), *Guðrúnarkviða* III (The Third Lay of Guðrún), *Oddrúnargrátr* (The Plaint of Oddrún), *Atlakviða (in grænlenzka)* (The [Greenlandic] Lay of Atli)—scholars think it is called Greenlandic by mistake—*Atlamál in grænlenzku* (The Greenlandic Lay of Atli), *Guðrúnarhvöt* (Guðrún's Egging), and *Hamðismál* (The Lay of Hamðir).

Preserved outside the *Codex Regius* are the following Edda-type poems: *Baldrs draumar* (Baldr's Dreams) or *Vegtamskviða* (The Lay of Vegtamr, a name of Óðinn) in a fragmentary collection of Eddic poems from the beginning of the fourteenth century (*AM 748, 4to*), *Rígsþula* (The Lay [or Thula] of Rígr) in *Codex Wormianus* of *Snorra Edda, Hyndluljóð* (Lay of Hyndla) in *Flateyjarbók, Gróttasöngr* (Song of Grótti, the Quern or Mill) in the *Codex Regius* and the *Codex Trajectinus* of *Snorra Edda*, and, finally, in paper manuscripts from the seventeenth century, *Grógaldr* (The Spell of Gróa) and *Fjölsvinnsmál* (The Lay of Fjölsvinnr). Also, there are a few bits of mythological poems found in the *Snorra Edda*, a few fragments of heroic poetry in the *Völsunga saga*, and *Hlöðskviða* (The Lay of Hlöðr) in *Hervarar saga*.

Apart from these, a few of the poems appearing in the *Codex Regius* also occur elsewhere; thus *Grímnismál, Hymiskviða*, parts of *Vafþrúðnismál, Skírnismál*, and *Hárbarðsljóð* in *AM 748, 4to*, and *Völuspá* in *Hauksbók*. The differences in these texts are almost always oral, not scribal, variants.

Names of the poems

Most Eddic poem names are made up of proper names of supernatural beings and heroes and a second element meaning "song" or "lay." There is some variation in the second element. Some occur only once like *senna* " dispute, flyting," *hvöt* " egging," *grátr* " lament," *þula* " list, thula," *söngr* " song," and *galdr* " song, magic spell." *Ljóð* " song, poem," occurs twice, *spá* " prophesy, vision," three times. Two endings are quite common: *mál* " speech, dialogue," mostly confined to poems in *ljóðaháttr*, about equally divided between the mythic-didactic and the heroic poems, and *kviða* " poem, lay," related to the verb *kveða* " to sing, chant, recite." *Kviður* are mostly in *fornyrðislag* and, excepting *Hymiskviða* and *Þrymskviða*, are heroic poems. Some scholars think *kviða* a Gothic loan-word.

Editorial principle

Is it possible to discover any editorial principle of the collector in this arrangement, apart from the obvious fact that the mythical poems are placed before the heroic ones? If a principle is not easily detected in the mythical poems, it is because they are not easily classified. Yet, it seems obvious that *Völuspá* is placed first because of its sweeping cosmological character. After that the grouping seems to be around certain gods. In a way Óðinn is the protagonist of *Völuspá*, and he is the hero of the poems following it up to *Skírnismál*, which deals with Freyr. Þórr is the hero of the rest of the poems, with the exception of *Lokasenna*.

The heroic poems are obviously arranged on a saga-principle or a historical basis. There are three groups: the first dealing with Völundr the Smith, the second with the two heroic namesakes, Helgi Hundings-bani and Helgi Hjörvarðsson. The third group deals with Sigurðr the Völsungr, his youthful exploits, his marriage to Guðrún Gjúkadóttir, and his murder. After that it tells of Guðrún's marriage to Atli (Attila) the Hun, the killing of her brothers, and of her vengeance. The cycle is brought to a close with her sons attacking Jörmunrekkr the Great, and their death.

Scholarly opinions of age and place

A sketch of scholarly opinion of the past may serve to indicate the extent of our knowledge—or ignorance—as to the age and place of origin of the Eddic poems.

The romantic scholars a century ago looked at the poems with awe and veneration, placing them in Scandinavia's hoary antiquity (*ca.* 400–800). In reaction the Danish iconoclast Edwin Jessen (1871) placed them in twelfth-century Iceland and denied them any high artistic merit.

Linguistic and metrical studies in the last quarter of the nineteenth century led scholars to place the poems after the loss of weak vowels in endings (the syncope period ending *ca.* 800) and to fix their language as West Norse. Then came the question, when and where in the West Norse area the poems had arisen, there being no external evidence except the Icelandic manuscript and the statement that the two lays of Atli were Greenlandic.

The Icelander Guðbrandur Vigfússon dated them *ca.* 800–1100 and placed them in the Viking settlements of the British Isles. His theory was most ably defended by the Norwegian Sophus Bugge, who saw Christian influence in the myths and Western influence in the heroic legends (the Helgi lays).

The German Karl Müllenhoff and the Icelander Finnur Jónsson opposed Bugge's theories of Western origin. Finnur Jónsson thought the poems pre-Christian and placed them in Norway, chiefly on the basis of nature description. The Icelander Björn M. Ólsen claimed they could just as well have been composed in Iceland and that the burden of proof rested upon those who would place them elsewhere.

The Dutchman Barend Symons (1906) reached a compromise, while the Germans Eugen Mogk and Andreas Heusler followed B. M. Ólsen in agreeing on the Iceland of 900–1000 or even as late as 1200 (Heusler). Heusler attributed the didactic poetry to Icelandic interest in skaldic art.

Dame Bertha S. Phillpotts (1920), believing that the *ljóðaháttr* poems, all in dialogue, had developed out of ancient cult drama in Scandinavia, placed these, as being older, in Norway, and the *fornyrðislag* poems in Iceland.

In the year 1917 a runic stone, containing magic formulas in some sort of alliterative verse (*ni s solu sot / uk ni sakse stain skorin . . .*), was found at Eggjum in Sogn. This stone, dated on archaeological grounds not later than 700, was shown by the Norwegian runologist Magnus Olsen to be written in the syncopated language of the Eddic poems.

The significance of this discovery was not lost upon Eddic scholars, though some of the older ones like the Swede Henrik Schück (1926) and Heusler (1929) continued to date the poems in the period 800–1200. Others like Gustav Neckel (German, 1923), Fredrik Paasche (Norwegian, 1923–24), and Erik Noreen (Swedish, 1926) would not only allow the poems to be moved back to the syncope period (650–700) but also began to question the linguistic dictum that no poem could be older than the syncope. Noreen, especially, showed that certain *ljóðaháttr* poems (*Skírnismál, Vafþrúðnismál, Fáfnismál,* but not *Sigrdrífumál*) could be turned into Primitive Old Norse without violating the metrical rules. In support of this, Birger Nerman (Swedish, 1931) dated some objects mentioned in the *Edda* as far back as 500.

If Scandinavian scholars tried to project the exclusively Scandinavian mythical poems back into the time before 700, German students of the heroic poems, especially Heusler and his disciples (G. Neckel, Hermann Schneider) have contended that the oldest heroic poems, *Völundarkviða, Atlakviða,* and *Hamðismál* (also *Hlöðskviða* of *Hervarar saga*) probably were linear descendants of German (Saxon) and Gothic poems from the Migration Period.

Heusler considered the fragment of *Sigurðarkviða* of this type, too, but the heroic elegies, dealing with the hard fates of Brynhildr and Guðrún, he considered of late specific twelfth-century Icelandic origin. Most recent scholars like the Dutchman Jan de Vries (1941–1942) and the Germans Hans Kuhn and Wolfgang Mohr (1938–1939) agree with Heusler as to the date of these poems but believe that they represent translations of eleventh- and twelfth-century German-Danish heroic elegies, a postulated genre, preceding the ballads in Denmark and the *Spielmannslied* in Germany. However that may be, there is no doubt that these poems show similarities in motifs to the ballads which, with the French dance, came to Iceland according to reports early in the twelfth century, and at any rate not later than 1200.

Seven centuries—500–1200—is a long time to stretch out a collection of poems not differing more from each other than the Eddic do. True, we find in them more variety in meter, style, and subject matter than in the three or at most four centuries of Old English poetry. But that should not be surprising in the land of skaldic verse.

Placing the heroic elegies within one century is surely reasonable and though, judging by the Old English lyrical laments (*Deor*, etc.), the century might just as well be the ninth as the twelfth, the contact with the ballads speaks definitely for the latter.

Scholars agree that the Helgi lays and the Sigurðr trilogy show unmistakable traces of the harsh and merry Viking life on ship and shore. But would it not be safer to date the oldest heroic poems to the same Viking age rather than to the Migration Period, even if they show traces of that period? It seems more reasonable to date the poems within the period *ca.* 800–1200 rather than to try to stretch them over so many centuries.

In order to explain how the oldest heroic poems could survive little changed from the fifth-century Gothic original, say, of the poem on Ermanric-Jörmunrekkr down to the ninth- or tenth-century *Hamðismál* of the *Edda*, Heusler developed a theory that heroic legend in Germanic tribes was identical with the heroic poem, and that there was no oral tradition or story existing outside the poem. In this specific case: the story of Ermanric (told first by Jordanes in his sixth-century history of the Goths) would be formulated and preserved only in the poem of which *Hamðismál* would be the direct descendant. This theory ignores the well-known fact that the poems are full of allusions, some of which are not understandable any longer, while others are cleared up by other heroic poems or prose tales. This has been clearly demonstrated in the case of *Hamðismál* by Hans Kuhn (1952). But if so, we must think of the heroic poems and the traditions clustered around them in the same way as we think of *Hervarar saga*, a *fornaldar saga* which has, indeed, preserved one of the oldest of the heroic poems, *Hlöðskviða*, though it was written in late thirteenth-century Iceland. The poems would, indeed, gradually become modernized; the oldest would die out or be replaced by new ones. Demonstrable cases are the two lays of Atli, *Atlakviða* the older, *Atlamál* the later. But in the old poems there would always be preserved in a more or less haphazard way some old motifs, some archaic verbal expressions, some old-fashioned objects (swords, goblets, etc.) just as the very names of the heroes were old and historical.

If one might trust the theories of German scholars, especially Heusler's disciples, practically all of the heroic poems would ultimately be " translations " from Gothic, South or West Germanic, and Danish originals, and no heroic poem would have originated in Norway or Iceland. Of course, there is not in any of these the slightest reference to the Icelandic scene, so why should they have been composed in Iceland? Similarly we might ask: why did the Icelandic Canadian immigrant Jóhann Magnús Bjarnason locate his plays in Granada, Venice, Russia, France, and Germany and his voluminous romance in Brazil rather than on the American prairie, where he wrote them? In both cases, I submit, we are dealing with immigrant escape literature. The modern Canadian escaped into modern romance, the Old Icelandic settlers into their beloved heroic legend.

It seems intrinsically more likely that the poems were composed in (Norway or) Iceland by a group of poets related in culture and vying with one another in treating topics and characters each from his own point of view. This point was well taken by the great Scottish scholar William P. Ker in his *Epic and Romance* (1897) ; it has been elaborated by Henrik Ussing (Danish, 1910), Fritz Askeberg (Swedish, 1944), and Martin Larsen (Danish, 1943–6). Larsen concludes: " Nothing speaks against the Icelandic—or if you will—Old Norse—origin of the poems : Iceland has had not only collectors and scribes, but also creative poets."

I do not, of course, mean to imply that Eddic poetry did not exist elsewhere in Scandinavia or elsewhere among Germanic tribes. The Icelanders brought it with them from Norway, and the oldest poems may just as well be Norwegian as Icelandic. And *Beowulf* and Saxo prove an unbroken heroic tradition in the East Norse area, especially Denmark, from the sixth to the twelfth century. But just as *Beowulf* is unmistakably English though it deals with subjects of the Scandinavian homeland, and just as the *fornaldar sögur* are unmistakably Icelandic though they are similarly oriented toward the Scandinavian East (*Austrvegr*), so we must grant that the related Eddic poems are most probably also

Icelandic, though the mythical and didactic poems may preferably reflect the nature of the Norwegian homeland and the heroic poems may range from the Goths and the Huns, the Burgundians and the Franks to Denmark, Sweden, and even Norway.

Criteria of age and origin

As may be seen from the preceding sketch, the criteria which scholars have tried to use in determining the age and origin of the poems are many and various.

Still, apart from the language, which is West Norse, and the manuscripts, which are Icelandic of the thirteenth century (cf., however, Seip's opinion, quoted above), very few are external facts. The two lays of Atli are called Greenlandic, but one of them is thought to be among the oldest poems, hence probably Norwegian. They might be so called because some one had learned them in Greenland, and *Atlamál* might have been composed there.

. Of external criteria there are two more: the relation of the Eddic poems to the skaldic poetry, which in the main is dated, and the relation to poetry outside Iceland or Scandinavia. There are echoes of *Hamðismál* in Bragi (ninth century), of *Völuspá* in Arnór jarlaskáld (1065), of *Hávamál* in Eyvindr skáldaspillir (*ca.* 960–70), of *Helgakviða Hundingsbana* I in Gísl Illugason (*ca.* 1100). Jan de Vries divided the Eddic poems in two groups—one before 1000, the other after 1150—because he felt he had observed that skaldic poetry avoided mythological kennings in the period 1000–1150. But Hans Kuhn and Jón Helgason (1953) disagree with him.

In and outside Scandinavia the only poetical genres comparable—apart from the West Germanic poetry—are the ballads. *Þrymskviða* has ballad style repetition; the heroic elegies have certain motifs in common with the ballads of Scandinavia.

Otherwise criteria are almost purely of the internal variety. They fall into two groups: criteria of facts and ideas expressed in the poems, and criteria of form and style.

Facts and ideas. Since Christianity came to Iceland in 1000, absolutely heathen poems should be older. Loan-words, if datable, would be valuable; loan-phrases might indicate transmission from a foreign language, as in the ballads. Yet *Rígsþula*, full of loan-words, has proved hard to date. Archaic objects, swords, goblets, cannot be used to prove the age of a poem, but they do indicate old tradition. Historical names are in the same category. Very rarely are historical events depicted in the poems, as perhaps the battles between Goths and Huns in *Hlöðskviða*; usually such events are personalized. The geographical scene fits a mountain country, Norway, Scotland, Iceland. But the orientation of the mythical poems, the fir and the reindeer-hunting in *Hávamál*, the hart in *Helgakviða Hundingsbana I* are all strictly Norwegian, while the volcanic eruption and earthquake in *Völuspá* are definitely Icelandic. So is the use in the same poem of *þollr* " fir " for *askr* " ash ": in Iceland there were no woods except birch, and the natives soon forgot the real meaning of the tree names. Occasionally there is another landscape, so the *grœnar brautir* " green roads " of *Rígsþula* would fit the emerald isle, Eire, as would the name *Rígr* and the custom of inviting a stranger to sleep with the housewife.

Form and style. The higher criticism of the last quarter of the nineteenth century coupled with contemporary metrical studies had high hopes that it would be possible to restore the poems to their original pristine form, always thought of as something better than what the manuscripts had to offer. Lines were streamlined by cutting pronouns, poems by cutting stanzas (or changing their order) attributed to an interpolating scribe. The proof should be in the pudding, but it turned out to be an even worse mess. Now scholars are content to take the poems as they are, realizing that nothing can be done about them, though obviously they often are far from perfect.

Yet the poems can be classified not only by the meter but also within the same meter according to the prevalent structure of the lines. Dame Phillpotts considered the *ljóðaháttr* mythical poems to be older than the ones composed in *fornyrðislag*. Later *ljóðaháttr* was not as commonly used as *fornyrðislag*.

In his history of Old English literature (1948) Kemp Malone assumed for Old English poetry that originally an alliterative line (two verses) was filled by one sentence (end-stopped style) and only later would the sentence be allowed to run into more lines (run-on style). He found the first style only in *Widsíþ* (before 700); after that the run-on style or enjambment prevailed. The same method was tried as early as 1908 on the Eddic poems by Gustav Neckel. He found end-stopped style in *Þrymskviða*, which he consequently thought one of the oldest of the mythical poems; now people tend to put it very late because of its ballad-like structure and fine preservation. He found, outside the *Edda*, completely run-on style in *Ynglingatal* and wanted to place it in the twelfth century, though according to tradition, corroborated partly by *Beowulf*, partly by Swedish archaeological finds, it should be among the oldest. So much for this criterion.

Another stylistic difference in the poems is the way the material is presented: in narrative, in dialogue, or in speech form. Most of the *ljóðaháttr* mythical poems are in pure dialogue, hence Dame Phillpotts thought them derived from ritual drama. The gnomic poetry, *Hávamál*, etc., is mostly in speech form. Of the heroic poems there were certain ones with mixed dialogue and narrative, like the Old English *Finnsburg* fragment and the Old High German *Hildebrandslied*. Heusler concluded that this was a common Germanic type, therefore of the oldest. Finally, there are heroic poems in which, for example, a heroine in a given situation is made to view her life in retrospect, usually with a good deal of nostalgia or lament in speech form, a dramatic monologue. This type Heusler considered the youngest and Icelandic; these poems show contact with the ballads.

At last, there is the consideration of preservation. Mutilated poems are likely to be old—so *Völuspá* and *Hamðismál*. Poems as perfectly preserved as *Þrymskviða* are more likely to be late. A Swedish scholar, Peter Hallberg, has even plausibly attributed it to Snorri Sturluson; it would, indeed, make a fine companion piece to his story of Þórr's journey to Útgarðaloki.

Mythical poetry—heathendom and Christianity

A major consideration for the dating as well as for the interpretation of the poems, especially the mythical ones, is their relation to Christianity, which was introduced in Iceland (1000) and Norway by King Ólafr Tryggvason with the aid of English and German missionaries. In this connection it should be borne in mind, however, that Hákon Aðalsteinsfóstri made some abortive attempts to keep his English Christianity in the teeth of considerable opposition in Norway, and that in Iceland there were several settlers who, coming from the Western Isles, brought Irish Christendom to Iceland, though most of them fell from the faith in the heathen community. This and earlier contacts of the Vikings with Western Christendom gave ample time for influence of Christian thought before the final victory of Christianity.

An inquiry into such influence on the Eddic myths was started when Bishop Anton Christian Bang of Christiania (1879) noted the similarity of *Völuspá* to the *Sibylline Oracles* and to the Book of Apocalypse.

Sophus Bugge, in his studies on the origin of Eddic myths (1881-89), went a good deal further, reducing most of them to Christian origin. The Alfaðir of several Eddic poems was God the Father; the innocently slain Baldr who went to Hel was Christ dying and descending to Hell; Óðinn hanging on Yggdrasill, sacrificed by himself to himself, was Christ on the cross sacrificed to God or himself; Miðgarðsormr spanning the world and biting his tail was Leviathan. Bugge based his thesis upon Viking contact with Irish-English Christianity; if he was right, that would give a *terminus a quo* for the poems, which he thought composed in the British Isles.

Bugge's Western theories were at once contradicted by the German Karl Müllenhoff and the Icelander Finnur Jónsson who both defended the native Norwegian or Germanic origin of the myths. The origin of the myths is, of course, not the literary history of the poems, but to dispel the idea that Bugge's Christian origin was favored, we shall hear a few other scholars on the subject of origins. Axel Olrik traced the Ragnarök myth in folklore and equated Loki with the bound giant (Prometheus) of the Caucasus (1902–14). The Germans Gustav Neckel (1920) and Franz Rolf Schröder (1924) assumed Hellenistic influence; Baldr, according to Neckel, was a vegetation god; according to Sir James G. Frazer (1911) one instance of the sacrificial king. Dame Phillpotts (1920) saw fertility drama in *Skírnismál*. Uno Holmberg(-Harva) (1922) connected Askr Yggdrasils with the world-tree in arctic myths and elsewhere. He was followed by Hugo Pipping (1925) who, with more learning than success, identified the Heimdallr of *Völuspá* with the world axis god. The astral-mythological work on Heimdallr by Åke Ohlmarks (1937) was much wilder, but his and Dag Strömbäck's (1935) work on magic (*seiðr*) shows conclusively traces of arctic shamanism in the folk beliefs of *Edda* and saga. This has been corroborated by Karl Bruhn's (1946) demonstration that the teaching of runes or mysteries in the *Edda* actually parallels similar didactic methods among the arctic shamans of Siberia, and probably also the mysteries of the Greek and the Irish. A very peculiar way of magic recital has been shown by the present writer (1951) to be common to the Finns, Lapps, and Icelanders. It looks Finno-Ugric, but might yet be of Germanic origin. We shall come back to that later.

Leaving all theories, we shall return to our theme, the mythical poems of the *Edda* and their relation to Christianity. We can be sure that they represented heathendom to their authors.

But how heathen are they? Are they older or later than the introduction of Christianity? Were they composed in defense of the old faith or against it? Or were they conceived in sovereign indifference to both faiths? One thing is clear: they are not composed against Christianity, which is curiously ignored. With more right one might claim that some of them were composed against the old faith, notably the very Aristophanic-looking *Lokasenna*.

We know in Iceland that Hjalti Skeggjason composed a derogatory ditty calling Freyja a bitch, for which he was promptly outlawed as a blasphemer by a heathen court. Conversely the heathen calumniated the missionary Bishop Friðrekr and his Icelandic aide Þorvaldr víðförli in a verse that cost the maker his life at the hands of Þorvaldr. These examples show that some minds were, indeed, fired with ardor both for and against the old faith at the time of the conversion.

Looking for this fire in the mythical poems, we might find it in the *Lokasenna*, which one might read as a biting satire on the old gods by a pagan who had had enough of their immoral and inefficient ways.

Another poem which has fire enough to be dated near the agitating times of the conversion would be *Völuspá*, greatest of all Eddic poems. This magnificent vision of the beginning and the end of the world, as well as of the rise of a new and better world, has sufficient points of contact with Christian thought to convince us that its author must have been familiar with Christianity directly or indirectly. As the poem is earlier than 1050, it is hard to believe that it could have been composed by a Christian. More likely its author was a late pagan thinker and poet trying to vindicate the old faith from within its own resources or to resurrect in his poetic dreams the long lost paradise of family solidarity.

Völuspá (The Prophesy of the *Völva*, i. e., Witch or Seeress), though mutilated and obscure, is one of the peaks in the mountain land of Icelandic literary history. It is a poem of inspiration, revealing in a series of swiftly changing scenes the course of the world from its chaotic beginnings out of the empty gap of the giants, through creation of the gods, earth, and men, to its and their ultimate doom and destruction in fire and water. The doom is inevitable, but out of the waves a new world will rise, to which gods and men will return to live in family solidarity and happiness. This was no haphazard development, as the poet sees it, but the result of the unethical behavior of the gods themselves. Having gotten into trouble, like the hero Sigurðr Fáfnisbani, through gold and women, the gods, Æsir, in the ensuing fight with the Vanir, another tribe of gods, have to choose between two evil alternatives: lose the goddess of love, sun, and moon to a giant, or break their given word to him and kill him. They choose the latter alternative and with it their ultimate doom. Full of evil forebodings Óðinn goes to a witch or a *völva* to ask her about the details of the coming doom. The *völva* sees one threatening event after the other, all portents of the end. She sees valkyries riding, Baldr's death through the mistletoe, his mother Frigg's weeping, Loki restive in bonds, a river of swords, several abodes of the dead—among them Náströnd, a hell for troth-breakers, oath-breakers, and murderers—and finally, a monster-bearing giantess in an iron wood. These visions are punctuated by the first refrain: *Vituð ér enn eða hvat?* "Do you know now, or don't you?" Then follows the part of the poem dealing with the fate of the gods: *ragnarök* (or less correctly: *ragna-rökkr,* "the twilight of the gods," familiar from Wagner's opera *Götterdämmerung*). It begins by cocks crowing in the abodes of the gods, giants, and Hel, after which follows the ominous refrain repeated throughout it:

> Geyr nú Garmr mjök   festr mun slitna
> fyr Gnipahelli   ok freki rinna.

"Now Garmr barks aloud before the Gnipa-cave; the chain will break, the wolf go free." The *völva* sees the world turn evil, cousins committing whoredom, brother fighting brother, in typical uprising against the strongest bonds of the "peace-family." Heimdallr blows a warning on his horn, Óðinn consults the magic head of Mímir, the world tree trembles on its roots. Loki and the wolf (Fenrisúlfr) break their fetters and join the ranks of the giants coming from the east and the fire-demon Surtr from the south. Óðinn fights the wolf and is killed but avenged by his son. Freyr fights Surtr, Þórr the Miðgarðsormr; they kill each other. There is a general holocaust (caused by Surtr) after which the earth sinks into the ocean. But the author of *Völuspá,* though critical of his gods, was too fond of them to let them end there. The best of them, Baldr the victim and Höðr the blind killer, come back to a newborn green earth, resuming a life of beauty and new family solidarity. Likewise, there is a place reserved for good men, and the poem ends by the disappearance of an evil dragon and the arrival of "the mighty one, ruler of all."

Nordal believes that this poet was inspired by the fear of the end of the world, probably preached in Iceland by missionaries just before the year 1000 when they thought the dread event would come. But he also believes that the poet was schooled in the best native traditions of inspiration, won or developed out of the old cult of Óðinn with its magical practices, paralleling the shamanistic methods of the Lapps and the Finns or the ways of a modern spiritualistic séance. Moreover, Nordal believes that there were more active ascetic methods of acquiring knowledge, probably also shamanistic, paralleling Óðinn's hanging himself in the tree (in *Hávamál*), wounded and given to himself in order to acquire the power of the magic runes. This aspiring to the higher knowledge of runes is also found in *Rígsþula*, an Icelandic poem, according to Nordal, linked with *Völuspá* in a prose introduction. Lists of the magic runes to be learned are found in *Sigrdrífumál*.

It is quite conceivable that in earlier times, when paganism was not threatened from the outside, men could treat their gods with less reverence than they would in a crisis, producing poems of such rollicking humor as *Hárbarðsljóð* and *Þrymskviða*. This is the argument of those who want to place the poems as far back as possible in Norway. Paasche points to a similar humor in the Vedic hymns and in the medieval poetry about St. Peter. Dame Phillpotts argues that, since flytings (disputes) occurred in real life and found their way into heroic poetry, there is no reason that the gods could not be represented as flyting. And H. Munro Chadwick (1932) points out that stories of gods are generally ruder than heroic legends—which certainly holds true in the Eddic poems.

On the other hand these poems might equally well have been composed after the zeal of the conversion had cooled to such an extent that the poets could begin to take renewed interest in mythical lore—as Snorri did in the thirteenth century, when he wrote the story of Útgarðaloki, companion piece to the humorous poems above. The question is, how early such a renaissance could occur. Heusler considers the Icelandic chieftain-clergy and the skalds of the eleventh and twelfth centuries fully capable of such an attitude. To Heusler and his followers the didactic-antiquarian poems, *Vafþrúðnismál*, *Grímnismál*, and *Alvíssmál* could not have been composed anywhere else than in Iceland. Where else could you find an audience of young skalds so sorely in need of instruction of mythological-skaldic vocabulary and terms?

The literary historian Jan de Vries (1941–42) follows Heusler in general in assuming an Icelandic antiquarian renaissance, but he puts it at 1150, a century and a half after the conversion. This assumption is based on his findings (opposed by Hans Kuhn and Jón Helgason, 1953) regarding the use of the mythological kennings by the skalds, who, according to de Vries, avoid them in the period 1000–1150. Mythic poetry, de Vries thinks, flares up before 1000 and then dies down to revive after 1150. He dates *Vafþrúðnismál, Grímnismál, Hávamál, Skírnismál, Hárbarðsljóð, Lokasenna, Völuspá,* and the lost Baldr poetry before 1000, but *Alvíssmál, Baldrs draumar, Hyndluljóð, Þrymskviða,* and *Rígsþula* in the period 1150–1200 (or 1250). The latter group, de Vries thinks, is Icelandic (except *Þrymskviða* and *Rígsþula*) ; about the first group Norway and Iceland may contend, though *Hávamál* more probably is Norwegian. The Icelandic Professor Einar Ól. Sveinsson's chronological order in *Íslands þúsund ár* (1947) is fairly similar, though he puts *Þrymskviða* and *Rígsþula* before *Völuspá* and the year 1000.

Classifying *Vafþrúðnismál, Grímnismál,* and *Alvíssmál* as didactic-antiquarian poems is alluring but ignores several fundamental traits about these poems.

Two other points may be and have been made. Though the poems seem quite unritualistic, they all are cast in the form of a contest frame story, where the god's opponent at the end forfeits his head. In this Dame Phillpotts (1920) saw vestiges of old ritualistic drama most fully exemplified in *Skírnismál,* a drama about the fertility god Freyr: how he falls in love with Gerðr by seeing her from afar; how he sends his messenger Skírnir to get her, sacrificing his good sword; and how this messenger finally secures her promise by threat of dire magic curses (one of two real curses in the *Edda*). Dame Phillpotts' theories are very tempting, for they would throw light on the peculiar habit, exemplified most fully in these poems but also prevalent in the heroic poetry: to express action in dramatic form (dialogue) rather than in narrative. Yet, scholars have not been convinced by her theories, no doubt partly because the dialogue form was also early and widely used in didactic poetry. The question narrows down to this: what here is being taught—skaldic terminology or magic religious knowledge.

In *Guðmundar saga Arasonar góða* (chapter eight) we are told the story of a crew in mortal danger at sea. The captain asked one after another, whether he did not know the true name of God. When finally one was found who knew, they were saved. This is Christian name magic. But the story suggests that the long list of names in *Grímnismál* and elsewhere may not have been there for antiquarian reasons, but for practical magic and religious purposes. If so, the poems are pre-Christian, and most probably they were.

We are here on the threshold of the magic element in the Eddic poems, which has been specially elucidated by Magnus Olsen in connection with his investigations into rune magic. Indeed, his interpretation of *Grímnismál* in this light is probably, of all, the most reasonable. The poem is spoken by Óðinn, placed between two fires by a foster-son who mistakes his identity and in the end pays for the fatal mistake with his life. But Óðinn is always considered the master magician among gods and men, his methods and achievements closely resembling those of the Finno-Ugrian shamans. Torture is one element in this system; in one case Óðinn actually hangs himself in order to acquire the wisdom of the runes (*Hávamál*). In this case he is tortured between two fires and the poem more or less represents the ravings and the hallucinations of his mind.

There is actually less magic in the Eddic poems than one would expect; we lack here parallels to the Old English and Old High German charms, except perhaps for the curses embedded in *Skírnismál* and *Helgakviða Hundingsbana* II. But apart from the name magic alluded to, there is in *Hávamál* the often-mentioned, typical description of Óðinn's hanging in the world-tree gallows, sacrificed to himself in order to learn the runes. As we saw, Bugge identified the situation with Christ on the cross, but it has a native parallel of ritual hanging, the victim also sacrificed to Óðinn, King Vikar in *Gautreks saga*. So Óðinn's hanging in the tree is probably a reflection of widespread initiation rites for magicians. Instead of real charms *Hávamál* contains a list of eighteen charms, the socalled *Ljóðatal*. A similar list of magic runes (*rúnatal*) makes up about half of *Sigrdrífumál*. This magic learning must have had deep roots in Norway and all Scandinavia, but that the Icelanders practiced it, too, is strikingly demonstrated by Egill Skalla-Grímsson, Viking, poet, and magician.

An interpretation of the meaning of *Ljóðatal, Sigrdrífumál, Rígspula,* and the introduction to *Völuspá* was made by Karl Bruhn (1946) in a study entitled " Education in Mysteries and Teaching in Scandinavia in Pagan Times." He looks upon the situations described in these poems as typical teacher-pupil (father-son in a spiritual sense) situations, similar to those current among North-Asiatic peoples practicing shamanism, but similar also to the primitive teaching of magical methods, practiced among Hindus, Celts, and Greeks. The topics listed in these poems are the same as those the shamans or magicians must master— and the same which Snorri's Óðinn, *galdrs faðir,* master of magic, claims to know to perfection.

The Lapp magicians (and the modern Finnish singers of *Kalevala*) sang incantations in a special ritualistic way: every line alternately, holding hands, and swinging their bodies until they fell into the shaman-istic trance, their souls, like Óðinn's, leaving their bodies. This same method of recital, which the writer found (1951) connected with a dream verse in *Sturlunga saga* where the rite was no longer understood, leaves no doubt that these Finnish-Lappish magic rites must have been practiced by the settlers of Iceland, no doubt in connection with *seiðr*, Óðinn's specialty.

But though the Scandinavians may have learned this practice and several others from their neighbors, expert as the latter were always considered in witchcraft, it does not follow that they accepted the whole training in magic from them. As a matter of fact, Lapps and Finns have been shown to borrow a not inconsiderable part of the Scandinavian myth, not to speak of material borrowings and loan-words. It is therefore quite possible that the alternate recital might be an arcane Germanic custom, as the two poets of *Widsíþ* indicate. One would probably be justified in so concluding, if the Finno-Ugrian scholars fail to produce parallels from the remainder of their widespread territory in Siberia.

Hávamál—Viking wisdom

If we look at the message of *Hávamál*, the greatest didactic poem of the *Edda* and one that embodies the wisdom of living in most direct form, there is no doubt about its heathen mark. The poem is surely pre-Christian. Another question is whether we can find in it anything point-ing to Icelandic rather than Norwegian origin. Some of the beautiful nature passages point unmistakably to the Norwegian scene, and so, it seems, does the unpresumptive philosophy of the poorest of cotters, though such poor cotters could, no doubt, have been found in Iceland too. There is a certain strain, recalling or rather foreshadowing Burns's " A man's a man for a'that ": Don't be ashamed of your shoes and breeches nor of a poor nag riding to a meeting, just so that you are washed and well fed. It is better to have a hovel and two goats than to go begging. And it is better to be alive, even maimed, than to be dead; a lame man can ride a horse, a deaf man may kill; alive, one can somehow get a cow. This is not only Norwegian cotters' wisdom; it is also truly ancient philosophy: Homer makes Achilles voice the very same thoughts about death. But it is far removed from the proud philosophy of the Vikings, who look with disdain at death, striving only for that which will survive man's death: his fame. The epitome of this philosophy is found in two famous stanzas of *Hávamál*, though one is enough to express the thought:

Deyr fé	en orðstírr
deyja frændr	deyr aldregi
deyr sjalfr it sama	hveim er sér góðan getr.

"Cattle die, kinsmen die, oneself dies the same; but fame alone will never die for him who gains a good one."

If one scrutinizes the remainder of the poem, most of it seems, indeed, to be Viking wisdom rather than cotters' and farmers' philosophy. There is little of the old family solidarity of *Baugatal*, though certain stanzas, like the famous one on the solitary tree decaying and dying, may be so interpreted. It is not the philosophy of the stay-at-home Norwegian but that of the roaming Viking, cut off from his kin, self-dependent, wary and suspicious, in need of striking up comradely friendship, and in need of deceiving and penetrating under the deceit of his enemies. It is quite fitting that it should be attributed to Óðinn, the god of the Vikings. Again, as Nordal has shown, Egill Skalla-Grímsson is the living embodiment of this Viking philosophy. Undoubtedly it was the philosophy of many of his countrymen no less than of the Vikings of the West. In that sense, then, *Hávamál* may be more Icelandic than Norwegian. Its influence in Iceland has always remained great.

Hávamál is really not a homogeneous poem but composed of several poems or fragments of different kinds. In connection with some realistic advice not to trust the fair sex, one is told the story of Óðinn's betraying the giant's daughter Gunnlöð in order to steal the poet's mead, an example of male treachery. There follows a general gnomic poem, *Loddfáfnismál*, so called because each of its twenty stanzas begins: *Ráðumk þér Loddfáfnir* "I advise you Loddfáfnir." Then comes the great magic adventure of Óðinn's hanging himself in the world tree to gain the runes, which is followed by a list, not of runes, but of magic charms or spells (*Ljóðatal*), all attributed to Óðinn and, as we have seen, no doubt belonging to his shamanistic practices.

Heroic poetry

The matter of the heroic poems has given rise to speculation as to their age and provenience.

Several points are here of interest: historical references; native Scandinavian and foreign origin of matter; the culture revealed in the poems; and tone, style, and form of the poems.

Some of the Eddic heroes are historical: so the Gothic king Jör-munrekkr of *Hamðismál*, Ermanricus of history, who died in 375 while the Huns were threatening his kingdom. Likewise the Burgundian king Gunnar (Gundaharius) of *Atlakviða*, who was defeated by Attila's (Atli's) Huns *ca.* 437. Memories of late fifth-century Hunnish-Gothic warfare are also preserved in the *Hlöðskviða* of *Hervarar saga*. Recently it has been conjectured that the matter of *Völundarkviða* may ultimately be of Gothic origin, because of the testimony of the Old English poem *Waldere*, making Wéland-Völundr the father of Widia who, in turn, is then identified with the *Gothorum rex fortissimus Vidigoia* of Jordanes.

From the Rhineland came the story of Sigurðr the Völsungr, but his historicity is doubtful, though the family feud, involving him and Bryn-hildr, might well have been patterned on conditions among the Merovin-gian Franks (so conjectures Gudmund Schütte).

About 725 the *Beowulf* poet alludes to the dragon-slaying of his father Sigemund Wælsing without mentioning Sigfrid-Sigurðr, who in Scandi-navia took over the dragon-slaying. A first skaldic reference to his Rhine-gold is found in 980, but in the *Edda* his life has become the axis around which most of the heroic poems, foreign and native, have been grouped.

The poems on Sigurðr fall into two well-marked groups: (1) poems and prose passages dealing with his youth, a trilogy, describing (a) the avenging of his father, (b) his dragon-slaying, winning of the hoard, and his flame-wall riding to release the sleeping *valkyrja* Sigrdrífa (Brynhildr), and (2) poems dealing with his death and especially the emotional reactions and the fates of the two women fighting over him: Brynhildr and Guðrún.

Doubtful though the historical connections of the three Helgi lays (*Helgakviður*) are, there is no question that the legends are native Scandinavian and older than the Sigurðr cycle, although here they are combined, Helgi Hundingsbani made the halfbrother of Sigurðr. Some of the place names point to the Baltic (North German) coast (Svarins-haugr), others to East Gautland (Brávellir). The personal names Helgi and Hjörvarðr are those of the Scylding dynasty of *Beowulf*, and the opponents of Helgi, the sons of Hundingr and Höðbroddr, may be paralleled by the Hundings and the Heaðobeards of *Widsíþ-Beowulf*, another proof of their fifth-century Baltic provenience.

In their present form the Helgi lays have features in common both with the trilogy of Sigurðr's youth and the mythic didactic poems. These features seem peculiarly Scandinavian, perhaps of the Viking age, as compared with the remainder of the heroic poems, the older heroic poems of Hamðir, Atli, Hlöðr, and Völundr, and the younger emotional laments of the Sigurðr cycle.

Most scholars, following the clue of the historical heroes in the *Edda*, believe that heroic poetry originated among the Goths or in tribes somewhere in the regions of Tacitus' Germania, who, in their opinion, led the other Germanic tribes (notably the Scandinavians) in culture during the Migration Period (*ca*. 300–500). The poems wandered north in more or less fixed form or translations, the Gothic poems probably over Austria, northwest Germany, and Denmark (Heusler-Neckel) until they reached their last refuge in eighth-century Norway and ninth- to twelfth-century Iceland, a typical relict or backward region.

This view has recently (1944) been vigorously attacked by the Swede Fritz Askeberg. In his opinion, continental Germany was not the cultural center of Germania when the heroic poems arose, but rather a fringeland, where waves of Germanic culture, springing up in Scandinavia, were shattered against the Graeco-Roman frontier.

Askeberg believes that the runes were invented by the Goths on the Vistula toward the end of the first century after Christ.* Thence the runes spread all over the Baltic and Scandinavia, only later reaching England and Germany. In the same way, during the famous Vendel period (sixth century) Baltic ornamentation spread to the Germans on the Continent, and with it, Askeberg believes, heroic poetry, which is much more likely to have spread from Scandinavia to Germany than vice versa, just as it demonstrably spread from Scandinavia to England on the testimony of *Widsíþ* and *Beowulf*. The Gothic and Burgundian legends, originating while these tribes were still neighbors on the Vistula, were preserved in the North because of the remaining relatives in Gotland-Gautland and Borgundarhólmr (Bornholm). Unique in Germanic heroic poetry is the patriotic feeling found only in Danish heroic poetry, but in Denmark heroic poetry must have flourished to a degree unequaled elsewhere (cf. *Beowulf*, Saxo) except among the intellectually alert Icelanders.

Also, Askeberg argues, the variety of meters found in West Norse poetry, notably skaldic verse, can be best explained—barring a foreign influence—as the development of a long native growth in a cultural center.

It is true that Askeberg cannot explain away all southern elements of

---

* The origin of the runes in the Alp regions is maintained by Helmut Arntz, *Handbuch der Runenkunde*, 1944.

the Sigurðr cycle, though he can demonstrate the northern features of the trilogy and its connections with the native Helgi lays. And when Brünhilde in the *Nibelungenlied* is said to be from Iceland and Sigfrid *von den Nederlanden*, Askeberg takes it to indicate interchange between North and South and not a steady northward current of legends and culture.

Finally, Askeberg is inclined to doubt the strict Heuslerian *Lieder-theorie* and to allow the possibility of prose and poem reports of the kind that later grew into the Baltic-oriented *fornaldar saga*. In this he is now supported by German scholars, old students of Heusler.

From the culture which they reflect and from their tone and style, the heroic poems have been divided into three groups: (1) the old heroic lays, *Hamðismál, Atlakviða, Hlöðskviða*, and *Völundarkviða*, (2) the three Helgi lays and the Sigurðr trilogy on his youthful exploits, and (3) the heroic elegies dealing with his death and the fates of the two women who loved him, Brynhildr and Guðrún.

Hlöðskviða alone reveals memories of international conflict in the Migration Period. In the others this conflict—which one might expect in *Hamðismál*, dealing with the death of Jörmunrekkr, and *Atlakviða*, dealing with the killing of Atli—has been metamorphosed into family or at least personal, not national, tragedies. The offenders in these poems perpetrate cruel deeds in their perhaps too human thirst for gold or land. This prompts the offended to take vengeance, unparalleled except in Greek legends and tragedies (slaughtered children are fed to parents who then are told what they have eaten). This is true also of *Völundarkviða*.

The authors of the old heroic lays admire the superhuman strength of character with which their heroes vindicate their honor at the point of death, but they are not interested in fighting in itself, which they almost always minimize. Their admiration is a matter-of-fact acceptance of heroism. These old poems lack both the sentimental lyricism of the heroic elegies and the Viking exuberance of the Helgi lays. They also lack the folklore trappings of the Helgi lays and the Sigurðr trilogy.

In form, these old heroic poems are narrative-dramatic and tend to express action in speech, though to a lesser extent than do the heroic elegies.

The three Helgi lays and the Sigurðr trilogy, relating his youthful exploits, seem to form a unit in the heroic poems. In them, three formal elements are fused: the heroic poem in *fornyrðislag* and narrative form;

the didactic poem in *ljóðaháttr* and dialogue form, and the intermittent prose characteristic of the *fornaldar saga*. In subject matter we find the following features: the flyting (quarrel), also occurring in the mythical poems, and numerous folklore elements, such as gods in disguise, shape-shifting, speaking animals and birds. The intermittent prose and the folklore elements will be found in Saxo and the mythical-heroic sagas (*fornaldar sögur*). These poems may, therefore, be late and represent the twelfth century. On the other hand there seems to be a clear case of Viking spirit in some of the poems, notably the very skaldic first Helgi lay.

Helgakviða Hjörvarðssonar, though placed between the two lays of Helgi Hundingsbani, is considered to be earlier in time, for its lovers, Helgi and Sváva, are reborn in Helgi Hundingsbani and Sigrún. The first lay of Helgi Hundingsbani is a skaldic eulogy of the young hero who is victorious both in avenging his father and in winning his bride, the *valkyrja* Sigrún, who in turn, riding through the sky, gives him magical help in battle. Tragedy comes in the second lay which tells partly the same story but adds the important detail that Helgi has to kill Sigrún's father and brothers to win her hand. When a surviving brother, with Óðinn's help, kills Helgi, Sigrún curses her brother and goes to Helgi's burial mound—but for one night only, for after that he does not return and she dies from mourning. This is the most dramatic of all the heroic love stories.

Though the tragedy in Sigurðr's life is precipitated only after he has married Guðrún Gjúkadóttir and has won the flame-wall-protected Brynhildr for his brother-in-law Gunnar, the success story of his youth, told in *Reginsmál* and *Fáfnismál*, is made ominous by his greatest achievement, the winning of Fáfnir's hoard of gold. From the very beginning this is a cursed hoard, destined to cause the death of every owner, from Hreiðmarr, Fáfnir, and Reginn to Sigurðr and the sons of Gjúki (Gjúkungar). Gold, women, and treachery are the causes of all evil in this heroic society no less than in the world of gods in *Völuspá*. There is much shape-shifting: the original owner of the hoard is a shape-shifting dwarf, and Hreiðmarr's two sons turn into an otter and a dragon, respectively. Here is folk-tale magic, too: Sigurðr drinks the dragon's blood and eats his heart to gain strength and power to understand the language of birds; but for their warning, Reginn would have killed him. But one of the strangest things about these poems is the exchange of conversation between Sigurðr and the dying Fáfnir. One expects Fáfnir

to heap curses upon his slayer Sigurðr, which he does, but one is totally
unprepared for Sigurðr's asking him general questions about the norns,
or in what place the gods and Surtr will fight it out between them, and
for Fáfnir's prompt answers.

After all the teaching which Sigurðr absorbs from the dying Fáfnir
one should, perhaps, not be surprised that *Sigrdrífumál*, the poem about
the Sleeping Beauty *valkyrja* on Hindarfjall whom Sigurðr awakens
from her magic sleep, is not a love poem but another educational session
for the young hero. Here he is taught the first commandment of family
solidarity, that one should not fall foul of his kinsmen and should save
his revenge for people not in the family. Here also he can learn the long
list of magical runes (*rúnatal*) which often should come in handy if one
could master them.

Is Sigrdrífa the same as Brynhildr? The author of *Grípisspá*, a survey
of Sigurðr's life, did not think so. But the collector of the poems (or
the author of the prose pieces) probably thought so, because he describes
Sigrdrífa's life in terms similar to those of *Helreið Brynhildar*. According to *Grípisspá*, Sigurðr met Brynhildr at Heimir's, and had a daughter
Áslaug, from whom Icelanders are descended. To make him forget
Brynhildr, Grímhildr (Gjúki's wife) gives him a drink of oblivion. Only
after that is Sigurðr ready to ride the flame-wall and win Brynhildr
by treachery for Gunnar.

The heroic elegies treat of the death of Sigurðr and the tragic fates
of his two women: Brynhildr, whom he deceives and who causes his
death but follows him on the funeral pyre, and Guðrún, who should have
avenged him on her brothers, but who, instead, was fated to marry Atli,
brother of Brynhildr, and exact the grimmest vengeance on him, when
he killed her brothers.

Brynhildr's saga is told in *Sigurðarkviða in skamma* and in *Helreið
Brynhildar*, Guðrún's story in three lays of Guðrún, *Atlamál* and
Guðrúnarhvöt. *Atlamál* is the longest of the heroic poems and the nearest
approach to, though still far removed from, a West Germanic heroic
epic like *Beowulf*.

The poets love to express the feelings and delineate the characters of
their heroines, mostly by letting them speak in dramatic monologues.
They are much less interested in action and narrative than they are in
describing a situation with their heroines emotionally contemplating their
past or the future. The sentiment is softer than in the old heroic poems;

there is a characteristic dwelling on womanly arts (tapestry-making, *Guðrúnarkviða* II) reminiscent of the ballad.

Similar dramatic monologues are common in Saxo and in the *fornaldar sögur* (death speech of the hero), making plausible a twelfth-century date for these poems.

Types of poetry

Embedded in the typical mythic, gnomic, and heroic poems of the *Edda* are several types of poetry, which stand out like colored bricks in a wall.

One of the oldest of these is the *þula*, a list of gods, elves, dwarfs, heroes, tribes, etc. This mnemonic device underlies much of the didactic poetry and appears as extraneous material in some of the others (cf. the list of dwarfs in *Völuspá*). The Old English *Wídsíþ* contains the earliest *þulur* on record; this type is closely paralleled by a stanza in *Hervarar saga* (*Eddica minora*). In the twelfth-century renaissance the *þula* grows into a veritable lexicon of poetic vocabulary.

Sometimes the gnomic poems flourish into long runs of precepts, like the rigmarole (priamel) in *Hávamál* 81 ff.:

At kveldi skal dag leyfa	Give praise to the day at evening
konu er brend er,	to a woman on her pyre
mæki er reyndr er,	to a weapon which is tried *

This run resembles the long truce formula *Griðamál* in *Grágás* and *Grettis saga*. Otherwise Icelandic law did not employ alliterative formulas.

Riddles can hardly be said to occur in the Eddic poems, but the situation of a god asking and a giant answering or else losing his head is similar to that of the riddles of Gestumblindi in *Hervarar saga*—the only Old Icelandic collection of riddles.

It may be that Skírnir's curse (in *galdralag*) and Sigrún's curse (in *Helgakviða Hundingsbana* II) represent the only true magic poetry in the Eddic poems. But there is a list of such songs, *Ljóðatal*, in *Hávamál* as well as one of magic runes, *Rúnatal*, in *Sigrdrífumál*. These lists show what we might have had, if the songs had been preserved. Egill's curse (*níð*) of King Eiríkr blóðöx is skaldic in form.

Closely related to the magic curse is calumny and slander (*níð, flím, flimtan, spott*) in verse. In the Eddic poems it is represented by the

---

* This and the following translations of the Eddic Poems are taken from Henry Adams Bellows, *The Poetic Edda*.

quarreling between heroes (or a hero and a giantess) in the Helgi lays,
and between gods in *Hárbarðsljóð* (Óðinn against Þórr) and *Lokasenna*
(Loki against the gods). These heroic boasting matches are old; witness
the flyting between Beowulf and Unferð. They live on in the sagas in the
form of *mannjafnaðr*, " man matching," the most famous example being
the verbal contest between the two royal brothers in *Heimskringla*,
Sigurðr and Eysteinn, sons of King Magnús berfœttr.

Opposed to these songs of hate are love songs, of which there are
many instances in the Eddic poems, as well as among the skalds. Actually, both love songs and calumnies were prohibited by law, the
enforcement of which was perhaps not observed.

One would expect to find in the mythic poetry some instances of
ritualistic cult songs as well as invocations or hymns to the gods. As a
matter of fact, *Skírnismál* and the frame story of some didactic poems
have been thought to represent ritualistic drama, though few scholars
have accepted that view. But if we may believe Adam of Bremen, the
ritualistic songs used at the temple at Uppsalir (Uppsala) in Sweden
would have been found too indecent for preservation. Perhaps the poem
of *Völsa þáttr* in *Flateyjarbók*, containing a phallus ritual, may give us
some hints about this suppressed poetry.

Invocations and hymns are even more strangely absent from the Eddic
poems, the chief examples being the beautiful invocation at the beginning
of *Sigrdrífumál*:

Heill dagr	Hail day!
heilir dags synir	Hail sons of day!
heil nótt ok nipt!	And night and her daughter now!
Óreiðum augum	Look on us here
lítið okkr þinig	with loving eyes,
ok gefið sitjöndum sigr.	that waiting we victory win.
Heilir æsir	Hail to the gods!
heilar ásynjur	Ye goddesses hail!
heil sjá en fjölnýta fold!	And all the generous earth!
Mál ok mannvit	Give us wisdom
gefið okkr mærum tveim	and goodly speech
ok læknishendr meðan lifum.	and healing hands, life-long.

Why, we ask, would such innocent and beautiful poetry be suppressed
if there was much of it? Or is this a reflection of the medieval Latin
invocation to God and the Muses?

Another and much more common type of invocation is the " Give
silence and listen to my song," which is not only an indispensable formula
of the skaldic praise poems, but used also in *Völuspá*:

Hljóðs bið ek allar	Hearing I ask
helgar kindir	from the holy races,
meiri ok minni	from Heimdall's sons,
mögu Heimdallar.	both high and low.

Metrics and form

In Eddic poetry we find three metrical measures in use: *fornyrðislag* (epic measure), *málaháttr* (speech measure), and *ljóðaháttr* (chant measure). They are all based on the old Germanic alliterative long line, and they all tend to be stanzaic. These forms, especially the *fornyrðislag*, have been practiced in Iceland up to the present day.

Fornyrðislag and *málaháttr* represent essentially the same meter, a continuation of the Germanic alliterative long line. This line was cut by a caesura into two half-lines or verses, each of which had two lifts or stresses usually separated by one or more unstressed syllables. The two verses were united to a couplet by alliteration, a kind of initial rime, most appropriate in a language stressing root syllables. Only the lifts could alliterate. In the first verse one or both lifts might alliterate (they were called *stuðlar*, " props or staves "), but in the second verse the first lift had to carry the alliteration (it was called *höfuð-stafr*, " head-stave "). Consonants could alliterate only with themselves, so, too, the consonant groups *sp*, *st*, *sk*, but vowels could alliterate with any other vowels. As a West Germanic example we quote two lines from the Old English poem *Widsíþ*, illustrating our rules:

> 'Ætla weold Hunum / 'Eormanric Gotum
> 'Becca 'Baningum / 'Burgendum Gifica.

The rules of alliteration are a *sine qua non* of all Icelandic poetry. Since Snorri's time Icelandic metricists have looked upon the verse (half-line), called *vísuorð* or *orð*, as a unit two of which make the alliterative couplet, the long alliterative line of the West Germanic metricists. It is only a different point of view, but it is reflected in the practice of printing Icelandic poetry:

'Ár var'alda	Of old was the age
þar er 'Ymir bygði;	when Ymir lived;
var-a 'sandr né 'sær	Sea nor cool waves
né 'svalar unnir;	nor sand there were;
'jörð fannz 'æva	Earth had not been
né 'upphiminn;	nor heaven above,
'gap var 'Ginnunga	But a yawning gap
en 'gras hvergi.	and grass nowhere.

This sample of *fornyrðislag* is from the *Völuspá*. Disregarding the unstressed onsets (anacruces), each verse tends toward four syllables, thus contrasting with the lengthy verse of West Germanic poetry. But *málaháttr*, occuring in the *Edda* only in the two lays of Atli, stands nearer to the West Germanic lines, tending toward five or more syllables in a verse. This is an example from *Atlakviða*:

'Atli mik hingat sendi	Now Atli has sent me
ríða 'örindi	his errand to ride,
'mar inum 'mélgreypa	On my bit-champing steed
'Myrkvið inn ókunna,	trough Myrkwood the secret,
at 'biðja yðr, Gunnarr,	To bid you, Gunnar,
at ið á 'bekk kœmit	to his benches to come,
með 'hjalmum aringreypum	With helms round the hearth,
at sœkja'heim Atla.	and Atli's home seek.

It has been suggested that the lengthy and irregular lines of this poem are archaic, while the shorter lines of *Völuspá* represent a secondary development. This tendency toward streamlining of forms, shortening, and syllable-counting, may result from skaldic influence. The skalds counted syllables from the first.

The two specimens are normal stanzas of eight verses (*vísuorð*) each. In the first stanza each couplet (long line) is one sentence, while the second stanza is one long sentence, with a subordinate clause beginning the second half (*helmingr* " helming ") of the stanza. But as a rule there is a syntactical break in the middle of the stanza dividing it into two halves, helmings. For skaldic verse this is obligatory.

Most Eddic poems have stanzas exceeding or falling short of this norm. Late nineteenth-century scholars, who discovered the metrical norms for the lines (E. Sievers's five types) and tended to cut irregular lines, also tended to assume losses or additions if the stanza was not normal. Now the tendency is to view such irregularity against the West Germanic background of stichic poetry. The irregularity of stanza length represents an archaic stage in the Eddic poetry and it is natural to find it in old poems like *Völundarkviða*.

Most of the heroic poems and a few of the mythological poems are in *fornyrðislag* or *málaháttr*. Such poems are often called *kviður* (pl.), a word related to the verb *kveða*, " recite."

Ljóðaháttr is a meter with no parallels outside of Scandinavia. It is built of three verses (half-lines), of which the first two are unified by alliteration to a couplet (like two verses of *fornyrðislag*) while the third has alliteration of its own (two lifts). Two such helmings make up a whole stanza of six verses. This is an example from *Hávamál*:

Hrörnar 'þöll	On the hillside drear
sú er stendr 'þorpi á,	the firtree dies
hlýrat henni 'börkr né 'barr;	All bootless its needles and bark;
svá er 'maðr	It is like a man
sá er'manngi ann;	whom no one loves,—
hvat skal hann 'lengi 'lifa?	Why should his life be long?

Ljóðaháttr is used preferably as a vehicle of speech poems or dialogue, dramatic or didactic; many of the mythological but very few of the heroic poems are composed in it. Such poems are usually called *mál* (" speech poems "?).

A variation of *ljóðaháttr* with an added line of the same structure as the last one or a repetition of it is called *galdralag* because it was used for magic purposes. Here is an example from a second helming of a stanza in *Skírnismál*:

'Heyri jötnar,	Give heed, frost-rulers,
'heyri hrímþursar,	hear it, giants,
'synir 'Suttunga,	Sons of Suttung,
'sjálfir ásliðar:	And gods, ye too,
hvé ek 'fyrir'býð	How I forbid
hvé ek 'fyrir'banna	and how I ban
'manna glaum 'mani	The meeting of men with the maid,
'manna nyt 'mani.	The joy of men with the maid.

We moderns may think that these two or three Eddic measures might be confines too narrow for the old poets to practice their art within. But whoever is able to read these poems aloud will soon find that the form is anything but monotonous. The reason for this is the freedom with which the poets fill their lines. In this respect *fornyrðislag*, and especially the fuller *málaháttr*, vies with hexameter or blank verse, if not in fullness, then in the marvellous ease with which the meter fits the sentence structure. The verse may be full or cut to the very bone of two words in a verse, but the patterns of stress are so various and allow the poet such latitude that the meter becomes a perfect instrument for his expression. It is this freedom of expression which makes the Eddic meters a complete antithesis to the meters of the skaldic poetry.

It is not known whether the Eddic poetry was recited or sung. There is no story of singing to the accompaniment of the harp like the charming tale of Cædmon in Northumbria. Yet the harp is mentioned in the heroic poems (Gunnar playing the harp in the snake pit) and in *Völuspá*. The word *ljóð* in *ljóðaháttr* and *Hárbarðsljóð* probably meant "song" and that, too, must be the original meaning of *galdr* in *galdralag* and *Grógaldr* (*gala galdr* "sing a magic song"). Clear is the meaning of *söngr* "song" in *Gróttasöngr*. From descriptions in the sagas we know that the poems used in sorcery rituals were sung, as their name implies; we may guess that they were composed in *galdralag* or *ljóðaháttr*. Melodies to *fornyrðislag* and *ljóðaháttr* exist, but they may be relatively late. They are found in Bjarni Þorsteinsson, *Íslenzk þjóðlög* (1906-1909, pp. 466 ff.).

Style

Though there is a good deal of variation in style and form to be found in the Eddic poems, ranging from the "free verse" of *Hárbarðs-ljóð* to the meticulous lines of *Þrymskviða*, the poems, nevertheless, stand out as a related group when compared with the West Germanic epic on the one hand and the contemporary skaldic poetry on the other. Because of the high artificiality of the latter group, Eddic poetry often seems nearer in spirit to the West Germanic group, with which it shares the specific poetic vocabulary differentiating it from the prose.

The Eddic poetry lacks the epic breadth and the slow movement of the West Germanic epics; it lacks, too, the stylistic features chiefly responsible for these: the variation and the enjambment of lines.

The movement of the Eddic poems is quick, often almost rushing. The swiftly changing scene is frequently brought about by repetition, which is reminiscent of the ballads (incremental repetition, as in *Þryms-kviða*). But this repetition is quite different from the West Germanic variation.

Variation is found in *Atlakviða*, rarely elsewhere. Sentences sometimes fill a couplet or a long line (*Þrymskviða*), rarely only a verse (*Atlamál*). Most commonly a sentence fills up the half stanza or the helming, sometimes the whole stanza; practically never does it run over into the next stanza.

The *kenning*, which will be discussed in connection with skaldic verse, is more in evidence in the Eddic than in the West Germanic poetry but much less so than in the skaldic poetry. The usage of it is far from uniform. It is employed more widely in *Hymiskviða* than in the other poems. *Heiti* are more common than kennings.

Skaldic Poetry

Skaldic poetry originating in Scandinavia

The trend of modern opinion seems to be that skaldic poetry originated in (West) Norway or in the Scandinavian Baltic. If so, it could
not have started until after the exodus of the English from Jutland-Angel
(fifth century). It appears fully developed in the poetry of Bragi hinn
gamli, a Norwegian flourishing *ca.* 800–850 (or *ca.* 835–900, cf. p. 6
above), the ancestor of an Icelandic family of skalds.

Origin as court poetry

Most scholars assume that skaldic poetry originated at the courts of
kings, the poems being praise poems to celebrate the deeds of these
kings. The Icelandic custom of visiting the kings of Scandinavia (primarily Norway) and England, does not seem essentially different from
the manners of the fictitious scop Wídsíþ, who is made to visit the famous
Gothic Ermanric and other Germanic kings famed in story before the
sixth century.

Origin in magic or epitaphs (erfiljóð)

But other theories of origin are not lacking, for the subject matter is
not invariably praise of kings. In the ninth century we find peculiar
shield poetry describing ornaments representing myths and heroic legends
(Bragi: *Ragnarsdrápa*). We find genealogical poetry (*Ynglingatal*),
mythological poetry (*Þórskvæði*), an epitaph, and a lot of occasional verse
along with the two praise poems of Þorbjörn hornklofi—the one in Eddic
meter and style (*Haraldskvæði*), the other in *dróttkvætt* (*Glymdrápa*),
a forerunner of the genuine praise poems.

From the tenth century we find instances of *dróttkvætt* used in runic
inscriptions for magic purposes. There is the copper box in Sigtuna,
Sweden, with a *dróttkvætt* curse for the thief who steals it, and there is
the famous curse of Egill Skalla-Grímsson, presumably cut in runes of a

magic number, designed to drive King Eiríkr blóðöx from his realm. This has been demonstrated by Magnus Olsen (" Troldruner," 1916), who also believes that the old custom of erecting a *bautasteinn* (runic stone) may have been replaced by the one of composing for the deceased an epitaph in *dróttkvætt*. In elaboration of this idea, it has been suggested that the epitaphs in *dróttkvætt* might be the point of departure for this form. Their purpose would have been to keep the dead from " walking back " and to insure the heirs unmolested ownership of the deceased's possessions and his good luck. And one would not be surprised to find obscurities, circumlocutions, tabu- and noa-words (like *lyng-fiskr*, snake), in a language of magic. In all these respects the style and vocabulary of the skalds recalls the language on the Eggjum stone (*ca.* 700), placed in a grave to prevent the dead from walking.

If one believes in the magic origin of skaldic poetry one should not forget the *dróttkvætt* dream verse in *Sturlunga saga,* which was to be recited alternately by two men in exactly the same way as the Lapps recited their magic formulas and the Finns their epic *Kalevala* (cf. p. 31). *Kalevala* is habitually sung, and tunes to *dróttkvætt* do exist, though they may be relatively late. A melody to *Þat mælti mín móðir* by Egill Skalla-Grímsson is found in Bjarni Þorsteinsson, *Íslenzk þjóðlög* (1906-09, p. 523).

Comparison of Eddic and skaldic poetry

It is useful to visualize the differences and similarities between the Eddic and skaldic poetry. There is the difference in meters: Eddic poetry makes use of the simpler ones: *fornyrðislag, málaháttr, ljóðaháttr,* while the skalds use *dróttkvætt* primarily or other meters even more elaborate (*runhent, hrynhent*). Still they occasionally use the Eddic meters and *kviðuháttr,* but never *ljóðaháttr.*

Even greater are the differences in diction and style, the elaborate diction appearing with the skaldic meters. The highly valued artistry of skaldic poetry must have been one reason that not only was the poetry remembered, but also the poets themselves: a skald's name would outlive his verse, while the makers of Eddic verse were always anonymous like the saga writers later.

One more fundamental difference: the Eddic poems are objective and epic; they tell an impersonal story. Skaldic poetry is mostly subjective and occasional, extolling the latest exploits of the king or commenting on some incident in the poet's own life. This makes for actuality in skaldic poems. They are rarely dialogic in the Eddic manner, but descriptive and expressionistic, driving home their points in images or sound-sketches of concentrated force. The king's sailings and battles are varied *ad infinitum*, strictly against Eddic conventional avoidance of battle scenes.

Skaldic poetry actual: historical value

The actuality of the king's eulogies derives from the circumstance that they must have been based on the king's recent feats. No poet would dare praise his chief for fictitious exploits; hence the poems were not only intended by king and court to be historical records, but they also became just that and owe their preservation to the fact that historians of the twelfth and the thirteenth centuries understood their value and quoted them as sources. No one appreciated them more than the famous historian Snorri Sturluson, and no one has preserved for us more of skaldic poetry than he in his *Edda* and his *Heimskringla*.

But the peculiar form and style of the skaldic poetry often militates against its historical value. The skald was not bent upon telling a connected story, but just a series of concentrated snapshots from the king's life: his valor in battle, his fleet sailing, or his generosity in the hall. True, an allusion to a specific event may be dropped now and then, but mostly the descriptions are so general that one feels that, but for the prose anecdote containing the verse, one would not understand the verse.

Uses of skaldic poetry: long court poems, occasional verse

We have seen that skaldic poetry was used for praising kings, chiefs, and friends, sometimes gods (*Þórr*); in shield poetry describing the legends or myths pictured on the shields, perhaps to honor the giver; in genealogical poems to honor the scion of a great family; and in epitaphs (*erfiljóð*) over men important to the poet, whether a king, a friend, or a kinsman.

These poems were mostly long and formal (*flokkar, drápur*), and so were their descendants, the historical praise poems of the twelfth century celebrating kings, heroes, and battles of the past, and the praise poems of saints, the only poems to continue this tradition after 1300—all the way down to the Reformation.

Less formal was the occasional poetry (*lausavísur*) in skaldic meters. Here the authors are not only the recognized skalds, but everybody who could turn an occasional verse, and their number seems to have been legion in Iceland.

We hear the exultant voice of the boy Egill, when his mother promises him that he shall get a ship and become a Viking; we hear him as a fullfledged Viking exhort his companions to a " commando " raid on Lund, Sweden; and, near death, we hear him lament his senility.

We have a nursery rime (*Hafr er úti*) and we may have a worksong, similar to one in *Gróttasöngr*, in the boasting ditty of an old Viking in his forge.

There are many dream songs, often of threatening import and adorned with ghastly repetition.

There is naturally much love poetry, and this in spite of the fact that it was strictly forbidden by law. From the sagas one might infer that the law was not enforced in this case. There is nothing unseemly about the love poetry that has survived. In more southern climes this poetry would seem unsentimental and subdued in feeling. Yet we have the spectacle of a betrayed husband who states his heartache in a stanza of this sort just before he cuts off his wife's fair head.

We have already spoken of the magic use the skalds made of *dróttkvætt*. Here Egill's curse is the shining example, but he could also use his craft for healing a spellbound maiden.

Related to the magic curses are lampoons (*flim*), also called *niðvísur*, designed to calumniate an opponent. These *niðvísur* are often composed in the simpler Eddic meters; their contents are often accusation of homosexuality. A good example is the stanza composed about Friðrekr biskup and Þorvaldr viðförli, early missionaries in Iceland. It says the bishop has given birth to nine children, Þorvaldr being the father. But instead of offering the other cheek, in Christian fashion, Þorvaldr killed two men to avenge the injury—in a good heathen manner.

Sometimes the calumnies would be strung along in a contest or a flyting which must have given the pattern on which the mythic and heroic flytings (*Hárbarðsljóð, Lokasenna, Helgakviður*) were moulded. These flytings are also related to the *mannjafnaðr*, the matching of men, of the sagas (cp. p. 39).

Sometimes the disputes would take the form of a harmless banter over ale-cups, as in the bridal at Reykhólar, but it could reach a more dangerous level if somebody thought his honor at stake. The banter which king Haraldr harðráði loved his poets to take part in was harmless enough, but tended to obscenity.

Saga verse: conventional mixing of prose and poetry

We already have (p. 46) mentioned the fact that a praise poem of a king would become incorporated in the twelfth- and thirteenth-century kings' sagas as historical evidence, a footnote. This became a literary convention in the later kings' sagas and in the thirteenth-century sagas of Icelanders, the verses of which are often suspect and may even have been composed by the saga-writer himself.

But the convention of mixing prose with poetry is even older than the kings' sagas. At the famous bridal of Reykhólar in 1119 we hear of a story-teller who composed a *fornaldar saga* with many verses and told it to entertain the guests. It was a fictional story, except for the name of the hero. We shall return to this story later.

Form: meters (hættir)

Like the West Germanic and Eddic meters, especially the *fornyrðislag*, all skaldic meters preserve the pattern of the alliterative couplet (or the alliterative long line in non-Scandinavian Germanic parlance) with alliteration falling on certain stressed syllables or lifts. In *fornyrðislag* with four lifts to the couplet, two in each verse (*vísuorð*), the alliteration *must* fall on the first lift of the second verse (*höfuðstafr*), and one or both (*stuðlar*) in the first verse. In skaldic meters the rule is the same: but here there must always be two alliterating lifts in the first verse.

Before we turn our attention to the typical skaldic meter *dróttkvætt*, it is convenient to look at certain other meters more closely related to *fornyrðislag*, and probably deriving from it through normalizing certain features like syllable-counting or by adding end rime.

In normalizing the Eddic *fornyrðislag*, there was a tendency among the skalds to make their verses (*vísuorð*) of four syllables (not counting the eventual onsets [anacruces]). This was the form used by some twelfth-century skalds and by Snorri in his *Háttatal*. The *málaháttr*, with a fuller verse than *fornyrðislag*, remains pretty irregular in the ninth-century court poetry of Haraldr hárfagri's skalds, though Snorri prunes it to five syllables a verse (*vísuorð*) in *Háttatal*.

In *Ynglingatal* by the Norwegian Þjóðólfr of Hvinir and in Egill Skalla-Grímsson's poems *Arinbjarnarkviða* and *Sonatorrek* the meter is *kviðuháttr*, with three syllables only in the odd verses (*vísuorð*) but the regular four in the even ones, a variation of *fornyrðislag*. A sample from *Ynglingatal*:

Varð framgengt	Fate did strike
þars Fróði bjó	where Fróði lived,
feigðar orð	word of doom
es at Fjölni kom.	awaited Fjölnir.

This type of verse occurs first as an irregularity in a stanza on the eighth-century runic stone of Rök, Sweden:

Ræið ÞiaurikR	Ruled Theodoric
hinn þormóði	the reckless brave
stillir flotna	steerer of fleet
strandu HræiðmaraR.	the strand of Hreiðmarr.

The fact that ninth-century skalds made a syllable-counting rule out of an irregular feature (*Ræið ÞiaurikR*) harmonizes well with the syllable-counting in regular *dróttkvætt*.

In Egill Skalla-Grímsson's *Höfuðlausn* we see *fornyrðislag* fitted with end rimes, a variation called *runhenda* or *runhent*. The translation is done by Lee M. Hollander in *The Skalds*:

Jöfurr hyggi at,	May the hero heed
hve ek yrkja fat,	how I herald his deed:
gótt þykkjumk þat,	was silence given
er ek þögn of gat;	so my song has thriven.
hrœrðak munni	Now I have stirred
af munar grunni	with heartfelt word
Óðins ægi	Allfather's-gift
of jöru fægi.	Eric to uplift.

Since the poem was composed in York (948) it is natural to assume, and has long been assumed, that Egill had heard some Old English rimed poetry similar to passages in Cynewulf's *Elene* and to the *Riming Poem*. Ultimately the rime (and meter?) was derived from Irish-Latin hymns as I have shown in my paper on " The Origin of Egill Skalla-Grímsson's Runhenda " (1954). This is a sample of the Irish-Latin *Rhythmus ad Deum*:

Sancte sator,	legum lator,
suffragator	largus dator.

Later, rime was extended also to the longer and more regular verses of *dróttkvætt* and *hrynhent*. Conversely, the " precious " (*dýrr*) assonances and inrimes of *dróttkvætt* were sometimes foisted upon the simple *fornyrðislag*, resulting in the variation *töglag* and others.

The most typical and most common skaldic meter is called *dróttkvætt*, a name obviously derived from *drótt* (OE *dryht*), meaning body of retainers, court; hence, a meter fit for the court.

As an example we can take Egill Skalla-Grímsson's curse stanza (which, according to Magnus Olsen, also was written with 72 (8 × 9) runes to enhance the magic effect). The translation is from Lee M. Hollander's *The Skalds*:

Svá sk*y*ldi 'goð 'gj*a*lda	May the powers repay the
—'gram reki b*önd* af l*önd*um,	prince and drive him from his

'reið sé 'rögn ok Óðinn,—
'rán míns féar hánum;
'folkmýgi lát'flýja,
'Freyr ok Njörðr af jörðum,
'leiðisk 'lofða stríði
'landáss, þanns vé grandar.

realm, for wroth are at the
robber all gods and Odin:
put to flight the oppressor
of people, Freyr and Njord, the
foe of freemen who de-
filed the holy thingmeet.

The metrical unit here is the three-lift verse (*vísuorð*: West Germanic half-line) made up of six syllables of which the last two always make a trochaic (feminine) ending. This number of syllables is fixed, though it is possible to replace a long syllable with two shorts (cf. English *full: fully* = - : ⌣ ⌣).

Two verses (*vísuorð*) are joined to an alliterative couplet (alliteration marked by ') with two lifts in the first verse (*stuðlar* " staffs," " props ") alliterating with the first lift in the second verse (*höfuðstafr* " headstave," " chief stave "). This rule of alliteration, essentially the same as in *fornyrðislag*, is also practically a *sine qua non* of all later Icelandic poetry.

But this is not all. The first verse in each alliterative couplet of *dróttkvætt* should have internal consonant assonance (i. e., similarity of consonants following a different vowel) in two stressed or half-stressed syllables, while the second verse should have internal full rime (inrime). Thus in *dróttkvætt* the odd verses should have assonance (*skothending*, e. g., *fold: field*), the even verses inrime (*aðalhending*, e. g., *old: sold*). Both assonance and inrime are marked by italics in the sample above. But these rules were not always strictly carried out. Exceptions are especially numerous among the oldest poets: Bragi, Egill, while it would be hard to find them in a polished eleventh-century poet like Sighvatr.

Two alliterative couplets make up the helming (*helmingr*, half-stanza) of four verses (*vísuorð*), while two helmings make up the whole stanza (*vísa*) of *dróttkvætt*, invariably of eight verses, except in *galdralag* where the last verse of the stanza is always repeated.

In the overwhelming majority of cases the helming is also a syntactic unit, making up one sentence, however involved in structure. The second helming sometimes represents a subordinate clause; rarely is a sentence confined within the alliterative couplet.

There are several variations of *dróttkvætt*, some of which are realized by varying internal rime (e. g., the *dunhent* of Egill) or adding end rime, others by cutting a syllable either at the end (*hneppt*, used by one settler) making a masculine ending, or inside the *vísuorð*. Thus arises *haðarlag* with five syllables (reminding one of *málaháttr*), used by

Vetrliði Sumarliðason (d. 999) in a poem (invocation or praise?) to
Þórr:

Leggi brautzt þú Leiknar	Legs of Leikn you smashed up
lamðir Þrívalda	lame struck Þrívaldi
steypðir Starkeði	stoop made Starkaðr
stóttu of Gjalp dauða.	stood o'er Gjalp lifeless.

But most of the variations do not appear until the twelfth century,
when interest in metrical variety—also apparent in Latin literature of the
time, cp. Saxo Grammaticus—grows by leaps and bounds. This is shown
by the *Háttalykill*, a *clavis metrica*, attributed to Earl Rögnvaldr kali of
the Orkney Islands and his Icelandic collaborator Hallr Þórarinsson.

There is, however, every reason to mention here the *hrynhendr háttr*
or *hrynhenda*, the first instance of which is attributed to a man from the
Hebrides who, late in the tenth century (986), got walled in by huge
ocean waves at sea and on the occasion composed the *Hafgerðinga-drápa*
(the Sea-Wall Poem) whose refrain was as follows (translation by A.
M. Reeves from *The Finding of Wineland the Good*):

'Mínar bið ek 'munka reyni	Mine adventure to the Meek One,
'meinalausan farar beina;	Monk-heart-searcher, I commit now;
'heiðis haldi 'hárar foldar	He who heaven's halls doth govern
'hallar dróttinn yfir mér stalli.	Hold the hawk's-seat ever o'er me!

Here we have a four lift verse (*vísuorð*) of eight syllables, while the
rules of alliteration, assonance, and inrime are the same as in *dróttkvætt*.
In all probability this stately verse derives from the same Irish-English-
Latin hymns which also gave rise to the rimed *fornyrðislag* or *runhent*
above, though the lines were not always combined with rime. Example
with inrime and without:

Sancte sator suffragator,	Vale frater florentibus
legum lator, largus dator	iuventutis cum viribus
iure pollens, es qui potens	ut floreas cum Domino
nunc in aethra firma petra	in sempiterno solio

The examples are from F. J. E. Raby, *A History of Christian-Latin
Poetry from the Beginnings to the Close of the Middle Ages* (Oxford
1953, p. 138 and 150). This Latin meter is trochaic tetrameter.

The meter *hrynhent* was to become very popular in court poetry, but
its most famous exponent was the Catholic praise poem *Lilja* by the
fourteenth-century monk Eysteinn Ásgrímsson.

Finally we must mention the meter called *stýft* or *hálfhneppt*, which may
be derived from *hrynhent* by cutting the feminine ending (A. Heusler).

Apart from a spurious verse of Haraldr hárfagri, the meter first occurs in a stanza of Björn Breiðvíkingakappi (*ca.* 997). The translation was done by L. M. Hollander for a forthcoming edition of *Eyrbyggja saga*:

Sýlda skark svanafold	Unfalt'ringly, my fraught ship
súðum þvít gæi-brúðr	furrowed the swan-road's
ástum leiddi oss fast	icy waters for she
austan með hlaðit flaust;	warmly loved me—from th' east:
víða gat ek vásbúð;	the helmsman much mishap
—víglundr nú um stund	whelmed; and now he lies
helli byggvir hugfullr—	cowering here in cold
hingat fyr konu bing.	cave, instead of her bed.

This meter, with its staccato cadence of an otherwise rhythmically free line (mostly of six syllables), was not only listed in the two *claves metricae* of Rögnvaldr and Snorri but is found occasionally used by skalds from the eleventh century onwards. It is also found in three long legendary poems of the Virgin Mary in the fourteenth century. The modern poet Stefán Ólafsson uses it. It reminds one of the staccato Skeltonic verse in English.

If the stanzas of *dróttkvætt* were artificial, the poems were not less elaborate structurally. The most common form of the court praise poem was the *drápa* in which stanza groups were marked off by *stef* (refrain) making up an introduction, middle part or parts, and a conclusion. A good example is Egill's *Höfuðlausn,* a *drápa* of twenty stanzas and two *stef,* the first occurring after stanzas six and nine, the second after twelve and fifteen. There were even more elaborate forms: Þjóðólfr Arnórsson composed a *drápa* of six *stef* (*Sexstefja*) about King Haraldr harðráði. A poem without a *stef* and of rather few stanzas was called *flokkr,* and not considered fit fare for kings and courts.

Form: poetical diction and style

Even more complicated than meters and structure was the poetic diction of the skalds. And in this diction there are two features of outstanding importance: the use of *heiti* and *kenningar,* both in endless elaboration of the nouns. In comparison with the all-important nouns, adjectives get rather little elaboration and verbs none at all. The skaldic style is a nominal style.

Heiti (usual meaning: " name " or " proper name ") is a term borrowed from Snorri's *Edda.* Though Snorri does not define it clearly, it obviously stands for uncompounded poetical nouns in contrast to the compounded *kenning* (also Snorri's term). An example from English would be the poetical *steed* as compared to the prosaic *horse*. A survey of the skaldic *heiti* shows that they represent (1) archaisms, (2) common words with a specific meaning, (3) new poetic creations, (4) loanwords, and (5) the so-called half-kennings. The two last-named categories are too rare to need much comment. Archaic words are often of common Germanic origin, e. g., *fúrr*, fire, *spjör*, spear. Many common words with specific meanings in prose get a generalized meaning in poetry; thus *brúðr*, bride, comes to mean " woman " in general, *brim*, surf, comes to mean " sea," *fólk*, folk, comes to mean people in fight, and then " fight, battle." For sea or ocean the skald could press into service such words as deep, flood, tide, expanse, surf, breakers, salt, wave, the wide one, the transparent one, the passable one, etc.

Related to these poetic *heiti* are proper nouns, especially of the gods; notably Óðinn is a god of many names (cf. *Grímnismál*). The multitude of Óðinn's names and the fact that his name is not used as a prop word in kennings for man has suggested connections with the old name magic and name tabu.

The newly created poetic words are mostly compounded words, often coinages of great beauty like *eygló*, " ever glowing " and *fagrahvel*, " fair wheel," both designations for the sun and both taken from *Alvíssmál*, a repository of such coinages.

In contrast to the simple *heiti* a *kenning* is always made up of two elements: a prop word and a definer. As a rule the definer precedes the prop word as a genitive or the first part of a compound; the prop word will not yield the meaning desired except when characterized by this genitive. The definer could also be called determinant.

The simplest type of kenning may be seen in combinations like *Óðins sonr*, son of Óðinn, where *sonr* is the prop word, *Óðins* the definer. In this type a man is defined by his origin, his property, or his work. It is common in West Germanic poetry (*bearn Healfdenes, Beowulf*).

In another type, very common, the prop word is a doer (*nomen agentis*), the definer the object of the doer's action. Thus *baug-broti*, " breaker of rings," a generous man (OE *beag-gifa*).

In a third group the meaning of the prop word remains little changed by the definer, though its meaning is specified. So in *hjör-lögr*, " sword liquid," i. e., blood, the blood remains a liquid (*lögr*), but sword indicates what sort of liquid it is. Even this type is found in OE: *gúð-wudu*, " battle wood," i. e., shield.

In the fourth group of kennings there is a radical change of meaning in the prop word, often a complete antithesis. Thus *lyng-fiskr*, " heather fish," is not a fish at all but a snake, crawling in the heather like a fish in the sea. Likewise, *Haka bláland*, " the blue land of Haki (a sea-king, pirate) " is not a land but its opposite: the blue sea. Two very common kennings for men or warriors belong to this group. In one the prop word means tree, wood or staff: *auð-stafir*, " staffs of wealth," i. e., men, in the other the prop word is some god's name, usually Týr, sometimes Freyr and Njörðr, practically never Óðinn or Þórr. E. g., *sverð-Týr*, " sword-Týr," a warrior, man.

The complexity of kennings could still be increased considerably by breaking up either the prop word or the definer, or both, into another two-element kenning. Thus the ship, " the horse of the sea," might also be termed " the horse of the land of Haki," or " the hart of the ride of the land of Haki." Furthermore, Haki, being a sea-king, could be called " the ruler of the swan-path," and so on theoretically *ad libitum*. In practice, however, kennings of more than three or four parts are rare; a kenning of seven parts is cited as the upper limit. These kennings are called *reknar*; one might call them " augmented " in English.

In the formation of kennings we sometimes have telescoped similes or metaphors; thus a wave-horse calls forth the picture of a ship running over the waves as a horse runs over land. But most of the kennings of group four, not least so when they are *reknar* (augmented), are more readily associated with riddles than anything else.

The solving of these riddles depended partly on ingenuity, partly on knowledge or learning. Ingenuity would tell you that a ship is the horse, steed, stallion, mare, stud of the sea, ocean, main, sound, channel, water, flood, and tide. But one would have to know the names of the sea-kings, like Haki, Meiti, etc., and one would have to be familiar with the old mythology and the heroic legends to understand the allusions of many kennings. This is the reason why Snorri started his *Edda* with a mythology and followed it up with several stories from the heroic legends.

Here we find explanations why gold is called Freyja's tears—Freyja once wept golden tears; or why gold is called Kraki's seed—Kraki sowed gold on Fýrisvellir in Sweden to delay his pursuers who could not help stooping for the red metal. Here, too, is the explanation why gold is called the Rhine metal—it is the famous legend of the Gjúkungar-Niflungs, who threw their gold into the Rhine. Many other kennings find their explanation here; for instance the complex and common kennings of poetry, referring to the story of the mead of poetry and how

Óðinn stole it from the giants. But there are also numerous kennings to the allusions of which we have lost the key forever.

Apart from *heiti* and *kenning*, both nominal elements, adjectives, *epitheta ornantia*, also played some role in skaldic verse, while the verbs were relegated to a relative insignificance. There was no variation in the West Germanic sense, but much harping on the same theme through variegated kennings, replacing not only simple nouns but also pronouns.

Though sentences were mostly confined to one helming, the structure was usually involved and the word-order free. True, for the last twenty years of his life E. A. Kock was gallantly trying to save the skaldic poetry from what he called the topsy-turvy style of Finnur Jónsson's editions, and other scholars have been busy demonstrating a pattern in the chaos. Pattern there undoubtedly is, but it is as intricate as the word order is unprosaic. In the brief compass of the helming one could have two or three strands of thought intertwined like polyphonic music, or intercalated one within the other like Chinese boxes. As an example we quote Hallfreðr's last stanza with Hollander's translation:

Ek munda nú andask	Dreadless would I die now—
—ungr vask harðr í tungu—	dagger-sharp my tongue was—
senn, ef sálu minni,	nor sad, if saved I knew my
sorglaust, vissak borgit.	soul was with my Maker:
Veitk at vættki sýtik	I shall not worry—well I
(valdi goð, hvar aldri)	wot that some time each must
—dauðr verðr hverr—nema	die—hell-fire I fear, though—
hræðumk	
helvíti (skal slíta).	for my God will keep me.

The polyphony is reduced to a duet—but what a duet!—in Egill's stanza, also in Hollander's translation:

Vasa tunglskin	Fearsom was't
tryggt at líta	to face or flinch
né ógnlaust	the angry glance
Eiríks bráa,	of Eric's brow-moons
þás ormfránn	when sharply
*enni*máni	they shot keen beams
skein *allvalds*	from under
œgigeislum.	the atheling's brows.

The ornate style of the *dróttkvæði* has long been compared with the Scandinavian animal ornamentation in metal work and wood-carving of the same period, most strikingly illustrated by the magnificent treasure of the Oseberg ship, now in Oslo, Norway. It has even been proposed that it was formed in imitation of this style (Hallvard Lie).

And it has also, and for good reason, been compared to the twisted style of polyphonic music that culminated in Bach. Although that is a daring comparison, it does help to understand the nature of skaldic poetry. Furthermore, it may be said that the style which Snorri refers to as *nykrat* is a style of baroque dissonance with deliberate mixture of metaphor (cf. Einar skálaglamm's " Hear, Earl, the blood of Kvásir ") while the style of *nýgörvingar* represents harmonic polyphony with consistency of metaphor, as illustrated above in Egill's stanza. Egill, himself, seems to have been a master of that style, while the skalds of his time and up to 1000 were usually addicts of the baroque style.

Development of skaldic poetry 900–1300

From Bragi hinn gamli onwards to the last representatives of court poetry in the thirteenth century we can follow the changing fashions in this genre with fair accuracy.

The changes in form are but slight. In the early poems (*ca.* 900–1000) the rules of consonantic assonance and inrime have not yet attained the regularity they have in the poems of Sighvatr and his followers.

Much more important are the changes in style. The style of the poets from Þorbjörn hornklofi with his *Glymdrápa* (*ca.* 900) to Eilífr Goðrúnarson with his *Þórsdrápa* (*ca.* 1000) is decidedly artificial and baroque, perhaps increasingly so, if we may believe the testimony of *Þórsdrápa*, the hardest of all skaldic poems. It looks as if the heathen style of *nykrat*-baroque kennings was being intensified just before the advent of Christianity, just as it is demonstrable (Jan de Vries) that references to heathen gods and old myths in kennings are more frequent toward the end of paganism.

With the introduction of Christianity the missionary kings, Ólafr Tryggvason (d. 1000) and Ólafr Haraldsson hinn helgi (d. 1030), naturally objected strenuously to continued use of the old gods' names, which they must have considered coming close to references to Satan and his devils. The effect is first seen in Hallfreðr vandræðaskáld's poems. But this pressure on the poets to keep mythology if not heroic legends out of their word-hoard resulted in a notably simplified style which we find at its very best in the poems of Sighvatr Þórðarson, court poet of King Ólafr helgi and his son. In Sighvatr's poetry the old gods are practically absent and the kennings are not only simple and lucid but noticeably reduced in number.

If the pre-Christian style is baroque, the eleventh-century style, ever so much lighter, may be called classical by comparison. But during the twelfth century there is an obvious reawakening of interest in the older baroque poetry as well as in old myths and legends and old, even Eddic, and new meters. This renaissance of the twelfth century is partly fed by, and partly, perhaps, in reaction to contemporary European (French-English) currents, as is obvious in the *Háttalykill* (*ca.* 1140) attributed to the Orkney Earl Rögnvaldr kali and the Icelander Hallr Þórarinsson.

As to meters, *töglag* and *hrynhent* appear in praise poems during the eleventh century, while even the humble *fornyrðislag* is restored to praise poetry by the skalds Gísl Illugason (1104) and Ívarr Ingimundarson (1140).

These renaissance strivings are intensified in the thirteenth century, where they culminate in Snorri Sturluson's *Edda*, written probably as a protest to the simple dance songs that must have been increasingly fashionable from the twelfth century onwards.

Egill Skalla-Grímsson (ca. 910–990)

Of all the Old Icelandic poets, Egill Skalla-Grímsson, who heads the list, was by far the most important. In him two races met: the tall, fair, popular Viking leader, and the dark, perhaps mongoloid, ugly and unsociable peasant or Lapp hunter type, taciturn, distrustful, and introvert.

His grandfather Kveldúlfr had in him a streak of the berserk; so did his ugly bald-headed father Skalla-Grímr. But the uncle Þórólfr and Egill's own brother Þórólfr both were fair heroes, friendly men of extrovert character, easily attracted to the splendor of the rising king, but not crafty enough to see through the wiles of backbiters nor meek enough to bow to the angry king. The uncle was killed by King Haraldr himself who thus started the feud between the two families which was to become not only the theme of *Egils saga* but symbolic for the whole tribe of emigrating Icelanders, who were thought to have fled the tyranny of the king.

Egill, born at the new home Borg, in Iceland, inherited the ugliness, the suspicion, and the cruelty of his forbears; he was inordinately avaricious like his father—but unlike father and grandfather he had the mighty Viking urge for adventure and travel in his blood. As a fighter and stickler for law and honor (if it be on his side) he stopped at nothing, courting trouble wherever he went. He possessed the loyalty of the Viking to king and friend. But he had also a surprising amount of sensibility or sensitivity, obvious in his shy attitude towards his beloved and his dark despair in the face of bereavement. This marked him as a poet, and the gift of poet's expression he had in a fuller degree than any of his contemporaries or successors, perhaps for centuries to come.

Just as two races fought in Egill's bosom, so two ages fought for possessing him. Receding into the background was the uneventful existence of the peaceful Norwegian farmer, loyal to his earth and to his gods—Þórr, Freyr, and Njörðr—loyal also to his kin, as *Baugatal* so eloquently testifies. In the ascendant was the new and dazzling Viking age, when men risked all for adventure, "fee and fame," under the brilliant leadership of the powerful but fickle god of warfare, magic, and poetry—Óðinn. Egill, the Viking, the sorcerer, and the poet must have felt thrice indebted to this god—and doubly hurt when Óðinn failed him. Egill's poems and his life testify to the fact that he did live according to the new Viking philosophy, best expressed outside his own poems in *Hávamál*.

Egils saga preserves *ca.* fifty occasional stanzas—mostly in *dróttkvætt* —by Egill, dealing with incidents in his life from the time he was seven, forming his first simple verses in anticipation of his coming Viking life, to the last ones, describing himself as a helpless and cold blind old man, now the butt of the temper of servant girls—he who formerly had been the entertainer of kings.

In these verses we find Egill boiling with rage when he feels wronged (Bárðr, Atli); we see him make use of his runic lore when he himself or others are in a fix, though he is never so successful a sorcerer as when he casts a spell upon Norway's land spirits to drive his archenemies, King Eiríkr blóðöx and his queen Gunnhildr the sorceress, out of their realm. We find him inciting his Viking followers to attack, see him summing up his victories: how many fought, and how many killed. Sailing in a storm is the theme of one of his finest stanzas, a theme long-lived in Icelandic literature. We find him playing with concealing the name of his beloved in a stanza when he cannot muster courage to ask for her hand. We see him in deep mourning for his brother, but brightening up marvelously when King Athelstan offers a ring to cheer him up. On this occasion we find him describing his ugly exterior with grim humor, a theme he reverts to not only in occasional stanzas—as when he receives his ugly head from King Eiríkr—but also in his larger poems. Nothing signalizes Egill so much as this preoccupation with himself and his looks.

In his feud against King Eiríkr and Gunnhildr, he had not only killed their henchmen, but also, according to the saga, their son, and, to top it off, had chased them out of Norway by his magic. Knowing Gunnhildr to be a sorceress of sorts, Egill would of course surmise that her magic would not let him rest until he was in her power. And sure enough; he had to sail to England and wreck his ship at the mouth of the Humber, while Eiríkr was reigning in York. Egill decided to take the bull by the horns; he went to York, seeking the help of his trusted friend Arinbjörn, a follower of the king. Arinbjörn advised him to follow the example of Bragi skáld and compose a *Höfuðlausn* (Head Ransom) to ransom his head. Egill composed a resounding *drápa* of twenty stanzas with two *stef* (refrains) in *runhent*, the meter of the Old English *Riming Poem*, perhaps in imitation of lost English poetry of that kind (cp. p. 49).

Though *Höfuðlausn* (*ca.* 948) is a conventional praise poem confining itself to general descriptions of Eiríkr's battles and his princely generosity, the new splendid form must have been enormously effective— for its resounding effect lingers even today. It also had the desired effect for Egill; he saved his ugly head and went his way.

The next great poem preserved in *Egils saga* is *Sonatorrek* (*ca.* 961), a lament over two sons that Egill had lost, one by sickness, the other—a favorite one—by drowning. Usually an *erfikvæði*, an epitaph, tells the life of the deceased. Not so here; this is Egill's own lament. The saga tells us that Egill was ready to starve himself to death in his grief; the beginning of the poem describes his difficulty in arousing himself from this torpor of mind. He feels utterly alone, his " fence of kin " broken down, leaving him open to attack. How gladly would he have attacked Ægir and Hel, but he is powerless not only against gods but also against men, a helpless man shorn of the support of his sons. Even against his chosen god he grumbles; Óðinn has deceived him in his ruthless fickleness; he does not sacrifice to him with pleasure after that. But—it must be admitted—Óðinn has given him recompense in another way; he gave him the spotless art of poetry and a temper that soon would transfer sneaking traitors into open enemies. For these things Egill is truly grateful; they give him strength to await death in equanimity. *Sonatorrek* means " difficult vengeance of sons."

Egill's third long poem, *Arinbjarnarkviða*—like *Sonatorrek* in *kviðuháttr*—is composed in honor of his best friend, who probably because he appreciated the genius in the erratic and avaricious poet, always was ready to aid him even at the cost of risking his life. Though not sworn brothers, Egill and Arinbjörn are one of the finest instances of Viking friendship.

In the beginning Egill asserts that he is slow to praise stingy niggards, in contrast to that he recalls the adventure in Eiríkr's court, where he braved the wrath of the king to win his ugly head, a priceless gift in spite of all its ugliness. But that feat could not have been done without Arinbjörn's help, and Egill would be eternally shamed if he did not requite that debt. And how easy Arinbjörn is to praise: three themes come thronging to the poet's tongue: his generosity first of all, and then probably his loyalty and bravery. But the poem is incomplete, except for a last stanza in which the poet says he has composed the poem in the early morning hours and that he has built a beacon of praise that will long stand " unbrittle in Bragi's town," i. e., it will be a *monumentum ære perennius*.

Kormákr Ögmundarson and other love poets

Kormákr Ögmundarson (tenth century), probably of Irish origin, is the best of the Old Icelandic love poets. He happened to glance at the feet of a girl, showing from under a half-closed door. This sealed his fate forever, starting him on singing her praises. Her kinsmen naturally reacted against the verses and wanted him to marry the girl. Kormákr seemed to be willing, but did not show up at the wedding. Modern interpreters have sensed here the poet who worships his ideal at a distance, but the saga attributes it to black magic, which sounds more likely for those days. Kormákr praises his beloved in quite extravagant terms. She is more worth than Iceland, Hungary, England and Ireland put together, and rocks will sooner float on water, mountains sink into the sea, than as beautiful a woman as she will be born again. (Cf. Horace *Epodes*, XVI, 25). When Steingerðr, his girl, married, Kormákr pursued her two husbands with calumnies. Kormákr's restlessness took him abroad; he praised Sigurðr Hlaðajarl (Earl of Hlaðir) in a poem with a curious device of allusion (*forn minni*). When killed, he still had a stanza about Steingerðr on his lips.

Other love poets were Hallfreðr Óttarsson who, like Kormákr, would not marry his beautiful but vain Kolfinna and Þormóðr Kolbrúnarskáld, nicknamed after his sweetheart, whom he had praised in a poem. The story of Gunnlaugr ormstunga and Helga fagra is most romantic, but his love-poetry was not on a par with Kormákr's. Björn Hítdœlakappi's saga tells how the poet Þórðr Kolbeinsson stole his sweetheart, Oddný

eykyndill; there is some love poetry by both suitors; most remarkable is
Þórðr's last stanza about his pining wife. Arnór Þórðarson jarlaskáld
was his son.

Court poets

In *Íslenzk menning* Nordal has scrutinized the important question
why, after Eyvindr skáldaspillir, the office of court-poetry became the
monopoly of Icelanders. He thinks it is mainly due to the fact that in
Norway no king took over the court of his predecessor, from Eiríkr
blóðöx (d. 954) to Haraldr harðráði (d. 1066), because the predecessor
always represented a hostile faction. Thus Eyvindr skáldaspillir, the last
of the Norwegian court-poets, at the court of Hákon góði, would have
nothing to do with his killers, the sons of Eiríkr blóðöx and Gunnhildr.
Eiríkr had, as we have seen, been eulogized by his archenemy, the
brilliant Egill Skalla-Grímsson, the first of the Icelandic court-poets, and
by Glúmr Geirason, also a poet to his sons. Kormákr praised not only
the sons of Eiríkr, but also Sigurðr Hlaðajarl, who was killed by them.
When the sons of Eiríkr were defeated by Hákon Hlaðajarl, eight
Icelanders flocked to his court, though not all were equally well received.
Of these Einar Helgason skálaglamm, a pupil of Egill, became a trusted
friend of the earl, while Þorleifr jarlaskáld became more famous, in
legend at any rate, for the *níð*, the black magic spell, which he finally
composed about the earl, than for his earlier praise.

When the ardent missionary king, Ólafr Tryggvason, broke the backbone of heathen resistance after Earl Hákon's death, there was more
danger than ever, not only that the Icelanders might lose their preference
at court but also that the court poetry tradition itself would be discarded.
This danger was averted by a happy accident.

The poet Hallfreðr Óttarsson (born *ca.* 965 in Vatnsdalr of the Northwest) had already praised Earl Hákon in a demonstratively heathen
poem (*Hákonardrápa, ca.* 990). Now he wanted to enter the service and
sing the praises of the young Christian king. He certainly did not have
the tact seemingly indispensable to win the favor of the impetuous king.
Fortunately, it seems that each recognized a kindred spirit in the other.
Thus was born a friendship and loyalty beyond death on Hallfreðr's
part. For Hallfreðr was a loyal soul, and from his verse it is obvious
that he needed more than a little persuasion to reject his old gods for
the friendship of the new White-Christ. Naturally the king was set on
baptizing his skald, but Hallfreðr would not be baptized unless the king

listened to his praises. Both won their point, and though Hallfreðr had to abstain from using heathen lore in his poems (cp. his *Ólafsdrápa* with his *Hákonardrápa*), he did save the day for the Icelandic court poets. And in the end Hallfreðr got to be so good a Christian that, when dying, he expressed the fear of hell in his last stanza.

Sighvatr Þórðarson

Loyalty to king Ólafr Tryggvason did not hinder Hallfreðr from eulogizing his vanquisher, Earl Eiríkr Hákonarson, at whose court there were several Icelandic poets—e. g., Þórðr Kolbeinsson—who afterward joined the court of Ólafr Haraldsson, later the sainted king of Norway. But the sainted king's chief poet, friend, and adviser was Sighvatr Þórðarson (*ca.* 995–1045). This remarkable man, a courtier and a diplomat of the best type, in addition to being the greatest master of *dróttkvætt* in his day, so consolidated the office of the Icelandic court poet that for a century and a half to come the Icelanders had no more rivals— any more than the Swiss guards at the Pope's Palace.

Sighvatr's father had been a skald to Earl Sigvaldi of Jómsborg and had joined King Ólafr Haraldsson on his Viking expedition in the West, just before he returned to claim Norway (1015). Sighvatr had been fostered at Apavatn in Grímsnes; legend has it that he was not precocious, but Snorri says that he was early a good poet. At any rate he became not only a prolific skald but one who has left us more remnants of his poetry than any other medieval skald. He was just grown when he joined his father and King Ólafr in Norway in 1015. For some reason, maybe his youth, the king would not lend him an ear, but Sighvatr overcame his resistance with a stanza which is the earliest on record, as well as with his poem *Víkingavísur* (Viking Verses).

So began a life-long friendship. The king, a sturdy, prosaic, somewhat suspicious nature, soon became convinced of Sighvatr's loyalty and wisdom. He made him his *stallari* (Marshal) and entrusted to him difficult diplomatic missions. But Sighvatr was no yes-man; he was frank and independent to the point of making friends with and eulogizing the king's staunchest antagonists. His impeccable character and frankness is most brilliantly exhibited in his remarkable *Bersöglisvísur*.

Apart from about thirty occasional stanzas, remnants of twelve poems have survived. There are four on King Ólafr, the first dealing with his Viking expedition (1014-15), another with the battle of Nesjar (1016). The third is a fragment, the fourth an *erfidrápa* (epitaph) composed about ten years after the king's death in 1030. None of these poems have the feeling of stanza twenty-six, composed by the poet returning from a pilgrimage to Rome and hearing of his lord being slain at Stiklarstaðr. " While Ólafr was alive, the high hills of Norway smiled on me—now the hillsides have a much unkindlier face." Þormóðr Kolbrúnarskáld, who fell with his lord at Stiklarstaðr, had some cutting words to say about Sighvatr's absence, but the king never doubted his man, and rightly so.

Among the most interesting things Sighvatr did were his *Austrfararvísur* (Verses on a Journey to the East), comments on a journey to Sweden in 1019. He had been sent there with the delicate mission of trying to compose border quarrels and cement the peace by arranging a marriage between his lord and the king of Sweden's daughter, Princess Ástríðr. The mission was a success, but his verses are not a record of that but rather of adventures by the roadside; they have a light journalistic touch and show his love of travel. He also made a journey to the West, France and England, but his so-called *Vestrfararvísur* (Verses on a Journey to the West) (1025–26) are quite insignificant. He did visit King Canute of England and Denmark and praised him in a poem now lost; the preserved *Knútsdrápa* (*ca.* 1038) is an epitaph.

These poems and the two he composed about Erlingr Skjálgsson (1026 and 1028–9) show him dealing out his praise to his lord's bitterest enemies; he could do that but he did not want to enter the service of King Canute.

Sighvatr was on a pilgrimage to Rome when his master was killed. After that he joined his son, Magnús, and to him he addressed his most original poem, *Bersöglisvísur* (The Frank Verses), composed in 1038 to warn the young king not to exact vengeance on the Norwegian chiefs who had fought his father at Stiklarstaðr. This unique poem shows Sighvatr's uprightness at its best as well as his shrewd statesmanship. It saved the day for the king, who took his advice. After that the office of Icelandic court poetry was, indeed, fully entrenched in Norway.

Court poetry after Sighvatr

After Sighvatr the road of the Icelandic court poets was smooth. No one esteemed them more than King Haraldr Sigurðarson harðráði (d. 1066), a connoisseur of skaldship and a poet himself. Among his twelve poets, Þjóðólfr Arnórsson was the leader, while Sneglu-Halli approached the role of a court fool. Best, however, was Arnór Þórðarson jarlaskáld, so called because he had served the Orkney earls. His *Hryn-henda* in honor of King Magnús góði was a splendid success; King Haraldr's verdict was that it would live as long as the North would stand.

There were some notable court poets in the twelfth century. Gísl Illugason praised the belligerent Magnús berfœttr (1104) in a *drápa* of *fornyrðislag*; Markús Skeggjason devoted another *Hrynhenda* to King Erik of Denmark (1104). Halldór skvaldri and Ívarr Ingimundarson praised Sigurðr Jórsalafari for his crusade to the Holy Land. Most important was Einar Skúlason, who eulogized Sigurðr Jórsalafari, Haraldr Gilli, and his sons: Eysteinn, Sigurðr, and Ingi. He also honored St. Ólafr with the poem *Geisli* (1153), the seventy-one stanzas of which are still intact, while the rest of his poems are mere fragments.

A couple of facts in Einar Skúlason's life point a prophetic finger to the future. An unheard-of thing happened to him in Denmark, where King Sven Grathe gave him no reward for his poem because the king preferred " fiddles and pipes " to his skaldship. Here for the first time we see the pipers and jugglers, the lowly mimes and musicians, victorious in their agelong competition against the high-brow skalds. Jugglers and pipers are first met with in Haraldr hárfagri's court, but they did not win the day until the thirteenth century.

But the twelfth century skalds had other and even more dangerous competitors: the clerks who from now onwards become secretaries and historians to the kings. Einar was a clerk himself, and his *Geisli* heads the saints' poems of the following centuries. Contemporary with Einar was Eiríkr Oddsson, author of a contemporary chronicle, and he was followed by Karl Jónsson, the historian of King Sverrir. *Sverris saga* has survived, but none of the many poems composed by his skalds. These poems had lost their functional value; they were a mere fossilized convention.

The same is true of court poetry in the thirteenth century. Here the Sturlungar loom highest, but their poetry, excellent though it is in crafts-manship, has been preserved only for special reasons. Snorri Sturluson's *Háttatal* (1222–3) survives only as a part of his *Edda*, and we have Sturla Þórðarson's *Hákonardrápur* (1262 *hrynhenda*, 1263–4 *kviðuháttr*) only because he inserted them for conventional ornamental purposes into his *Hákonar saga*. The case of Ólafr hvítaskáld, his brother, was similar. Sturla and Ólafr were nephews of Snorri.

Jón murti Egilsson, son of another nephew of Snorri and tenth in a descending line from Egill Skalla-Grímsson, was destined to be the last of the court poets. He praised King Eiríkr Magnússon, the last king to be so honored, in 1299. *Skáldatal* (Poets' List), a list of court poets, enumerates 110 Icelandic court poets over the period of 350 years, from Egill to Jón murti. That is on the average ten skalds to a generation.

Háttalykill and Háttatal

In the twelfth century we meet for the first time a type of poem which, in the centuries to come, is emulated by many learned Icelandic poets. This is *Háttalykill, Clavis Metrica* or Key of Meters, composed in the eleven-forties. It is a list of Scandinavian heroes and Norwegian kings, leading up may be to the latest ruler in whose honor it may have been composed, though we do not know, as the poem is incomplete. Since the latest edition by Jón Helgason and Anne Holtsmark (1941) we are not sure of the authors either, but accept the old and most likely view that they were a young otherwise unknown Icelander, Hallr Þórarinsson, and Rögnvaldr kali, Earl of the Orkneys. By birth a Norwegian, though his mother was from the Orkneys, he had carried on trade with England and then joined Sigurðr Jórsalafari, who helped him to the earldom. Later he went on a pilgrimage to the Holy Land, meeting *en route* fair Ermingerðr of Nerbón (Narbonne) in France, whose praise he sang in skaldic verse with troubadour spirit.

Háttalykill is not only a praise poem but primarily a *clavis metrica*, a key to the meters of skaldic poetry. There are two samples of each meter (*háttr* pl. *hættir*), perhaps one by each collaborator. Preserved are only forty-one double stanzas, many fragmentary. Listed are, as a matter of fact, the old well-worn meters, *fornyrðislag, kviðuháttr, málaháttr, ljóðaháttr, dróttkvætt, hrynhent*, and *runhent* and *hneppt* or *stýft*, but the new *hættir* are rarely meters in our sense, but variations of the old ones, obtained chiefly by two means: on the one hand, rimes and inrimes, on the other, rhetorical figures. A. Holtsmark and Jan de Vries have shown that both features may be derived from eleventh and twelfth century *artes poeticae* and *rhythmicae* of the schools. *Núfuháttr* alone breaks the bonds of *dróttkvætt* by adding a tail to each helming; such tails were common in troubadour meters, but Snorri did not admit them.

Obviously Rögnvaldr kali had a clerk's education; he tells us as much in the stanza enumerating his nine accomplishments (*íþróttir*): among them runes, books (i. e., Latin books), playing the harp, and composing poetry.

Snorri's *Háttatal* (List of Meters) was composed (1222–3) to praise his royal friends Earl Skúli and King Hákon, rulers of Norway. But like *Háttalykill* it was at the same time designed to demonstrate to aspiring students some 100 odd meters, old and new. As a matter of fact, most of the meters were, again, old, from our point of view, the new thing about them being a variation of some sort. Often this variation is obtained by using different figures of speech; thus, the number of sentences within a stanza may be varied from sixteen to one (*sextánmælt: langlokum*), the use of adjectives may be regulated, the use of antitheses and juxtaposition (*refhvörf*) is another figure of speech. Then there are variations in the use of assonances, inrime and end rime; here we seem to be getting closer to real metrical changes. Finally there are variations in syllable length or syllable count throughout the verse, and, the device to fit a *dróttkvætt* or a *hrynhent* verse with a masculine ending (*stýft*) instead of the usual feminine one.

If we look only to the length of the verses, we might perhaps classify as new *príhent* (36), three types of *stúfar* (49–51), three types of *kimblabönd* (59–61), and *draughent* (65).

But though Snorri creates his meters in basically the same way as Rögnvaldr kali, there is a world of difference in their method of classification. Rögnvaldr has seemingly no classification. Snorri classifies his meters according to a strictly logical order, beginning with *dróttkvætt*, ending with the lesser (i. e., more short-lined) meters of the *Edda*, and variations of them, e. g., *runhendur* of all possible types, but always with running, never alternating, rimes.

That Snorri, like Rögnvaldr, was influenced by the *artes poeticae* and the school rhetorics of the twelfth century, is made doubly likely by the fact that his nephew Ólafr Þórðarson hvítaskáld went the whole way and wrote a *Málskrúðsfræði*, a Rhetoric, after the current pattern of school rhetoric, using its learned Graeco-Roman terminology but illustrating with examples from skaldic poetry, some of them from Snorri himself.

Though skaldic court poetry, fossilized in convention, gave up the ghost in the thirteenth century, skaldic art did not. That it survived is probably more than anything due to the impulse it got from Snorri's *Edda*. The artless popular ballads would likely enough have won out in Iceland as elsewhere in Scandinavia if Snorri's marvellous textbook had not marked the trend of national taste for centuries to come. After Snorri, no Icelandic poet could get his *Edda* out of his mind, whether he tried to follow its precepts, as the *rímur*-skalds did, or reacted against it, as did the writers of sacred poetry.

No doubt, the *Edda* represents the culmination of the twelfth century renaissance in skaldic poetry. That renaissance, reaching back to old poetical forms, to the old myths, to the old poetical diction in the *þulur*, seemed mainly nationalistic. Still, we must not overlook the international current of Latin learning stimulating the native lore. Maybe there would have been no *Edda* without the twelfth-century *artes poeticae* and *rhythmicae*.

Epic praise poems. Twelfth century onwards

We have already mentioned the historical praise poems that sprang up in the twelfth century. Their intrinsic value is less than their significance as a link between the court praise poetry and the epic *rímur*. They are also symptomatic of the twelfth-century historical interest that was to culminate in the sagas. In the skaldic poetry the epitaphs are, probably, the immediate ancestors of these poems.

Perhaps the oldest of these poems is *Ólafs drápa Tryggvasonar*, wrongly attributed to Hallfreðr vandræðaskáld. Though the poet stresses the king's missionary work, the poem is not legendary as is Einar Skúlason's somewhat earlier *Geisli* (1153). Another secular poem on Ólafr Tryggvason is Hallar-Steinn's *Rekstefja* (*ca.* 1200?), whose author may have learned from *Háttalykill* his meter and his way of addressing his poem to women—a southern mark.

Being a kind of *kappatal* (list of heroes), *Háttalykill* might have spurred Haukr Valdísarson to composing *Íslendingadrápa*, a list of Icelanders, later celebrated in the sagas.

The battle of Hjörungavágr, in which the Jómsvíkings were beaten by Hákon Hlaðajarl, was sung by two poets, the Icelander Þorkell Gíslason in *Búadrápa*, celebrating the Viking who jumped overboard with two chests of gold under his arms, and the Orkney Bishop Bjarni Kolbeinsson (d. 1222) in *Jómsvíkingadrápa*, which treats the love story of Vagn Ákason. This latter *drápa*, perhaps the best of its class, is obviously touched by courtly love; the refrain goes: " The wife of the noble lord kills all my joy; a highborn lady gives me great grief," voicing the subjective plea of the courtly poet. Bishop Bjarni has also been credited with *Fornyrðadrápa* or *Málsháttakvæði* (Lay of Proverbs), a poem using proverbs as its medium of expression and breathing the same southern spirit of love.

Krákumál is a romantic description of the Viking Ragnar Loðbrók's death, told in the dying hero's words. Reminiscing, he begins every stanza with the refrain-like *Hjuggu vér með hjörvi*—" We struck a blow with our sword." This poem, partly misinterpreted (drinking from enemies' skulls instead of from drinking horns), made a deep impression on early romantics in France and England who thought it specially revealing of Viking philosophy!

Sacred Poetry

Introduction

The Icelandic sacred poetry of the twelfth, thirteenth, fourteenth, and, to some extent, the fifteenth centuries is a hybrid flower deriving its form and diction from the skaldic poetry—the meter is mostly *dróttkvætt*, sometimes *hrynhent*—but the spirit from contemporary currents of thought in the Catholic Church. It is really a marvel that the church hymn forms did not break through earlier, but the Icelandic chieftain-clergy probably saw nothing incongruous in breaking with the established rules of the Church in this field as in many others, and the true hymn forms did not appear until the fifteenth century.

In diction the conventional kennings were kept, even though they contained the time-honored references to the old myths and names of the old gods—a circumstance which compelled Jan de Vries to set *Plácítusdrápa* after 1150. Perhaps the twelfth century renaissance in Europe, with its appreciation of the classical myths, helped the clergy to an appreciation of their own, though if so it was a specially Icelandic point of view. The kennings, for God, especially, and for other members of Christian myth and legend were naturally a virgin field where the authors of sacred poetry could and did exercise their ingenuity. Thus, by variations of " sky " in " ruler of the sky," Gamli kanoki of Þykkvibœr unfolds before our eyes the rich fluctuations and the rigors of the weather in South Iceland. But from this early skaldic form there is a continuous development to the full and conscious absence of kennings that marks the fourteenth century *Lilja*.

From fashions of thought in the Church come shifting attitudes towards God and saints. Thus, first of all, White-Christ is thought of as a victorious king and that not only because he has ousted Þórr and other old Norse gods but primarily because the Church stressed that aspect of him in the Harrowing of Hell (*Niðurstigningar saga*). But

during the twelfth century—the age of the Crusades—there was a reaction to this glorious and victorious king of heaven in favor of the
God-man, or the man suffering for our sins on the cross. Thus, Anselm
of Canterbury writes: " It is far sweeter to see You born into the world
by the Virgin Mother than seeing you born in splendor by the Father
before the Morning Star, to see You die on the cross, than seeing You
ruling angels in heaven.—Nowhere do I perceive Christ more truly than
where He hangs on the cross." Already *Harmsól* and *Líknarbraut* are
touched by this new thought—*Lilja* follows along the same lines—but
this point of view culminates in Hallgrímur Pétursson's *Passíusálmar*.

With concentration on Christ the man there followed a transfer of
interest to the group of people surrounding Him in the manger and on
the cross: Mary, who after 1200 begins to be represented as weeping,
mater dolorosa, his favorite disciple John, and others. The adulation of
Mary was given impetus by St. Bernhard's Cistercians in the twelfth
century; it came to full flower in fourteenth- and fifteenth-century Iceland. These centuries were also, in Iceland, the ages of the other saints,
the Apostles and the martyrs, though John, Peter, Nikulás, and Thomas
à Becket had already been praised in the thirteenth century.

With the Church tradition, too, came symbolism, sometimes allegory,
and conceits, such as: *flœðar stjarna* = *maris stella* (i. e., Mary) ; *friðar
sýn* = *visio pacis* (i. e., Jerusalem) (*Geisli* 1153); the sun betokening
God (*Harmsól, Sólarljóð, ca.* 1200); the hart betokening Christ
(*Plácítusdrápa*, 1150-80, *Sólarljóð*, cf. the Icelandic *Physiologus*); and
the sails of Óðinn's wife (i. e., Frigg or Freyja = Venus) hanging on
ropes of passion (*þrá-reipi*) (*Sólarljóð*).

Like much sacred poetry in Western Christianity, the bulk of the
Icelandic religious verse seems more or less uninspired and dull, at
least to the non-faithful reader. A few peaks rise in solitary brilliance
over the plateau: the Death Prayer of Kolbeinn Tumason (1208), the
Song of the Sun from about the same time, and Eysteinn Ásgrímsson's
Lilja (The Lily *ca.* 1350).

Twelfth-century drápur

From the twelfth century four sacred poems and some fragments
survive. *Geisli* (Sun Ray) is the earliest, Einar Skúlason's *drápa*
(seventy-one stanzas) to Saint Ólafr, the ray (*geisli*) from the sun of
pity (God), born from the sun of the sea (Mary). It is a eulogy of the
saint and his miracles more than of the king, though his battles, adorned

with the conventional ravens and wolves, are not quite forgotten. Nor does Einar forget to allude to his skald's reward in this world and that to come. The poem was recited in the cathedral in Niðarós (Trondheim) in 1153 (or the winter 1153–54).

We have mere fragments of a *Jóns drápa postula* and a *Kristsdrápa* (?) by Nikulás Bergsson, abbot at Munkaþverá, a great traveler who returned from a pilgrimage to Rome and Jerusalem in 1154 and died in 1159. The fragments are marked by the conventional Catholic prefiguration theory.

Harmsól (Sun of Sorrow), a *drápa* (of sixty-five stanzas in *hrynhent*) on Christ; the "sun of sorrow," was composed by Gamli kanoki at Þykkviboer monastery (founded 1168). The author is penitent, though not wallowing in his sins; his meditations on Christ culminate in the scene of his return on the Day of Judgment, when sinners should beware. His kennings have already been commented upon (p. 69). His poem closes with a request to the reader to pray for his soul. Fragments of a *Jónsdrápa* are also credited to Gamli.

Plácítusdrápa, slightly incomplete, recounts a popular medieval legend about a long-suffering man whom God deprives of wife and sons, restoring them to him in the end only to have the whole family suffer the martyrs' death. Heavy with kennings, the poem was thought by early commentators to be older than *Geisli*, while J. de Vries for that very reason puts it about 1180. It is preserved in a manuscript of about 1200.

Leiðarvísan (Showing the Way), a *drápa* (forty-five stanzas) celebrating Sunday, tells a popular story of a "Sunday Epistle" falling to earth on Sunday in Jerusalem and commanding the day's sanctification. In support of this claim the *drápa* enumerates all the great things having befallen on a Sunday. The celestial letter was and is a well-known motif. The anonymous author mentions as his helper a certain Runólfr (Ketilsson, priest, fl. 1143?). The poem is indebted to *Plácítusdrápa* and *Geisli*; F. Paasche dated it *ca.* 1150, J. de Vries after 1180.

Thirteenth-century drápur

In the thirteenth century the tradition of sacred *drápur* is continued. Fragments are found of *Jónsvísur* (*postula*) by Kolbeinn Tumason (d. 1208), a *Kristsdrápa* (?) by Ólafr svartaskáld, *Tómasardrápa* (Thomas à Becket) by Ólafr hvítaskáld, some indefinable bits in the *Fourth Grammatical Treatise*, and an anonymous fragment of a *Nikulássdrápa*.

More or less complete are *Líknarbraut* (fifty-two stanzas) and *Heilags anda vísur* (eighteen stanzas), the first extant translation of a Latin hymn: *Veni creator spiritus*, as recently shown by Einar Ól. Sveinsson.

Líknarbraut (The Way of Grace) is a poem about the cross. It is a meditation on Christ's passion—we hear the nails driven into his hands and feet and meet the weeping Mary. The poem is more emotional than its predecessors, the style more subjectively direct. It is a stepping stone to the great *Lilja*; F. Paasche rates it very highly.

Didactic poetry and Sólarljóð

Some of the thirteenth-century religious and didactic poetry does not fall in the current of the above *dróttkvætt-hrynhent drápur*, but employs Eddic meters. The translation *Merlínusspá* from Geoffrey of Monmouth's *Prophesy of Merlin* was rendered in appropriate *fornyrðislag* (after *Völuspá*) by Gunnlaugr Leifsson, the monk (d. 1218). Probably after 1250 falls the anonymous translation of *Disticha Catonis*, called *Hugsvinnsmál*. The *ljóðaháttr* of *Hávamál* makes a fine vehicle even for this late Roman wisdom.

In *ljóðaháttr*, too, is *Sólarljóð* (Song of the Sun), from *ca.* 1200 (or after?), anonymous, the greatest Catholic monument before *Lilja*. It is an epic didactic and visionary poem, uniting some of the spirit of *Hávamál* and *Völuspá* with that of the Catholic *exempla, visio,* and allegory. The thought is wholly Catholic-medieval: do good, and you shall be saved.

Sólarljóð are the words of a father, returned from death, to his surviving son. He begins by a series of *exempla*, brilliantly illustrating the ways of evil or blundering men and their fates after death. After a short admonition to pray, addressed to his son, the father reviews his pleasant, if wayward, life up to the day of death, when Hell stood ready to drag him down. Dying, he sees the sun, a vision he describes in seven famous stanzas, all beginning: *Sól ek sá* (" I saw the sun "). This sun is " the true star of day," *versus Lucifer*, i. e., Christ. The blood-stained rays and the red ocean in which the sun sinks are awful reminders of the Day of Judgment. When the sun is no more, death comes and the soul flies away—as a star of hope—while the body lies in state awaiting burial. On its way through the seven heavens the soul is first waylaid by the dragon and his satellites who hope to get it, but it is succored by the sun-hart (i. e., Christ) and the seven star-angels, led by St. Michael. Then, soaring, it looks into two worlds, giving thumbnail sketches of what it sees in each and leaving us in no doubt where we should wish to go. This episode ends with a prayer to the Trinity to keep us all from misery. The final episode of the poem is made up of some seemingly allegorical sketches whose exact meaning eludes us. The penultimate stanza gives the name of the poem, and the last one, where father parts with son, echoes the famous *Requiem æternam dona eis, domine: Dróttinn minn / gefi dauðum ró / ok hinum líkn er lifa*. Though related to the Catholic vision literature, the visions here are subordinated to the main theme and much subdued in tone, if compared with European counterparts (e. g., *Visio Tnugdali = Duggals leiðsla*). But just as Dante reflected his own time in the *Divina Commedia*, so, Paasche holds, *Sólarljóð* mirrors the troubled Sturlunga age with its crimes and lawlessness, but also with its deep religiosity reflected not only among churchmen, as in the saintly bishop Guðmundr góði or as in the knightly religious chieftain Rafn Sveinbjarnarson (d. 1213)—a type of man who well might have composed *Sólarljóð*—but also among the greatest antagonists of the Church like the chieftain Kolbeinn Tumason.

Intending to rule the Church, this chief had forced the election of Guðmundr góði to the bishopric of Hólar. But once bishop, Guðmundr became recalcitrant and anathemized his patron. A little later, it was on the Nativity of St. Mary, September 8, 1208, the church bells of the nearby Hólar Cathedral rang to evensong, but Kolbeinn Tumason, excommunicated enemy of the Church, soon to die, could not hear them. Then he composed three stanzas in *runhent, Heyr þú himna smiðr* ("Listen, Creator of Heaven") a Death Prayer to the Son of the Virgin, whose direct emotional appeal we seek in vain elsewhere in the sacred poetry, except in *Sólarljóð* and in the Latin hymns of the Church.

Fourteenth-century drápur

When we reach the fourteenth century, the sacred poetry in skaldic meters is the only skaldic poetry surviving and in a considerable bulk at that, judging by Finnur Jónsson's edition in *Skjaldedigtning II*, but Jón Helgason suggests that some of the anonymous poems may be of the fifteenth century.

Striking at first glance is the fact that the saints are now altogether in the foreground, among whom the Virgin Mary looms the largest, with eight poems in her honor: two praise poems, *Lilja* and *Máríudrápa*; one lament, *planctus* (*Máríugrátr*); and five legends, all (but one?) from the prose *Máríu saga*. Of holy maidens, Catherine gets a whole *drápa* (by a Kálfr skáld = Vitulus vates), and thirty-two other saintly virgins share in the honors of another praise poem (*drápa*).

Of the Apostles, Peter and Andreas get one praise poem each (the latter a fragment), and all thirteen get one stanza each of *Allra postula minnisvísur* (A Toast to All Apostles), each stanza being a toast with a two-line exhortation to drink appended to the eight-line *dróttkvætt* stanzas, e. g.,

> Drekki hér drengir inni
> dýrligt Jákobs minni.

Then there is a fragmentary (?) *Heilagra manna drápa* (Lay of Saints), perhaps in honor of all saints, though only seven saints' legends appear in the surviving stanzas.

The one "saint" who can, to a certain extent, compete in popularity with the Virgin Mary is the Icelandic beggar-bishop Guðmundr inn góði. There was agitation to get him canonized. His bones were disinterred in the year 1344; Abbot Arngrímr Brandsson of Þingeyrar composed his *vita* in Latin and a *drápa* in his honor (1345). Two other men, Einar Gilsson (lawman 1367–69) and Abbot Árni Jónsson of Munkaþverá, joined in the chorus, so that the good bishop had no less than six poems dinning his merits, but to no avail.

Eysteinn Ásgrímsson and Lilja

There is no space to discuss these poems here in detail, except the great poem *Lilja* and its composer, Eysteinn Ásgrímsson. It must have been composed 1343–44, since it has influenced the above-mentioned *Guðmundardrápa* of Arngrímr Brandsson.

In the year 1343 a monk, Eysteinn Ásgrímsson, was imprisoned, perhaps for breach of chastity and for beating up his abbot at Þykkvibœr in Ver. Released shortly afterwards, he was sent to the monastery of Helgafell. In 1349 an Eysteinn Ásgrímsson was made *officialis* at the Skálholt bishopric; he collaborated with the bishop and went with him to Norway in 1355. There Eysteinn remained until 1357, when he with another man was made inspector of the Skálholt bishopric and, as such, incurred the enmity of the bishop to such an extent that the bishop excommunicated him. In 1360 the inspectors returned to Norway and here Eysteinn died on March 14, 1361, at the monastery of Helgisetr, in Niðarós.

If all these facts refer to the same man, they reveal a violent character, sometimes in open revolt, sometimes guiding his Mother Church. Most commentators have accepted this colorful personality at its face value, but the last editor of *Lilja*, Guðbrandur Jónsson, separated the sinful rebel from the high churchman and gave the poem to the latter. But it has since been pointed out by Gunnar Finnbogason that the first half of the fourteenth century was a time of growing depravity in the church and the monasteries, as a result of its decisive victory over the secular chieftains about 1300. It has also been shown that Abbot Arngrímr Brandsson of Þingeyrar had a career of revolt and rehabilitation similar to that of Eysteinn. Indeed, he seems not only to have been his boon-companion in beating up the abbot of Þykkvibœr, but also the first to appreciate and imitate *Lilja* in his above-mentioned *Guðmundardrápa*.

Lilja (The Lily), a *hrynhend drápa* of one hundred stanzas, has traditionally been interpreted as a poem in honor of the Virgin Mary; the name " Lily " and the number of stanzas being the same as the number of letters in Ave Maria supports this common view. But Guðbrandur Jónsson points out that only 10 per cent of the stanzas (st. 86-95) deal exclusively with Mary, while elsewhere the poet dedicates his poem to God, Christ, or to Christ and Mary. Actually the poem " over-runs " or surveys most of the history of the world as understood in Western Christianity. After an invocation to God and Mary this history starts with the Creation and the Fall of the Angels, to be followed by the Creation of Adam and Eve, their Temptation and Fall. Immediately after that follows the Annunciation and the Birth of Christ. Then comes Christ's temptation and, the most important passage, his Passion and Crucifixion, occupying the exact middle of the poem—where the two refrains of the *drápa* meet. Here, too, we meet the *mater dolorosa*. Now follows the Harrowing of Hell, the Resurrection, and, finally, the Last Judgment. The rest of the poem (st. 75-100) is chiefly contrite self-reproach, with a prayer to and the adulation of the Virgin Mary. The poem shows that Eysteinn knew his Scriptures, but was not an original thinker. With his emphasis on sin and grace, he is nearer to the *Passíusálmar* than to *Sólarljóð*.

But the poem also testifies to the fact that he was a great poet, able to inspire his work with the spark of life. An important means to this end was his dropping of the kennings—to make his poem easier to understand and more immediate in appeal. It lends to his style a newborn ease yet does not make his composition less majestic. The stately lines are still a fit vehicle to glorify God and the Virgin. His narrative is swift, his pictures apt, his humorous-sarcastic description of the devil incisive. The brilliance of his poem may be somewhat cool, though some of the best critics have emphasized his dept of feeling and his sincere repentance.

Certain it is that his poem won such a popularity that everybody was supposed to learn it by heart and recite it, if not daily, then at least once a week. The admiration of the people for this poem finds a natural and beautiful expression in the proverbial saying "everyone would have liked to have composed *Lilja*." The poets of the fifteenth century paid the poet a similar tribute with their imitations—scorning, as they did, all older poetry for this modern marvel. The leaders of the Reformation did essentially the same by granting *Lilja* a place in their anthology, *Vísnabók* (1612), in an expurgated form, to be sure. The Protestants had, indeed, nothing to match it until Hallgrímur Pétursson's *Passíusálmar* appeared.

Fifteenth-century poems and authors

The sacred poetry of the fifteenth century and up to the Reformation (1550) has been discussed and edited chiefly by two scholars, Jón Þorkelsson and Jón Helgason, though Páll E. Ólason also has made notable contributions. Jón Þorkelsson was a pioneer in a virgin field trying to collect every scrap of matter and fit it into a meaningful picture. He had great powers of combination, but neither time nor inclination to be overcritical. Jón Helgason, on the other hand, is a critical perfectionist who has felt it his duty not only to establish a thoroughly reliable text of the poems but also to weed out or point out for what they are worth tenuous connections between authors and poems made by his predecessors and earlier workers or amateurs in the field.

According to Jón Helgason, there are no certain authors' names preserved in the field of sacred poetry of the fifteenth century. Jón Máríuskáld, earlier identified with Jón Pálsson, pastor of Grenjaðarstaðr (d. 1471), as an author of *Máríulykill*, is a fictitious person. In a verse from the first half of the sixteenth century, attributed to Jón Arason, four poets then living are identified as being the best poets each in his own quarter of the country. They were: Einar Snorrason Ölduhryggjarskáld (d. 1534) in the West, from whose poetry nothing has survived; Jón Hallsson in the South (d. 1538), author of one secular poem on old age; Sigurðr blindr in the East, who composed *rímur*—among them *Hektors rímur* in collaboration with Jón Arason—and was long assumed to be the author of the sacred poem *Rósa* (which has recently been plausibly attributed to Sigurðr Narfason at Fagridalr in the Northwest— P. E. Ólason) ; and Gunni Hallsson Hólaskáld of the North (d. *ca.* 1545), a not too certain author of *Ólafsvísur*. Towards the end of the Catholic period two authors emerge in a somewhat clearer light: Hallr Ögmundarson (1501–39), a priest in the West Fjords, author of *Gimsteinn, Máríublóm, Náð,* and *Nikulásardrápa,* and Jón Arason, Bishop of Hólar, usually considered the greatest poet of his time, and usually thought to be the author of *Ljómur, Niðrstigningsvísur, Krossvísur,* though Jón Helgason allows him only *Píslargrátr* and *Davíðsdiktr* for certain.

The subject matter of the poetry

The two volumes of Jón Helgason's edition, *Íslenzk miðaldakvæði,* contain one hundred sacred poems, five times as many as the preceding fourteenth century could show, though some of those may belong after 1400. Since most of this poetry is anonymous, it is most conveniently classified according to subject matter.

First there is poetry dealing with the Creation, the Fall of Man, the Redemption, and the Last Judgment. This continues *Lilja's* theme directly, and we find its meter continued in *Rósa* (133 stanzas), though the author of *Ljómur* employs a new meter, used previously(?) only by Skáld-Sveinn, and at the same time also by Jón Arason, if he is not the author of *Ljómur*. Altogether there are seven poems on this subject.

Then there is poetry on Christ and the Holy Cross, of which *Píslargrátr* is, and *Niðrstigningsvísur* and *Krossvísur* may be, by Jón Arason, *Máríublóm* (Mary's Flower, i. e., Christ) and *Gimsteinn* (Gem, i. e., the Cross) by Hallr Ögmundarson. There are fifteen poems on this theme about equally divided between Christ and His Cross.

As in the preceding century Mary is, by far, the most popular figure— about 150 * churches were dedicated to her in Iceland. No less than forty-five poems deal with her. The first, *Náð,* by Hallr Ögmundarson, tells the story of her mother Anne (i. e., *Náð* = Grace), popularized in Western Christendom by Jacobus de Voragine's *Legenda Aurea* in the thirteenth century. A dozen poems deal with Mary's own story. Among them are four of exuberant praise, three of them macaronic, singing the Annunciation of Mary's glory. Then there are three, one of them called

---

* The count of churches is taken from Jón Þorkelsson's *Om Digtningen*. Though not absolutely correct, it is no doubt representative of the relation in the distribution of churches between the saints.

Máríugrátr (Mary's Lament), praising her, but dwelling on her five sorrows (planctus). Another three contemplate her five or seven joys. The dozen is completed by two poems, of which the first, *Heyr mig bjartast blómsturið mæta*, has a graphic description of Christ on the Cross and the sorrowing Mary. Another dozen or so tells Mary legends, borrowed mostly from *Máríu saga*.

Then we find a *clavis metrica, Máríulykill*, attributed to Jón Máríu-skáld, thus continuing the line of Rögnvaldr kali and Snorri even in the sacred poetry. The original *clavis* seems to have been only about thirty-six stanzas and as many meters in the old sense of the word, among them none of the new hymn meters. The expanded poem, seventy stanzas, has more elaboration of the old and a few new meters.

The remainder of the Mary poems, starting with the exuberant maca-ronic eulogy, *Salutatio Mariae*, are mostly praise and prayers, for oneself, one's family, or for all of mankind, mingled sometimes with the invoca-tor's sense of unworthiness, sometimes with his holier-than-thou attitude towards those who waste their efforts on worldly paramours. Most of the Mary poems are anonymous, though several are attributed to authors.

In comparison with the great number of poems dedicated to Mary, the Apostles come off rather poorly. There is *Tólf postula kvæði*, dedi-cated to all of them, two poems on St. Peter, two on St. Paul, three on St. Andréas (Andrew), and one each for Jóhannes (John), Jacob (James), Thomas, and Bartholomeus. This predilection of the poets for St. Andréas, patron saint of Scotland, may be accidental, but it has a curious parallel in the preceding century—provided these poems do not belong to the fifteenth—where we find two poems on Mary and one *Heilagra meyja drápa* (Lay of the Holy Virgins) starting with an invo-cation to St. Andréas, besides the usual to God and Mary. But measured in church-ownership he trails in popularity after Peter (fifty-eight), John the Evangelist, and John the Baptist (*ca.* twenty each), with only thirteen churches.

Of the saints only St. Nikulás and St. Ólafr seem to have been more popular than the Apostles; each has four poems in his honor, while the former owns forty churches, the latter fifty-two or more. Two poems are devoted to Mary Magdalene and St. Cecilia; the rest of the saints—Agnes, Barbára, Christefórus, Dóróthea, Hallvarðr, Laurentíus, Magnús Eyjajarl (Earl of the Orkneys), Margrét, and Thomas à Becket—get one. Several of the poems are macaronic, making a strange impression.

Meters old and new

As stated before, some of the sacred poetry in *dróttkvætt* or *hálf-hneppt*, assigned by Finnur Jónsson to the fourteenth century may be from the fifteenth. Otherwise, with the exception of *fornyrðislag* in *Krossþulur*, the purified *hrynhent* or *Liljulag* reigns supreme among the old meters in the period 1400–1500. It is cultivated by the best poets: e. g., Sigurðr Narfason, Jón Arason, and Hallr Ögmundarson.

All the more striking is the flood of new hymn meters: ninety-seven per cent of the poems show up in this fashionable garb—there are about forty-five varieties of meters represented—borrowed from or formed by analogy with Latin, Scandinavian(?), German, and French hymns and sequences.

Curiously enough, we do not find the time-honored Ambrosian hymn quatrain employed in Icelandic sacred poems, though we find it in the Latin-Icelandic *Þorlákstíðir* (*Officium St. Thorlacii*) in a manuscript from *ca.* 1300, but probably composed as early as the first quarter of the century:

Adest festum percelebre   mentem lumen irradiat
quo effugantur tenebre   gens devota tripudiat.

Still, we do find a related ballad quatrain used once in the poem about the Norwegian St. Hallvarðr, and in about half a dozen legendary ballads, admittedly of Scandinavian origin (Norwegian [?], Danish). Under such circumstances one wonders whether the poem about St. Hallvarðr might not be of Norwegian origin, too. But if the Ambrosian quatrain was banned from native Icelandic hymns, we feel certain that the reason must be that it was associated with the ballad quatrain, which since the twelfth century had been so thoroughly secularized in Icelandic dances, *rímur*, and ballads. The development in Iceland was in this respect different from that in the other Scandinavian countries, for here the Ambrosian-ballad quatrain remained in use for saints' lives and other legendary matter. And, conversely, because of this survival of the Ambrosian meter in hymnal use in Scandinavia, we find there much less experimentation with other sacred meters than in Iceland—until after the Reformation.

Of other popular hymn meters we find the famous *Pange lingua gloriosi* stanza (the Thomas of Aquinas version) reproduced in *Hæstur Guð með heiðri skapti* (*Agnesardiktr*), though the translation *Tunga mín af hjarta hljóði* does not appear until after the Reformation. Likewise the stanza, used already in the eleventh century (Peter Damianus) but made famous by Archipoeta's *Mihi est propositum*, appears not only in the Latin-Icelandic *Þorláks-* and *Jóns-tíðir* (*ca.* 1300) but also in *Dýrðarlegast dyggða blóm* (translated from a Latin original in *Analecta hymnica* XXXII, p. 166).

In half a dozen cases there is identity or similarity with German pre-Reformation hymns, and though I have found no exact parallel to *Ljómur* among the Latin or the German hymns, its form is a perfect illustration of the German *Lied*-form (of *Minnesänger* and hymnwriters alike), with its two equal parts at the beginning (*zwei Stollen des Aufgesanges*) and its different end (*Abgesang*), the whole stanza riming abc/abc//dddd. But *Ljómur* is far from being an isolated case; about half of the meters (stanza forms) fall into this three-part form, at times symmetrical, as in *Pange lingua*, at times asymmetrical, as in *Ljómur*, obviously a later form. About half a dozen stanzas are clearly made up of two symmetrical parts, like *Mihi est propositum*, while the rest is more or less irregular or asymmetrical. A sequence stanza is often asymmetrical, but if two such are joined they make up a symmetrical two-part form.

The earliest sequence found in Iceland is probably the Latin-Icelandic (or Orkney?) twelfth-century poem in honor of St. Magnús Eyjajarl: *Comitis generosi*. The extremely popular sequence form *Stabat mater dolorosa* appears in the early (?) thirteenth-century Latin-Icelandic *Officium Thorlaci* (*Þorlákstíðir*) but not in Icelandic until the seventeenth century (Stefán Ólafsson). Sequences in the vernacular have not been mentioned except after the Reformation (in the *Graduale*, 1594). Still, there are at least two clear cases in *Íslenzk miðaldakvæði*. One is *Ágæt vil eg þér óðinn færa*, identical with the eleventh century French sequence *Verbum bonum et suave*. The other is *Nikulám skulum heiðra hér*, adapted from a known Latin sequence. In a descriptive note this sequence is referred to as " *prósa* " which might point to French origin. Two other poems are very probably sequences. The first, *Allra kærasta jungfrú mín*, has alternating eight and five line stanzas, sixteen in all. The second, *Fýsir mig að fremja dikt*, has twenty stanzas of equal (asymmetrical) build, but an odd end stanza slightly different in structure. There may be other cases too. One poem, *María mærin svinna*, is very reminiscent of a German *Leich* in its irregular form.

The chief element of stanza structure is, of course, the rime. We find it arranged in a variety of ways: the old row-rime (*runhent*, a couplet or more), the more recent alternating rime (1200–?), the split rime (abba), and other arrangements (e. g., the asymmetrical aab or aaab of the sequences). But in addition to these common European building blocks, the Icelandic hymn poetry also preserves religiously the common Germanic alliteration to cement two lines together (an odd line usually has its own alliteration). There may be some slackening of the rules of alliteration, and the rime is not always pure in the poetry of the period any more than it is in its Latin patterns. But there is no such wholesale decay or rejection of these two principles as we find in the earliest slavish translations of Lutheran hymns and to some extent in the Icelandic ballads.

Otherwise the Lutheran hymns, both in Germany and Iceland, are of the same three-part and two-part construction that we find in the pre-Reformation sacred poetry in Iceland—forms that from now on dominate not only the sacred but also, probably, the secular poetry in Iceland even up to the present. It is, therefore, not surprising to see some of the fifteenth-century meters actually surviving the Reformation, though probably zealously avoided by the Reformation leaders themselves. Those that I have found surviving are: *Tunga mín af hjarta hljóði* (= *Pange lingua*), *Jesú móðirin jungfrú skær* (= *Heimili vort og húsin með*), *Hæstur heilagur andi* minus the refrain (= *Einn herra eg best ætti*), and *Heyr þú Jesús hjálpin mín* (= *Játi það allur heimur hér*).

Others have survived as profane and popular songs: *María meyjan skæra* (= *Ó mín flaskan fríða*), *Bjóða vil eg þér bragsins smið* (= *Út á djúpið hann Oddur dró*), *Sannur Guð með sætri grein* (= *Keisari nokkur mætur mann*), and *Dýrðarlegast dyggða blóm* (= *Mihi est propositum*). Likewise *Stabat mater dolorosa* (= *Hjöluðu tveir í húsi forðum*, " Hrakfallabálkur "). Still others have been resurrected in the twentieth century by the two great medieval scholars and poets, Jón Þorkelsson and Jón Helgason.

The fifteenth century has commonly been given a very low rating in the history of Icelandic literature as, generally speaking, elsewhere. But it must not be forgotten that, as demonstrated above, it did give birth to the forms of the Modern Icelandic lyric.

Skáld-Sveinn and heimsósómar

Apart from the bulk of the sacred poetry, already described, there are a few other poems preserved from Catholic times, such as a couple of hymns on day and night, gospel verses, prayers, etc. More important, and on the border of sacred and secular poetry, are the *heimsósómar* or satires on this world, *de contemptu mundi*, of which the one by Skáld-Sveinn (fl. *ca.* 1500) is the earliest and best. It is an impressive poem (in the meter of *Ljómur*), lashing out against the arrogance and lawlessness of the chieftains of that time. The description of the vicious contemporary conditions, no doubt fitting the second half of the fifteenth century, is nothing less than superb, securing the otherwise unknown poet a rank among the best. The theme was one which remained popular throughout the sixteenth and seventeenth centuries, a favorite of the orthodox Lutherans who always were at war with the Devil, the flesh, and this world. It was often combined with praise, sometimes nostalgic, of the past, and deprecation of the present generation (*heimsósómar, aldarhættir, aldasöngvar, heimsádeilur*).

Jón Arason

Jón Arason (1484–1550) was born in Eyjafjörðr of good stock; he was ordained priest in 1507, and became bishop of Hólar in 1522. He introduced printing in Iceland and had the first books printed, though they are lost. As the last Catholic bishop in Iceland, he was beheaded in 1550, a martyr to his faith. His life was really the history of Iceland for a quarter of a century. He was not only the greatest personality of his age but has also long been considered the best poet, though the devotional poetry traditionally ascribed to him is perhaps not quite on a par with the earlier *Lilja* and the later *Passíusálmar*. But if, with Jón Helgason, we are to limit his canon of religious poetry to *Píslargrátr* (Christ's Passion, in *hrynhent*) and *Davíðsdiktr* (David's Psalm 51 = *Miserere*) in the *Ljómur*-meter, depriving him of *Niðurstigningsvísur* (Harrowing of Hell), *Krossvísur* (The Cross), and *Ljómur* (The Bright Poem, on Creation, Fall, and Redemption), his reputation will inevitably suffer a decline, for *Ljómur* is, by far, the best poem attributed to him. It compares favorably with *Lilja* on the same theme and, in artistry, with Skáld-Sveinn's *Heimsósómi* in the same meter. And since Jón Arason's *Davíðsdiktr*, in the same meter, suffers by comparison, it would be tempting to give *Ljómur* to Skáld-Sveinn, who thereby would eclipse Jón Arason as the best poet of the period and the creator of this popular and beautiful new meter. But if the bishop composed *Ljómur* he, who otherwise follows the Bible and conventional Catholic doctrine, completely evades the doctrine of eternal damnation by letting Mary and John intercede and obtain salvation for all the damned. Though I know of no parallel, this may not have been a unique feat of thought in the age of Mariolatry. But it shows how great an optimist the poet was. That optimism would go well with the character of Jón Arason, for it is no less evident in his secular poetry, which in some respects is no less important than his sacred poetry.

His secular poetry is—apart from the *rímur* he composed in collaboration with Sigurðr blindr—mostly *lausavísur*, occasional verse, personal humorous comments on current events or himself; the one on his horse Móalingr seems to be the first *hestavísa* (horse verse) recorded, the beginning of a long-lived genre. With few exceptions, such *lausavísur* (occasional verse) had not been preserved since the Age of the Sturlungs (though no doubt composed), but from now on they remained a steady stream up to the present. A stray stanza, if genuine, shows that the bishop could blow the trumpet of indignant satire (*heimsósómi*) like (though not as well as) Skáld-Sveinn. But most of the bishop's humorous verse is light-tempered banter (in ballad or *vikivaki* [?] meters) about his adversaries, of whom he did not think too highly, and about himself, whom he playfully depicts as "staff-carl" (a tramp). Even when arrested and confronted with the ax, there was no panic in his manly but bitter comments. That he was essentially a hero of the Old Icelandic type, a man of great good luck (*gæfumaðr*) is indicated in the last verse greeting to his son Ari: "He who is not burdened with sorrows and care (*harmar*) will be a man of good fortune." In a way it recalls *Hávamál*: *Meðal snotr / skyli manna hverr* "Middling wise / a man should be."

Secular Poetry of the Later Middle Ages

Introduction

Late medieval secular poetry in Iceland was of two kinds: popular and learned. The learned branch, the discussion of which we shall defer to the end, was represented by *háttalyklar* (metrical keys) in continuation of Snorri Sturluson.

Popular poetry (*ca.* 1200–1550) comprised three genres—dances, *rímur*, and ballads—as well as minor things like folktale poems, prayers, charms, riddles, and rigmaroles (*þulur*).

Danzar: Dances

Dance (*danz*) is mentioned for the first time in Iceland (and Scandinavia) by Gunnlaugr Leifsson, a monk, at the beginning of the thirteenth century: "The game was popular before the saintly Jón became bishop [in 1106] that a man should sing to a woman in the dance amorous and erotic songs, while the woman was to address love songs (*mansöngvar*) to the man. This sport the bishop abolished and prohibited strictly," though he was not quite successful. Doubt has been cast on this statement, but if correct it establishes (French) dancing in Iceland before 1100.

This passage, from the older *Biskupa sögur* (I, 237), is supplemented by several instances from the *Sturlunga saga* referring to dancing in the years 1119, 1121, 1232, 1255, and 1258. The later *Biskupa sögur* of Bishop Árni (1269–98) and Bishop Laurentíus (1323–30) state the fact that these worthies did not approve of dancing any more than did the saintly Bishop Jón. In contrast to this, Bishop Guðmundr the Good of the thirteenth century does not seem to have minded dancing among his men.

The terms used—apart from *danz*—are *danzleikr* and *hringleikr*, showing that it was some kind of a ring dance like the French *carole*.

If dancing was actually older than this in Iceland, *hringleikr* would be the word for it. But *danz* is of French origin; the Norwegian *Konungs-skuggsjá* uses the verb *danza*, while *Sturlunga saga* always uses the term *slá danz* " strike up the dance." *Danz* can also mean a ditty (or a poem) used for dancing. *Sturlunga saga* relates a feud of 1220–21 in these terms: " The Breiðbœlings mocked Loptr and composed many dances (*danza marga*) and many other lampoons (*spott*) about him." In 1245 the followers of Kolbeinn ungi Arnórsson were practicing dance-making (*danza-görðir*) to the chagrin of his enemies. But most famous is the story of Þórðr Andrésson riding to this death on December 26, 1264, singing aloud this dance (*danz þenna*):

> Mínar eru sorgir/ þungar sem blý.
> Mine are the sorrows/ heavy as lead.

(Guðbrandur Vigfússon, *Sturlunga* II, 264; ed. Jón Jóhannesson I, 533) This sounds like a ballad refrain, and it was so used in seventeenth century *vikivaki*.

There are several lampooning ditties preserved in the *Sturlunga saga* that one might suspect as coming under the head of *danza-görðir*, " dance-making," but they all seem to be composed in old skaldic meters (*runhent*) except the ditty from 1221, one of the many dances (*danza marga*) referred to above:

Loptr er í Eyjum
bítr lundabein,
Sæmundr er á heiðum
etr berin ein.

Loptr is out in the Islands
gnawing the puffin bones,
Sæmundr is up in the highlands
eating berries alone.

(Guðbrandur Vigfússon, *Sturlunga* I, 249; ed. Jón Jóhannesson I, 284). This quatrain anticipates the ballad meters which emerged in the sixteenth century, and which were probably alive from the thirteenth century onwards, perhaps even as old as the twelfth century, at least their characteristic refrain (*viðlag*).

Rímur: Metrical romances

Still, the first poetry to emerge after these earliest dances was not the ballads (*fornkvæði, sagnadanzar*) but the related *rímur* (" rimes ") or metrical romances. The earliest datable *ríma* is *Ólafs ríma Haralds-sonar* by Einar Gilsson in *Flateyjarbók* (*ca.* 1390). It is a narrative or epic poem telling its story in sixty-five quatrain stanzas. References in some of the earliest *rímur* prove that, like the ballads, they were actually used for dancing. Such references linger into the seventeenth century, though by that time the practice had probably been given up.

The legacy of the dances to the *rímur* was the metrical form. There appear in *rímur* before the Reformation eight basic meters (A-H) of which five show four-lined stanzas of some sort while one (*afhent*) is two-lined and two (*braghent* and *stuðlafall*) are three-lined. The origin of these lastnamed meters is obscure, but most of the quatrains are derivable from the four-lined dance or ballad meters current in Iceland, Scandinavia, and England.

The following translations are designed to reproduce the meters in English. They are made by Páll (Paul) Bjarnason of Vancouver, B. C., one of the few American-Icelandic poets who has attempted to transmit the Icelandic poetical form to English.

The most common stress pattern in the ballad stanzas was four stresses to the odd and three to the even lines, the rime scheme being abcb.

Ríka álfs kvæði (The Ballad of the Rich Elf) :

Eirek nefni eg kónginn þann,
stýrir beittum brandi;
Engilsól hét dóttir hans,
ólst hún upp í landi.

Eirekr, widely hailed as king,
swings a hefty sabre;
Engilsól his child remained
inland with a neighbor.

This pattern is reproduced not only in the *skáhent* with identical rime scheme, but also with the rime scheme abab in *ferskeytt*, the oldest of all *rímur* meters, the most commonly used, and the one most teeming with variants.

Ferskeytt (*rímur*) :

Ólafr kóngur örr ok fríðr
átti Noregi at ráða;
gramr var æ við bragna blíðr
borinn til sigrs ok náða.

Ólafr king, so fine of feature,
fated was to tower
over Norway's every creature
as a kindly power.

Skáhent (*rímur*) :

Skikkju bil hún skipar mér til
að skemmta á hverju kveldi;
seggurinn má hjá seima Gná
sitja undir feldi.

Each day she will order me
to act the gallant lover;
in the shade beside the maid
sitting 'neath a cover.

A related meter with two stresses only in the even lines is found in the ballad *Tristrams kvæði* and copied in *úrkast*:

Svo skal búa hennar ferð
sem segi eg frá;

Thus be planned as I command
her ocean trips;

blá skulu segl á skipunum	blue shall be the sails on all
sem hún er á.	her stately ships.
Úrkast er mér undraleitt	*Úrkast* forms an ugly mood
þó efni eg brag;	that I detest.
varla mun hér veita greitt	Seldom will be very good
það vísna-lag.	a verse so dressed.

Two ballads, *Kaupmanna kvæði* (Ballad of Merchants) and *Sonar harmr* (Sorrow of Son), display a rime scheme aabb and an equal length of the riming lines (four stresses). This pattern is copied in the *stafhent* of *rímur*:

Kann eg öngvan kvæða mátt	Mine is not the magic art
að kveikja af nokkurn dýran hátt;	to metrify each runic part;
stundum hef eg *stafhent* lag	I prefer the *stafhent* style
það styttir nokkuð fyrir mér brag.	to stem the phrases that beguile.

But this meter is also a regular skaldic half-strophe in *hneppt runhenda af hrynhendum hætti* found in *Háttatal* 91 and in the lampoon (dance?) *Vetrungs fæðist efnit eitt* in *Sturlunga saga*.

Samhent in *rímur* differs from this only in carrying the rime through the four lines (aaaa).

There are no parallels to the two-lined ballad stanzas in *rímur*. But *rímur* have developed one two-line meter, *afhent*, and two three-lined meters, *braghent* and *stuðlafall*. Both *afhent* and *braghent* have in common a first line prolonged by two stresses while the other lines are of normal four stress length:

> *Afhent* verður óðarlagið fyr ýtum glósa;
> vill það ekki vífið ljósa.
>
> Tyros love the *afhent* ode and often use it.
> Women, more refined, refuse it.
>
> Ferjan hlýtur úr fræðanausti hin fimmta að renna;
> *braghent* lag er bezt að kenna
> ef blíðar þjóðir hlýða nenna.
>
> From its berth of basic lore the brew is flowing
> *braghent* mead is best for showing
> to brethren with a thirst for knowing.

In *stuðlafall* the first line is prolonged by one stress only:

> *Stuðlafalls* þó stofna gjöri eg rímu;
> það má skilja þjóðin hrein
> þar á kann eg öngva grein.

Stuðlafall though still I sway to riming.
It is well that all should know
in that field my stock is low.

Rime patterns are: in *afhent*, aa; in *braghent*, aaa or A(assonance)aa, and abb; in *stuðlafall*, abb. Theoretically *braghent* might be derivable from *afhent*, by the addition of one line, or *vice versa*. But since *braghent* is pretty common, but *afhent* and *stuðlafall* extremely rare before the Reformation, it looks as if *braghent* would be the oldest form.

If the stanza form and the end-rime were a legacy of the dances, the strict syllable counting, the alliteration, and the inrime were inherited from the skaldic poetry. In the quatrains the odd and even lines were always tied by alliteration; there were two to the odd and one to the first stress of the even lines. In the two- and three-lined stanzas the first line always had its own alliterative pattern, the rest of the stanza another pattern.

The diction and the style of *rímur* were also taken from the skaldic poetry. There is the same use of *heiti* and *kenningar* as found in the skalds or the *Snorra Edda*, a book the poets no doubt knew and used, for they often refer to their art as *Eddu-regla*, *Eddu-list* or simply *Edda*, and commonly avow moderation in its employment. But though both *kenningar* and *heiti* were employed and understood by the *rímur* poets, there is a gradual development away from the old classic style towards a stereotyped phraseology where the meanings of the components of a kenning are increasingly forgotten. This tendency toward muddle-headed phraseology was not confined to the realm of kennings but was also detectable in recurring tags and in recurring epithets for heroes and villains, for ladies and hags or troll-women. But such faults the *rímur* shared with other metrical romances of the Middle Ages.

As the form so the matter of *rímur* can be shown to be woven of mixed strands, native and foreign. But before trying to unravel them we must pause for a closer definition of the genre *ríma* (sg.) and *rímur* (pl.). The *Ólafs ríma* is a short narrative poem, but most *rímur* tell a story of considerable length. A prose saga of many chapters would be turned into *rímur* (or a *rímur*-cycle) of equally many *rímur* (cantos), each single *ríma* corresponding to a chapter. The different *rímur* of one cycle would often, and increasingly so, be composed in different meters. Finally, though there is no introduction to *Ólafs ríma*, there soon developed a habit of prefacing at least one *ríma*, later all the *rímur*, of the cycle with a *mansöngr*, originally a love song addressed to a woman or the female audience.

The question is now: were there any epic poems from which the *rímur* poets could have learned to tell an old story in verse? The answer is yes. In the first place they could have learned this from the native epic praise poems which arose in the twelfth century and which we have already discussed (e. g., *Jómsvíkingadrápa* p. 67). In the second place they could have learned it from the foreign epic ballads (*fornkvæði, sagnadanzar*), which we must assume to have been current from the thirteenth century onwards though not appearing in MSS until the sixteenth. But though the roots of the *rímur* are thus clear, they soon developed into something different, the long narrative poem not previously found in Icelandic.

The *mansöngr* is a feature as peculiar to *rímur* as the introductory lyric stanza or refrain to the ballads. It is most commonly a love song in which the poet voices his praises of his lady or pours out his lament over the vicissitudes of love. He may deplore his lady's indifference, his own insignificance or his old age. A favorite device is to cite a row of illustrious personages suffering from love's pangs or ladies' whims—as a consolation. Later, especially after the Reformation, when the original purpose of the *mansöngr* was obscured, it might be used for most anything; such as comments on the story, enumeration of colleagues, dedication to a patron, and so on. But originally the *mansöngr* was, clearly, a reflection of the medieval courtly love tradition, whether it came by way of the Orkneys (*Jómsvíkingadrápa*), or perhaps as a branch of the German *Minnesang*, over Norway.

Foreign love and romance vied in popularity with native Viking adventure and, to some extent, old myths (*Þrymlur, Lokrur*). Only half so popular were folk and fairy tales and the Norwegian kings' sagas, while native Icelandic themes trailed far behind. This is obvious from a classification of *rímur* before the Reformation:

Sagas of Icelanders	3
Sagas of Norwegian Kings	10
Heroic-Mythical sagas and the *Edda*	20
Sagas of Chivalry with *Karlamagnúss saga* and *Þiðriks saga*	19
Folk tales and Fairy tales	10
Mock-heroic *Skíða ríma*	1

Even in descriptions we can sense the difference between native and foreign matter. Accounts of sailing and battle are in the tradition of the skaldic poetry, while the descriptions of gorgeous and fantastic festivity derive from the foreign romances.

Thirty-seven *rímur* (cycles) are preserved from the period *ca.* 1350–1460, all anonymous except *Ólafs ríma* (*Völsungs rímur* and *Skíða ríma?*). From 1460–1520 eleven *rímur* are preserved, among them those of Sigurðr blindr, an older contemporary of Jón Arason, and highly esteemed in his time and after (*Hektors rímur, Mábilar rímur*, etc.). From the period 1520–1560 fifteen *rímur* have been preserved, among them *rímur* by Árni Jónsson, who shows some effect of the Reformation. We can discuss none of these *rímur* here, except the interesting *Skíða ríma*.

Skíða ríma

Skíða ríma was by its last editor (Jón Þorkelsson) attributed to Svartur Þórðarson á Hofsstöðum (...1462–77...) (older sources say Einar fóstri) the poet of Ólöf Loptsdóttir (ríka) and Björn Þorleifsson, who held the manor Skarð á Skarðsströnd after her father Loptr ríki. Svartur also composed *Skaufhalabálkur*, an Icelandic Reynard the Fox. Whoever the author, he was familiar with the region around Skarð. The author makes his protagonist, the tramp Skíði, whom he describes in burlesque terms, walk between chiefs of the neighborhood, carrying flattery and slander as well as his scrip and staff. Coming to an inhospitable place, he has to eat his own food and sleep on the floor. Forgetting to cross himself, he dreams that Ása-Þórr comes for him and brings him to the court of Óðinn, who wants to add him to the roster of his heroes. For a while things go well. Skíði is even offered in marriage the famed Hildr Högni's daughter, whom he betroths with a dirty hand. Unfortunately, Skíði, forgetting God in the evening, now comes to mention his name, thus scandalizing the heathen gods. When this happens for the third time, pandemonium breaks loose. The tramp fights and kills most of the gods and the heroes, until, finally, he awakens with a jolt, bruised and broken-nosed but with a new steel cylinder to his staff and his scrip full of " thrice " ancient butter, which proves fatal to the dogs of the place. This is not only the sole mock-heroic poem among the *rímur* but also the first in the Icelandic literature, though there are a few mock-heroic skaldic verses. B. K. Þórólfsson, the greatest authority on *rímur*, doubts the identification of *Skíða ríma*'s author, but agrees to the above date, believing the *ríma* to be a parodic reaction to the extravagant adventures of the early *rímur* (cf. *Don Quixote*).

In conclusion let us say a few words on the poetical and cultural

worth of the *rímur*. Excepting *Skíða ríma* and a stray passage or stanza
here and there, there is by common consent little first rate poetry to be
found in the *rímur*, though this judgment, made by nineteenth and
twentieth century critics has been found to be too harsh, not only by
several modern poets but also by the great student of *rímur*, Sir William
A. Craigie. There is much solid workmanship and, due to the rigorous
form, the *rímur* compare favorably with contemporary metrical romances
in other lands, at least those in English. Also, because of the increasingly
strict form, the *rímur* became a school for poets and a depository of
linguistic tradition whose importance for Icelandic poetry, even today,
could hardly be overestimated. They represent, indeed, the backbone
of the poetical tradition and have kept unbroken the connection with the
most ancient poetry. At the same time they served well their immediate
purpose, which was to entertain the people with tales from their past
and from contemporary European literature and thus to keep alive the
flickering spirit of heroism and romance during the long centuries of
national decline. Probably no product of the national genius is so
peculiarly Icelandic as the *rímur*.

Ballads: fornkvæði, sagnadanzar *

Though the ballads must have been contemporary with the earliest
rímur and must have helped to give them form, they do not emerge in
manuscripts until the early sixteenth century. Indeed, two of the most
important manuscripts date from 1665 and *ca.* 1700. The following
comments will be confined to the sixty-six ballads edited by Svend
Grundtvig and Jón Sigurðsson, though a few have been published since,
among them some humorous ballads. A new edition *Fornir dansar* was
published by Ólafur Briem in 1946.

As shown before (p. 85), the ballads were closely related metrically
to the old dances of the thirteenth century and the earliest *rímur*, though
differing from the latter in not counting syllables and in disregarding
rules of alliteration.

About forty-four per cent of the ballads are in rimed (or half-rimed)
couplets, not found in *rímur* but common in England and Scandinavia,
a form there associated with the oldest ballads. About thirty-six per
cent are in the quatrain meters, discussed under *rímur*, of rather loose

* Both these terms are modern. But as *Tristrams kvæði* and other instances show,
they were often called *kvæði* to distinguish them from the older *drápur* and the
contemporary *rímur*.

structure, but mainly with four stresses to the odd and three to the even lines, though some (e. g., *Tristrams kvæði*) have only two stresses to the even lines. The rime scheme is abcb. Two ballads (*Kaupmanna kvæði*, see *rímur*) have four stresses in all four lines riming aabb.

About twenty per cent—all but one of the couplet type—show what I call connective repetition from stanza to stanza. There are four types of this repetition: (1) the last line of the preceding stanza is repeated *in toto* as a first line of the following stanza, (2) the end of the second line *and* the last line are repeated, (3) the end of the second line *only* is repeated, and (4) the end of the last line is repeated. In the only quatrain ballad that has this repetition, a fifth line is added to the end of the stanza and repeated as the first line of the next stanza. This sort of repetition is not found in English ballads, but is not uncommon in Danish ballads. Elsewhere in Icelandic poetry it is found in a hymn of 1665 and in *Grýlu kvæði* from the seventeenth century onwards. A similar repetition in Middle English poetry has been thought to be of Celtic or French origin.

With four exceptions the Icelandic ballads have refrains (*viðlög*), thus agreeing with the Danish but differing from the English ballads, which are usually without refrain. The refrain may be one line, or two, or even more; its lines are often of irregular length. The refrain of a couplet is usually split by the second line of the couplet, while the refrain of a quatrain usually comes at the end, but there are irregularities.

Fourteen ballads also have what is called *stef-stofn* or a refrain base, an introductory stanza from which the *stef* or *viðlag*, "refrain," is derived. This stanza is usually lyrical, often marvellously expressive of the mood of the ballad, but not as a rule connected with its story. Thus it is analogous to the *mansöngr* of the *rímur*. Scholars have long assumed that this part of the ballad was a direct descendant of the oldest dance stanzas, presumably of French origin.

The ballads differ from all Icelandic poetry—except some sixteenth century Lutheran hymns—in these points: they disregard the rules of alliteration, use poor rimes (assonances), and introduce a number of foreign word forms, a fact indicating that they were introduced by imitative word of mouth rather than by regular translation. But if they lack the formal refinement of the *rímur*, they compensate by their naive simplicity of approach—though they are, perhaps, rarely as naive as the Danish and English ballads. Still the usual and well-known charms of ballad artistry do not fail in Iceland any more than elsewhere; perfect poetical gems are to be found there though only the classic *Tristrams kvæði* need be mentioned.

When compared to the ballads of the Scandinavian sister countries, the Icelandic ballads are not only comparatively few (cf. the 500 Danish) but also comparatively meager in subject matter. Of the sixty-six ballads there is one on a theme from an Icelandic saga (*Gunnars kvæði* from *Njála*), one from a king's saga (*Ólafs vísa* [*Haraldssonar*]), one from a French romance (*Tristrams kvæði*), and none whatever from the heroic-mythical sagas and the Eddas—all themes most fully represented in the Faroese and Norwegian ballads (*Kæmpeviser*) and spread from there to Denmark and Sweden. But a glance at the subjects of *rímur* (p. 89) will show the reason: in Iceland these themes were always retold in *rímur*.

Apart from these, sixteen ballads derive their themes from folk- and fairy-tales, dealing with elves, nixes, a woodsprite, a sea-troll, the might of song, of harping, and of runes; the power in names, shape-shifting, and, finally, legends. Among these was the most popular and still best known of the ballads *Ólafur liljurós* (Clerc Colwin). Here, too, belongs the *Gauta kvæði* that Kemp Malone so ingeniously connected with *Deor*.

But the majority of ballads—about forty-six—deal with the life of ladies and lords from the Danish age of chivalry and, if localized, they are laid in Denmark. Among these there are a few on Danish twelfth century characters, like King Valdemar, his queen Soffia, and his concubine Tove. Esbern Snare was one of his men. One poem, *Bjarnasona kvæði*, treats of a killing in Norway, dated in 1206.

These kinds of ballads (*riddaravísur*) were unique for their subject matter in Iceland, since there were too few knighted lords there ever to be felt as a specific class. The collection of the ballads may, however, have been compiled for some of these few trying to follow the fashion of the mother-country. For other Scandinavians the Icelandic ballads are important by representing an older stage of balladry than now is to be found anywhere else.

Since most of the knightly ballads seem connected with Denmark, it was natural for Finnur Jónsson to assume that they came directly from Denmark, during the fifteenth century. He did not note the telling similarity in connective repetition. Knut Liestöl noted that some of the ballads had closer parallels in (West) Norway, and therefore concluded that most of them, even if ultimately Danish, made their way over Norway, some in the thirteenth, most in the fourteenth century. If connective repetition belongs to the fifteenth century, Liestöl must be wrong about such ballads. However, it may be a century older.

The ballads were a southern flower transplanted on arctic soil. They always retained their exotic appearance and were never fully assimilated. But they fill their niche in the garden of Icelandic literature with distinction.

Other popular forms

Apart from dances, *rímur* and ballads with their often delightful lyrical refrains the secular poetry of the fourteenth, fifteenth and six-teenth centuries includes some (lost) love poetry (*afmors-* and *bruna-vísur*) always under attack from the clergy, and a few occasional verses (*lausa-vísur*), comments on a passing event or the times.

The nature and love lyrics, so common in contemporary Europe, are conspicuous by an almost complete absence in Iceland. Still, there are verses in the late sagas or *fornaldar sögur* that would come under this head. So would the beautiful lyric heard by Fiðlu-Björn in a fairy rock, if it dates from before the Reformation.

There also was a body of poetry in the Eddic *fornyrðislag*, now used chiefly for nursery rimes and folk-tale poetry. An early representative is the fragment of a *Grýlu kvæði* (Ogress Ballad) from 1221, but after the Reformation these poems are continued in ballad meters. Of the fifteenth century is the fabliau *Skaufhalabálkur*, which, if inspired by *Reynard the Fox*, only recounts the last foray of the fox and its death. Later, probably from the sixteenth century, are the so-called *sagnaljóð* (folk-tale poetry) and *ljúflingsljóð* (fairy-tale poetry), also in *fornyrð-islag*, whence the new name *ljúflingslag* for the meter. Both versify Icelandic folk tales of the period; both, not least so the last-named, are lyrical and of an unusually light touch. The same carefree romantic spirit is also found in the simplest Mary legends, and is perhaps related to the optimism in Jón Arason's (and Einar Sigurðsson's?) poetry.

It remains to mention the riddles (*gátur*), and the nursery rimes proper (*þulur, barnagælur*), of which some are still in *fornyrðislag*, others in a free style riming verse which recalls the early Latin sequences or the German *Leich*.

Loptr ríki Guttormsson: Háttalykill

The learned secular poetry of the fourteenth and fifteenth centuries is represented by one poem only: the *Háttalykill* (*Clavis metrica*) of Loptr

Guttormsson inn ríki (the Rich) (*ca.* 1375–1432), so-called because of his enormous wealth, due partly to his rich ancestry and partly to the Black Death (1402). He was knighted by the Danish king, and he loved to ride between his eighty farmsteads surrounded by his henchmen. His first love and paramour was the highborn Kristín Oddsdóttir, by whom he had four sons, though for some reason (a stay abroad?) he never married her. His wife, no less highborn, bore him four children. His descendants kept up the family traditions of wealth and nobility and became, besides, so prolific that most Icelanders are now descended from them. One would have thought that Knight Loptr, in voicing his love-lament to Kristín, would have favored the ballads then in vogue among the gentry of the Danish motherland. Instead, we find him harking back to the skaldic tradition and Snorri—Nordal thinks, in conscious revolt against the free measures of the ballad. However that may be, it is certain that by his complicated and ornate *háttalykill* (*ca.* 1410–20), which with its random verses may be compared to a sonnet sequence, he set a fashion, followed not only by the sacred and learned author of *Máríulykill* (*ca.* 1430) but also, after the Reformation, by the " popular " *rímur* poet Hallur Magnússon. From then on there was an unbroken row of *háttalyklar* of skaldic, lyric, and *rímur* forms up to the voluminous *Bragfræði* (Metrics) of *rímur* finished by the Rev. Helgi Sigurðsson in 1888, containing over twenty meters in almost 2000 variations.

But if Loptr ríki was thus a typical transmitter of the skaldic tradition, he was also a typical representative of the romantic love fashion of his day. Snorri's *Háttatal* had been a poem in praise of kings; Loptr ríki's was an expression of courtly love with a praise of the paramour, not his wife, and a lament over the lost love. It was no doubt composed after each of the lovers was married to another person. Jón Helgason doubts the authenticity of Loptr ríki's *Háttalykill* as well as of *Máríulykill*.

Note: *Háttalykill* of Hallur Magnússon is wrongly attributed to him, it belongs to the seventeenth century.

Literature of the Clergy

Latin alphabet introduced

We shall now trace what part the Icelandic church and clergy played—more or less directly—in the production of literature. Its first important part was introducing the Latin alphabet for writing books, a virgin field, for the runes were always restricted to monumental and magic purposes. Sermons and homilies must have been preached from the very first in the native tongue by the missionaries, and since there were Englishmen among them, such as Rúðólfr in Bœr in Borgarfjörðr, they may have started the Icelanders on writing their homilies in their native tongue as was the custom in England.

Icelandic bishops

By the middle of the eleventh century the Icelanders had become ambitious enough to choose their own bishop with a seat at Skálaholt in the South. Here the first two bishops, father and son, Ísleifr Gizurarson (1056–80) and Gizurr Ísleifsson (1082–1118) laid the foundation of the new church. The latter's popularity was such that he could even introduce the tithe law in 1097 and, in order that the country might never be without a bishop, he generously gave up a quarter of his jurisdiction to a new bishop, Jón Ögmundarson, at Hólar in the North (1106–21).

Schools and learning at the sees

Schools were operated at both sees, but we know nothing about the one at Skálaholt, now Skálholt, beyond the fact that many chieftains sent their sons to be educated there. At Hólar, Bishop Jón brought two foreigners, a native of Gautland (Götland) to teach Latin grammar and a Frenchman, Rikinni, to teach Gregorian chant and Latin versification. This paradise of learning was not without its snake in the shape of Ovid's *De arte amatoria* to tempt a young clerk, but such a book was not tolerated by the saintly bishop any more than the impious and sexy dancing which seems to have come in the wake of the French cantor. The new learning attracted not only budding clerics, but also a deft maiden and a skilled carpenter, Þóroddr Gamlason rúnameistari, who both became expert Latinists by listening to Latin being taught. In this one should not forget that in the Iceland of 1100 there was no great social cleavage between the chieftains and the farmers or even the farm-hands, for pioneering life had proven such a social equalizer that by this time even the slaves had been set up in freedom to shift for themselves.

Astronomy and computus

The maiden and the carpenter at Hólar were not the only examples of learning spreading outside the circle of clergy. Stjörnu-Oddi, apparently a farmhand in the North, became interested in astronomy and made observations far ahead of his time. Still, most of the literature on chronology and calendar science is, no doubt, attributable to the clergy. Before Christianity was introduced the Icelanders had counted time in 52 weeks in a year of 364 days. By the tenth century they had discovered that this was too short a year and added one week to the summer, sumarauki, every seventh year. This reform was duly recorded by Ari inn fróði. It was the task of the twelfth-century chronologists to bring this native counting into harmony with the ecclesiastical Julian calendar. According to modern scholars they did solve it in a brilliant fashion.

First Grammatical Treatise

Grammarians and rhetoricians of eleventh and twelfth century Europe rarely dealt with any language but Latin, and it was most unusual if anyone, like the Englishman, Ælfric, wrote his Latin grammar in the vernacular. But in twelfth-century Iceland (ca. 1140–80) there was a grammarian who devised a modified Latin alphabet for his mother tongue and wrote his treatise—the so-called First Grammatical Treatise—in the vernacular. Moreover, this man, though he knew Hebrew, Greek, and Old English scripts—in addition to the Latin one—was so unorthodox that, to the amazement and delight of modern linguists, he actually invented a perfect phonological orthography for Icelandic. As a model observer and theoretician he seems to have had no peer in Western Christendom, until perhaps fifty years later when Brother Orm appeared on the English scene with the Ormulum. Both men wanted to create a practical spelling for their countrymen to ease the art of reading and writing. But fate was not particularly favorable to either; Orm was ignored, and, though the Icelander started a school of spelling no one followed him in detail.

Málskrúðsfrœði (rhetoric)

This first anonymous Icelandic grammarian was followed by several others, but only the last one, the rhetorician Ólafr Þórðarson hvítaskáld, nephew of Snorri Sturluson, deserves to be mentioned. He wrote Málskrúðsfrœði (Rhetoric) in the European school tradition, with the Latin terminology (barbarismus, etc.) but in Icelandic, and with examples from the skaldic poetry. His work in stringency of method does not measure up to his uncle's Edda which, though wholly native, obviously owes much to the European vogue of rhetorics in the twelfth century.

Other centers of learning

The schools of the two dioceses, at Skálholt and Hólar, were not the only centers of learning. The school of Haukadalr was run by Teitr, son of Bishop Ísleifr; his most important pupil was Ari inn fróði. No less important was the school of Oddi, founded by the chieftain-priest Sæmundr inn fróði (1056–1133) who was the first Icelander (and Scandinavian) to study in France (Bec?) and the first Icelander to write in Latin. His son, Loptr Sæmundarson, married the king of Norway's daughter; their son was Jón Loptsson, the most powerful chief in Iceland towards the end of the twelfth century. He fostered Snorri Sturluson. The traditions fostered by these schools were aristocratic and critical.

Monasteries: the Church militant

Other centers of learning sprang up with the seven monasteries— the first one at Þingeyrar—established in the period 1133–1226. In the latter half of the twelfth-century Iceland seems to have been flooded by a wave of religion which culminated about 1200 and did not begin to recede until the twenties of that century. The writings at the school of Þingeyrar, hagiographic and uncritical, were borne on this wave of religion. About 1200 a census revealed the presence of some 425 priests in a population of about 80,000—one priest for less than 200 souls. At the same time Iceland had its two saints: Þorlákr Þórhallsson, born 1133, Bishop of Skálholt 1178–93, exhumed 1198, and Jón Ögmundarson, born 1052, Bishop of Hólar 1106–21, exhumed 1200, though neither of them were sanctioned by the Church. The first Code of Church Law, dating from 1122–33, had embodied the peculiar compromise with the chieftains of the earliest Church in Iceland. Towards 1200 the European *ecclesia militans* was in no mood to compromise. Already Bishop Þorlákr Þórhallsson had tried to wrest the time-honored ownership of the churches from the chiefs (originally the Church had encouraged them to build churches on their estates!), but his attempt had foundered on the resistance of Jón Loptsson. The fight was carried on relentlessly by Bishop Guðmundr Arason of Hólar (1203–37), but with his impractical saintliness all he gained was to be repeatedly chased from his see, for even his claims to sainthood were ignored by the Church. It was reserved for the eminently practical Bishop Árni Þorláksson of Skálholt (1269–98) to gain the ascendancy over the chieftains and to write a second Code of Church Law, which did not differ from the European Canon Law. With the ruling that this, God's Law, was to prevail over the Law of the Land, in case of a clash, the Church was now made the wealthiest and most powerful institution of the country, and it remained so for two centuries and a half (1300–1550).

Homilies, books of instruction, saints' lives

Already the *First Grammatical Treatise* mentions " sacred translations " among works in the mother tongue. Since there exists in a manuscript from about 1200 an Icelandic *Hómilíubók* (Book of Homilies, ed. Wisén, *Den Stockholmska homilie-boken*) it seems likely that some such work was meant. It is true that only sixteen of the fifty-six homilies have been identified as translations (e. g., from the *Homiliarum* of Paulus Diaconus) but whether that is due to disappearance of the Latin originals or to the originality of the Icelandic (-Norwegian) clergy is still an open question. Perhaps F. Paasche's words about the lives of saints are equally applicable to the homilies: " It has been a common practice to classify these as ' translations ' but the truth is that a great number of them contain considerable independent work in the shape of Icelandic theology and even polemical theology " (*Homiliu-bók*, CCImÆ, VII. 16). In any case these homilies are based on the Bible, the apocryphal Gospels, the lives of saints, and the history of the early Church.

A *Physiologus* (Bestiary) and an *Elucidarius* (Manual of Theology) date from about the same time as the *Hómilíubók*. Most of the *Postula sögur* (Lives of the Apostles), *Heilagra manna sögur* (Lives of Saints) as well as *Máríu saga* (Life of Mary by Kygri-Björn) date from the thirteenth century, though some are earlier, some later. Most are, presumably, translations; most, too, are anonymous, though a few Icelandic authors are mentioned by name, like Kygri-Björn. A good deal of the matter of these three huge collections is Icelandic; the sagas must have been made for the monasteries where such *legenda* were prescribed for mealtimes and evening wakes. Style and language of these devotional works is very uneven; the Latin original shimmers through in many places as well as the florid and involved style (the learned style), but the early homilies are written in a surprisingly idiomatic Icelandic. Much work remains to be done to write the history of these legendary sagas and determine the sequence of the two or more versions that often occur of the same sagas, but when that has been done they will probably, like the sacred poetry, be found to reflect contemporary currents in the Church. They are often the foundation on which the sacred poems are based. As devotional works they have been praised by modern Catholics (Sigrid Undset).

Íslenzk Æfintýri (exempla)

It remains to mention an interesting collection of *exempla*, called *Íslenzk æfintýri* by the editor Hugo Gering. Part of these " adventures " or tales is a translation of Petrus Alfonsi, *Disciplina clericalis*, part are stories credited to the fertile Dominican preacher, Jón Halldórsson, a Norwegian student at Paris and Bologna and Bishop of Skálholt (1322– 39). A couple of adventures, reputedly happening to himself, were related in his *þáttr*, written shortly after his death.

Legendary kings' sagas

Legendary sagas of the missionary kings were written in the monastery of Þingeyrar, during the second half of the twelfth century. They are treated with the kings' sagas, but here we must stress their importance as patterns, especially for the hagiographical bishops' sagas, written shortly after 1200. Apart from Abbot Karl Jónsson, who was really a secular writer, we know the names of three hagiographers at Þingeyrar: the monks Oddr Snorrason (late twelfth century) and Gunnlaugr Leifsson (d. 1218 or 1219), and the priest Styrmir Kárason inn fróði (*ca.* 1170–1245), who later became closely associated with Snorri Sturluson. It is true that the first book of miracles about Bishop Þorlákr had been written and read at the Althing in 1199. But the following year the " saintliness " of Jón Ögmundarson of Hólar (1102–21) " came up," and the hagiographer Gunnlaugr Leifsson at Þingeyrar lost little time in composing his saga.

Jóns saga helga

Jóns saga helga was written in Latin at the instigation of Bishop Guðmundr Arason, the Good, in the period 1203–11. The Latin original is lost, but an Icelandic translation is preserved in two versions, of which the first is a close translation, the second an abbreviated copy, pruning not only some of the legendary matter of the first but also its ecclesiastical metaphors and learned style. The first version may belong to the first half (quarter ?), the second to the second half of the thirteenth century. *Jóns saga helga* is our only source for the activity of the church in the first quarter of the twelfth century: our information about the school at Hólar, the learning, and the dancing, comes from it. It also contains the miracles, *Jarteinir*, of Jón helgi. The activity of the hagiographers of Þingeyrar and Hólar seems to have started the southerners at Skálholt on their intense saga-writing in the first and second decade of the century. But because of lingering respect for the critical traditions of Sæmundr and Ari, their sagas were much more sane than those of the North.

Hungrvaka

Hungrvaka (Appetizer) was written in Skálholt during Bishop Páll Jónsson's tenure of office (1195–1211) but after the sanctity of Bishop Þorlákr had been acknowledged (1198). It treats the lives of the first five bishops and is written with admiration for them and with an unostentatious piety. The unknown author wants primarily to whet the hunger of his readers for more information about his worthy subjects and to draw their minds from occupation with less essential reading matter. Which matter, we wonder. Apparently not laws, sagas, or genealogical lore, for he claims it to be his second purpose to entice young men to read these things. The " sagas " were probably those of Þingeyrar. Still, it looks as if a *Landnáma* compiler from the first quarter of the century (Styrmir) had to defend himself against this very criticism, so maybe *Hungrvaka's* author was frowning on too much interest in secular matters in general.

Þorláks saga helga

Þorláks saga byskups is found in two forms. The older version, like *Hungrvaka*, was written in Skálholt (1202–11) under the auspices of Bishop Páll Jónsson. He was the son of Jón Loptsson of Oddi; his mother was Ragnheiðr Þórhallsdóttir, sister of the sainted bishop and concubine of the chieftain of Oddi. When the saint began to work miracles, Bishop Páll had a book of his miracles read at the Althing (1199) in order to have his sanctity recognized. Now he had his uncle's life composed with due emphasis on the holiness of his ascetic life but with studious avoidance of his uncle's dramatic clash with his father at Oddi. Actually the bishop had not only waged and lost the first skirmish in a war of church patronage which was to last unremittingly throughout the following century but he had also threatened to excommunicate Jón Loptsson for his illicit relations with his sister. It was precisely this very understandable omission which prompted a later writer (after 1222) to add a part, dealing with the bishop's fight against the Oddaverjar. That constitutes the later version of the saga.

Jarteinabœkr

Three *Jarteinabœkr* (Miracle Books) recount the miracles of St. Þorlákr. The first, of 1199, has already been mentioned; it is preserved in a contemporary manuscript. Another dates from the times of Páll Jónsson, a third from about 1300–25. The language of the miracles is spotless, sometimes racy. The miracles savor very much of the humble people. Actually they give in some respects a better and more realistic picture of everyday life in Iceland than any other sources available to us. They breathe the quiet religious fervor of the late twelfth century in its most dignified form.

Páls saga

The group of the bishops' lives of Skálholt from the first decade of the thirteenth century comes to a close with *Páls saga byskups*, written shortly after his death. The style of this sympathetic saga so much resembles that of *Hungrvaka* that scholars agree they must be by the same author, perhaps Ketill Hermundarson, friend and servant of the bishop, later abbot of Helgafell (d. 1220). *A priori* one would think it likely that Bishop Páll had entrusted the composition of *Þorláks saga* to the same author, but such is hardly the case, for the point of view of that work is more ecclesiastical and the style more rhetorical—with balance and alliteration—than the simple, manly, though pious style of *Hungrvaka* and *Páls saga*. On the other hand, the difference in style may be due to the difference in subject only, for *Þorláks saga* is in reality a saint's life, not a bishop's saga. No less a biographer than the Venerable Bede is known to have wielded those two styles for different subjects. The second version of *Þorláks saga* (with *Oddaverja þáttr*) has been attributed to Hallr Gizurarson, priest, lawspeaker, and abbot of Helgafell and Þykkvibœr (d. 1230).

All the above-mentioned sagas follow a faulty chronology, with a shift of seven years back. This timing has been called the chronology of Þingeyrar, because it is first found in *Sverris saga* by Karl Jónsson, abbot of Þingeyrar. Jón Jóhannesson has shown (in *Skírnir* 1952) that it is derived from a Lotharingian computist of the eleventh century by the name of Gerland.

Style of the Church militant

The two sagas following, dealing with bishops whose rule falls within the thirteenth century, and written, probably, during the period 1230– 1310, differ markedly in style from the earliest group of bishops' sagas, dating from the first two decades of the century. They deal with prelates, one saintly, the other worldly, in full fight against the secular chieftains of the time, and they are markedly similar in style to the contemporary secular sagas of the *Sturlunga* collection. Perhaps it might be called the style of the Church militant.

Guðmundar saga Lambkárs

Guðmundar saga Arasonar hins góða—he was a bishop of Hólar 1203– 37—is found in several versions of a somewhat complicated history. His life up to the time that he became bishop (1160–1203) was written by his friend and secretary Lambkárr Þorgilsson (d. 1249), who seems to have died before he could tackle the bishop's *vita* itself. This so-called *Prests saga* (Priest's Life) has been incorporated into the *Sturlunga* collection, and it forms the beginning of a full Life of the Bishop, compiled *ca.* 1300 from many sources and preserved only in two versions, called the " Oldest " and the " Middle " saga by Guðbrandur Vigfússon, the earliest editor, while modern editors would reverse this order. The last-named version has an interesting preface stating how a collection of letters, located in a church in Eyjafjörðr (Laufás), was burnt up (1258) before they could be utilized by the writer.

The composition of the *Prests saga* is full, annalistic, and sometimes clumsy, but it contains, in addition to the miracles worked by the incipient saint, a wealth of good stories. One such is the tale of Guðmundr's and his fosterfather's shipwreck. The storm was so terrific that the skipper had to canvas the crew for a man who knew the highest name of God. In the wreck Guðmundr broke his leg and his fosterfather lost his chest of books which, however, after due invocations on the part of the owner, drifted ashore so that the books could be dried. Both the Priest's saga and the Bishop's saga are comparatively secular in style. Both give an unforgettable picture of the saintly bishop, maltreated by his enemies, but irrepressible, traveling all over the country with a horde of beggars and tramps, leaving a trail of consecrated springs (*Gvendar-brunnar*), the names of which still linger, though their potency may have vanished among his heretical countrymen.

Árna saga

Árna saga byskups is the life of Árni Þorláksson, Bishop of Skálholt 1269–98, the man who carried the struggle of the Church, begun about a century earlier by the saintly Þorlákr, and waged with more Godly spirit than worldly wisdom by Guðmundr the Good, to a victorious end. The saga, based upon contemporary speeches and letters, is among the most trustworthy and best sources for the history of the period. It is defective at the end, breaking off in the winter 1290/91. Scholars have attributed it to the bishop's nephew and successor, Bishop Árni Helgason (1304–20). As in *Guðmundar saga góða* the style is more secular than clerkly.

New style

In the first sagas of the fourteenth century there is a new spirit and a new style, though the break with the preceding secular group is not so sharp as that between the secular and the earliest pious group. This style is clerical, reflecting the spirit of the church that has attained its goal and can therefore indulge in some good-humored self-criticism and banter.

Laurentíus saga

Laurentíus saga is the life of Laurentíus Kálfsson, Bishop of Hólar (1324–30), written by his friend and confidant, Priest Einar Hafliðason (d. 1393), who also wrote *Lögmannsannáll*. The life is detailed and well written; it is our chief source for the period. The author has a fresh sense of humor, not least in evidence in anecdotes about other clerics, learned and otherwise. He delights in explaining to us why the learned Jón flæmingi (from Flanders) wanted to live with a scarecrow of a woman and how sorely pressed some of the country priests were when *visitatores* of the bishopric were examining their reading knowledge of Latin. He writes as if the spirit of Chaucer might have been brewing in Iceland; his style reflects the new spirit, but it never comes to a flowering.

Guðmundar saga Arngríms

Another *Guðmundar saga Arasonar* was written by Arngrímr Brandsson (d. 1361), abbot at Þingeyrar, shortly after 1350. It was written in Latin, obviously to propagate the good bishop's holiness in higher places. For that reason it contains a short description of Iceland. The Latin original is lost, but its learning and heavy, florid, rhetorical style has left its mark on the Icelandic translation, further adorned with *Guðmundar drápur* by the author and others. Naturally, the saga stresses the bishop's miracles, but there is little new in it. This is the last of the bishops' sagas: it reverts to the hagiography of the earliest ones. Not only self-criticism but corruption is discernible in the church of the fourteenth century; both Arngrímur Brandsson and Eysteinn Ásgrímsson, the famed author of *Lilja*, had transgressed heavily before they, as repentant sinners, were restored to grace and power within their church.

The Earliest Historiographers

Sæmundr inn fróði and Ari inn fróði

The founder of the school at Oddi, Sæmundr Sigfússon inn fróði (the Learned) (1056–1133), was the earliest historiographer of Iceland. He wrote a Latin Chronicle of the Norwegian Kings; it is now lost but was used by subsequent writers, such as the poet who eulogized Sæmundr's grandson in *Noregskonungatal* (List of the Norwegian Kings).

But the man who was to become the father of Icelandic history, writing in his native tongue, was Ari Þorgilsson inn fróði (the Learned) (1067/8–1148). He was a priest-chieftain from the West but had been educated at Haukadalr by Teitr Ísleifsson, son of the first Icelandic bishop. In the twenties of the twelfth century Ari wrote *Íslendingabók* or *Libellus Islandorum* (the Book of the Icelanders), for the bishops then in office, perhaps to serve as a historical introduction to their new Code of Church Law. But only a revised second edition has come down to us.

The first part of Ari's revised book deals with the highlights of early Icelandic history: the settlement, four of the chief settlers, early legislature, the establishment of the Althing, and the division of the country into quarters. The settlement of Greenland (and Vínland) was another important event to be mentioned, but though a chapter on a calendar reform in the tenth century seems curious to us it was important to the churchmen of the time and it fits in completely with Ari's great preoccupation with chronology, for in his *Íslendingabók* he laid the foundation not only of Icelandic chronology (list of lawspeakers) but apparently of Norwegian as well (the omitted list of kings). Recent scholarship has tended to throw doubt on his chronology, but most medieval writers, notably Snorri, followed it and praised him highly for his sagacity and accuracy. The latter part of Ari's book deals with church history: the introduction of Christianity, a list of foreign bishops, and

[106]

lives of the two native bishops: Ísleifr, father of Ari's teacher Teitr, and Gizurr, his personal friend.

Ari's book, as preserved, is a severely concise history of Iceland, but not dry as dust. Ari can tell a story, quote a ditty or a speech if the spirit moves him. The work is thoroughly documented. Ari was careful to mention his informants and tell where they had their knowledge from. In dating the finding of Greenland, he cites his uncle and claims that the latter had the information from a man who himself accompanied Eiríkr inn rauði (Eric the Red) out there. Listing of sources had, of course, been a commonplace among historians since Bede, but few seem to have taken the sifting of truth as seriously as the " Father of Icelandic history." And with his implied and explicit motto, " nothing but the truth," he set a fashion among the writers of the twelfth century. The popular and entertaining *fornaldar sögur* (comparable to Geoffrey of Monmouth's *Historia Regum Britanniae*) had to wait a century and a half before they were thought fit for the parchment.

Before we can appraise Ari's influence, we must cast a glance at his lost works. In the preface to the second edition of *Íslendingabók* he says: " I wrote this one covering the same ground, with the exclusion of the genealogies (*áttartala*) and the lives of kings (*konungaævi*)."

Later writers often referred to Ari for details in the kings' sagas, especially in matters of chronology. And Snorri devoted most of his preface to *Heimskringla* to telling what Ari wrote and why he (Snorri) thought it so important. Snorri may have been referring to the *konungaævi* in the older *Íslendingabók*, if we assume that this was a list of kings with their respective years of reign. The other possibility would be that Ari actually wrote a separate work on the kings. Scholars have not been able to decide the question. In either case Ari's critical acumen set a very important standard for all following writers of the kings' sagas.

Landnámabók (Book of the settlements)

What happened to Ari's omitted genealogies (*áttartala*)? Interest in genealogical lore (*áttvísi, mannfræði*) was always intense in Iceland, and we know that in Ari's time it was not only assiduously studied, but also put to writing. The sagas always leaned heavily upon genealogy, but the chief repository of such lore relating to the period before 1100 was *Landnámabók*. It is a work enumerating about 400 noble settlers, with their claims of land, their farmsteads, often their origins in the old country, and always their descendants in the new. Scholars who think Ari wrote nothing but the two *Íslendingabœkr* agree that his genealogies must have found their way into the *Landnámabók*. Others attribute that unique work to Ari himself, following the testimony of Haukr Erlendsson, Lawman, who wrote his version of *Landnámabók* ca. 1330–34. Says Haukr:

" Now the settlements in Iceland have been covered according to the writings of learned men, first Priest Ari the Learned son of Þorgils and Kolskeggr the Wise. But this book I, Haukr Erlendsson, wrote after the book written [ca. 1260–80] by Sturla Þórðarson, Lawman, a most learned man, and after another book written [ca. 1225] by Styrmir [ca. 1170–1245] the Learned; I took from each book whatever it had more than the other, but to a great extent they contained the same matter."

This clear statement of Haukr has never been in dispute except as far as it concerns Ari, because Sturla does not mention him in his version. But all preserved versions of *Landnámabók* agree that Kolskeggr inn fróði (the Learned) " dictated " part of the work. That part shows marks of special authorship, being sketchier than the rest. But since Ari and Kolskeggr were contemporaries, it seems most likely that Ari was the chief author and Kolskeggr his collaborator.

Why did Ari write *Landnámabók*? No one knows. It would clarify matters if we knew that Ari had been traversing a good deal of Iceland, say, in the retinue of Bishop Gizurr when he was organizing the parishes of his young church (H. Hermannsson). For *Landnámabók* is far more than a genealogical work; it is above all a historical topography of Iceland so astoundingly minute and correct that it is difficult to account for such a work unless the author travelled widely in collecting the materials for it. That he also collected information at the Althing is likely enough. Kolskeggr's dictation covered the remote Eastern Quarter.

But *Landnámabók* is even more than genealogy and historical topography. It also abounds in excellent thumbnail sketches of character and dramatic incidents. It seems obvious that many of the family sagas are here, in extract or in a nutshell.

William the Conqueror had his *Doomsday Book* compiled for the advanced political purpose of pressing the last penny in taxation from his subjects. But even if *Landnámabók* was connected indirectly with the organization of the early Church, it is impossible to discover behind it any motives except great family pride and avid interest in knowledge. It is, indeed, a unique work and a fitting monument for the nation that produced it.

At this point we can better appraise Ari's influence. With the ecclesiastical history in *Íslendingabók* he inspired the saner bishops' sagas after 1200; with his list of kings in the lost *Íslendingabók*, he set the pattern for the kings' sagas; and with his *Landnámabók* he set the stage and provided matter for many of the family sagas (*Íslendinga sögur*) of the thirteenth century.

It remains to sketch the subsequent history of *Landnámabók*. Styrmir wrote his version after 1222, probably stimulated by Snorri; his purpose was, partly, to meet the slander of foreigners (Norwegians) regarding the origin of Icelanders.

After the middle of the thirteenth century (1260–80?) Sturla Þórðarson wrote an enlarged and recast version of the book to serve as an introduction to his history of Iceland. Ari's and Styrmir's books had started at the border between the Eastern and the Southern Quarters, proceeding clockwise around the island. Sturla started by telling about the discovery of Iceland and the first settlement of Ingólfr Arnarson— in the middle of the Southern Quarter. He also composed *Kristni saga*, a history of the conversion, to bridge the gap between *Landnámabók* and the historical sagas of the *Sturlunga* collection. Though Haukr Erlendsson, as already stated, used *Styrmisbók* as well as *Sturlubók*, he followed the arrangement of the latter and kept *Kristni saga* as a continuation. Since both Ari's original and *Styrmisbók* are lost, we would be at a loss to know the original arrangement of *Landnámabók* but for the fact that it is preserved in the so-called *Melabók* (*ca.* 1300), although it is now only a fragment.

The Kings' Sagas

The origins and Eiríkr Oddsson

As already stated, the origins of the kings' sagas go back to the writings of Sæmundr inn fróði and Ari inn fróði—both no doubt inspired by medieval European Latin chronicles, though only Sæmundr used that language. Judging by the poem *Noregskonungatal*, Sæmundr's survey went down to the death of King Magnús the Good (1047). It is not known how far down Ari brought his list of kings, but his writing in the vernacular and his critical attitude towards sources (informants) and chronology marked his followers in the aristocratic schools of Haukadalr and Oddi.

His critical methods were to some extent emulated by Eiríkr Oddsson, the first writer of contemporary history. In that capacity he was also the first to write a real *saga*, as his book was called in *Morkinskinna*. He was in Norway during the sixties of the twelfth century collecting materials for his book *Hryggjarstykki* (Back-Piece, Back-Flap?) "about Haraldr Gilli reigning 1130–36 and two of his sons [d. 1155 and 1161], and about Magnús the Blind and Sigurðr Slembir until their deaths." The two last-named died in 1139, and if the time reference is limited to them, the book covered only nine years. But if, as is more likely, it refers to all the kings mentioned, it covered the period 1130–61. The book was lost, but one gets a fair idea of it from borrowings in *Morkinskinna* and *Heimskringla*. Like Ari, Eiríkr lists his informants, his work is very detailed and secular, but if he was not a cleric, he would be the exception among the twelfth-century authors.

Nordal has pointed out that Sigurðr slembir, before he claimed Norway, stayed a winter with Þorgils Oddason of Staðarhóll in Northwest Iceland. Some of the prince's later companions hailed from this region of the Northwest, among them possibly Ívarr Ingimundarson who wrote an epitaph on Sigurðr. Assuming that Eiríkr Oddsson also hailed from the Northwest would throw light on two things: why he happened to get interested in Sigurðr slembir's life and why his book set the pattern for the abbot of the neighboring monastery of Þingeyrar.

Oldest Ólafs saga helga

The anonymous author of the *Oldest Ólafs saga helga* certainly was a cleric, probably a monk of the monastery of Þingeyrar (founded 1133) which in the second half of the twelfth century became the most active center of writing in Iceland. The monks of Þingeyrar quoted Ari and paid lip service to his principles, but, with the exception of their abbot, Karl Jónsson (1169–1213), they were more inspired by the hagiographical tradition of the church and its principle of admitting everything redounding to the glory of their subject, regardless of factual truth. To the monks no one could have seemed as eminently worthy of treatment as the King Saint, Ólafr Haraldsson, the missionary who supposedly died for his faith in 1030. His cult had early led to a *Vita* and a *Book of Miracles*, the skald Einarr Skúlason had recently (1153) eulogized him, and now (perhaps 1160–85) he got his first saga, written from the rich and conflicting traditions still existing about him in Iceland. Only seven fragments of this saga survive—but we know it from descendants once removed—the fragmentary *Ólafs saga helga* (*Flateyjarbók* III, 237 ff.) by Styrmir Kárason hinn fróði (the Learned), an inmate of Þingeyrar up to 1207 (d. 1245), and the complete *Legendary Ólafs saga helga*, both from the first half of the thirteenth century. The legendary saga is so called because it contains a great number of miracles; otherwise it is surprisingly secular, though not without the hagiographer's touch nor his learned style. The composition is unwieldy, but the saga's literary reputation has suffered because of comparison with Snorri's brilliant work. In Styrmir's version it furnished Snorri not only with a basis for his work but also with many a good story and sharp repartee. Its historical value is great: it is the first work to use skaldic poetry as a source and, even more important for the future of the sagas, to open its doors to oral tradition.

Karl Jónsson: Sverris saga

Abbot Karl Jónsson was seemingly very different from his subordinates. Following Eiríkr Oddsson's lead, he wrote realistic contemporary history, the first life of a reigning king, *Sverris saga*. He was in Norway 1185–88 to write the beginning of his saga (*Grýla*) from dictation of the king himself. Back home, he continued the story and not invariably from

Sverri's point of view. Scholars are not agreed whether he himself
finished the book after Sverri's death (1202), but it seems most likely,
since he lived to 1213. Norwegian scholars have emphasized the king's
initiative, claiming that he was the man who started the Icelanders on
Norwegian historiography. It is true that Sverrir used the saga as his
mouthpiece, not least so through his many remarkable speeches. Still,
one can hardly assert that he did more than embrace with understanding
what the Icelanders (Eiríkr Oddsson) had already launched. That they,
like Sverrir, were influenced by the vogue of Latin chronicles in twelfth-
century Europe goes without saying. Formerly the skalds had been
royal historiographers; now the responsibility was shifted to the aristocratic clerks. But though *Sverris saga* was written by a cleric about a
cleric usurper of the throne, the two of them sometimes indulging in
unctuous moralizing, it is primarily the picture of the great war-lord and
leader which emerges from its innumerable battle scenes. Thus the
ideology of the skalds is perpetuated in the secular kings' sagas. And
Sverrir did not only destroy his fellow-king, he also defied the Church
militant and died in its ban, though at peace with himself.

Oddr Snorrason and Gunnlaugr Leifsson

About 1190 a monk of Þingeyrar, Oddr Snorrason, wrote a *Life of
Ólafr Tryggvason* in Latin. Though this original is lost, the saga survives
in Icelandic translation from about 1200, preserved in one Icelandic and
two Norwegian copies. This work is in some ways more hagiographic
than the *Legendary Ólafs saga helga*, which more likely inspired it; the
style shows marked influence of the Latin original. When tradition failed
him, the pious Oddr seems to have had recourse to the Bible or saints'
lives, but he could occasionally tell a good, even a splendid, story, like
the tale about the battle of Svoldr.

Towards 1200 Oddr's work was expanded by another brother of the
monastery, Gunnlaugr Leifsson (d. 1218). He, too, wrote in Latin and
was translated, but nothing remains of his work except fragments incorporated into the works of later writers. The part about the introduction
of Christianity in Iceland was utilized by Sturla Þórðarson in *Kristni
saga*. Gunnlaugr was even more of a hagiographer than Oddr; he composed the lives of Saint Ambrose and " Saint " Jón of Hólar, and he
loved to display his learning in long edifying speeches placed in the mouth
of the royal missionary. He revealed his taste in translating Geoffrey
of Monmouth. Fortunately the hagiographic kings' sagas came to an
end with his work.

Norwegian works

A few years (*ca.* 1180) before Karl Jónsson started work on *Sverris saga* two Latin surveys of Norwegian history had been written in Norway. The first, ranging from Haraldr hárfagri (Fairhair) to the death of Saint Ólafr (1030), was written by a certain Theodricus monachus (monk) of Þrándheimr (Trondheim). He wrote a Latin chronicle in which he cited the Icelanders as his main source. The abbot of Þingeyrar probably took the book home with him; it was used by Oddr Snorrason.

The second Latin survey was probably written in eastern Norway, mostly from local traditions; it is partly known from *Historia Norwegiae* (from *ca.* 1220). Here the list of kings started with the Ynglingar and went down to Saint Ólafr.

The last decade of the twelfth century saw the composition of *Ágrip af Noregskonunga sögum* (Survey or Resumé of the Norwegian Kings' Sagas), written in Þrándheimr, largely from local traditions, perhaps for King Sverrir, to serve as an introduction to his saga. It spanned the time from Halfdan svarti (the Black) to 1177, the date of Sverrir's coming to Norway. This was the earliest survey—barring Ari's *konungaævi* (Lives of Kings)—written in the vernacular; it was used by several Icelandic writers of lost kings' sagas about and after 1200.

Other works from ca. 1200

About or shortly after 1200 a number of individual kings' sagas (or sagas connected with them) seem to have been written apparently in imitation of *Sverris saga* and the two *Ólafs sögur*. There were sagas of Haraldr hárfagri (Fairhair), Hákon góði (the Good), Hlaðajarlar (the Earls of Hlaðir), one of Jómsvíkingar, and one of Hákon Ívarsson. There was, possibly, a saga of Magnús góði (the Good), and Haraldr harðráði (the Hard), and there were sagas of Magnús berfœttr (Barefoot) and his three sons: Eysteinn, Sigurðr, and Ólafr. Finally, there were sagas of Hákon herðibreiðr (the Broadshouldered) and Magnús Erlingsson to fill the gap between *Hryggjarstykki* and *Sverris saga*. In these sagas the oral traditions were no doubt utilized to the fullest extent to make them as interesting as possible. Most of them are now lost but have been utilized by the writers of the fuller histories that now became fashionable: *Morkinskinna, Fagrskinna*, and *Heimskringla*.

To this group, too, belong *Færeyinga saga* and *Orkneyinga saga*, the latter an extensive survey of the earls of Orkney up to the middle of the twelfth century. Both sagas are well composed but have been preserved only in a patched-up form: passages in the original texts, used by Snorri in *Heimskringla*, have been replaced by his text.

Different from all these but probably from about the same time is *Skjöldunga saga* about legendary Danish kings. It has ties not only with Snorri's *Ynglinga saga* but also his *Edda*. It may be a product of the school of Oddi.

Morkinskinna

After so many special kings' sagas had been composed there seems to have been an urge to combine them into broad and detailed historical works. The first of these was *Morkinskinna* (Rotten-Skinny, book of rotten vellum), treating the period from Magnús the Good (1035-47) to Sverrir (1177) but defective at the end. *Morkinskinna* contains some of the best writing found in kings' sagas before Snorri; its style often matches the best of the family sagas, of which it incorporates no less than thirty *þættir* or short stories, mostly relating to the Icelanders at the Norwegian court. Among these we have the stubborn hero Halldór Snorrason, the pious pilgrim Auðunn vestfirzki, and the burlesque figure of Sneglu-Halli. We also meet the well-versed Icelandic saga-teller, who regales King Haraldr and his court with the king's own exploits in the Mediterranean (*Útferðar saga* Haralds harðráða), but as told in *Morkinskinna* this part seems to have attracted a good many motifs from contemporary chronicles in western Europe (S. Nordal, J. de Vries). *Morkinskinna*'s author used skaldic verse expertly; he knew and copied *Hryggjarstykki*, but bits from *Ágrip* and some of the *þættir* were probably added later. In its original form *Morkinskinna* dates from *ca.* 1220.

Fagrskinna and Böglunga sögur

Fagrskinna (Fair-Skinny, book of fair vellum, also entitled *Noregskonunga tal*) is a detailed survey which covers the period from Hálfdan svarti (the Black) to Sverrir (1177). The author used the many special sagas mentioned above and he was well versed in skaldic poetry, quoting it profusely; we owe the preservation of *Haraldskvæði* and *Eiríksmál* to him; it has been suggested that he found them in Norway (J. de Vries). In dealing with the missionary kings he was even more of a rationalist than Snorri, but he was not so good a storyteller. His interest in warfare and foreign relations may reflect the point of view of his master, if he wrote for King Hákon Hákonarson, as Norwegian scholars are inclined to believe. It was this saga which King Hákon had read to him on his deathbed—after he became tired of listening to the Latin saints' lives. *Fagrskinna* seems to have been written just before Snorri's *Heimskringla* (S. Nordal).

Böglunga sögur deal with the period 1202–17 in continuation of *Sverris saga*. They are similar to it in style as one would expect of contemporary history. In part they are known only from a sixteenth-century Dano-Norwegian translation.

Snorri Sturluson

We come now to an author who, standing head and shoulders above his predecessors, raised the sagas about the kings of Norway to their ultimate perfection. He did more. If he wrote *Egils saga*, as many scholars now believe (S. Nordal), he brought the family sagas also to a previously unattained peak. It is hardly an exaggeration to say that in his day he overshadowed other saga-writers almost as much as his ancestor Egill had towered over his skaldic brethren of old. And though he aspired in vain to become himself a great poet, he became the greatest critic of the old poetry, building for it a fortress safe against foreign encroachment for a long time to come.

This man was Snorri Sturluson.

Snorri came of prominent and strong families. His father Sturla, descended from the famous chief Snorri goði after whom he named the boy, was a rather unscrupulous opportunist who at his death had amassed considerable wealth and power. Snorri's mother, Guðný, was descended from Egill Skalla-Grímsson. The two had three gifted sons, Þórðr, Sighvatr, and Snorri, who were to stamp their family name, *Sturlungar*, upon the age (cf. *Sturlunga saga*). Snorri, the youngest, was born in 1179, but by a providential accident he came to be brought up by the powerful Jón Loptsson of Oddi, son of a Norwegian princess. Here, in the aristocratic and critical school of Oddi, where the European learning of Sæmundr fróði mingled with the native family traditions and the proud lineage of the princess, Snorri received his education—and his first interest in the kings' sagas.

At the age of twenty Snorri made a rich match (1199), acquiring with his bride first his ancestral seat at Borg in Borgarfjörðr. Later he came into possession of Reykjaholt (now Reykholt), a great estate nearby, which he held until his death. Here he led the life of an ambitious, splendor-loving chieftain, playing for high stakes in the turbid politics of the day, feuding even with his own brothers if they crossed his path. He loved many women and formed shifting alliances, but he was somewhat lacking in generosity and faithfulness to his dependents. He was even more lacking in unscrupulous harshness towards his enemies, for at heart he was a mild and reasonable man. His ability to see both sides of an issue was as fatal for the political leader as it was a great boon for the understanding writer. For if Snorri could not assert himself as a leader in his amoral age, this ability gave him a wonderful detachment when he began to describe the individuals born of it.

In 1218 Snorri went to Norway and was well received at the court of Earl Skúli Bárðarson and his nephew, King Hákon Hákonarson (1217–63), then a boy of fourteen. Snorri paid a visit to Sweden, too, visiting a noble lady in Vestr-Gautland (Västergötland). In the spring of 1220 when Snorri wanted to return to Iceland, a misunderstanding had arisen between the semi-royal family of Oddi and the Norwegians; the Earl threatened warfare, but Snorri offered to mediate. This was accepted, and he left Norway laden with honors, but as a king's agent in Iceland he was a rank failure. Instead of wooing friends for Norway he composed the poem *Háttatal* in honor of his royal friends (1222–23). There followed a decade or so of relatively quiet years, during which he must have written his books. But after 1235 the civil war which cost Iceland her independence flared up afresh, and Snorri fled to Norway in 1237. Here he revisited his friend, the Earl, but broke with King Hákon, and went back to Iceland without his leave. Shortly thereafter the Earl rebelled against Hákon, but lost. Hákon wrote a letter to the arch-enemy of the Sturlungs, Snorri's erstwhile son-in-law, Gizurr Þorvaldsson, and bade him send Snorri back to Norway or " liquidate " him. In the fall of 1241 Snorri was cut down in his own home by one of Gizurr's henchmen.

Apart from *Háttatal* and several other poems, now mostly lost, Snorri has long been credited with writing (the Prose or Younger) *Edda* and *Heimskringla*. Others have even attributed *Egils saga* (p. 115) to him, and recently Sigurður Nordal, the greatest living authority on Snorri, has bolstered that theory with weighty arguments. Nordal thinks that Snorri wrote *Edda, Egils saga, Ólafs saga helga*, and the beginning and end of *Heimskringla* in that order during the years 1222–30/5.

In writing his *Edda* Snorri aimed at two things: to compose an incomparable praise poem for his royal benefactors and to write a textbook for young skalds which would guide them to the difficult metrics and exotic diction of the old " classic " skalds. With this work he placed himself squarely against the tide of the popular ballads and the hymnals of the church. But for all his national antiquarianism he was not untouched by the fashions of the time. He knew, of course, the *Hátt-alykill* of Rögnvaldr and Hallr. More important, he was inspired by the contemporary vogue of rhetoric, and his dialogue form was conventional. Looking upon the gods as kings and giving them Asiatic (Trojan) origin was, even then, conventional medieval " free thought," perhaps imported by Sæmundr fróði, but certainly adopted by Ari fróði and Snorri.

Snorri's textbook of poetics falls into three parts: mythology (*Gylfa-ginning*), skaldic diction (*Skáldskaparmál*), and a metrical key (*Háttatal*). Recent scholarship has tended to prove that they were written in reverse order. *Háttatal* (List of Meters) is an enumeration—in 102 stanzas—of all " meters " known to or invented by Snorri, but most of the varia-tions are rhetorical or stylistic rather than metrical. Snorri took great pride in this poem, which in spots sparkles with his artistry and through-out displays his methodical stringency; but were it not for its metrical value and Snorri's commentary, its loss would not have troubled us. In *Skáldskaparmál* (Poetic Speech) Snorri dealt with two main features of the poetic language: uncompounded poetical nouns (*heiti*) and com-pound circumlocutions (*kenningar*). If his classification falters at times, it is less to be wondered at than the fact that this pioneer work still remains the best introduction to the difficult field of skaldic poetry. Everywhere Snorri quoted examples from the old masters, and it is astounding how few of these recur in *Heimskringla*. It looks as if Snorri knew the whole corpus of skaldic poetry by heart.

If *Háttatal* and *Skáldskaparmál* are tough reading, even for specialists, *Gylfaginning* (The Beguiling of Gylfi) has long been the joy of readers of every age and background. Here Snorri relates within a frame story fence of his own—designed to keep the wolf of clerical intolerance at bay—the story of the old gods and the heathen world, as he was able to piece it together from several Eddic and skaldic poems, cult traditions, and popular superstitions. Including this mythology in a textbook for poets was demanded because of constant poetical references to the myths. Óðinn was, indeed, the god of poetry no less than of magic and warfare and poets were ever alluding to his conquest of the poetic mead from the giants. Fortunately, Snorri gives us far more than the bare necessi-ties of skaldic exegesis; witness the tragic tale of Baldr's death, the comic masterpiece of Þórr's journey to Útgarðaloki, and the somber eschatological drama of Ragnarök. But above all Snorri succeeded—at the eleventh hour—in catching the vanishing myths and the oldest ideologies of our race in an impressive cosmological panorama, always alive to us through the wizardry of his art.

A glance at *Heimskringla* (*orbis terrarum*, so called after the beginning *Kringla heimsins*, but otherwise *Noregs konunga sögur*) reveals the astounding fact that the *Ólafs saga helga*, spanning only fifteen years of time, makes up one third of the whole work. This above all, but also many other things, for instance the existence of separate manuscripts of the *Ólafs saga helga*, prefaced by Snorri himself, go to show, as suggested by Eiríkr Magnússon and proved by Sigurður Nordal, that the saga was written separately and before the rest of *Heimskringla*.

When Styrmir fróði (the Learned) of Þingeyrar joined the household of Snorri in Reykjaholt (*ca.* 1220) to become something like his private secretary, he was probably inspired by Snorri to undertake a new edition of *Landnámabók* to silence the slanderous tongues of hostile Norwegians. In turn Styrmir must have intrigued Snorri considerably as the living representative of the hagiographic spirit of Þingeyrar. Indeed, Styrmir brought books from the monastery, among them, no doubt, his copy of *Sverris saga* and his own uncritical and much expanded *Ólafs saga helga*. This was based on the so-called *Mid-Ólafs saga helga*, an expanded copy of the *Oldest Ólafs saga helga*. Snorri, schooled in the fastidious aristocratic traditions of Oddi, must have recognized Styrmir's work for the *rudis indigestaque molis* it was, and he decided to cut it mercilessly. This he did, though not, like Ari, leaving only a skeleton of truth. Having just finished *Egils saga* he was satisfied with nothing less than full-blooded figures, psychologically correct and interesting, moving on the broad canvas of his history. He exerted his artistry to the utmost to make his characters be true to history and life alike.

In his sources Snorri found conflicting representations of his hero, some making him out a saint, others the very opposite. Out of these Snorri created a character in development, always rare in the sagas. According to Snorri, there was no great difference in character between the two half brothers, Ólafr Haraldsson and Haraldr Sigurðsson, and if one was remembered by posterity as the Hard (*harðráði*), the other as the Saint, it was primarily because of the difference of their final aims and acts. Haraldr was killed trying wrongfully to win a foreign realm, Ólafr won his sainthood fighting to regain his legitimate kingdom, lost to perfidious chiefs and people disgruntled by the king's harsh missionary methods. Consonant with this view Snorri's saint performs no miracles until near the end of his career.

If the fifteen short years of the Saint's reign—treated in much greater detail than *Egils saga*—make up one third of *Heimskringla*, it is obvious that the introduction and the sequel in most cases represent a severe cutting of Snorri's sources. Still, this does not hold for the very beginning, the semi-mythical and heroic *Ynglinga saga,* based as it is on the poem *Ynglingatal* by Þjóðólfr of Hvinir. It is in some ways a companion piece to *Gylfaginning* and *Skáldskaparmál* but written from a historical not a mythological point of view. In writing it, Snorri's knowledge of the mythical-heroic *Skjöldunga saga*, probably written to glorify the Oddaverjar, must have been useful.

The cuts in *Heimskringla* are most pronounced where the sources flowed fullest, as in *Ólafs saga Tryggvasonar* and in the period from the Saint's death to King Sverrir (1030–1177). No doubt some good stories have been lost in this process, but their loss is not so noticeable, for the whole is—with few exceptions—marked by Snorri's style, his saga-like objectivity, his aristocratic sense of dignity and proportion, his keen psychological insight, and his unexpressed but nevertheless pervasive philosophy of history and life. It seems a constant wonder that Snorri's troubled age should have been able to produce so serene an observer—but it is no doubt due to the rationalist amorality of Snorri and his times.

Snorri was without the slightest doubt one of the most critical historians of the Middle Ages. He paid no empty tribute to Ari and his stringent method of source and fact-finding in his prefaces to *Ólafs saga* and *Heimskringla*. But in dealing with his vast material, most of it consisting of written works, Snorri found his main criterion of truth in the court poetry, whose nature he knew better than anyone else. And, as stated in connection with the *Edda* (p. 117), he seems to have known the whole body of court poetry, from Bragi to his day, by heart. Snorri was not the first historian to use skaldic poetry for source material, but he was the one who perfected the method to the utmost.

Excepting the general remarks in his prefaces, Snorri does not, as would a modern historian, discuss his sources or the reason for his selections, omissions, and additions. He follows *Sverris saga* in having his characters voice their minds and motives in speeches often both long and effective. He has a sure sense for the dramatic incident, the pointed remark. We find him forever polishing, rationalizing, and dramatizing. He is—as the sagas in general (and not a few of the contemporary Latin chronicles of Europe)—seemingly neutral and objective in his narrative, and he has an unusual knack of showing the two sides of a controversy or a character. But his chief trait is possibly his pragmatism: demonstrating cause and effect until the line of development stands out crystal clear before our mind's eye.

These qualities made Snorri a classic author. In his own day people apparently threw away his source books to keep his own works. And in nineteenth- and twentieth-century Norway *Heimskringla* has long been a best seller. No medieval historian can rival him in his hold on the present. Indeed, it is only recently that Norwegian historians have been able to penetrate the magic armor of his art to come to the understanding that his philosophy of history was probably not correct.

With Snorri the sagas of the kings of Norway came to a brilliant end. What followed was mostly compilations with his works as the core. He was, however, directly imitated by the unknown author of *Knýtlinga saga*, a chronicle of the Danish kings covering the period *ca.* 940–1187. This unknown author of *Knýtlinga saga* also quoted Ólafr hvítaskáld (d. 1259), Snorri's nephew, as a source.

Sturla Þórðarson: Hákonar saga

Sturla Þórðarson (1214–84) was the son of Snorri's brother Þórðr; a peace-loving man, though he could not avoid the factional skirmishes of the times. Summoned to Norway in 1263 after the fall of the Icelandic Commonwealth for having opposed King Hákon Hákonarson in Iceland, he found his royal adversary dead and succeeded by his son Magnús lagabœtir (the Law-emender). The young king frowned upon him until, by chance, he heard him tell a story. He found his story-telling so interesting that he allowed him to recite the poems he had composed about his father and himself. After that the king commissioned Sturla to write the life of his father Hákon, *Hákonar saga Hákonarsonar*. Written during the years 1263–5, it is a detailed but rather uninspired work, based on the testimony of the king's friends and helpers, probably also on the royal archives. But out of consideration for his patron, Sturla had to deal diplomatically with the earl's rebellion, for the king was married to the earl's daughter. Sturla followed the convention of quoting his own and other skalds' poetry, though the verses now had lost all historical value. After this task was completed Sturla helped the king with a new Code of Laws for Iceland (*Járnsíða*), which he presented to the Icelanders in 1271. This law replaced the old office of the lawspeaker with the one of lawman, a royal officer who became the supreme judge of the country. Sturla became the first lawman of Iceland.

In 1277–8, when Sturla was again in Norway, he wrote the saga of King Magnús lagabœtir himself who died in 1280. This saga, most of which has been lost, was the last of the kings' sagas.

The Sagas

Definition of saga

Saga is etymologically the same word as the English (old) " saw "; it means something said or told, a tale, a story or narrative *in prose*, in a wide sense. In length it varies from short stories (*þættir*) of a page or so to that of a full length novel (*Njála*).* In subject matter it also ranges widely. The translated saints' lives are sagas, as are the biographies of the native bishops and the records of their miracles. Eiríkr Oddsson's *Hryggjarstykki* is a saga, and so are later historical works treating of a contemporary period (e. g., *Sturlunga saga*). Sagas, too, are the so-called *fornaldar sögur*, treating mythical figures or heroes from the heroic age of Continental Scandinavia. The histories or chronicles of the Norwegian kings are sagas, kings' sagas, and so are *par excellence* the sagas of the Icelanders or family sagas, dealing with Icelandic heroic farmers of the saga age (870 or 930–1030). Sagas, finally, are translations and imitations of French and Anglo-Norman romances and stories of chivalry, adventure and phantasy, called *riddara sögur* (knights' tales) and *lygi sögur* (lying tales), always in prose even though their sources may have been in verse. These types range from pure history to wild fiction, but practically all the fictitious sagas purport to be historical and deal with semi- or pseudo-historical figures. But in a narrower sense some of the heroic *fornaldar sögur*, the kings' sagas, the sagas of the Icelanders, and some of the historical Icelandic sagas would represent the most typical saga literature.

Origin of types

Which of these types is the oldest? If we look at the still extant

---

* The Icelanders have given their sagas pet names which scholars should know: E(i)gla, Eyrbyggja, Fljótsdœla, Glúma, Grettla, Hrafnkatla, Landnáma, Laxdœla, Njála, Reykdœla, Sturlunga, Vatnsdœla.

[122]

works alone, Ari's *Íslendingabók*, a concise chronicle of Iceland, from *ca.* 1120–30 is the oldest. But reports of saga-telling go much further back. The recounting of one's own feats or news from abroad at a meeting, like the Althing, occurs at times in the family sagas (*ca.* 1000). A *locus classicus*—to which we shall revert (p. 126)—concerns the telling of the *Útferðar saga* (the Story of the Expedition) in the Mediterranean of Haraldr harðráði at his own court (*ca.* 1050) by an Icelandic youth who claimed to have learned the saga from a retainer of the king. This is, then, a king's saga. At the celebrated bridal of Reykhólar, Northwest Iceland, in 1119, a *fornaldar saga,* embellished with verses, was told by the author himself, while another storyteller, a priest, entertained with the saga of a skald, possibly a family saga. From other sources we know that *fornaldar sögur* were popular at the courts of Norway and Denmark. The Danish Saxo Grammaticus credits the Icelanders with a considerable part of his stories.

Fornaldar sögur are oldest

From the above record it might seem idle to guess which of the types, family, kings', or *fornaldar sögur* would be the oldest. One may, for instance, assume that contemporary storytelling, recounting one's own feats or news always existed to some extent. Still there would be a long step from such reports to a king's saga or a family saga. More likely the *fornaldar sögur* or the heroic-mythical sagas represent the oldest type of oral-"literary" form. Though highly fictional, they cluster around the earliest memories of the Scandinavians and lead us back—like the heroic Eddic poems—not only to Norway but even farther *i Austrveg*—into the Baltic or the South.

These Baltic memories seem, curiously enough, as near to the hearts of the Icelanders of 1100 (–1300) as they were to the author of *Beowulf* about 700–50 A.D. In both cases they had been cherished for more than two centuries after the settlement of the new land. But this consideration does not speak well for a theory which would derive the Icelandic prose-verse saga from the Irish prose-verse " saga." Such a theory is of course very tempting, since only Ireland and Iceland are known to have cultivated such a form. A. Heusler flirts with the idea, but K. Liestöl rejects it even in the case of the *fornaldar sögur,* though that genre would no doubt come closer to the fantastic-romantic Irish " saga " than the objective-realistic Icelandic family saga. And it must be conceded that folk tales and folk-tale motifs did jump the barrier from Irish to Icelandic and *vice versa.*

Conditions favoring oral tradition

All scholars agree that conditions favoring storytelling and rich oral tradition in Iceland were many and various. With true poetical insight Nordal has said that the seed of the Icelandic saga writing was the Icelanders' moving from the old country to the new. After that they might feel that they had two fatherlands or none, but the mind was forever detached from the present, becoming a fertile ground for nostalgia and introspection. The authors of the *Iliad-Odyssey* and *Beowulf* were emigrants too.

Like the Vikings the settlers of Iceland were after " fee and fame " but a good deal of fame was connected with the old country, above all the family ties. To be of noble birth was always important; the best, however, was to be able to trace one's family to the famous royal lines of antiquity, like the Skjöldungs of Denmark (Oddaverjar) or the Ynglings of Sweden and Norway (Ari fróði). But even if few could claim such distinction, family ties with the old country were always kept up and cultivated. For a very long time the Icelanders kept one foot, so to speak, in the Norwegian homeland. They were famous travellers and globetrotters.

Traditions were strengthened by the homogeneity of Icelandic society, and it helped when the farmstead belonged to the family for generations. Migrations always were a hazard to the accuracy of the traditions; hence relatively few genealogies extend behind the time of the settlement, and the sagas transplanted from one district to another were apt to lose much of their local color, notably the very helpful place names. Examples are the *Hávarðar saga* and the two accounts of the Greenland-Vínland sagas, oral variants kept respectively in the West and North of Iceland. Examples, too, are the stereotype stories of Icelanders on Viking raids or abroad.

An age of peace (1030–1150) is often assumed to have followed the feuds of the heroic saga age (930–1030). Historians are prone to attribute it to the pacifying influence of Christianity, but such an influence is out of the question until, at most, the end of the period. More likely the peace was connected with an economic expansion where there was still room for small farmers, like freed slaves, and where the lords had not yet grown over-strong. But the peaceful aristocrats of this period must have looked back with admiration to the time when the pioneer giants stalked the land.

The importance of the Althing for the gathering of news, entertainment, and saga-telling has often been stressed and is corroborated by several well authenticated facts. Strange as it may seem, the isolation of the farmsteads may also have acted as a powerful incentive for news-gathering, for the people were always hungry for news. In part Icelandic hospitality was due to this very starvation.

Less stressed, but no less significant, is the fact that in Iceland, always scantily populated (*ca.* 40–80 thousand), the individual could never get lost in the crowd. That, according to W. P. Ker, was what happened to the individual in the Old French *Chansons de geste*. Indeed, the Icelanders might be accused of never discovering the woods because of the prominence of the trees. Not only are most family sagas more or less biographical—often behavioristic character studies of note—but the kings' sagas, too, depict individual kings, their retainers and their enemies. " Burckhardt considers it a great event when the Italians during the Renaissance began to write Lives of Great Men, for in Northern Europe people wrote only about saints, kings, or prelates . . ." But did the European Renaissance create any " life " better than *Egils saga?* (Nordal, *Snorri Sturluson*, p. 258).

The prevalence of skalds and skaldic poetry in Iceland was likewise of paramount significance in preserving oral tradition strong and intact. Often enough an occasional poem would be the kernel of an anecdote, a cluster of such might make up the backbone of a skald's life. Even more important for the kings' sagas were the praise poems of the court poets. One might be tempted to ask: why did not the skalds themselves start telling and writing the kings' sagas? The answer is that they often enough carried news from the Norwegian court to Iceland, and thus a good bit of the oral traditions underlying the kings' sagas would ultimately be traceable to them. Still, nothing could be more extremely different than composing a skaldic verse and telling a story; we are told about Sighvatr that though he composed verse as fluently as other people talked, he was not a good speaker. Thus it was reserved for the clerics to introduce the *writing* of the kings' sagas in imitation of saints' lives or the prose Latin chronicles. But no sooner had they taken this step than they found skaldic poetry indispensable. Eiríkr Oddsson, not having to depend upon it as a source material, used it for ornamentation. The author of the *Oldest Ólafs saga helga* used verse as a source, but no one exploited it to the limit as Snorri Sturluson did, himself a court poet.

The free-prose theory

While scholars agree about the existence of a rich oral tradition in Iceland there is disagreement about the extent to which the oral form is actually represented in the sagas as we have them now.

To an untutored and unsophisticated Icelandic reader the genesis of a saga was a simple thing. The saga happened; that is, the events of it took place; it was told as it happened, and it was later written down as told. Hence, the saga was naturally true—at least the family and the kings' sagas—sceptical people could always entertain a doubt about the *fornaldar sögur*.

Scholars have, naturally, realized that there could be many a slip betwixt the cup and the lip, considering the fact that there was usually a gap of two to three centuries between the events and the writing down of the saga. Nevertheless, many scholars have come quite close to adopting this naive Icelandic point of view, though their arguments for it have often been anything but naive. They have argued that it should not have been harder for interested and semi-professional storytellers to memorize their stories than for the lawspeaker to memorize the law, especially in an unlettered age, when people were constrained to use their memories. That there were such storytellers is indicated by many references in the sagas, though none is more graphic and instructive than the *Þáttr af Íslendingi sögufróða*, the classic instance of saga-telling.

This famous short story or episode (*þáttr*) tells the story of a young Icelander who came to the court of King Haraldr harðráði. He came in the fall and offered to entertain the court with his sagas. All went well until Yuletide; then the young saga-teller seemed to be losing heart. Asked by the king whether his stories were running low, he had to admit that they were; in fact, he had only one story left and did not dare to tell it, for it was the saga of the king's own exploits as a Varangian chief in Byzantium and in the Mediterranean (*Útferðar saga Haralds harðráða*). " But that is the very story I want to hear," said the king, and arranged for the youth to tell it all during the twelve days of Yule; the king would not show whether he liked it or not. Actually the king was highly pleased with the performance, and asked the boy where he had learned the story. He had learned it bit by bit at the Althing during several summers, listening to Halldór Snorrason telling it, but Halldór had been a close friend and trusted retainer of the king. This event must have taken place somewhere near 1050, a century before any of the kings' sagas was put to writing.

There is no reason to doubt the essentials of this story. It indicates the existence of semi-professional saga-men, an institution parallel to that of the court poets, though probably much less conventional. It gives insight into the methods of these semi-professionals. The question is: Did the *Útferðar saga*, as originally told by Halldór Snorrason and repeated by the saga-man at the king's court, live more or less intact on the lips of saga-tellers until it was written down in *Morkinskinna* about 180 years later?

The believers in the oral tradition sagas, also called the free-prose theorists, would tend to answer this question in the affirmative. They contend that the short *þættir* and many of the shorter family sagas had already taken essentially the form they now have at some time during the long period of oral tradition, after which they had been handed down orally and put on parchment by a scribe.

The free-prose theorists—notably the late Andreas Heusler and the Norwegian folklorist Knut Liestöl—have pointed out numerous characteristics of the sagas, especially the family sagas, characteristics which seemingly find their best explanation in such a theory. A few of these may be mentioned.

One very striking feature—even more common in folk tales—is the convention of triads. It was recognized even by the Old Icelanders in the saying, "Everything happened thrice in olden times."

Another striking point is the demonstrable difference between sagas dealing with contemporary events—like the sagas of the *Sturlunga* collection—and the family sagas. The contemporary sagas are so chockful of detail as to become positively confusing; the number of unessential persons mentioned is, especially, very great. By contrast the family sagas—with long tradition behind them—have sloughed off a great amount of detail and thereby have been improved. Still, in most family sagas there is left a hard core of details, notably the genealogical matter, which, to a modern reader, is expendable dead weight. But it was an important part of the tradition and was therefore retained. It goes without saying that this difference is no less understandable from the point of view of the book prose theorists: assuming the sagas to be written by authors who presumably would not be tempted to overload their old sagas with facts as they would if they were writing a contemporary chronicle.

Another feature of the oral saga was that it could split up into two (or more) variants. Such oral variants would be different from the mere scribal ones. There are many variants, but whether oral or scribal has been a much debated point.

The book-prose theory

In contrast to the free-prose theorists the book-prose theorists hold that the sagas are essentially written compositions attributable to authors —though most of them anonymous—in the twelfth and the thirteenth centuries.

This school of thought was represented by the late B. M. Ólsen and is now most vigorously espoused by Sigurður Nordal and his disciples in Iceland (e. g., E. Ó. Sveinsson), editors of the *Íslenzk fornrit* (1933–). Since they have written mostly in Icelandic, their arguments have not received the publicity abroad which they deserve. It is to be hoped that the present work may play a part in popularizing their views, which are essentially the same as those of the Frenchman Joseph Bédier as compared to his predecessor Gaston Paris.

The book-prose theorists do not deny the richness of the oral tradition, but they rightly point out that only writings will submit to investigation, a point too often forgotten by their opponents. And as they believe that most storytellers used their own words in telling a saga, so they contend that the form of the saga as we have it in the manuscripts is mostly due to the individual author who collected the oral tradition, using oral tales as well as written sources, if they existed, to form his own saga. They claim that the *Útferðar saga*, stock example of the free prose theorists, has demonstrably received motifs from the written chronicles of the twelfth century (J. de Vries, S. Nordal).

Nordal has emphasized the unthinkability of assuming scribes who could record minutely and without change what they heard from a supposedly perfect saga-man. He has also stressed the fact that the modern Norwegian " family sagas " adduced by Liestöl to explain the Icelandic sagas are in no way comparable to these artistically. Says W. P. Ker about the latter's high artistic quality : " The art of them keeps up with the newest inventions in fiction and is familiar with secrets of workmanship about which Flaubert and Turgenev are still exercised." And : " The sagas are not by any means pure Northern work outside of the common literary influences. If they comply little with the ordinary tone of Latin education, it is because their authors made it so."

If the traditionalists are prone to stress the monotony of the saga style, the book prosaists are liable to accentuate the individuality of the sagas.

Each saga has to be studied on its own to yield its secrets. " There are primitive sagas, chronicling oral traditions without mastering the material (*Bjarnar saga Hítdœlakappa*),* there are well-composed sagas, stressing the historical and antiquarian element (*Egils saga*), there are novels, often perfect works of art, either completely heroic-Icelandic in spirit (*Hœnsa-Þóris saga, Hrafnkatla*) or suffused with the foreign romantic element (*Gunnlaugs saga, Laxdœla, Njála*). There are sagas based on native folklore (*Grettla*), troll sagas, adventure and lying stories influenced by the *fornaldar* sagas and the sagas of romantic chivalry. There are rewritten sagas where the old and the new is often inextricably mixed." (Nordal, *Skírnir* 1941).

In the so-called *Sturlunga* prologue (of which more p. 155) there is a statement which, in one of the recensions, could be taken to mean that all sagas about Icelandic events were written before *ca.* 1200. This statement, actually referring to the sagas within the *Sturlunga* collection, was by several scholars—including Finnur Jónsson—wrongly taken to refer to the family sagas. Now Finnur Jónsson and the traditionalists (free prosaists) with him thought that sagas, written down in the earliest period, presumably in their pristine state, little changed from the oral composition of the old saga-man and not far removed from the original true story, represented the family sagas in their most perfect, classical form. Unfortunately, so the theory ran, most of these early sagas were spoiled by scribes of the thirteenth century who interpolated them and recast them according to their declining taste. Then, towards 1300, there was another period of saga writing in which the sagas were definitely not classical—due to the dying out of good reliable oral tradition and due to the increasing taste for the lying sagas and the foreign (French) romances. The splendors of a work like *Njála*, undeniably to be dated in the post-classical period, were credited not to its final composer but to the fine lost works on which it was presumably based.

The book-prose theorists have thoroughly upset this picture. According to Nordal no family saga is older than 1200, while the latest ones date from about—or even after—1350. More important still, whereas Finnur Jónsson and the traditionalists thought that the kings' sagas had been inspired and modeled on the family sagas, Nordal demonstrated the very opposite. But the kings' sagas had long been recognized to be works of real writers, many of them known by name, some writing from contemporary sources, others working from oral traditions, skaldic

---

* The examples are mine. S. E.

verses or, later, from older written works. Such was the method of Snorri, the greatest writer of all, and, like a modern historian, he always rejected loose traditions when they conflicted with the verses.

Nordal has, furthermore, shown that of the oldest group of family sagas several are directly connected with the kings' sagas; thus *Fóstbrœðra saga* and *Bjarnar saga Hítdœlakappa* have connections with *Ólafs saga helga,* and *Hallfreðar saga* is tied up with *Ólafs saga Tryggvasonar.* Then for decades the two genres run side by side. But while the kings' sagas culminate with Snorri's works, the family sagas have two great peaks, first Snorri's (?) *Egils saga* in the twenties and then the great but anonymous *Njáls saga* in the eighties or nineties of the thirteenth century. Following *Egils saga* are such excellent sagas as *Gísla saga* and *Laxdœla saga,* while *Njála* is followed by the well-nigh perfect novelette *Hrafnkels saga* and the huge haunting *Grettis saga,* the last-named belonging to the first quarter of the fourteenth century, if it is not later.

In Nordal's arrangement we have thus a development of the literary type from primitive beginnings over a long period of flourishing to a decline and end, whereas according to Finnur Jónsson and the traditionalists there was a hypothetical oral perfection at the beginning, after which came nothing but decline.

Among the things which the book-prosaists are likely to stress is the unity of the written work, a classic instance being E. Ó. Sveinsson's work on *Njála* (*Um Njálu,* 1933). But perhaps the most radical difference between the traditionalists and the book-prosaists is the latter's insistence on the purely and arbitrarily fictional element in the otherwise realistic-looking sagas. The traditionalists, like the Icelandic readers and listeners, were loath to admit that a story-teller or a saga-writer would ever intentionally deviate from what he saw as a truth, unless he was under the influence of his art like the great author of *Njála* (and hardly even then!), or inspired by the fictional genres: *fornaldar sögur, lygi sögur* and *riddara sögur.* Thus because *Hrafnkatla* was a perfectly reasonable-looking, realistic saga, it was supposed to be a traditional saga from about 1200—of a tradition even more dependable than *Landnáma*—while Nordal has shown (1940) that it is purely fictitious and later than *Njála.*

Working from another angle, the historian and antiquarian Barði Guðmundsson agrees that the sagas are literary compositions, not codified traditions. But he thinks that he has been able to establish so close a parallelism between some of the sagas and contemporary history (as represented by *Sturlunga saga*) that he would define the sagas as disguised contemporary history, if not *romans à clef*. He has treated *Ljósvetninga saga* and *Ölkofra þáttr* from this point of view, and one must admit that the satires *Ölkofra þáttr* and *Bandamanna saga* seem especially inviting to such an interpretation. But Barði Guðmundsson's main thesis, not yet demonstrated in detail, is that the chieftain Þorvarðr Þórarinsson (d. 1296) of Valþjófsstaðr in the East was the author of *Njáls saga*. In his new edition of *Njáls saga* (1954) Einar Ól. Sveinsson rejects this hypothesis on rather weighty grounds.

The spirit of the sagas

The sagas chronicle the memories of a heroic heathen society and reflect its spirit. True, this society of farmers, great and small, their goodwives, their farmhands and slaves, is several degrees nearer to the realism of a workaday world than the heroes of the *Edda*, who loom oversize through the romantic haze of distance. But there is a fundamental similarity of outlook, the goals are similar, the problems similar. We saw that the seeking of fee and fame was a common Viking objective, but such an objective was no less urgent in the Icelandic society of the saga age. One might say that the prime preoccupation of every man was to gain a good name and, having won it, to keep it. The moral code of the heathen was no less strict than that of the Christians, though the heathen *goðar* apparently never were the watchdogs of virtue that the Christian priests turned out to be. In reality heathen society was the main enforcer of the moral code; no one could with impunity challenge the opinion of the crowd. This seems like a paradox, since the heathen code was individualistic and proudly independent, whereas the Christian code was submissive and humble. But however proudly and independently the heathen individual might act, he could never escape the laws of common heathen decency instilled in him from childhood. The more independent a man was the more he would have to conform to the conventional code of honor.

This code of honor had grown out of the tribal clannishness at home in Scandinavia and the freedom of Viking enterprise. A man must defend his family and his dependents and take vengeance, if a member was killed or hurt in any way, bodily or mentally. You could overlook much as long as your opponent did not act out of spite to you and your honor. But once your honor was injured, even to the slightest degree, your sense of dignity would not allow you to rest until restitution was made. A wise man did not have to act at once: " a slave takes vengeance at once, the coward never," was an Icelandic saying. And the punishment did not have to fit the crime, but rather your injured honor: you could let a lesser man personally guilty go scot-free, if your honor was better served by striking a greater man out of the ranks of his kindred. With all the feuds and killings chronicled in the sagas—their main subject matter— one might jump to the conclusion that the Icelanders were a blood-thirsty lot. That, however, would be a decided mistake; they were not after blood but after restitution of honor. Hence, as a rule, there was little cruelty connected with these feuds. The Vikings may occasionally, even habitually, have been a cruel lot—God knows that the suffering monks and churchmen did not paint them in bright colors; but then, I suppose, we would not get a bright picture either, if the Germans were left to write the history of the brilliant and brave commando raiders of the last war. There is no denying that the author of *Egils saga* describes his hero's wind-pipe-biting and thrusting-out-of-eyes with considerable glee, but we must not lose sight of the fact that these picaresque traits are reflections of Egill's werewolf (or berserk) ancestry. Even so, his rough adventures pale beside the tales of torture told about the two missionary kings. One hears of a spirited fighter who cut down a man for no reason except the fact that he stood in an ideal position for his axe. This hero of *Fóstbrœðra saga* became the object of Laxness' satire in *Gerpla*. But torture of an enemy does not seem to occur until the embit-tered civil war of the *Sturlung* Age, when towards the end such things did happen. The incident of torture told in the late *Hrafnkatla* is probably to be accounted for on that score. Even so, there is nothing even in thirteenth-century Iceland to compare with the cruelties devised in feudal France and England for the enemies of the lords and for the hapless rabble (cf. the *Old English* [*Peterborough*] *Chronicle* A. D. 1137–54).

The Old Icelanders were fatalists, and a strong undercurrent of fatal-ism runs through many of the best sagas. It was an old and ingrained belief; the heathen gods were subject to fate no less than humans, and even in Christian times fate did not relax her grip. Sometimes fate was bound up with certain things that became her symbols, like the fatal gold of the Nibelungs in the *Edda*. There are fatal swords in *Gísla saga* and *Laxdœla*; in other sagas, such as *Njála* and *Grettla*, fate becomes a somber leitmotif.

But subject to fate though the heroes were, they never must allow themselves to submit to it. Instead they must rise—and usually they did

rise—to the fateful occasion as to the greatest opportunity to test the
mettle of their proud spirits. A Scandinavian hero would not lament
his fate but meet misfortune with a silent challenge, death with a wry
grin. The heroes in homespun were no exception. A chieftain threatened
his tenant with death because the tenant had harbored the chieftain's
outlaw. The tenant's answer was, " My clothes are bad, and it is no
concern of mine whether I wear them a shorter or longer time—but I
would rather die than fail to help my friend in any way I can." (*Gísla
saga*).

The reactions of the heroes to fate give them tragic significance, en-
hancing their greatness at point of death or in defeat. Another fact contributing to the greatness of the sagas is the frequency with which the
tragic dilemma arises in them. A man is given two choices and neither
good, but he has to make the choice. A man must decide whether not
to avenge his wife's brother or to kill his sister's husband. He takes the
latter choice. The sister then first decides to avenge her husband, out-
lawing her brother and causing his death, but later she wants her
brother's killer destroyed.

Such were the tragedies furnishing the matter of the Icelandic family
sagas. Without the tragedies the sagas would not have been estimated
highly any more than a scoop without news-value. Actually the sagas
follow Aristotle's definitions of tragedies fairly closely, though none of
the saga-writers, as far as we know, were at all familiar with the theories
of the great philosopher. The similarities of the sagas to the Greek
tragedies and epics from which Aristotle drew his observations must be
ascribed to the similarity of the heroic societies out of which the two
literatures grew.

Style and composition of the sagas

The sagas are prose narratives with occasional skaldic verses, and
the prose diverges as much as possible from the verse style. The prose
is so plain, so completely non-lyric, that it does not even allow an
occasional ornamental adjective. " He grasped his fine sword " would
not be saga style; it should be: " He grasped his sword, it was a fine
weapon."

The sagas employ certain devices of composition and style which lend
them a distinctive character. They name a great number of persons, and
when a man " is named to the story " or introduced, his genealogy is
usually given and he may be described in a few words; sometimes the

opinion of others is cited. This introducing of persons is a trait most tiresome to the modern reader. In *Njála* there are named *ca.* 600 people, but only about twenty-five are main characters. No other saga is as " modern " in this respect as *Hrafnkatla*, where only twenty-four people are mentioned of whom eight are the main characters.

The sagas are usually told in as chronological an order as possible, though, when two strands of story coincide, the author must tell first one then the other. There are several conventional modes of starting a story or a chapter: " There was a man called N son of N," " Now the tale is to be told that . . ." " Now the tale turns to - - -" etc., etc. " Once upon a time " does not belong to the saga style, but to the folk tales.

The sagas are written in a factual or matter of fact style, making the action swift, lucid, and dramatic. Apart from the weakness for genealogy and personal history, mentioned above, the sagas are remarkably free from any digressions not absolutely essential to the story. (A good deal of the genealogical matter is essential.) Descriptions of nature are rare, occurring only as integral parts of the story. Psychological descriptions and moralizing harangues are conspicuous by their absence, likewise any kind of learned digressions.

One of the most marked characteristics of the sagas is the objective neutral point of view of their authors. One might jump to the conclusion that since they were written about feuding families, presumably by their descendants, who themselves were engaged in the internecine warfare of the thirteenth century, they would take sides violently for or against the warring heroes. Nothing is further from the truth. If the writers were biased, they strove valiantly and successfully to conceal their animus and to view events and personalities from a detached and dignified, humanistic point of view. In this respect the saga-writers compare favorably with the Italian renaissance humanists, and like these, they extended their humanist point of view to treatments of their old religion, though as a matter of fact they were probably as convinced Catholic Christians as any of their day and age. Only one pre-Christian deity may be said to have survived: the impersonal but powerful fate. And fatalism is quite prevalent in some of the best sagas.

The detached point of view made the saga-writers especially fine evaluators and describers of character. When introduced, a person may be described in a few words, or a thumbnail sketch may be given at some high point in the narrative (cf. Egill at the English King Athelstan's

court). But characters were mainly described by their acting and inter-
acting upon other characters, very often by their speeches, sometimes
by comments of others or public opinion, represented by the gossip of
the countryside. The method of description is always external, dramatic;
thoughts are practically never revealed, except in speeches—and not
always then. In spite of this purely behavioristic method, it is really
uncanny how deep a saga-writer can dig into the psychology of his
subjects, and that as often by reticence as by the spoken or written word.
One of the main charms of the sagas is precisely how much one can and
must read there between the lines.

The Family Sagas

The oldest family sagas

The oldest Icelandic family sagas seem to have been written in the period 1200–20, either at the monastery of Þingeyrar or in the surrounding districts of the West and Northwest, though not all of them seem inspired by that monastery. Three of these sagas deal with court poets— of the two missionary and saintly kings, whose sagas had been written by the monks of Þingeyrar in the last quarter of the preceding century. The sagas of Þormóðr Kolbrúnarskáld (*Fóstbrœðra saga*) and of Björn Hítdœlakappi, both poets of Saint Ólafr, are both primitive, each in its own way, but the saga of Hallfreðr vandræðaskáld, poet of Ólafr Tryggvason, is already approaching the classic saga style of *Egils saga*. Primitive, too, though unconnected with the saintly kings, is the saga of Kormákr the Skald, and probably earlier than *Egils saga*.

It is generally believed that *Fóstbrœðra saga* and *Heiðarvíga saga* are the oldest of all. Both show peculiarities and awkwardness of style compared to the later classical sagas. The author of the first, apparently a learned clerk, perhaps a physician, adorned his work with poetical effusions, theological and anatomical digressions, the like of which is not found elsewhere in the sagas. The matter of the digressions is paralleled in the learned literature of the twelfth century; the anatomical interest may be due to the circle around Hrafn Sveinbjarnarson of Hrafnseyri, Vestfirðir, the most celebrated physician of his time in Iceland and Scandinavia (Nordal). With these ornaments cut off, the saga is very nearly classical in style; such is the case with the copy in *Hauksbók* (after 1300), long believed to represent the original. The opposite has only recently been proved by Nordal and S. B. F. Jansson.

Heiðarvíga saga is now hardly more than a torso, since most of the first part is preserved only as retold according to the burned manuscript by Jón Ólafsson in 1729 and only the fragmentary second part is preserved in the old manuscript. A lost leaf of this saga, found in the Icelandic National Library in the summer of 1951 by the young scholar Magnús Már Lárusson did not add materially to our knowledge of the saga. In spite of that the saga is stylistically noteworthy. And just as the author's powerful symbolism about the quartered meat and stones served the hero by his mother to egg him on to vengeance may have come from his monkish legends, so he also introduces a few Latinisms in his style. His predilection for speeches is marked; indeed, it completely runs away with him when the wise man of the saga is advising the hero how to act. Here speech and narrative become inextricably mixed. Otherwise there is much unevenness in narrative and composition, and in general the work reflects pristine robustness unmatched by some of the later and more conventional sagas.

Uneven composition marks *Bjarnar saga Hítdœlakappa*, written probably in the monastery of Hítardalr. It opens with a Viking adventure story laid in Garðaríki (Russia), has a middle sagging from the weight of more or less interesting local traditions, but ends with a fine flourish. If this author seems sometimes embarrassed by the richness of his tradition, the opposite seems true of the author of *Kormáks saga*. But both authors seem to have had trouble in expressing themselves in writing, not least so the author of *Kormáks saga*. His work has been judged primitive by several sagacious scholars.

All the early sagas obviously rely heavily on tradition, often tradition supported by skaldic verse. But only *Fóstbrœðra saga*—minus the digressions—and *Hallfreðar saga* may be said to represent the good classical saga style so common in the following period.

To the earliest period likewise belong many of the so-called *Íslendinga þættir*, short stories of Icelanders, usually incorporated as episodes in the kings' sagas. They deal with adventures of the Icelanders at the kings' courts or in travel abroad. About thirty such *þættir* are already found in *Morkinskinna*, dating from *ca.* 1220. Some of these are real gems of story telling. The *exemplum* of *Brandr örvi* and the pilgrim's tale of *Auðunn vestfirzki* show clerical influence; the latter is one of the most popular of the *þættir*, and deservedly so. Of great literary importance is the tale of the Icelandic saga-teller at King Haraldr harðráði's court, elsewhere (p. 126) quoted, while the story of the love-lorn skald Ívarr at King Eysteinn's court is psychologically interesting. Then we have the superb character delineation of Halldór Snorrason, the humorous tale of Hreiðarr, the fool, and, last but not least, the rollicking farce of Sneglu-Halli, the last-named tale being the only one that has some smutty overtones.

The early classical saga period

The early classical saga period may be said to begin with the writings of Snorri Sturluson (*ca.* 1222–25) and come to a close with the third quarter of the century. It seems thus to be wedged in between the *Landnáma* version of Styrmir fróði (1222–30) and that of Sturla Þórð-arson (*ca.* 1270–80). Many of the intervening saga-writers found help and inspiration for their sagas in Styrmir's (or Ari's) *Landnámabók;* most of the resulting sagas were utilized by Sturla in his *Landnámabók.*

Even if Snorri were not the author of *Egils saga*, as he probably was, it still would herald the new school of Borgarfjörðr in saga-writing, a school combining the critical attitude of Haukadalr-Oddi with the avid collector spirit of Þingeyrar. In Snorri's study in Borgarfjörðr the gullibility and the hagiographical invention of the Þingeyrar monks were replaced by scepticism, aristocratic dignity and true poetical creativeness.

Egils saga was followed by three great sagas in the West: *Laxdœla saga* in Dalir, *Eyrbyggja saga* in Snæfellsnes, *Gísla saga* in Vestfirðir. Judging by literary relationships, the sagas were written in this order during the years 1235–55, though *Eyrbyggja* in style and composition seems to represent a more primitive stage than *Egils saga*. Both *Gísla saga* and *Laxdœla* were inspired by the heroic spirit of the Eddic trage-dies (Sigurðr—Brynhildr—Guðrún); but, while *Gísla saga* is marked by an unusually Christian tinge, *Laxdœla* is also visibly touched by the new spirit of courtesy and romance—quite lacking in the other sagas. In the third quarter of the century there followed in Borgarfjörðr the rustic-realistic *Hœnsa-Þóris saga* (the romantic *Gunnlaugs saga* is even later) and in Húnaþing the rollicking satire *Bandamanna saga* and the proud family saga of the Vatnsdœlir.

It is hard to decide whether the *Eiríks saga rauða* (also called *Þorfinns saga karlsefnis*), also belongs to this period. In its present form it cannot be older than 1263 and may, if it has used Sturla's *Landnáma*, belong to the last quarter of the century. On the other hand there are indica-tions that Sturla might have used an older (?) form of it. Connections with *Ólafs saga Tryggvasonar* (of Gunnlaugr) and legendary interest might even indicate composition during the first quarter of the century. The somewhat uneven style would not militate against that view. It was written on Snæfellsnes probably among the descendants of *Þorfinnr karlsefni* (Rev. Ketill Þorláksson is suggested as the author by Halldór Hermannsson). It has literary ties with *Eyrbyggja*.

The *Grænlendinga saga* of *Flateyjarbók* (*ca.* 1390) seems to be an oral variant of *Eiríks saga*, but the differences are such that the free prose theorists did not recognize it as the same story. It may represent the traditions in Skagafjörðr, while *Eiríks saga* gives the version current on Snæfellsnes. Apart from the manuscript there was no indication of date, and the work was usually thought to be late (after 1300). But Nordal thinks that the two works were written about the same time, the two authors writing without knowledge of each other, hence the differences.

Egils saga

Egils saga (*E(i)gla*) is a family saga, with special emphasis on the biography of the Viking skald Egill Skalla-Grímsson. How his family rose against the tyranny of the rising monarch of Norway, how it was composed of two strains, dark and fair, and how this dualism was reflected in the temperament of the hero himself, has been amply discussed under Egill Skalla-Grímsson, the Skald (p. 57). Here attention is focussed rather on the composition and the art of the saga.

An introductory portion is mainly concerned with the uneven struggle between the emigrating family and the king, climaxed by the killing of the fair Þórólfr and the settlement of the ugly Skalla-Grímr at Borg in Borgarfjörðr. Here a new generation grows up and the old one is reborn: the fair Þórólfr and the dark and ugly Egill, who is especially destined to carry on the feud with the royal family.

After Egill becomes the center of attention, the saga moves swiftly from one highlight in his story to another: his grotesque killing of Atleyjar-Bárðr, the king's henchman; the famous scene in King Athelstan's court after the loss of his brother in the battle of Vínheiðr (= the unidentified English site of Brunanburg), his timid approaches to his brother's beautiful widow, and his fight for her honor and money. Egill's revenge is then climaxed in his killing of the king's son and his magic act to drive the king and the queen, Eiríkr and Gunnhildr, out of Norway. The reaction comes with Gunnhildr's magic counterstroke and Egill's narrow escape at York, where he paid for his head with *Höfuð-lausn*. After that, the saga is filled with various adventures, the hero fighting for his honor, for his friends, and for gain, until fate strikes him with the loss of his sons, a blow to which he would have succumbed but for his daughter's help and his own resiliency of spirit. When age creeps upon him he longs for one final spree, that of sowing his silver at the Althing and hearing—he was blind by then—the assembled crowd fight for it. But when this truly Odinesque design is thwarted, he follows his father's precept and buries his chests of silver.

That the feud against the royal family is told from the Icelandic rather than from the royal (Norwegian) point of view has been emphasized by scholars who deny the common authorship of *Egils saga* and *Heimskringla*. But it is really natural enough, for few writers were more adept than Snorri in seeing and expounding an opponent's point of view. The slander of Hildiríðarsynir and the verbal joust between Arinbjörn and Gunnhildr about Egill's life at York are cases in point. Now, Gunnhildr is a woman much slandered in the sagas and, since she was Egill's most implacable enemy, one would not expect her to be whitewashed in his saga, but the fact is that *Egils saga* comes nearest of all to presenting her point of view unbiased. The author of *Egils saga* is as fond of speeches as is Snorri in *Heimskringla*, a trait he has learned from *Sverris saga*. But the greatest similarity between *Egils saga* and *Heimskringla* is found in their logical structure and pragmatism, probably the most eloquent mark of Snorri's authorship. He forges his rich material, local traditions of the best kind, Egill's verses, and whatever written works he could use, into a masterpiece of medieval scholarship and art.

Nordal places *Egils saga* just before *Ólafs saga helga* in the canon of Snorri's works. Like the early sagas it is written in connection with the kings' sagas: Snorri gives in it a miniature history of Norway and some glimpses of English history—things only a travelled man could do without risking the errors of other sagas in descriptions from abroad. Like many of the earlier sagas, it is a skald's saga, based on his verse. The author of *Egils saga* was pragmatic and nationalistic, as Snorri would have been after his unpleasant experiences in Norway in 1220.

Laxdœla saga

In *Laxdœla saga* (*Laxdœla*) one finds folk-lore, the old Viking spirit of *Egils saga*, the heroism of the Eddic poems, and the new romantic spirit mixed as so many ingredients in a cocktail. It is one of the longest sagas, but it is well constructed, except perhaps for the somewhat rambling introduction. It is a family saga, where one generation after another steps into the spotlight, from the queenly Auðr djúpauðga, the first settler, to the *chevalier* Bolli Bollason, who at the end of the saga dares to ask his aging mother Guðrún whom in her heroic-romantic life she has loved the most, and receives the famous answer: " I was the worst to him I loved the most."

It is of course these famous loves of Guðrún which have captured the imagination of readers and writers in Iceland and abroad. The story of her loves is prefigured by two episodes; one, about an ominous sword destined to strike the best of the family; the other, Guðrún's own dreams signifying her four marriages.

What is fated comes to pass. Guðrún is first married against her will and beneath her station to a man whom she quickly leaves. There follows a marriage of love, but the husband is shortly after drowned at sea. Now follows the greatest courtship of her life: the romantic hero Kjartan Ólafsson, accompanied by his kinsman and foster brother Bolli, begins to frequent Guðrún's home. But Kjartan is not only an ardent lover, he is also proud and ambitious, and he breaks up his courtship to go to the Norwegian court, there striving in accomplishments with the greatest sportsman of the age, King Ólafr Tryggvason himself. Guðrún wants to go with him, but he asks her to wait the conventional three " winters " betrothed to him. Though Guðrún refuses, she actually waits longer, and it is only during the fourth year that she yields to the entreaties of Bolli, when he tells her that Kjartan probably will marry the king's sister. So when Kjartan returns, it is too late, but he takes another beautiful girl, Hrefna, and gives her the fine headdress (*motr*) he had intended for Guðrún. The surface waters are smooth enough, but there are raging currents of jealousy and regret in the deep. There are incidents. Guðrún has a regal sword and the *motr* stolen from Kjartan, and he takes a hot-headed and humiliating vengeance. The stage is set for the climax of the story, Kjartan's killing done by his foster brother Bolli. Guðrún's rejoicing is to not a small extent caused by the fact that Hrefna is now widowed. The next step in the feud is, of course, the killing of Bolli by Kjartan's brothers after their mother, Egill Skalla-Grímsson's daughter, has given them a substantial egging. At Bolli's killing one of the slayers walks up to the pregnant smiling Guðrún wiping the blood of his spear on her garment and remarking that she must be carrying his avenger under that very garment. Having brought up her boy, Bolli, to carry out that duty, Guðrún marries, for the fourth and last time, a chieftain who, however, is soon lost at sea. After that the destiny of Guðrún is fulfilled and she awaits her death as a nun at the monastery of Helgafell.

The author of *Laxdœla* seems to have been a man growing up in the Old Icelandic Viking tradition but receiving a strong impulse as a youth and mature man from the spirit of courtesy which was victorious at the Norwegian court from the twenties of the thirteenth century onward. He belonged to the next generation after Snorri.

Eyrbyggja saga

Eyrbyggja saga's (or *Eyrbyggja*) real name is " the Saga of Þórsnes- ingar, Eyrbyggjar, and Álptfirðingar," that is: the story of the inhabi- tants of Þórsnes, Eyrr, and Álptafjörðr, and as a matter of fact it is the story of a whole countryside, not a biography or a family saga or a complex of events (like *Njála*) but a mixture of all this. It is among the longest of the sagas. The author was obviously a critical historian and antiquarian. He sifted his sources but lost no opportunity to acquaint us with ancient customs: law, religion, and temple rites. His realistic tales of the revenant and the wonders of Fróðá still make us shudder. He was a master at character drawing and adept at unifying his scattered material. His style is lucid, cold and clear, his outlook realistic and heathen. But for the fact that he quotes *Laxdœla*, and thus must have written about or after the middle of the century, his style would seem to range him even before Snorri. He is absolutely free from any taint of the romantic which so strongly affects *Laxdœla*.

Nordal believes that *Eyrbyggja saga's* author was in deliberate reaction against his times, frowning upon the newfangled romantic-chivalrous fashions that obviously had a free play in *Laxdœla*. His contrasting of the prudent, almost niggardly-seeming Snorri goði with the dandy Þorleifr kimbi is a clear case in point.

Gísla saga

Of *Gísla saga's* two versions the shorter is by common consent older and better. Though short and not without compositional faults, it is one of the most moving of sagas. Several strands are discernible in it. Its tragedy, as in *Laxdœla*, is modeled on the heroic poems of the *Edda* (the Sigurð-cycle). Like *Grettis saga* it is an outlaw story, both heroes being victims of inexorable fate in spite of their rich endowments of brawn and brains. But in *Gísla saga* there is an additional Christian element already contained in the many verses of the saga, most of them attributed to Gísli but probably most composed by a twelfth-century cleric. Many verses are recited by Gísli's dream-women, one bright, bringing solace and Christian moralizing, the other dark and gory, a personification of paganism. And if the bright dream-woman is a symbol of Christianity, Gísli's own wife, Auðr, often acts more like a good Christian than most of the saga women. Thus when she has to choose between the loyalties of kin and marriage, between brother and husband, she chooses her husband. Faced with the same choice at Atli's court, Guðrún Gjúkadóttir chose her brothers in a true Old Germanic family fashion. Faced with the same choice Gísli's sister first has him killed to avenge her husband and thereupon exacts vengeance on her brother's slayer (cf. p. 133).

The pity of it is that it is an unguarded remark of Gísli's wife which starts the wheel of fate turning. First her brother was murdered by Gísli's brother-in-law, then Gísli struck back in a similar fashion, and finally he was outlawed and hounded by a second brother-in-law, who married Gísli's widowed sister. The somber tale of Gísli's outlawry is warmed by his wife's self-sacrificing heroism and enlivened by several humorous episodes for comic relief. In Gísli's last stand the good wife is still by his side, wielding a dangerous club, but after his death she goes to Rome, not to return—another indication of a clerical author?

Bandamanna saga

Bandamanna saga is preserved in two versions but the relation between the two is not clear. It is in many ways unique among the sagas. Its events are laid after the usual saga age (930–1030) and instead of extolling its heroes, it is the most vicious satire, indeed the only satire of the *goðar* in existence. In that respect it recalls *Lokasenna* among the mythical poems of the *Edda*. It is rather short but well composed. It tells how the prosperity of the up-and-coming merchant Oddr Ófeigsson is suddenly threatened by a procedural flaw in his otherwise just law-suit, how the chieftains pounce upon him like vultures to get his money, and, finally, how his estranged, aged but shrewd father comes to his aid by bribing the chieftains and setting them at each others' throats. The situation of the chieftains' airing their dirty linen in public is the most dramatic in any saga; it has been borrowed from the shorter and more primitive *Ölkofra þáttr* (or *vice versa?*); it has in turn been dramatized by the modern writer Gunnar Gunnarsson in *Rævepelsene* (The Foxes, 1930). The social satire is easily understood against the background of the last days of the Icelandic Commonwealth (–1264) with its impoverished and grasping chieftains. Identification with known thirteenth-century public figures would *a priori* seem likely and has been attempted by Barði Guðmundsson, though without certain results.

Spreading of saga-writing

Immediately after the appearance of *Egils saga* saga-writing seems to have spread to districts outside the West of Iceland. In the winter of 1230–31 Snorri's nephew, Sturla Sighvatsson, was with him, busily copying his sagas. He must have taken them to his father's manor in Eyjafjörðr, and shortly after, the first saga of that district, *Víga-Glúms saga*, was written there. Like *Egils saga* it is a biography, but the hero bears a curious resemblance to Sighvatr Sturluson, Snorri's brother. If the saga was written at the monastery of Munkaþverá, Glúmr's old farmstead, the monastic spirit has had no influence on the heathen fatalism and the Viking orientation of the saga.

From Eyjafjörðr saga-writing seems to have spread east to Þingeyjarþing. Here *Reykdœla saga* was written, perhaps a decade later, and *Ljósvetninga saga* another ten years later. While *Víga-Glúms saga* relates feuds between chieftains in Eyjafjörðr, the two last-named tell of the struggles between the mighty rulers of Eyjafjörðr and the smaller fry towards the East. Both sagas have been cited by the free-prose theorists, *Ljósvetninga saga* as a particularly lucid specimen of oral variants. But the last editor, Björn Sigfússon, has claimed them as written variants.

Did the saga-writing of the East (Austfirðir) not start until after 1230? Most free-prose theorists think of *Droplaugarsona saga* as the oldest of all the sagas, written down before 1200, for it alone of all the sagas gives a genealogical list of four men, from the hero Grímr to " Þorvaldr, the man who told this saga." Unfortunately the list is corrupt; either one man's name has to be changed (which the traditionalists do) or one (or two) missing links must be added to the genealogy. By assuming a missing link, B. M. Ólsen thought the saga-writer might have lived as late as 1250. Jón Jóhannesson, latest editor of the sagas of the East, considers *Gunnars þáttr Þiðrandabana* to be the oldest (*ca.* 1200–25), having been composed at Helgafell monastery in the West, early enough to be used by the author of *Laxdœla* and to set going the saga-writing in the East. It was followed by *Droplaugarsona saga*, written in Fljótsdalr or by an emigrant from Fljótsdalr before 1240. *Vápnfirðinga saga* he thinks written outside of the district (*ca.* 1225–50) by some descendant of Þorkell Geitisson (perhaps Snorri Sturluson's friend Loptr Pálsson of Hítardalr [1224–42]). He places the defective *Þorsteins saga Síðu-Hallssonar* near the middle of the century because of a supposed influence on *Bandamanna saga* (and *Ölkofra þáttr*). Others have thought it later than *Njála* (i. e. after 1300). From the second half, perhaps the last quarter of the century, would be the realistic-romantic *Þorsteins saga hvíta* and the folk tale *Brandkrossa þáttr*, the first designed to be a new introduction to *Vápnfirðinga saga*, the second serving in the same capacity for *Droplaugarsona saga*. The heroic *Þorsteins þáttr stangarhöggs* and the realistic *Hrafnkels saga Freysgoða* close the list, the latter dating from about 1300.

The late-classical period

We take the late-classical period of saga-writing to span the last quarter of the thirteenth century and perhaps the first quarter of the fourteenth. Some of the very greatest sagas date from this very time; sagas like *Gunnlaugs saga, Hrafnkels saga, Njála,* and *Grettla*. Still, this period is characterized by changes which differentiate most of these sagas from those of the middle period, not to speak of the beginnings of saga-writing. There is increasing stress on chivalrous romance, well-exemplified in *Gunnlaugs saga* and *Njála*, though *Njála's* romances are somewhat cool. There is a Christian tinge in *Njála* not so common in sagas, except perhaps *Gísla saga*. Both *Njála* and *Grettla* show, besides, a vulgarization of taste contrasting with the dignity of the earlier sagas. The addition of *Spezar-þáttr* in *Grettla* also ranges it with the late classical period.

But what all these sagas have in common is, perhaps, the strong element of fiction and the great art of their composition. This has of course long been noted about the dramatic *Njála*, but only recently it has been appreciated about the shrewdly composed *Hrafnkatla*. It is so realistically written that it was claimed by the traditionalists as a perfect example of an oral saga, exceptionally well preserved, written down about 1200—and more reliable than *Landnáma*. It is Nordal's merit to have unmasked this supposedly perfect and true oral saga and to have demonstrated that it is an equally perfect specimen of a novelette and practically completely fictitious.

Nordal, too, has shown the sovereign liberties which the author of the rustic-realistic *Hænsa-Þóris saga* takes with the distances of his district, thus proving the saga to be a historical novel, probably the earliest of this group, though not by any means the best.

One thing is very intriguing: no family sagas seem to have been written in the South until the mighty *Njáls saga* is composed in the last quarter of the century—and few after that (e. g., *Flóamanna saga*). Did the critical spirit of Haukadalr-Oddi keep the South from doing anything after the early bishops' lives except genealogical lore? We do not know, but *Njála* is full of genealogies which are independent of *Landnáma*.

Gunnlaugs saga

Gunnlaugs saga is by far the most popular of the Icelandic sagas today outside of Iceland. The reasons are not far to seek. It is short and of simple construction, the array of secondary persons is much smaller than in most sagas, except *Hrafnkatla*. More important, it is a romance where Viking valor and love are mingled in proportions which the world was taught to like and demand by Tegnér's *Frithiofs saga*. Gunnlaugr ormstunga (the Snaketongue) is a Viking after the world's heart, hardy, headstrong, but courteous, fighting for his love rather than to settle a moot point of honor, risking his life to bring his dying enemy a drink. Helga the Fair, sitting like a swan on the wave, inactive while fought about by the eagles, finding solace in death by unraveling the precious mantle Gunnlaugr gave her, is much more closely related to Ophelia and Gretchen than most of the realistic saga-women. In fact, this sentimental display of feelings falls decidedly out of the true saga style and speaks of lateness. The plot is very similar to that of the primitive *Bjarnar saga Hítdœlakappa*, but the difference in treatment is significant. The tragic fates of Gunnlaugr and Helga are fore-shadowed in a dream at the beginning of the saga in a manner reminiscent of *Laxdœla* and *Völsunga saga* (*Nibelungenlied*). The two early skald and love stories, *Kormáks saga* and *Hallfreðar saga vandræðaskálds* are less closely related to *Gunnlaugs saga* than to *Bjarnar saga*.

Njáls saga

Njáls saga (or *Njála*) has long been considered the greatest of the sagas of Icelanders, and with good reason. It is the work of an author who seems to have had the last line of the saga in mind when he wrote the first. It is not a biography, not a family saga, but a complex chain of dramatic events fashioned by the skilful artist into a mighty trilogy, ruled by inexorable fate. The first part of this trilogy is the tragedy of Gunnar, the second the burning of Njáll and his sons, the third the vengeance exacted by Kári. This three-domed architecture is supported and thrown in relief by many secondary pinnacles and niches, all blending into one harmonious whole. One of these subsidiary structures is the three-act tragedy of Hallgerðr, another the three-act tragi-comic warfare between the housewives Hallgerðr and Bergþóra, another still the comedy of the chicken-hearted but big-mouthed Björn, companion of Kári. Njála teems with living characters often arranged in couples for contrast. There is the benevolent wise Njáll paired with the perfect romantic hero, Gunnar; there is Njáll's wife Bergþóra, strong, sane and faithful, against the beautiful, headstrong, and sinister Hallgerðr, Gunnar's wife. But Hallgerðr is no mere dark, evil spirit; her character has a complexity that reminds one of the Hamlet type, in so far as to have made her an everlasting source of controversy. Most characters of Njála are of the realistic type, neither all white nor all black, but it does have characters approaching that type, too—thus the almost saintly Höskuldr Hvítaness-goði, and the well-nigh Mephistophelian Mörðr. Yet, the latter has a redeeming feature, loving his wife to distraction. This tendency to excess, also noticeable in occasional vulgarity of style, shows the lateness of Njála. There are unmitigated scoundrels like Skammkell, simpletons like Otkell, shrewd rogues like Hrappr, great and good men like Flosi (whose lot it is to burn the wise Njáll and his sons), romantic heroes like Gunnar and Kári, not to mention the favorite rustic Viking Skarpheðinn, whose tongue can be as sharp as his broad ax Rimmugýgr. Though the roster of Njála's women is great, one is hard put to find a truly romantic idyl, unless it be Hallgerðr's brief middle marriage. The description of the king's adulterous mother, Gunnhildr, and of her paramour's subsequent marital difficulties has a decidedly monkish-clerical flavor. Njáll's wife is not romantic but a good housewife, and her famous remark at the burning shows what stuff she is made of. She and many other women are alert guardians of the old code of honor and do some magnificent things when there is vengeance to be done, though none excels in egging like the young, proud Hildigunnr, inciting her uncle to kill Njáll and his sons. Leaving the characters and focussing on the scenes and incidents of the drama there would be much to report. There is pageantry at the Althing with heroes recently returned from abroad rich in fee and fame, their colored clothes and courtly demeanor turning the heads of maidens and winning the admiration of the crowd. A peaceful picture. Another year the Althing is in turmoil through the legal bouts between a good lawyer and a shyster, each trying to outwit the other in the tangled maze of legal procedure. When the shyster succeeds in blocking the case, there is recourse to more tangible weapons and pandemonium breaks out. These are but interludes between some of the great acts, like Gunnar's killing and the burning of Njáll and his household. And such events do not come to pass without great portents to prefigure the tragedy.

It is interesting to watch how the author moves his puppets on the chessboard of fate. Just as he himself implies the end of his rigidly unified book by its beginning and just as he over and over again indicates the march of events with foreboding hints, so from the beginning he sees his heroes doomed to their tragic fate. Nowhere is this clearer than in the case of the great seer and wise man Njáll. In his benevolent wisdom he maps the course of his good friend Gunnar; he fends and parries at every step, but all in vain. Fate marches on, and when she has trampled Gunnar under foot, the turn inexorably comes to Njáll himself and his sons. Thus the greatest prophet and the deepest thinker turns out to be the greatest fool—as human kind of all ages is likely to find out.

Njála's author must have been a great pessimist, and with good reason, for had he not witnessed the decline and fall of the Icelandic Commonwealth as Thucydides had witnessed the internecine struggle of the Greek republics? But Thucydides may have been more optimistic, thinking that his history might be a lesson to others. *Njála's* author suffered from no such illusions, though he allowed his hero to hint, in true Christian fashion, that perhaps God would not let him and his folks burn both in this world and the next. To that extent, then, Njáll did become a Christian, but he remained true to the old code of honor when he chose death rather than living in shame, unable to avenge his sons. And certainly *Njála* holds out no reward for the righteous on this side of the grave.

But if *Njála's* author had no illusions of regaining a Paradise lost, he certainly did re-create the beloved past in his wonderful book, by dint of his great art. Nothing, perhaps, astonishes us more than his way of conjuring up the colorful life of the Althing now lost for ever, by copying long formulas out of the dead and dry-as-dust lawbooks and endowing them with the life of his spirit.

Hrafnkels saga

Hrafnkels saga (or *Hrafnkatla*) is probably later than *Njála*, since *Njála's* author seems not to have known it. Its composition is unique for conciseness and clearness, but the style, though good, is hardly on a par with the composition. The clearness is partly due to the fact that it does away with genealogies and minor characters. Instead of these it uses place names to good effect. No other saga is proportionally as rich in dialogue (53 per cent). *Hrafnkatla* was written to prove that over-bearing tyranny does not pay; but it also shows how an arrogant man may be tamed and brought to his senses by misfortune. Hrafnkell emerges from the saga a wiser and better man. The fact that his character develops is very rare in sagas; we find such development in Snorri's Ólafr helgi and in the wise Njáll, who turns Christian before his end. Otherwise the sagas usually display Aristotelian-like unchanging characters. It is astonishing how, within the narrow confines of the saga, the author succeeds in drawing the characters of eight people, giving the reader the impression that he knows their whole lives. In this the saga vies with the best modern novelettes. Unlike *Gunnlaugs saga, Hrafnkatla* has no trace of the romantic spirit, its heroic realism being so convincing that even book-prosaists like B. M. Ólsen took it to be a saga of tradition, dating from *ca.* 1200. It is Nordal's merit to have shown that it is pretty nearly fictitious and about a century later.

Grettis saga

Grettis saga (or *Grettla*) is the latest of the long Icelandic family sagas, and not the least by any means. The present saga, dating from *ca.* 1320, seems based on an older one written probably by Sturla Þórð-arson (d. 1284). It bears the mark of a learned though not very critical author. He has used *Sturlubók* (of *Landnáma*) and a number of older sagas and he has collected the rich folklore—ghost, troll, and half-troll stories—that had attached themselves to the name of this second most famous outlaw in Iceland—Gísli Súrsson being the first and Hörðr Grímkelsson the third. Two of these folk tales, the story of the revenant Glámr and the story of the trolls at Sandhaugar (especially the latter), have long been recognized to be related to the story of Beowulf's fight with Grendel (the identification was made by Guðbrandur Vigfússon when he first read the Old English poem *Beowulf*). But the author of *Grettis saga* has not been satisfied with native matter; he has enriched his saga with an episode, *Spezar þáttr*, about the vengeance that Grettir's brother exacted for him all the way " out " in Mikligarðr (Byzantium). This highly romantic episode was almost bodily lifted from *Tristrams saga*, which was translated into Norwegian as early as 1226 for King Hákon. But apart from this ending, *Grettis saga* is far from romantic, for it is written to prove that good endowments and good fortune are two very different things. Grettir is the strongest man of the land and not ill-disposed, though headstrong and impetuous. After a rather ominous childhood he grows up to become a prodigious worker (when he works at all!) and a valiant fighter, a typical savior type, whether he tackles Vikings and bears in Norway or ghosts and trolls in Iceland. But, like many benefactors of mankind, Grettir cannot save himself. Ill luck haunts him. On one of his missions of mercy he inadvertently starts a fire where people perish, among them the son of a prominent Icelandic chieftain. The chieftain has Grettir outlawed and his long life of excommunication begins. His adventure with Glámr marks another turning point in his career, for Glámr's spell cuts his further development and starts the life-long nightmare of fear of darkness—a typical Icelandic malady. There are many more adventures still, but, like the large boulders which Grettir was supposed to have lifted and raised up all over the mountains of Iceland, they are but beacons on his road to extinction. He and his brother, stationed on the rocky island fastness of Drangey in Skagafjörðr, are finally overtaken by sorcery, treachery, and death.

Though the sententiousness of *Grettla* is tempered with a great deal of broad humor (another sign of lateness), some of it of the earthy kind, the fundamental note of the work is one of fatalistic pessimism not unlike *Njála*'s. There is this significant difference: Njáll fights fate, but Grettir drifts. It is, again, the atmosphere of the fall and decline of the Commonwealth. And for centuries to come Grettir came to be the symbol of the frustrated nation, so well endowed, so hard of luck. In the words of the saga: " Good gifts and good luck are often worlds apart."

Post-classical sagas

In the post-classical sagas, written mostly 1300–1350, a single work even as late as 1500, the door was flung open to influence and borrowing from *fornaldar sögur* and the romances of chivalry.

In the first place, some new sagas were written in this spirit, like the adventurous *Finnboga saga ramma* and *Þórðar saga hreðu*, the antiquarian *Kjalnesinga saga*, the folkloristic *Bárðar saga Snæfellsáss*, the humorous *Króka-Refs saga*, and the romantic love story *Víglundar saga*.

In the second place, there was a tendency to rewrite old sagas, adorning them with incidents and motifs borrowed from the above sources, Viking exploits, breaking into burial mounds, etc. This was most easily accomplished in episodes taking place in foreign lands; hence some sagas, like *Gísla saga*, were furnished with adventurous introductions, others, like *Grettla*, with a romantic end laid in Mikligarðr (Byzantium), though lifted from *Tristrams saga*. Others were completely rewritten in this fashion: thus to some extent *Grettis saga* though it remained a classic, likewise *Harðar saga, Hávarðar saga, Svarfdœla saga*, and *Þorskfirðinga saga*—all representing a mixture of old and new matter, and none so good as *Grettis saga* though some of them can boast really interesting characters.

To what length such rewriting could go is well demonstrated in the fantastic *Fljótsdœla saga* written as late as 1500 to round out the sagas of the East of Iceland and based chiefly on the classical *Droplaugarsona saga*. It is the last of the sagas and as such of no mean interest. That it should fall short of its illustrious pattern is perhaps less remarkable than the fact that it kept so well within the saga style that it deceived scholars as late as the nineteenth century.

Sturlunga Saga

The compilation

Sturlunga saga (or *Sturlunga*) is a collection of sagas dealing with
the contemporary or nearly contemporary history of Icelanders during
the twelfth and the thirteenth centuries. It was compiled about 1300 by
one of the sons of Narfi Snorrason from the manor Skarð on Skarðsströnd, probably Þórðr Narfason, Lawman at Skarð (d. 1308). It
represents a tendency, increasingly common during the fourteenth century, to collect within one manuscript as many sagas of one type—or as
much miscellaneous matter—as possible. *Hauksbók* is a miscellany from
about 1330 compiled by Lawman Haukr Erlendsson; *Flateyjarbók* (*ca.*
1390) is a compilation of kings' sagas; *Möðruvallabók* (*ca.* 1350) a
collection of family sagas.

In such compilations the individual sagas were often left more or less
intact, though many a scribe—Haukr among them—was given to shortening and turning into his own style.

The compiler of *Sturlunga saga* was interested in the history of his
country during the last two centuries. Hence he took all the individual
sagas dealing with it, arranged them in chronological order, cut them
if they overlapped, or entered them in alternate bits into his text. If he
had hoped to give a rounded and well-proportioned history of the country—somewhat like Snorri's *Heimskringla*—he failed miserably. His
work is in reality a *rudis indigestaque molis* and even more so because
of his attempts to scramble the individual sagas into a chronological
whole.

To unscramble the individual sagas from this scrap heap has been
no easy task, and the work of editors has not been made easier by the
fact that the collection has been preserved in two different manuscripts
(*Króksfjarðarbók* (I), *ca.* 1350 and *Reykjarfjarðarbók* (II), *ca.* 1400),
both of which are now very defective. Fortunately, both were copied
while still relatively intact, but the two manuscript classes were too often
mixed up.

A few short items in the collection are by the collector himself, namely the introductory *Geirmundar þáttr, Haukdæla þáttr* and some genealogies. Otherwise the sagas are as follows, in the chronological order of the collection:

Þorgils saga ok Haflíða

This saga of Þorgils Oddason and Haflíði Másson deals with a feud, arising *ca.* 1120, between two mighty chiefs of the Northwest, and with the success of the churchmen in composing the quarrel. The scene where the two lords ride with their forces to the Althing expecting a fight, won the applause of W. P. Ker. The story of the bridal at Reykhólar in 1119 is not only well told but is, in many ways, an important document of literary history (see p. 123). Since the author goes on to quote King Sverrir's views on " such lying tales " as were on the program of entertainment at Reykhólar, he could not have written the saga before the last quarter of the twelfth century. The last editor of *Sturlunga saga* is even tempted to put credence in the contested reference to 1237 as a *terminus post quem* for the composition of the saga.

Sturlu saga

It deals with Snorri's father, Sturla Þórðarson in Hvammr (Hvamm-Sturla), his quarrels and feuds with his neighbors in 1148–83. It is overloaded with detail, but the author succeeds in giving several anecdotes and situations that not only show up the rather shady character of his subject but also reveal him as a grim humorist. The author must have been very close to the events and if he was a friend of his hero he did not spare him in the least. The saga is too badly written to be credited to Snorri. It might date from the first quarter of the thirteenth century.

The Priest's saga of *Guðmundr góði* has been treated with the bishops' sagas (pp. 103–104).

Guðmundar saga dýra

The saga of Guðmundr dýri or the saga of the Burning of Önundr is laid in the years 1185–1200; the burning of Önundr by Guðmundr occurred in 1197, after which the arsonist entered the monastery of Þingeyrar, where he died in 1212. This saga looks more like a collection of material than an articulated composition. Perhaps it was never finished, but such as it is, it was probably put together after 1212. It is an apology for the firebrand, the next one in Icelandic history after Flosi in *Njála*.

Hrafns saga Sveinbjarnarsonar

The Life of Hrafn Sveinbjarnarson has been preserved as a separate work, but only the latter half of it (1203–13) was incorporated in *Sturlunga saga*. The author, a contemporary friend of Hrafn, writes the story to clear his memory of slander. He may not be equally fair to Hrafn's opponent and killer (1213), described as a man who cannot control his wickedness. The author is obviously a clerk; like the hero, he is interested in medicine. Hrafn may have been the greatest *medicus* of Scandinavia in his time. The saga was probably written not long after 1228.

Íslendinga saga

The Saga (or Sagas) of the Icelanders forms the backbone of the *Sturlunga* collection. It was written by Sturla Þórðarson, probably as a part of a grand history of Iceland, beginning with his *Landnáma* and *Kristni saga* and supplementing such historical works as existed in his day: *Þorgils saga ok Hafliða, Sturlu saga, Prests saga Guðmundar góða, Önundar saga dýra,* and *Hrafns saga*. That this is so seems clear from the fact that he avoids repeating matter from these sagas. To begin with, that is to say during the years 1184–1200, his saga is thus very sketchy, it is chiefly a history of Sturla's sons, Þórðr, Snorri, and Sighvatr, but it gains in breadth and scope as the years roll by. The end is in dispute, some (B. M. Ólsen) setting it at 1242, others (F. Jónsson, P. Sigurðsson) at 1255, where there is a gap of three years in the saga. But the latest editor (Jón Jóhannesson) believes that Sturla skipped these three years because they were fully treated in *Þorgils saga skarða*. He believes that the end of *Íslendinga saga* is sketchy for the same reason as the beginning is, namely, that Sturla in both cases was only supplementing existing sagas, here *Þorgils saga skarða* (1241–58), written (by a certain Þórðr Hítnesingr) 1275–80, and *Þórðar saga kakala* (1242–49), written shortly after 1271. If this is true, Sturla must have written his *Íslendinga saga* during the last years of his life (1271–84) and very likely left it unfinished. This theory would explain a certain unevenness of the composition: omissions here, too many details there. Sturla's artistic instinct was not quite up to par with that of his famous uncle Snorri; he suffered too much from the common Icelandic fault of not seeing the wood because of the trees; besides, the wealth of the contemporary material was much harder to handle than Snorri's writings or traditions of the past. And this is not to say that he does not write well, for he does—and has left us many a brilliantly executed scene, many a moving tale, and some highly humorous anecdotes. His characters breathe real life. In the foreground are full-scale portraits of the actors of the tragic drama, the Sturlungs. There is his quiet but efficient father Þórðr, the brilliant, ambitious, but weak-kneed Snorri, and the humorous realistic man of action, Sighvatr, who loves to take the wind out of the sails of his ambitious brother. But Snorri's ambitious intrigues never put the mark as high as the foolhardiness of his nephew Sturla Sighvatsson. Aiming to subdue the country in one fell swoop, he foundered on the determined resistance of the prudent and cunning Gizurr Þorvaldsson, who all but wiped out the Sturlungs: father and son, Sighvatr and Sturla, and the greatest of them all, Snorri Sturluson. Gizurr did succeed in making himself the master of the country, but only as an earl under the king's sovereignty (1262). There are hundreds of others, great and small, but all, somehow, endowed with a strange life. Sturla, himself, was one of the actors of the drama, and he describes himself with the same seeming detachment as his worst enemies. If he was biased he studiously avoids showing it.

In connection with Sturla and his *Íslendinga saga* one must mention the so-called *Sturlunga*-prologue, by the collector, but perhaps based on an older prologue by Sturla. It states: " Most sagas, taking place in Iceland before Bishop Brandr Sæmundarson died (1201), were written, but sagas taking place after that were to a small extent written, before (i. e. until) Sturla the Poet Þórðarson dictated the Sagas of Icelanders, for which he utilized information from learned men, those who lived while he was young, but some things from letters written by people contemporaneous with the heroes. Many things could he himself observe and hear of great events in his own day . . . "

In this prologue, " most sagas " was long mistakenly interpreted as referring to the family sagas (*Íslendinga sögur*), so e. g., Finnur Jónsson, who for that reason dated most of them before 1200. Actually the statement concerns the *Sturlunga* collection only and was first correctly interpreted by Guðbrandur Vigfússon.

Svínfellinga saga

Of the other sagas of the collection *Svínfellinga saga*, recording the events of 1248–52, is especially noteworthy not only because it alone of the sagas of *Sturlunga* takes place in the Southeast but also because it is the only saga colored by a certain manly sentimentality, reminding in that respect of *Njáls saga*, which hails from the same district. It was probably written towards 1300.

Arons saga

The saga of Aron Hjörleifsson, chronicling the life of a thirteenth-century hero, was actually later than the *Sturlunga* collection, though often included in it by editors. It was probably written towards 1350. Much of the matter was already recorded by Sturla Þórðarson in his *Íslendinga saga*; the fourteenth-century author has somewhat increased the dimensions of his hero.

The style

The style of most of the sagas in the *Sturlunga* collection, notably the style of Sturla himself, was almost always secular. Only when he describes the fate of Bishop Guðmundr the Good does he momentarily succumb to the ecclesiastical point of view, revealed in a devotional flavor of the style. Otherwise he is the hard, detached humanist observer, studiously neutral, but obviously an admirer of the great men of his age and their great deeds. To us these deeds may appear in a dubious light and, indeed, the wisdom of the family feuds must have seemed dubious even to the actors themselves. Often enough they must have felt like Paul that they did not do the good they wanted to do but the evil they did not want to do. Thus, in the Norwegian court—and in order to prevent an invasion of Iceland—Snorri may have suggested that it would not take him long to turn the Icelanders to a friendly submission to the Norwegian crown. But in *Heimskringla* he wrote that famous speech of Einar Þveræingr epitomizing the resistance of the people to foreign encroachment, a speech still ringing in Icelandic ears during and after World War II.

And here, incidentally, we have the salient point. The actors of the great drama of the Sturlung Age were fighting for the noble ideals of heroic life: independence and greatness in the individual. They lost this fight in the arena of everyday life and sold their ancient birthright of freedom for a dangerous security, a deadening peace. But they succeeded in making their literature, the sagas, a flaming torch of these ideals, destined to illuminate the dark centuries to come in the nation's life—and to flare up afresh in mighty revivals under more favorable circumstances.

Fornaldar Sögur

Name and definition

Though the name *fornaldar sögur*, sagas of antiquity, is not old (it was coined by the first editor of the sagas) it is a very apt name, for many of these sagas deal with the oldest memories of the race in the North and, to some extent, in the surrounding Germanic lands. They have also, in English, been called the mythical-heroic sagas, which is apt, as far as it goes, for, like the Eddic poems, whose tradition they continue in many respects, they deal with myths and heroic legends, a few of which vie in importance with the Eddic poems themselves. Some of them have also been called Viking sagas because they deal with raids and adventures of the Vikings, both in the West (*Vestrvegr*) and, preferably, in the East (*Austrvegr*). As stories of adventure in strange exotic lands they are filled with folklore motifs of various kinds: ghost stories, troll stories, and fairy tales. They are as fantastic as the family sagas are realistic; and while the family sagas (and the heroic legends among the *fornaldar sögur*) are mostly tragedies, the happy ending comes as natural to these sagas as to a Hollywood movie. They are obviously always composed for the sake of entertainment.

Origins and oral tradition

Though the *fornaldar sögur* as we have them are later than the kings' sagas and the family sagas—they belong roughly to the period 1250–1350 or perhaps 1400—there is plenty of evidence to prove that of old they were popular for oral entertainment or story-telling not only in Iceland but all over the North. Likely enough some of the sagas with which the expert Icelandic youth entertained King Haraldr harðráði about the middle of the eleventh century were of this type. But the first *fornaldar saga* to be mentioned by name is *Hrómundar saga Grípssonar*, told, verses and all, for the sake of merrymaking by its author Hrólfr from Skálmarnes at the bridal at Reykhólar 1119, described in *Þorgils saga ok Hafliða* (p. 153). The author of that saga, feeling that he has to apologize for mentioning such trifles, tells us that such *lygi sögur*, lying stories (cf. contemporary churchmen's *mendacium* about Virgil's *Æneid*), were specially appreciated by no less a personage than King Sverrir himself. About half a century later we find Sturla Þórðarson able to gain the graces of the king and queen of Norway by telling them another *lygi saga*. It seems that he had the story *Huldar saga* with him in manuscript, though he is said to have told—not read—it. From then on people began committing these entertaining though disreputable stories to the parchment.

Sagas in Saxo Grammaticus

By an indirect road some sagas of this type did get " published " even earlier than most kings' and family sagas. These were the *fornaldar sögur* used by the Danish Saxo Grammaticus in his *Gesta Danorum* (*ca.* 1200). Saxo pays due tribute to the Icelandic saga-tellers in his preface, and when Axel Olrik cast doubt on this clear statement, awarding most of the Norse sagas to Norwegians, he was misled by the view of Finnur Jónsson and others that the best family sagas existed already before 1200, hence the uncritical *fornaldar sögur* could not have been told by Icelanders. But this, as we have seen, was a fallacy, and there is nothing to disprove Saxo's own words.

In many cases the sagas adopted by Saxo have been altogether lost in Iceland; thus *Haddings saga, Fróða saga, Haðar saga, Eiríks saga málspaka, Friðleifs saga, Ála saga frœkna, Þorkels saga aðalfara.* On the other hand sagas like *Hrólfs saga kraka* and *Ragnars saga loðbrókar* have survived also in Iceland. The differences between the two groups, Icelandic and Danish, are often considerable.

The scene

The scene of the *fornaldar sögur* is chiefly the North. There are eleven sagas laid in Norway, five in Denmark (plus the seven borrowed by Saxo, though some of them may owe their localization in Denmark to him). Four sagas deal with East and South Germanic matters in closest connection with the old heroic poetry, while the nine sagas of adventure are vaguely localized in Norway, Denmark, and Sweden, with Viking raids to England, rarely Ireland, often Finland and Bjarmaland (Perm in Russia), even more frequently to Garðaríki (Russia), with an occasional jaunt to Mikligarðr (Byzantium) and Tattaria. This localization of the raids is quite similar in all the sagas and it is noteworthy that, just as *none* of the sagas take place in Iceland itself, so few of the raids are in the West. Apparently the *Vestrvegr* was not by any means as romantic as the *Austrvegr*.

From the above stated facts the *fornaldar sögur* may roughly be divided in three classes: those closest to the heroic poems of the Edda, the Viking sagas, and the wild adventure sagas. The first two classes may occasionally preserve some old historical memories, at least the names, the latter are frankly fictitious fantasies.

The chief sagas

Most important among the heroic sagas is *Völsunga saga*, based to a great extent on the heroic Eddic poems on Helgi Hundingsbani, Sigurðr Fáfnisbani, Guðrún, and Brynhildr, Atli, and Jörmunrekkr. It is especially valuable because it has preserved for us, in prose narrative, the lost poems of the *Codex Regius*. The introductory story, about Sigmundr the Völsungr and his incest-begotten son Sinfjötli, begotten to help him carry out the avenging of his father, is unknown from elsewhere, though it was probably an old tale, since *Beowulf* refers to Fitela as Sigemund's sister's son (*nefa*). In the nineteenth century *Völsunga saga* was to become the inspiration of Richard Wagner and William Morris.

Nornagests þáttr covers partly the same ground as *Völsunga saga*. The 300 years old Nornagestr comes to the court of King Ólafr Tryggvason, tells him his old tales, gets baptized, and dies.

Hervarar saga ok Heiðreks konungs has preserved poetry on a par with the oldest of the Eddic poems: *Hlöðskviða* dealing with the folk battles between Goths and Huns on the banks of the Dniepr (*á stöðum Danpar*) and on the plains north or east of the Carpathian Mountains (*Harvaða fjöll*). It also contains a splendid poem about Hervör's nightly visit to her father's mound to fetch his magic sword. Finally, it contains the oldest collection of riddles in Old Norse: *Gátur Gestumblinda*, sometimes called *Heiðreks gátur* (The Riddles of Gestumblindi or Heiðrekr). The wisdom of King Heiðrekr is being tested by the disguised Óðinn, who naturally wins the contest. *Hervarar saga* is a composite story starting with the tale of the magic but fatal sword Tyrfingr, ending with the strife of the half-brothers Hlöðr and Angantýr. It has unmistakeable parallels in the Old English *Widsíþ*. The saga is followed up with a much younger chronicle of Swedish kings in historic times (up to 1118).

Hrólfs saga kraka deals with a mighty fifth-century Danish king, praised not only by Saxo but also by the Old English emigrants, as *Widsíþ* and *Beowulf* show. Though marked by its lateness in style and language, it contains many old motifs, some derived from the heroic poetry (*Bjarkamál*). It it episodic, but it ends in the grand heroic manner with a fight about the king's hall, where king and retainers vie with each other in gaining a glorious death defending the hall against overwhelming odds. This matter is also, to a certain extent, found in Snorri's *Edda* and in *Skjöldunga saga*.

Ragnars saga loðbrókar deals with another Danish king, famed in story, of the much later Viking age. He is known to have raided France in 845, and after that his exploits and those of his sons grew mightily in the chronicles of western Christendom. They were all familiar to the authors of the Orkney *Háttalykill*. King Ragnar was supposed to have been laid in a snakepit by the English King Ella and to have recited a death poem, *Krákumál*, in which he boasts that he will die laughing. Ragnar was the husband of Áslaug, daughter of Sigurðr and Brynhildr, a fiction forgetting the famed sword that separated the two in bed but designed to connect *Ragnars saga* with *Völsunga saga*, of which it forms a continuation. This fiction also gave many Icelanders a very noble origin.

One of the Norwegian sagas, *Hálfs saga ok Hálfsrekka*, probably represents the oldest legends from that country, clustering around several long poems. King Hálfr and his heroes are typical Vikings, who come to a tragic end through fire and sword, unlike most of the later Viking adventurers, as e. g., Örvar-Oddr, who for 200 years goes unscathed and victorious from one adventure to another.

Gjafa-Refs saga ok Gautreks starts by telling a marvellous yarn about a primitive peasant family in Gautland committing suicide out of stinginess by jumping over a cliff. It goes on to describe an almost equally stingy earl in Norway who never allows himself to accept a gift, knowing the proverbial " Gift calls for reward." When put in this awkward position by Gjafa-Refr, the stingy earl pays by giving advice as to how to get a great gift for a small one (cf. *Auðunnar þáttr vestfirzka*). Apart from this the saga contains an episode on King Vikar and the hero Starkaðr the Old, one of the most famous heroes in the North (cf. Saxo).

Friðþjófs saga is the love romance among the *fornaldar sögur* as *Gunnlaugs saga* is among the family sagas. It is concise and comparatively realistic; there is little of the supernatural in it and few adventures.

Scholars have thought that it was based on the Eastern romance *Flóres ok Blankiflúr*. It became the basis of E. Tegnér's famous nineteenth-century poem of the same name. He told the story in cantos of different meters, in imitation of the Icelandic *rímur*.

It would lead too far to list the remainder of the sagas. Suffice it to say that in *Örvar-Odds saga* the Viking adventures are commensurable in number, if not always in variety, with the twelve ells stature and the 200 years of the hero. Yet Örvar-Oddr was of the family of Hrafn-istumenn, the ancestors, too, of Egill Skalla-Grímsson and his clan in Iceland, to which any Icelander would be proud to belong. Not so the hero of *Göngu-Hrólfs saga*. For though his name is that of the famous Rollo of Normandy, who had plenty of proud relatives in Iceland, there is no attempt to connect him with the historical figure: he is, indeed, as fictitious, and intentionally so, as the great marvels that happen to him. From such a fantasy there is hardly a step to the marvellous romances of chivalry (*riddara sögur*) and to the hybrid of *fornaldar saga* and *riddara saga*, the *lygi saga*. Indeed, *Göngu-Hrólfs saga* and several others from the collection of *fornaldar sögur* may well be looked upon as such hybrids.

Romances of Chivalry and Lygi Sögur (Lying Stories)

French romances and chansons de geste in Norway

While the Icelanders were already experienced in writing kings' and family sagas, the king of Norway (Hákon Hákonarson) prodded his clerks to introduce cosmopolitan chivalry in Norway by translating the best of the Anglo-Norman metrical romances. The beginning was made by a certain Brother Robert, probably an Englishman, who translated the Anglo-Norman poet Thomas's *Tristan* into pompous but indifferent and rather clumsy prose. This was in 1226. There followed translations of Marie de France's Breton Lays (*Strengleikar*), three romances by Chretien de Troyes: *Erec, Ivain,* and *Perceval,* as well as many others. During the second half of the century the *chansons de geste,* dealing with Charlemagne, were united into a bulky *Karlamagnúss saga* done, no doubt, by different translators. These earliest romances of chivalry belong as clearly to the Norwegian court as the book of royal etiquette *Konungsskuggsjá* or *Speculum regale.* The latter was to teach the theory of chivalry, the sagas to demonstrate its practice. In one important point they were indebted to the earlier Icelandic sagas: but for them, they would not have been written in prose, since they were translated from metrical originals. In another very important sense they became part and parcel of Icelandic literary history; most of them were preserved only in Iceland where they became one of the most important strands from which the *lygi sögur* of the fourteenth and fifteenth centuries were fashioned.

Sources of romances in Iceland

Closely related to Arthurian romance was Geoffrey of Monmouth's famous *Historia regum Britanniae* dating from 1137. Part of it, Merlin's Prophesy (*Merlínusspá*), was translated as early as 1200 by Gunnlaugr, a monk of Þingeyrar. In general its presence at Þingeyrar may have helped to launch the kings' sagas there. Dr. Leach believes that the rest of Geoffrey's *Historia* was translated not much later but at least before the middle of the century in Iceland. The translator prefixed a *Tróju saga* (based on Dares Phrygius and Dictys Cretensis) to Geoffrey's *Breta sögur*, thus following the medieval scholarly theory of Trojan origin for royalty everywhere (as in Virgil's *Æneid*). This theory, by the way, is first found in Iceland in Ari fróði's genealogy, which is earlier than Geoffrey's history.

If most of the above-mentioned works introduced the matter of France and the matter of Britain to Iceland, the *Trójumanna saga*, the *Rómverja saga*, and the *Alexanders saga* (translated by Bishop Brandr Jónsson [d. 1264] from Philip Gautier's *Alexandreis*) introduced the matter of classical antiquity into Iceland.

The Crusades had opened the way even to the Orient, and it is certain that the Eastern tales of *Barlaam ok Josaphat* (a version of the Buddha legend) and *Flóres ok Blankiflúr* (influencing *Friðþjófs saga*) came by way of England to Norway and Iceland.

But what was the origin of a goodly number of Byzantine and Oriental romances, seemingly making their way into Iceland during the fourteenth century? Had they been floating in oral tradition since the days of the Varangians (*ca.* 1100), or did they seep through the learned channels of the church? In view of the fact that the originals could mostly not be found (Leach, Schlauch), Icelandic scholars have proposed that they were native concoctions made out of foreign, mostly classical-ecclesiastical matter. Their vogue would be co-existent with that of the *exempla*, whose chief exponent in Iceland was the Dominican monk, later bishop, Jón Halldórsson.

Development of romances in Iceland

According to Einar Ól. Sveinsson, who has made the most thorough study of *riddara sögur* and *lygi sögur* in Iceland, mostly based on their internal relationship, the development of the genre is somewhat as follows:

The Icelandic *lygi sögur* derive both from the Norwegian school of Abbot Robert's translated romances and from the native *fornaldar sögur* from the last quarter of the thirteenth century. The strand of the genre which derives from the *fornaldar sögur* is easily discernible from the first to the last. Here belong, in the period 1300-50, *Vilmundar saga viðutan,*

Þjalar-Jóns saga, Hrings saga ok Tryggva, and *Sigurðar saga fóts*; in the period 1400–1500, *Álaflekks saga, Sigurgarðs saga frækna, Valdimars saga,* and *Jóns saga leiksveins.* The influence of chivalrous romance on these sagas is slight for their chief characteristics are native motifs and native style.

The Icelandic romances of chivalry, *riddara sögur,* begin *ca.* 1300 with *Konráðs saga keisarasonar* and *Mágus saga jarls,* the older and shorter version. Though based on foreign matter, *Mágus saga* on a French poem, the style is fairly saga-like and native, clearly distinct from the Norwegian school of Abbot Robert.

Klárus saga, attributed to the story-telling of Jón Halldórsson, Norwegian bishop of Skálholt, and written after his death 1339, perhaps towards the middle of the century, marks a new departure in the style of these sagas. It is verbose and clerical, learned and vulgar at the same time. The same style is seen, too, in the bishop's *Ævintýri, Jónathas saga,* and *Markúlfs saga ok Salómons.* It is most likely a reflection of the strong Norwegian element in the church. From the second half of the thirteenth century there was almost a continuous row of Norwegian (or foreign) bishops at Hólar; the same was true in Skálholt, from Jón Halldórsson onward almost up to the Reformation. This Norwegian influence became especially strong after 1325.

About 1350, slightly later than *Klárus saga,* the two sagas *Kirjalax saga* and *Rémundar saga* seem to have been written. These sagas strive for the pompous high style of the oldest Norwegian romances as well as for the clerical learning of *Klárus saga,* and they have also been influenced by *Alexanders saga.* The result is an ornate style, verbose and subjective, but lacking the experienced clerical touch of *Klárus saga.* Here belong sagas like *Gibbons saga, Nítíðu saga, Viktors saga ok Blávus,* and *Sigurðar saga þögla.* In all probability these sagas mirror the society of the wealthy aristocrats of the fourteenth and fifteenth centuries, otherwise only represented by the ballads of the same time. *Kirjalax saga* represents the aristocratic taste for classic antiquity, Greek motifs and matter, which are so prominent in these sagas. And this taste holds sway for a century and a half, as the titles of *Dínus saga drambláta* and *Sálus, Nikanórs ok Hektors saga* from about or after 1500 prove. It looks as if this "classicism," diluted though it was, may have kept out of Iceland the miraculous and other-worldly matter of the Arthurian romances. They are strangely absent in Iceland.

A bibliographical note on the lygi sögur

When Dr. H. G. Leach made his pioneering survey of the *lygi sögur* in his *Angevin Britain and Scandinavia* (1921), he found " more than 150 romances professing to be records of chivalry in foreign lands." Dr. M. Schlauch, in her brilliant study *Romance in Iceland* (1933), limited her observation to about 110 of these sagas. Since then the *Handritaskrá Landsbókasafnsins* (1937) has revealed the names of about 115 new sagas, bringing the total number up to nearly 265. Most of these 115 sagas will probably be found to have been written after the Reformation, perhaps even after the time when Árni Magnússon brought his collection to a close in Iceland. Dr. Leach had already pointed out a number of romances derived from Germany through Denmark after 1550; likely enough many of the Landsbókasafn sagas will fall into that group, being derivable from German-Danish *Volksbücher* or chapbooks. Here is still a wide open field for study. To try to write the history of the *lygi sögur* after the Reformation would be premature. Suffice it to say that they actually survived into the nineteenth century, which produced not only most of the learned and popular editions of the *lygi sögur* but also the only mock-heroic example of the genre, Benedikt Gröndal's *Heljarslóðar-orrusta*, a masterpiece.

Lygi sögur and rímur

Like the *fornaldar sögur*, the *lygi sögur* always provided popular subjects for composing *rímur*, and it is instructive to note the numerical relation between the two genres. According to Björn K. Þórólfsson, there are about 115 *rímur*-cycles dating from before 1600. After that there are about 900 *rímur*-cycles preserved, by nearly 330 known poets. There would thus seem to exist about 1000 *rímur*-cycles as against 35 *fornaldar sögur* and 265 *lygi sögur* or about a combined number of 300 *fornaldar* and *lygi sögur*. The relation would thus be three or four *rímur*-cycles to one saga. A glance at the list of manuscripts at the Landsbókasafn reveals the fact that one saga often served several poets as a subject matter, thus we find five *Ambáles rímur* by as many poets made from the unique saga which, in England, was to become *Hamlet*.

The literary motifs of lygi sögur

As in fairy tales the hero often starts with a handicap: he is exposed or exiled or he is a scorned and slow-witted *kolbítr*. As in Greek romances, there are amorous stepmothers, always rejected, but the wicked stepmother, foreign to the family sagas, is all-important in fairy tales and *lygi sögur*. Her most common weapon is *álög*, spell or enchantment, by which she will transform her stepchildren into monsters or animals, she herself usually being a witch or troll in disguise. Stepmother trouble may lead to parricide, unknown in the family sagas. While dragon or monster-slaying is a common beginning of a hero's career, vengeance of a father, common in Edda and saga, is rare in the *lygi sögur* (Amlóði, Hamlet).

When ready to embark on adventure the hero makes a solemn vow— *heitstrenging*—to accomplish the most difficult feats. This motif was common in life and literature alike, as the *Battle of Maldon* and the *Jómsvíkinga saga* show. In French romances the mock-heroic vows of the *Pelerinage de Charlemagne* were most famed and imitated. A stock adventure is saving a damsel in distress from giants, dragons, other monsters or, French fashion, a heathen prince at the head of an army. To win a princess a combat with her father or relatives may be necessary, if not a difficult quest: *sendiferð, forsending*, again a fairy-tale motif. Robbing a dragon-guarded treasure was a common motif, likewise the breaking into the burial mound of an old Viking, who as a living ghoul fights for his hoard. Usually the hero must open the mound and be lowered into it by a rope and fight while the rope-tender gets cold feet and absconds.

While hunting for adventure, the hero may run into another woman of this world or the other and beget a child by her—to be sent to him when grown, if a boy. This may lead to the father-son combat of Hilde-brand and Hadubrand (cf. *Ásmundar saga kappabana*). But the tragic end is rare, normally the *lygi saga* has a happy ending, with a marriage and a reign over a kingdom for ever after.

Supernatural elements and magic

The *lygi sögur* abound in supernatural elements and magic. There are giants, dwarfs, trolls and ghouls (*skessur* and *draugar*), the last-named of the solid physical characteristics of Icelandic folk belief at all ages. Causing storms, fogs or confounding darkness by walking or by waving a cloth or a pole withershins seems to be a native art, while the windbags of Gautan and Ógautan recall the same instrument of the *Odyssey*. At times the magic storms are real, at times only illusions. The ability to change shapes, perhaps implied by the going berserk of the realistic sagas, and one of Óðinn's master arts, is extremely common in the *lygi sögur*. The shapeshifters are called *hamhleypur*. The most common spell in the *lygi sögur* as well as in Icelandic folk tales is the *álög*, a wish and a behest. It is similar to but not identical with the Irish *geis*; the two differ in that the Irish often fail to make it clear who, if any one, imposed the original tabu and what will be the consequences, if broken. Also, the Irish *geis* is often negative, while the Icelandic is always positive. In the sagas the *álög* may be imposed by a dying opponent (e. g., Glámr), a rejected woer, a witch, a troll, but above all by the wicked stepmother. Unlike conditions in the family sagas, illness often plays a considerable role in the hero's life; it may be caused and cured by magic remedies, a drink, a life-giving stone, or by going to a certain place such as India.

French influence

Motifs due to French influence are as follows: a wooer's betrayal of his lord; an innocent queen, falsely accused by enemies; an envious courtier plotting; accusations of disloyalty or of illicit relations with lord's daughter; a queen prodding her king to action by invidious comparison with other " great " kings; a love-affair between a human and a supernatural being (Marie de France); combats against heathen Saracens; heathen princess converted and married to hero; the imperial palace of Miklagarðr (Byzantium) turning on pillars; a cure of a poisonous wound; chastity tests (*Möttuls saga*); a witless rustic hero resembling Chretien's Perceval (*Vilmundr viðutan*).

Latin influence

It has been claimed (Schlauch) that, excepting *Trójumanna saga* and *Rómverja saga*, the Latin or classical heritage in the *lygi sögur* was less a matter of plots than that of a general setting borrowed by the learned Icelanders from Latin works on geography, Paradise and India, the monsters of antiquity, lapidaries, bestiaries, medicine and magic. Actually, the plots of Greek and Byzantine romance, so common in the *lygi sögur* after 1300, should rather be considered part of the Latin book-learning than survivals of oral tales carried to Iceland by the illiterate Varangians. The typical Greek romance was a tale of dispersal of families or lovers to be reunited after many troubles and tribulations, frequently by means of telling their lives and thus recognizing each other, after the pattern of the Greek drama. Authors of *lygi sögur* seized avidly upon the motifs of *ævisaga* and *fagnaðarfundur* (biography and reunion). The type occurs earliest in the legendary *Plácítusdrápa* (and *-saga*) of the twelfth century. Other common traits of the Greek romances are: a long quest for a princess (sometimes unseen) and a long list of pompous musical instruments in descriptions of feasts.

Whether the Oriental matter can be separated from this Latin-Greek Byzantine material seems rather doubtful. We have seen that *Flóres ok Blankiflúr* affected the *Friðþjófs saga*, and it is believed that the Buddha legends affected not only the pious *Barlaams saga* but also the farcical *Dínus saga dramblátá*. The legend of the snake-infested Babylon is found not only in *Alfrœði íslenzk*, the encyclopaedia, but also in *Konráðs saga keisarasonar*, where the description reminds of legends of how to enter Paradise (cf. H. R. Patch, *The Other World in Medieval Literature*).

Difference in spirit between saga and lygi saga

The heroic spirit, running through Edda and saga, is to some extent preserved in the chivalrous romances and the *lygi sögur*. Battle and fighting, glossed over in the Edda, given reasonable space in the sagas, are exaggerated in the romances as a chief means of covering a knight with glory. Crude though these fights may be, they are a mark of the heroic spirit, and one of the main reasons why the common people preferred the romances to legendary and devotional matter: " The gospels are no fun," complained the old hag, " there are no fights in them."

Still, the old tragic greatness of Edda and saga is forever lost. There a hero fought a losing battle against fate, winning an undying fame in so doing. In romance and *lygi saga*, no matter what the odds and complications, the hero vanquishes his enemies, wins his lady, and lives happily ever after. If a Viking occasionally saves a damsel in distress, the romantic hero may make it his chief business. Yet one must concede that swooning, sighing, weeping, and humiliating oneself for one's lady, if commonplace in French romances, were rare in the *lygi sögur*. Likewise, if the French romances excel in the description of love as a powerful emotion and tend to become psychological documents of note, the Icelanders, demanding action, cut such descriptions as mere twaddle. Another attitude, quite foreign to the ideology of Edda and saga, but characteristic of the *chansons de geste*, was the bigoted feeling of the Christian-patriotic Frenchman against his foe, the heathen Saracen. To a Frenchman his antagonists might be good knights, if they were not paynims! In the North neither religion nor, as a rule, patriotism mattered. An individual pitted against an individual, if both were good enough, was all that counted. So much for the heroic code as compared to the code of love and Christianity.

Another profound difference between Edda and sagas on the one hand and the *lygi sögur* on the other was the realistic air of the former and the romantic-fantastic outlook of the latter. The splendor of description, the variation of adventure could be all the more intensified because, in their decline, the Icelanders could never hope to visit the marvelous foreign lands except in imagination. The once great globe-trotting Vikings had now—with very few exceptions—turned into stay-at-homes that had to be content with their dreams. They were more avid than ever for news from foreign parts, but their critical faculties were sapped, and they could let their imaginations run riot with the flotsam and jetsam which the great tide of foreign romance carried to their shores. They did not create good literature out of this romantic matter, but they kept their interest in reading and writing and even their sanity by escaping from dire reality.

The Reformation

Political-economic effects

Although the fifteenth century was a time of comparative stagnation, it brought, in the sacred poetry, the new measures that were to dominate not only the new evangelical hymns but also, to a great extent, the lyric poetry of the succeeding centuries.

With the sixteenth century came the Reformation and with it a threat to the language and the native culture greater than any since the advent of Christianity.

The Reformation was ushered in, ominously enough, by the death of Bishop Ögmundur Pálsson of Skálholt in 1541 and the beheading of Bishop Jón Arason and his sons on November 7, 1550. The latter event marked the end of all resistance, though the conversion was hardly more than nominal, except in the case of the leaders. To begin with, the revolution was more in the political economy of the country than in religion, which had to wait for the educational activities of a Bishop Guðbrandur Þorláksson to strike firm roots.

The first effect of the Reformation was the sudden shift of power from the old Catholic Church to the Protestant king. After the Church, about 1300, had succeeded in gaining supremacy over native law and the secular chieftains, it had been in constant growth so that, by the end of the period, it had amassed almost one half of all the real estate of the country. The bishops wielded not only the highest ecclesiastical authority but also, toward the end of the period, the supreme temporal power. It is true that stubborn chieftains always managed to fight against the encroachment of the Church, but the Church in turn was ever ready to take advantage of their carnal weaknesses and force them to submission. Hence some of the chieftains were only too glad to side with the reformers and the king. Withal, the Church had become closely integrated with Icelandic nationality and its institutions; the sees and the monasteries had become cultural centers of importance.

[170]

The Reformation began, significantly, with the plundering of the monastery at Viðey, on Whitsunday, 1539. Such plunderings had an obvious appeal to the king's men, who persisted in them even after the Reformation and under protest of the Lutheran clergy. The first Lutheran superintendent of Skálholt, Gissur Einarsson (1542–48), succeeded to some extent in stemming the tide, but his weak successor, Marteinn Einarsson (1548–56), had to give in to their rapacity, resigning his see in protest. The king's men not only appropriated all the real estate of the Catholic bishops and the monasteries, but they also robbed the see of Skálholt of the rich fishing farms near Bessastaðir, substituting real estate elsewhere of little value. It is calculated that after the Reformation the king amassed one sixth of all real estate in Iceland. The representative of the king in Bessastaðir would gladly have reduced all the king's tenants to the status of the villein peasantry in Denmark but succeeded only in the immediate neighborhood. It was this exploitation, together with the fateful trade monopoly, which started the country on an economic decline from which there was no recovery until the nineteenth century.

Bible translations

The first concern of the reformers in Iceland, as elsewhere, was translating the Bible and educating the common people to read it. Hence, there was an unrealized proposal to establish schools for children at the monasteries. But after 1552, there were established Latin Grammar schools at the two sees to educate the parsons, who in turn became the instructors in their parishes. Though reading was fairly common in Catholic times, it was not compulsory as was the knowledge of the *Credo, Paternoster,* and *Ave Maria.* After the Reformation, the memorizing of Luther's smaller *Catechism* became compulsory for all, obviously an incentive for many to learn to read it. Moreover, the printing press, first introduced by the last Catholic bishop, Jón Arason, was to become a great weapon of propaganda in the hands of the reformers. Important books to disseminate the new faith were printed, both abroad and in Iceland, but no one was a more energetic publisher than Bishop Guð-brandur Þorláksson at Hólar who, for half a century, continued to pour forth religious and devotional books of various kinds, most of which dominated the field of religious practice for the next two hundred years.

Apart from the thirteenth-century Norwegian Bible translation of *Stjórn,* there seems to be good evidence to prove the existence of a

"Gospel Book" (*Guðspjallabók*) or a ritual, printed (and perhaps translated) by Jón Arason. If so, the claims of the reformers to the first Bible translations must be accordingly modified. Though this book was lost—perhaps frowned upon by the reformers—it may have left traces on later books of its kind.

The first full translation of the New Testament was the work of Oddur Gottskálksson (1500 or 1515–56), the son of a Norwegian bishop of Hólar and an Icelandic mother. Educated in Norway, Denmark, and Germany and secretly converted to Lutheranism, he became the private secretary of the last Catholic bishop of Skálholt (*ca.* 1534–36). Here he started his translation, working in a cowshed to keep warm and out of the way of the crusty old bishop. The New Testament, printed in Denmark in 1540, is the oldest book printed in Icelandic and still preserved. Its significance among the Icelandic Bible translations was, of course, paramount. It was not only used by Guðbrandur Þorláksson in his Bible and in all succeeding editions, but it has been claimed by experts that there is relatively more of Oddur's translation preserved in the last Bible translation (1908–12) than there is of Luther's Bible in the latest German editions. Though the language shows some German influence on vocabulary and syntax, it was in general forceful and clear, a worthy upholder of the Old Icelandic religious prose tradition.

As a basis for his translation, Oddur used the *Vulgata*, a Latin translation by Erasmus, and Luther's translation (probably the Nürnberg edition of 1524). He may also have used the Swedish version of 1524 (Magnús Már Lárusson).

Though the New Testament was not nearly as epoch-making in Icelandic literary history and the history of Icelandic prose as were similar works in Germany, Denmark, and Sweden, where no prior prose works of note existed, the fact that the translation was made was of great importance for the future of the Icelandic language. It was precisely at this fateful juncture that the destinies of Norway and Iceland parted company. Instead of utilizing the Icelandic Bible text made by their own countryman, Oddur, the Norwegians adopted the Danish Bible and Danish devotional works, thus cutting their cultural roots in the old soil. The effect was a deplorable decline in literature and language during which the continuity with the old language was irretrievably lost.

Attempts to translate or publish other parts of the Bible were negligible until Bishop Guðbrandur Þorláksson published the whole Bible at Hólar in 1584. This was the greatest work of that most energetic publisher among the reformers.

Guðbrandur Þorláksson was born in 1542 at Staðarbakki in Mið-fjörður, the son of a Catholic priest and his mistress, who were married shortly after the Reformation. After being graduated from the Latin School at Hólar and teaching there for a year, Guðbrandur went to Copenhagen to study theology at the University (1560–64) with the leading professors of the time, some of whom were said to vie in learning with Tycho Brahe himself. Guðbrandur became a typical humanist scholar, knowing Latin and Greek, if not Hebrew; he was a mathematician, an astronomer, and a surveyor, the first to determine the geographical position of Iceland and map the country reasonably well. And he was musician enough to print the notes in his *Hymnbook* and his *Graduale*. Back in Iceland, Guðbrandur served as a headmaster of the Skálholt school and as a parson at Hólar before, finally, he became bishop at Hólar in 1571, an office he held until his death in 1627.

Guðbrandur used what he found well enough translated by his predecessors, above all Oddur Gottskálksson's New Testament and certain books of the Old Testament translated by Gissur Einarsson. There were other translations, but so poor that he either could not use them or had to change them considerably. His own translation was done spasmodically, when he could find time from the pressing tasks of the bishopric and his own voluminous business. He was a skillful translator, writing in a clear and easy style, though his work was naturally subject to the same objections, due to the German-Danish element, as Oddur's translation. The printing of this monumental work was done with great care; it was adorned with woodcuts and ornamental initials, some of which may have stemmed from the bishop's own hand, though most were of foreign (German) origin. The printing of the Bible took two years. It was printed in 500 copies that sold for the amount of two to three cows each, and was published in 1584.

This Bible was revised by Bishop Þorlákur Skúlason (1637–44) after the Danish Bible, resulting in a deterioration of the language, and the two revised editions following it before 1800 (" Steins-biblía " 1728 and " Waisenhúss-biblía " 1747) reflected the same general decline, especially " Steins-biblía."

Sermons and service books

In addition to the Bible, the leaders of the Reformation translated several books for divine service in the church and in the homes. Among the earliest was a book of sermons, the *Postilla* by Antonius Corvinus, translated by Oddur Gottskálksson and published in 1546. It was intended for parsons to read from the pulpit or to be read in the homes. The author was a popular preacher in Germany; his book inaugurated a long series of postils in Iceland, though only that of Jón Vídalín won lasting fame, due to its high literary quality. Next came *Ein kristileg handbók* (A Christian Manual, 1555), a manual for clergymen, containing collects (*óracíur*) for the whole year, funeral sermons, prayers, and hymns, compiled and translated by Marteinn Einarsson, bishop of Skálholt. Another " book with collects, epistles, and gospels in the vernacular " was compiled by Ólafur Hjaltason, bishop of Hólar, printed there in 1562. This ritual, often called the " Gospel-Book of Ólafur Hjaltason " to some extent set the pattern for all following rituals.

The Lutheran hymns

The Lutheran hymns were a new genre of poetry which could have revolutionized all poetry in Iceland had not some of the reformers, notably Guðbrandur Þorláksson, had the foresight to see and curb their dangerous tendency, turning them into native channels.

Tradition has long credited Bishop Ólafur Hjaltason with translating some hymns, but only recently has their existence been proven (by Magnús Már Lárusson). Otherwise the oldest hymnal is *Lítid Psálmakver* (A Small Hymn Book), translated by Marteinn Einarsson of Skálholt and added to his above-mentioned manual of 1555. It has been deemed " not very creditable to the bishop, since the translations are extremely bad, both as to form and language " (Halldór Hermannsson). It was followed by *Nokkrir Psálmar* (Some Hymns 1558), translated by Bishop Gísli Jónsson of Skálholt, " very similar to the first one both as to impurity of language and crudity of metrical form " (Hermannsson). Marteinn's thirty-five hymns were mostly by Luther or other German reformers, translated from the originals or from the Danish. Gísli's twenty-one hymns, by the same authors, were translated from the Danish only, likewise apparently those translated by Ólafur Hjaltason.

Halldór Hermannsson may have been a trifle too harsh a judge of Bishop Marteinn's hymns. For though simple and not quite faultless metrically his hymns compare quite favorably with similar translations in Scandinavia, which all seem to strive for prosaic simplicity and strict adherence to the originals. But the translations of Gísli are, indeed, the very poorest of these versions: they have no alliteration and hardly any rime, and are slavishly literal in the worst sense of the word, swallowing words and idioms wholesale. Such violations of form were nowhere to be found in Icelandic poetry, except in the "free versions" of the fifteenth-century ballads; but in poetic spirit most of the ballads were vastly superior to the hymns. And such a break with the native poetic tradition did not reappear before the "atom poets" of the twentieth century.

Guðbrandur Þorláksson revolted against the prosaic strivings of his predecessors and made a sincere attempt to put the hymns on a respectable basis compared to all other Icelandic poetry. He did this in *Ein ný Psálma Bók* (A New Hymn Book, 1589) as he tells expressly in the preface. His aspiration was not only to provide a book for the church service, but to replace with his hymns the "vain songs, *rímur* on trolls and champions, smutty and burning love songs, mockery and lampoons, invective and sarcastic songs," so popular among the common people at feasts, bridals, and wakes, since such hymns, according to him, had won popularity on all festive occasions in Germany and Denmark. He was convinced that this could only be done by exercising as much care in composing the sacred songs as was bestowed upon the despised secular poetry. Hence he did not try his own hand at the composition, but entrusted it to those who were specially blessed with the gifts of poetry. As such he singled out the Rev. Ólafur Guðmundsson of Sauðanes (1537–1609), a poet whom the good bishop seems to have overestimated a good deal in entrusting him with most of the translations.

The book contained more than 300 hymns of which only ten were signed by Icelandic authors, though eleven others may be Icelandic. A few stemmed from Hans Thomissön's Danish hymnal (1569). About seventy were translations of time-honored Latin Catholic hymns. But the great majority were translations of German Lutheran hymns, probably out of a hymnal from Strassburg, extant in many editions from the sixteenth century.

How did the translators succeed in carrying out the editor's wishes concerning the Icelandic metrical rules and the poetic diction? Only to a limited extent. They usually preserved the alliteration, but rime was often replaced by assonance. Worse, the natural stress of words was frequently violated; stressed syllables were often rimed or in assonance with unstressed ones. The diction frequently left much to be desired. Nevertheless, the book was an improvement on the earlier hymnbooks. Although the good bishop's ranting against the secular poetry was apparently an echo of German and Danish sentiments, the point was well taken, for the Icelandic secular poetry proved to be a tough opponent. He reiterated his attacks with *Ein Ný Vísnabók* (A New Song Book), but with similar lack of success. His hymnal was re-edited with small changes down to the middle of the eighteenth century.

If Ólafur Hjaltason reformed the church service, Guðbrandur Þorláksson fixed it for two centuries with his *Graduale, Ein Almennileg Messusöngs Bók* (Graduale, A General Mass Hymnal, 1594). This *Graduale* or *Grallari* as it was commonly called in Iceland, went through nineteen editions and was replaced by the hymnbook of 1801; in many churches it was used even down to the middle of the nineteenth century (Hermannsson). In the first edition the old Latin mass service was a good deal curbed, at least so that parsons could choose whether to use the Latin or the vernacular. But this was unpopular, and in the second edition of 1607 the Latin service was considerably increased. Guðbrandur was guided by the Danish *Graduale* of Jespersen (1573), both editors following the Church Ordinance of Christian III, dated September 2, 1537, composed by the German scholar Dr. Johann Bugenhagen Pommeranus.

The Lutheran hymnals continued in altered form the office of the Catholic Church. In general they also continued the meters current in the medieval sacred poetry and introduced into Iceland during the fifteenth century. They did differ in their revolt against the saintly subject matter: the great Mariolatry of the fifteenth century was curtailed or changed to adoration of Christ himself. The powers of the Devil were re-emphasized. The extreme prosaic form was also, as we have seen, characteristic of the Lutheran hymns.

Guðbrandur Þorláksson tried once more to come to grips with the " immoral " secular poetry, this time on its own terms. In *Ein Ný Vísnabók* (1612) he offered religious and didactic poetry, partly from early Catholic times with due correction of popish heresy (e. g., the beloved *Lilja* here printed for the first time), and partly poems composed by his contemporaries, foremost of whom was his friend the Rev. Einar Sigurðsson of Eydalir, comprising about half of the stout volume. By versifying the gospels in popular (*vikivakar*) meters rather than in the hymn measures and, more important, by turning Old Testament themes into the arch-secular form of *rímur*, the good bishop, though worn and disappointed by his long career of poorly received publications, had some hope of success. It was a new and signal failure. The Bible *rímur* had no chance against the time-honored themes of *fornaldar* and *lygi* sagas, the spirit of Christian devotion no chance against the spirit of heroic romance.

The spirit before and after the Reformation

After this survey of the activities of the Protestant reformers in Iceland, we shall pause and see the effect of the Reformation in contrast to Catholic times.

Though the accumulation of wealth by the Catholic Church was probably as pronounced in Iceland as elsewhere, there is no indication of any revolt against it except among the wealthiest chieftains. In general, the common people seem to have been content to revel in the richly ornamented churches and the ornate Mass, where Gregorian chant, illumination, and incense cast an irresistible religious spell over the congregation. The saints, the apostles, and the Virgin Mary were ever ready with their aid and intercession in return for votive offerings. Sins could be expiated in many ways: by good works and penance, or by direct payment to the Church; those who died in sin might have their stay in purgatory shortened by soul masses financed by their descendants. In such a system there was little reason for despair, except for the most inveterate sinners and enemies of the Church. This may be the reason that the Devil cuts a poor figure in folk tales laid before the Reformation, and why the last generation of Catholics seems so optimistic in outlook.

After the Reformation, the change for the common man must in many ways have been for the worse. The number of churches decreases as does the number of church holidays. The king's men rob the churches of valuables and saints' relics, breaking down crosses and statuary of the saints. The Latin Gregorian chant is to some extent replaced by congregational singing as poor in content as in execution. The parson reads an orthodox Corvinian sermon from the pulpit. Strictly forbidden recourse to Mary and the saints, the common man is to turn to a God as dread and distant as the king. There is no working off one's sins by good deeds nor atoning by payment to the Church, nor is there a purgatory to mitigate the hellish prospects after death. One may be saved only by the grace of God, but God is primarily not graceful at all, but a dread and just sovereign whose wrath no one can hope to soften. The Devil and his ilk now loom a good deal nearer than before; hell is much more of a threat. No wonder that some people begin to think that it is wiser to propitiate the evil powers and have their help in this life than to fight them in vain both on this and the other side of the grave. The soil is obviously ripe for the age of sorcery, the seventeenth century, with its black magic and sorcerer hunting in imitation of the witch hunting of Europe, with the significant difference that most of the Icelandic magicians were male.

Still, Lutheran orthodoxy did have its saving graces. It saved the erring genius, Jón Magnússon, plagued by black magic and devils, from utterly losing his mind. It inspired Hallgrímur Pétursson to his almost mystical union of love with his suffering Savior and to his magnificent contemplation of death. It, too, inspired Jón Vídalín's brilliant and eloquent attacks on the flesh, the world and the Devil. For most of the common people it, no doubt, offered an anchor of safety in the vicissitudes of an ever worsening world. And for the young it gave wholesome, sincere advice in some of the best didactic verse in the language.

The Icelandic Renaissance

Interest in learning

Looking back, the Lutherans claimed to see nothing but dense ignorance in Catholic times. But though their criticism must be taken with reservations, it cannot be denied that interest in learning was increased after the Reformation. We have already seen how reading was spurred by dissemination of printed books and the need for people to learn Luther's *Catechism*. On the higher levels, the leaders were not immune to the aspirations of the Renaissance and the budding natural sciences. The writing of annals was resumed by the Rev. Jón Egilsson (1548–1636) in the South and the farmer Björn Jónsson á Skarðsá (1574–1655) in the North. Both were connected with the sees, and though the bishops usually were more interested in Lutheran propaganda than native lore, Oddur Einarsson of Skálholt is on record as the earliest collector of Icelandic manuscripts. Among the native lore history, personal history, genealogy, and law bulked large.

What interest in grammar there was was obviously of foreign origin: the concern with orthography (Sigurður Stefánsson) everywhere followed in the wake of printing and the conventional attempts to derive the vernacular from Hebrew (Oddur Oddsson). More important was the interest in geography, spurred by the discoveries of the fifteenth century. Guðbrandur Þorláksson determined the geographical position of Hólar and made a map of Iceland, published in *Theatrum orbis terrarum* by A. Ortelius and G. Mercator. This map remained the best map of Iceland for a long time to come. The bishop made another map of Greenland and the Arctic. Sigurður Stefánsson (1570–95), rector of Skálholt, also drew a map of the North Atlantic and Greenland, but the fine work, *Qualisqunque descriptio Islandiae*, ascribed to him and destined to be buried in a German library until 1928, was actually written in 1589 by Oddur Einarsson (1559–1630), later bishop of Skálholt.

Sigurður also wrote *De geniis, umbris, spectris, larvis et monstris montanis* used by later writers on folklore, but now lost.

Arngrímur inn lærði

Most important of all writings on native lore and destined to lead to a real renaissance of Old Norse studies and the Viking spirit, first in Scandinavia, later, throughout the Germanic world, were the books of Arngrímur Jónsson inn lærði (the Learned).

Arngrímur Jónsson (1568–1648), born in Víðidalur of the Northwest, was a close relative of Bishop Guðbrandur, who helped him through the Latin School of Hólar (1585) and the University of Copenhagen (1589), after which he became headmaster of the Hólar school, chaplain at the Cathedral, and generally the bishop's right hand man. When the bishop fell ill in 1596, Arngrímur was appointed to officiate for him. When he died in 1627, Arngrímur was, as a matter of course, offered the bishopric, but he declined.

In 1561 there appeared in Hamburg a verse description of Iceland by a certain Gories Peerse or Gregorius Peerson, who obviously tried to cater to his public by telling them sensational stories about the savages of the distant island. And even more reputable authors, in their ignorance about the country, were not averse to publishing stories that had little basis in fact and often amounted to calumnies of the country, at least from an Icelandic point of view. Annoyed by this trend, the good bishop of Hólar had long hoped that some of his scholars would rise to refute the calumniators. It was reserved for the learned Arngrímur to do so in his *Brevis commentarius de Islandia*, a complete refutation of Gories Peerse and his boon companions, fittingly polemic in tone, but objective and instructive as to the real facts about the country, its inhabitants, and its culture. Arngrímur went to Copenhagen to publish the book (1593). It was reprinted with an English translation by R. Hakluyt in 1598. Arngrímur was to write two more polemic retorts: *Anatome Blefkeniana* (1612) and *Epistola pro patria defensoria* (1618), but fortunately he also found time to write something more constructive—the books *Crymogaea* (1609) and *Specimen Islandiae historicum et magna ex parte chorographicum* (1643). The first-named comprises a description of Iceland, its political and cultural history, the lives of its great men, and recent events. The last-named is partly polemic, but covers otherwise the same ground. Both books received a fairly wide circulation: *Crymogaea* was printed in extract in London in 1625. Arngrímur also wrote a book on Greenland in Latin ; it was not printed, but was used by later authors.

The scholarly world of Scandinavia was just ripe for the message of Arngrímur the Learned. In the Romance countries the Renaissance had pointed the way back to antiquity, to the illustrious examples of Greek and Roman literature. It had stimulated learning and imitation of the classic writers. In Scandinavia the Old Icelandic writings took the place of the Greco-Roman classics, becoming in the imagination of scholars and, as it turned out, in reality the classics of Scandinavian antiquity. And they were sorely needed. True, the Danes had their own Saxo Grammaticus. But the Swedes had nothing and the Norwegians only Snorri's *Heimskringla* which they by now began to translate into the modern idiom. Actually these translations first called attention to the promise of the Old Icelandic literature for the history and the antiquities of Scandinavia. Arngrímur's writings fullfilled this promise to a certain extent ; his correspondence with Scandinavian, notably Danish, scholars was also of great importance.

During his stay in Denmark (1592–93), Arngrímur had met two men who were to become royal historiographers. When one of them, Niels Krag, achieved the office, he lost no time in asking Arngrímur to collect manuscripts in Iceland. In 1596, this was reinforced by a royal command for Arngrímur to collect anything that might come in handy for writing the history of Denmark. Working fast, Arngrímur had his report ready in 1597. This report contained two long histories of Norway and Denmark and two short ones of Sweden and the Orkney Islands. This was compiled and digested from twenty-six vellum manuscripts, and care was taken to follow the Icelandic tradition even when it ran counter to Saxo or the opinion of modern scholars. This Icelandic point of view did not gain universal credence until about 1700 (Þormóður Torfason, Ludvig Holberg) ; after that it was the reigning opinion up to the present century. A definitive edition of all of Arngrímur's Latin works was published 1950-57 by Jakob Benediktsson in *Bibliotheca Arnamagnaeana.*

Ole Worm

Arngrímur's friend, the historiographer Krag, did not live to carry out his plans. After him Dr. Ole Worm (1588–1654), a physician and polyhistor of note, was to become the greatest promoter of Old Icelandic studies in Denmark. He was primarily interested in runes, but as he was convinced that the language of the runes was identical with

Icelandic, or as he called it the Old Danish tongue—to oppose the Swedes who called it *lingua Gothica*—he did his best to elucidate and publish the Old Icelandic literature. He helped to bring out Peder Claussön's (Friis) translation of *Heimskringla* (1633). He wrote and published *Runir seu Danica literatura antiquissima, vulgo Gothica dicta* (1636), deriving the runes as a matter of course from Hebrew, but printing also there the first specimens of Old Icelandic poetry (*Höfuðlausn* and *Kráku-mál*) with commentaries by Icelandic helpers. Worm carried on a voluminous correspondence with Arngrímur the Learned and other Icelandic friends in Latin. Never mastering the language fully, he also put some Icelanders to work on glossaries (Magnús Ólafsson) and the grammar of the language (Runólfur Jónsson, whose grammar was printed in 1651).

The activity of the Danish scholars, notably that of the royal historiographers, led to a collection of manuscripts in Iceland. The Swedes soon joined in this activity but carried on an uphill fight against their privileged Danish brethren. The search culminated with Árni Magnússon's great and, generally speaking, exhaustive collection.

Icelandic studies, 1600–1750

The interest in native lore kindled by Renaissance scholars like Arngrímur the Learned was to grow throughout the seventeenth century until it culminated in two great figures about 1700 and after: the historian Þormóður Torfason and the book collector and bibliographer Árni Magnússon.

The bishops Þorlákur Skúlason (1597–1656) of Hólar and Brynjólfur Sveinsson (1605–75) of Skálholt were both interested in Icelandic studies and both were collectors of manuscripts. Unfortunately, the former prevented the latter from establishing a printing press in Skálholt and there publishing Old Icelandic sagas. Brynjólfur had to be content with sending his most treasured manuscripts—among them the Eddic poems and *Flateyjarbók*—to the king for eventual publication.

About 1650, King Frederik III had asked Bishop Brynjólfur to come to Copenhagen and publish Icelandic manuscripts. The bishop declined but, as already mentioned, he sent some manuscripts to the king and broadcast the king's call for more manuscripts to the nation. The king established the office of an *interpres regius*, but the first incumbent was a shortlived drunkard. The second one, however, Þormóður Torfason (Torfaeus) (1636–1719), was not only a hard worker and a genuine scholar but a robust personality as well, whose checkered career there is unfortunately no space to consider here. Torfaeus collected manuscripts in Iceland and kept professional scribes to copy them. First, he translated many of the Old Icelandic sagas into Latin for his royal patrons— for he survived two of his kings. Later he wrote Latin historical works, based on the manuscripts, on the Faroe and Orkney Islands, on Vínland and Greenland (1705–1706), on Danish kings of antiquity, and finally his chief work: *Historia rerum Norvegicarum* (1711) in four folio volumes.

This was really a great historical synthesis from the Icelandic point of view, earning Torfaeus a well deserved reputation among scholars and in learned circles. Moreover, it was a historical view which was to prevail far down into the nineteenth century, if not even longer. If it is definitely uncritical from our point of view, no one could see that at the time except Torfaeus' exceptionally critical and learned friend, Árni Magnússon, who often helped him with his great history. The next great writer of Norwegian history, Ludvig Holberg, stood on Torfaeus' shoulders.

Árni Magnússon

Though Árni Magnússon (1663–1730) wrote very little himself, he is one of the greatest figures in Icelandic literary history because of his unique collection of Icelandic manuscripts. His critical bent was revealed in an early attack on witch-hunting as well as in numerous critical notes on his manuscripts. As a student at the University (1683–85) he helped Thomas Bartholin collect material to write *Antiquitatum Danicarum . . . libri tres*. After Bartholin's death, Árni Magnússon became a secretary in the Royal Archives, later (1701) a professor of Danish antiquities, the first to hold that chair. At that time he was busy helping Þormóður Torfason with his historical writings. In 1702–12 he and the lawyer Páll Vídalín were commissioned to make an inventory of all real estate in Iceland. This took them all over the country and gave Árni a unique opportunity to look for his coveted manuscripts. He acquired the remnants of the collections of the late bishops, Brynjólfur Sveinsson and Þórður Þorláksson, and the living bishops, Björn Þorleifsson and Jón Vídalín, helped him readily. When Árni left Iceland in 1712, his manuscripts remained behind in Skálholt as a result of the Sveco-Danish war. He received his fifty-five cases of books in 1720. When Þormóður Torfason died, Árni bought his sixty-two volumes of manuscripts. In general, it was his practice to purchase manuscripts from anyone and at any price. He kept two secretaries to copy and care for the collection. On October 20, 1728, Copenhagen caught fire. Árni thought himself safe, but eleven days later the fire caught up with him and his collection. Heroic efforts could save none of his printed books, but perhaps one third of his manuscripts survived according to the estimate of Finnur Jónsson, later bishop, who helped to save them. This torso is now the Arnamagnaean Collection in the University of Copenhagen. Fortunately, these were the oldest manuscripts, but the loss of manuscripts concerning later times in Iceland was appalling and irreparable. " Here go writings nowhere to be found in the wide world," was Árni's sad comment on the conflagration. No wonder that he was a broken man after that. Yet he set to work at once writing his friends, trying to fill the gaps, and he might have had some success had he not died, himself, shortly after (1730). Árni Magnússon had married a rich widow " who was a secret housecross for him " in order to indulge his collecting. He gave the collection to the University of Copenhagen after his death and provided money for editing the rich treasures.

Among Árni Magnússon's contemporaries were many annalists and scholars. His collaborator Páll Vídalín excelled in law; Jón Thorchillius, rector of Skálholt, wrote on literary history; and Jón Halldórsson (1665–1736), parson of Hítardalur, amassed materials and wrote voluminously on the ecclesiastical history of the country. He was not only the carnal but also the spiritual ancestor of the two scholars and bishops, son and grandson, Finnur Jónsson (1704–89) and Hannes Finnsson (1739–96).

Secular Poetry, 1550-1750

Introductory remarks

The secular poetry after the Reformation may be divided in three parts: the old *rímur*, the new *vikivakar* for dancing, and other lyric forms, mostly new.

But here a warning is in order. Just as it is impossible to separate the poets themselves into sacred and profane, so there is often no hard and fast boundary between the sacred and secular lyric, although the extremes may be clear enough. In general, the first two generations after the Reformation (Einar Sigurðsson, Ólafur Einarsson) tend to be sacred in outlook (in response perhaps to Guðbrandur Þorláksson's call) while the third (Stefán Ólafsson) is secular with a strong tinge of the Renaissance. Hallgrímur Pétursson belongs to that third generation and can be almost as worldly as Stefán, but he is also the supreme hymnodist of the whole period. After the two great men there is a decline with secular poetry perhaps slightly predominating, though its final representative Páll Vídalín cannot compete with Stefán Ólafsson.

Rímur (1550–1750)—metrical romances

The *rímur* received a fresh impulse toward complexity in metrical form by the first post-Reformation generation: Hallur Magnússon (1530–1601) and Þórður Magnússon á Strjúgi (fl. 1575). Hallur named several meters in his *rímur*, but a *Háttalykill* of *rímur* (seventy-four meters) attributed to him, belongs to the seventeenth century. Þórður carried the inrime to its logical end in *sléttubönd* (in *Rollants rímur*, ca. 1590). In this meter, every word in the first half of the quatrain (*ferskeytt*) rimes with a corresponding word in the second half, and the whole can be read backwards as well as forwards:

Mettur rómur, meyrnar mér   dettur ómur heyrnar hér,
máttur glettu-góma,   háttur sléttu óma.

[185]

Before the Reformation, inrime was one of the chief means of variation, either within the line (transversal) or between lines (longitudinal). After the Reformation it was supplemented or even supplanted by consonantal assonance. With this artificiality in meters, that increased their numbers up to the nineteenth century, went growing professional pride of the poets, who now started to sign their names, though often in acrostics or runes. One would have believed that the *rímur* would lose in popularity what they gained in art form, but the opposite was true. During the period they were composed by lay and learned alike, the greatest (Hallgrímur Pétursson) and the most insignificant, except as it seems by some "highbrow" poets of the East (Stefán Ólafsson and Bjarni Gissurarson). They were widely enjoyed, and they were as immune to the strictures of the pious Danish Order of House Discipline at the end of the period (1746) as they had been to the fulminations of Bishop Guðbrandur at its beginning. He had indeed bowed to their supremacy when suggesting the new genre of Bible *rímur*. And after 1600 their supremacy was such that almost all occasional verse (*lausavísur*) was cast in the popular quatrain form (*ferskeyttla*). One might also have thought that the difficult form would restrain the productivity of the poets, but again that was not the case. Jón Guðmundsson in Rauðseyjar (*ca.* 1575–1650) at an advanced age gave his number of *rímur* as 189; Guðmundur Bergþórsson in 1701 reckoned his total as 232, adding another 24 before his death.

Apart from the new Bible *rímur*, the topics of *rímur* remained much the same as before: *riddara sögur* and *lygi sögur*, to which would now be added foreign chapbooks of related matter. A few were humorous, mostly burlesque, like Þórður Magnússon's *Fjósa ríma* and the *Grobbians rímur* of Jón Magnússon (1601–75) with matter of German origin. After the Reformation, *mansöngur* lost its original meaning of love song and could be used for any topic whatever by the poets.

Vikivakar

A new dance form replaced the ballad during the second half of the sixteenth century. This was the so-called *vikivaki* (Engl. wigglewaggle?), a stationary ring dance of bodies rocking forwards and sideways, men and women holding hands and singing more or less long poems thereto. This dancing—first described by Arngrímur Jónsson in *Crymogaea* (1609)—became enormously popular during the seventeenth century but was rooted out by the pious clergy before the end of the eighteenth in response, apparently, to the Order of House Discipline (1746).

The form of the *vikivakar* is related to that of the ballads. As in the ballads, there is always a refrain-stem (*stef-stofn*), a stanza of two, three or four (or more) lines from which matter is taken for a refrain (*viðlag*), variously worked into all the stanzas of the poem. But unlike the ballad stanzas, the average stanzas of the *vikivakar* are much more complicated in form. There are many four-line stanzas, a great many of six and eight, quite a few of ten and more. When long, the stanzas become complicated structures woven of two distinct strands: the refrain in bits, sometimes overlapping and variegated, and the stanza parts proper, often two lines together inserted between the parts of the refrain. One would think such complicated structures late; on manuscript evidence they are at least earlier than 1676 (*Litars bátur leita má*, Ólafur Davíðsson, *Íslenzkir vikivakar*, p. 232). An earlier and simpler example is Einar Sigurðsson's "Kvæði af stallinum Kristi" (*Emanúel heitir hann*, in Bishop Guðbrandur's *Vísnabók*, 1612, p. 105).

The refrain-stems are obviously often old ballad verses and share in the lyric mood of the ballads. Many of them are beautiful, indeed. But apart from the refrains, the *vikivakar* share more the precious and ornate diction of *rímur* and *dróttkvæði*. At best they are brightly scintillating structures, at worst they are turgid and obscure, but rarely do they lose the powerful swing of the dance rhythm. They are indeed music in words.

In spite of the skaldic diction and obligatory alliteration, rime is the main structural element of the *vikivakar* stanzas, mostly alternating or run-on rime.

As one would expect from dance songs, several of the *vikivakar* are composed in praise of women, not least of their bodily charms. If they often have an erotic tinge, they are seldom obscene. In some the opposite sexes mock each other; others are pure love poems. Many are seriously didactic with good Christian counsel to the girls and the boys. And there are not a few purely religious poems in the lot, in response, perhaps to Bishop Guðbrandur's call for sacred songs on all festive occasions. The above-mentioned poem by the Rev. Einar Sigurðsson (1538–1626) would fit that description. And there are several parsons among the authors: Ólafur Jónsson á Söndum (1560–1627), Hallgrímur Pétursson (1614–74), Bjarni Gissurarson (1621–1712). Of laymen may be mentioned: Björn Jónsson á Skarðsá (1574–1655), Steinunn Finnsdóttir í Höfnum (1641–?), and Guðmundur Bergþórsson (1657–1705).

A special kind of *vikivaki* is the ornate and rhythmic *Tröllaslagur* (Troll dance) first reported as old by Magnús Ólafsson í Laufási (1573–1636). The enormously popular *Grýlu kvæði*, designed to thrill children, if not scare them, were always cast in a ballad form.

Lyric poetry

Apart from *rímur* and *vikivakar*, the secular lyric would use alliterative riming stanza forms similar in structure to those of the fifteenth-century sacred poetry and those of the Lutheran hymns, mostly representing foreign songs and to a lesser degree native invention. The border between sacred and secular was always fluid, and it stands to reason that Protestant wags might parody Catholic hymns. Stefán Ólafsson's profane use of *Stabat mater dolorosa* and *Út á djúpið hann Oddur dró* might be cases in point. One poet only attempts the classical hexameter and pentameter (*Ó þú feigðarfox, fölvan eg meina þig dauði,* by the Rev. Jón Guðmundsson (1558–1634) in Hítardalur), but the leonine hexameter was used by Hallgrímur Pétursson and others. A few other classical meters might be used in translations from the classics, as well as by those who actually wrote Latin poetry, and they were quite numerous, but change of meter was not unusual in translations. As in *rímur* and *vikivakar*, there was a development from simpler to more complex forms, clearly visible by comparison of grandfather and grandson: Einar Sigurðsson and Stefán Ólafsson. Even the styles of the two contrast: Einar is classical and simple, Stefán twisted and baroque.

Some of the themes are very old: the epitaph, both as a praise poem and lament, going back to the earliest skalds. It increased in vigor and religiosity during the period. Instances are: the poem on Jón Arason and his sons by Ólafur Tómasson (1532–95), Eiríkur Árnason's *in memoriam* of his wife (d. 1559), and Hallgrímur Pétursson's great poems on the death of his daughter, Steinunn.

Some of the heroic poems of the *Edda* and the *fornaldar* sagas had been cast in an autobiographical form, but real autobiographical poems appeared first after the Reformation (Einar Sigurðsson, the Rev. Jón Bjarnason, Presthólum [*ca.* 1560–1630], and Jón Indíafari).

Many themes bear testimony to the fact that they, like the hymns, have grown out of constant preoccupation with three enemies: the Devil, the flesh, and the world, all equally tempting and all forbidden. The Devil and his ilk, the sorcerers and the ghosts that they raise to harass or kill their enemies, were fought both by lay *kraftaskáld* (poets wielding magic powers) like Jón Guðmundsson lærði and by learned exorcists of the church itself, like the Reverends Magnús Pétursson (1603–86) and Jón Daðason (1606–76) who frowned upon the efforts of a tyro like Jón lærði, considering him no better than a black magician. The poems have telling titles, " Devil-scare," " Shield," " Angels' Coat of Mail," and " Turks' Lullaby," designed to put to eternal sleep the damned " Turks " from Algier, who in 1627 had raided Iceland for slaves. Some of these exorcist poems are long and eloquent, others, like the extemporaneous wishes or curses of the *kraftaskáld*, short and pithy; such verses were attributed to Hallgrímur Pétursson. These were the poetical symptoms of the age of sorcery. A more serious manifestation of it was the burning at the stake of twenty-five sorcerers, mostly men, in the period 1625–85. Though magic was pre-Christian in Iceland, this particular wave came from abroad, the practice having flared up in Catholic and Protestant countries alike shortly after the Reformation.

Love was suspect as a temptation of the flesh and rarely found expression, except in beautiful refrains or brazen *vikivakar*. Indeed, the only personal love lyrics of the period seem to be those of Páll Jónsson (Staðarhóls Páll) and Stefán Ólafsson. In Páll's poetry we first meet the European courtly love tradition of the paramour in a setting of nature; the poet finds her as a beautiful flower in a garden. In another poem, he takes a morning walk and finds a beautiful grove, observing its development from daybreak to noon, and its withering in the afternoon storm. This has been interpreted as an allegory of his first tempestuous but shortlived love affair; but in any case, it is the conventional motif of the round of human life. The love letter he wrote in his old age was less conventional and surprisingly serene. Although there may be doubt whether Stefán Ólafsson's two love poems are actually personal, they are both beautiful laments for a lost love.

None of the three anathemas of the seventeenth-century orthodoxy were as constantly before the vision of the poets as was the world. From the Catholic Skáld-Sveinn there was an unbroken and variegated row of satires of this world (*heimsósómar, heimsádeilur, aldarhættir, aldasöngvar, tíðavísur, tímarímur*) that persisted to the nineteenth century. To many the world was dark because they compared it to the heavenly Jerusalem (Bjarni skáldi). Others saw the present world in decline in comparison with some good old times of the past. To some this was the Catholic past with its ornamented churches, illuminated manuscripts, and statuary—now all broken and burned (Einar Sigurðsson, Bjarni skáldi, Ólafur Einarsson); to others still it was the ancient Icelandic heathen world, a daring humanistic point of view, taken by no less a Christian than Hallgrímur Pétursson himself. Often the satire took the concrete form of attacking or lamenting the decline of Iceland itself, and predicting its quick ruin. Þórður Magnússon á Strjúgi seems to be the first to voice this sentiment (*Reyndar verður stutt stund / að standa náir Ísland*). It was echoed by the Rev. Ólafur Jónsson á Söndum (1560–1627) and others. But there were also those who, like Einar Sigurðsson, in reaction to this praised the country, thus inaugurating the patriotic theme that was to be powerfully developed in Eggert Ólafsson and culminate in the poetry of the nineteenth century.

There were many more ways of attacking the world in earnest: pointing out the uneven lot of rich and poor, the mutability of man's lot, false friends and false fortune; but this must suffice by way of example.

Fortunately, however, there were also all kinds of escape or even revolt from the world. *Rímur* and *vikivakar* often represented such an escape, as did the worldly pleasures of beer and wine, tobacco, and— horses. The first convivial song actually appears in the poetry of the pious and moderate Rev. Ólafur Jónsson á Söndum, the use of this theme was continued in the West by Hallgrímur Pétursson and in the East by Ólafur Einarsson and Stefán Ólafsson. The earliest tobacco verses are attributed (with some doubt) to the Reverends Einar Guð-mundsson (1585–1649) and Jón Jónsson á Melum (1596–1663) but they were taken up by Hallgrímur Pétursson and Stefán Ólafsson, who himself seems to have introduced the praise of horses (*hesta-vísur*, " horse verses "). And, indeed, if Stefán Ólafsson was not the author of these humorous genres, he did more than most to make them popular.

Toward the end of the period the Rev. Benedikt Jónsson í Bjarnanesi (1664–1744) listed three desirable worldly things in his escapist *heims-lystarvísur*: good horses, ordained parsons for the fair sex, and fair girls for the men. His nineteenth-century imitators substituted sailing a good boat for the preaching parson, but to the poets of our period sailing the sea was no more attractive than nature itself. Thus Magnús Ólafsson (1573–1636) and Guðmundur Erlendsson (1595–1670) saw the sea only as sinister in their sailing poems, and Björn Jónsson á Skarðsá (1574–1655) only the harsh aspects of winter. But the optimist Stefán Ólafsson and his friend Bjarni Gissurarson seem to have begun to see and appreciate nature to some extent in their poetry, especially Bjarni in his fine poems on the sun.

Poetical epistles both in Latin and in Icelandic are, apparently, first preserved from this period. The two secretaries of Bishop Brynjólfur, Stefán Ólafsson and Bjarni Gissurarson write to each other. A great many of the latter's epistles have been preserved.

Topsy-turvy style

In Europe the revolt of the Reformation and the Renaissance had been not only in doctrine, but also in form. Thus Erasmus had used irony as the instrument of his satire in *Moriae Encomium*, which was belatedly emulated by Þorleifur Halldórsson in his *Mendacii Encomium* (1703, published by Halldór Hermannsson, *Islandica* 1915) and was translated into Icelandic by Hjörleifur Þórðarson in 1730. The antecedent of this literature is found in Sebastian Brant's *Narrenschiff* (1494).

Likewise Rabelais had evolved a grotesque and burlesque style in attacking the vast learning of the Catholic clergy and the notorious immorality of the monks. The Rabelaisian spirit and style was not slow in spreading to Germany, the source of the Lutheran Reformation.

In Iceland there was no real Protestant or Renaissance satire, although there are some echoes of it in the translated sermons. But the topsy-turvy style, burlesque and grotesque, did, somehow, penetrate to the country and was there used for humoristic purposes. Introduction of this new comic style was made easier because of the already existing mock-heroic *Skíða ríma* and in continuation thereof the *Fjósa ríma* of Þórður Magnússon á Strjúgi. But the " paradoxes " (*öfugmælavísur—Verkehrte Welt*) of Bjarni skáldi were the essence of topsy-turviness, and their vogue in Europe (France, Germany, Scandinavia) seems to me understandable only if they were a harmless, playful outgrowth of the anything but harmless Renaissance satire. In Iceland the topsy-turviness of the *öfugmæli* paradoxes was only exceeded by the satirical epigrams of Æri-Tobbi (Mad-Tobbi, i. e., Þorbjörn vitlausi, fl. *ca.* 1650) who actually used nonsense words to fill his lines, of which many a modern poet might be proud. Topsy-turvy exaggeration is pursued in Bjarni skáldi's " Lundúnarkvæði " (a mock-encomium *urbis*), in Jón Guðmundson í Rauðseyjum's " Lákakvæði " (the mock-adventure journey of a drinking keg), in Hallgrímur Pétursson's " Þráðar-leggsvísur " (listing the impossible things that one would rather do than winding a " leg " of yarn), and in Bjarni Gissurarson's " Hrakfallabálkur " (a chain of unheard of disasters happening to an unhappy man).

Less topsy-turvy but still burlesque is the style of the great humorist of the age, Stefán Ólafsson. His mood may vary from genial horseplay to biting satire of his farmhands or his thriftless neighbors, but his style is usually baroque-realistic. One almost suspects that he may have derived his point of view from Denmark, where the lot of the poor villein peasants was no better than in Germany or in western Europe in general.

Jón Guðmundsson lærði

Jón Guðmundsson lærði (1574–1658) well represents the superstition and learning of his age. In spite of his nickname " Learned " he was not a learned man but a lay autodidact. Hailing from the witchcraft-ridden Vestfirðir, he began his career by laying a ghost with his *Snæ-fjallavísur*, a forceful bit of magic poetry. But if he won the admiration and thanks of those concerned, he also incurred the enmity of church and state, whose watchdogs took the first opportunity to snap at him and chase him all over the country, even out of it. Even Ole Worm's interest in his runes could not save him from the fate of spending his last years in misery in a sort of island asylum granted him by friends, like Bishop Brynjólfur, in the East of Iceland. Here he wrote most of his variegated works : his own life in verse, poems and articles on fairies and " mountain folks " (*útilegumenn*), books on medicine, an omnibus on superstition called *Tíðfordríf* (Pastime), notes written for his benefactor the bishop, and a natural history of Iceland, the first one attempted in the vernacular, called *Um Íslands aðskiljanlegar náttúrur* (On the Diverse Natures of Iceland). This supplemented in several ways—notably in the discussion of the whales—the Latin work written by Bishop Gísli Oddsson on the same subject : *Annalium in Islandia farrago* and *De mirabilibus Islandiae*, 1637–38. It was published by Halldór Hermannsson in *Islandica* XV, 1924.

Jón Ólafsson Indíafari

Jón Ólafsson Indíafari (1593–1679), hailing from Vestfirðir and dying there in his old age, was among the first to write an autobiography in Modern Icelandic : *Æfisaga Jóns Ólafssonar Indíafara*. It comprised chiefly the memories of his travels in Denmark, England, and India. It is the only representative in Iceland of the great Renaissance travel literature. This work is not only of considerable historical value for the countries concerned—whence an English translation was issued by the Hakluyt Society in 1923—but it is written with such verve and such captivating naiveté that when belatedly published (1908–1909), it took the public by storm and inspired progressive authors, like Þórbergur Þórðarson, to imitate its style. As a musketeer in the service of the enterprising Danish monarch, Jón knew his king and master personally and could at times break through the barriers of baroque society to the simple comradeship of an Old Icelandic skald. Jón's observations must have been keen and his memory sharp, for he wrote the book in his old age (1661) without the benefit of contemporary journals. The language is vigorous—full of sailor's jargon and foreign words. It is also evident that Jón's style had fallen into the ruts of the German-Danish habits of the time. Both facts contribute to the burlesque-naive tinge of the work which constitutes its greatest charm for modern readers.

The *Æfisaga* (Life) was published by Sigfús Blöndal, 1908–1909.

Jón Magnússon

Jón Magnússon (1610–96) was certainly the most characteristic and probably the most important writer in the age of sorcery and witchcraft. As a parson at Eyri, Skutilsfjörður in the Vestfirðir, he was in 1655 stricken by a strange malady caused, in his opinion, by the witchcraft of two of his parishioners, father and son. Unable to clear themselves, they were burned at the stake, but as the parson did not recover, he now accused a daughter of the family, who, when cleared, claimed damages from the parson. It was then that he wrote his *Píslarsaga* (Passion Story), a most astounding description of his sufferings, an apology of his acts, and an angry *J'accuse* against the leniency of the secular officers handling the case and cases of witchcraft in general. When the *Píslarsaga* was belatedly published (1914) its eloquence and seemingly absurd claims fascinated the incredulous public. But as in many other cases it was reserved for Nordal to give it its critical due: " It is truly a great cultural document—in my opinion the greatest literary monument left in any country by the raging age of witchcraft—a record of the disease and a rich fountain of genuinely popular language. But it has many more facets than that. The author's rich style and never faltering phantasy rank him with the most gifted of our writers. There is much more to writing the best passages of the *Píslarsaga* than being half-crazy or a master of popular speech. These passages vie with similar spots in the writings of Strindberg and Fröding where these great men describe their insanity. And the *Píslarsaga* bears eloquent testimony not only to the spiritual malady of the writer's age but also to its strength: the great orthodoxy in the history of Icelandic Christianity. In these confessions *de profundis* we can gauge the power of this type of religion under a test not to be matched in the ordinary religious writings of the sixteenth to the eighteenth centuries."

The *Píslarsaga* was published by Sigfús Blöndal 1912–14.

Páll Jónsson

Páll Jónsson (1535–98), often nicknamed Staðarhóls-Páll, was one of three brothers, all prefects in the North and West, descended from Loptr ríki. His brother Magnús Jónsson prúði (1532–91) helped to revolutionize the *rímur* with his *Pontus rímur* (1564). Páll's lyrics were as subjective and picturesque as his own personality, he being as rash and impetuous as his brother was steady. He fell passionately in love with a granddaughter of Bishop Jón Arason, Helga, a proud and eccentric lady whom he wooed in fervent poems in the courtly love tradition. Once married they are said to have lain together for six weeks at a stretch. But reaction was bound to come, and they were soon fighting like cats and dogs, the poet venting his spite and disdain in verses that now were more in the native *níðskáld* (invective) tradition. When she left him for good, his mood at first seemed to mellow, if we may believe his poem " Hugleiðing og heilræði " (Reflection and Good Advice), but soon he was bringing a suit against her, charging her with stubbornness, contention, and insubordination. After a while Páll was sending poetic epistles to a daughter of Bishop Guðbrandur Þorláksson, this time in vain. Páll's occasional verses bear ample testimony to his quick temperament, his courage, and his wit. Those who knew him best felt that there was a heart of gold under his blustering exterior.

Einar Sigurðsson

Einar Sigurðsson (1538–1626), parson and poet, was not only one of the greatest spiritual poets of his age, but also the ancestor of a numerous progeny of common people, parsons and poets. His son and grandson, Ólafur Einarsson and Stefán Ólafsson, counted among the best poets of their day. The son of a poor parson, he too, eked out a meager living as a parson in the North, having married twice and had many children by both wives. But fortune smiled on him after his first-born, Oddur Einarsson, became bishop of Skálholt, and invited the whole family there. Soon after (1590) he gave his father the fat parsonage of Eydalir in the East, and here he raised his family, became a well-to-do man and a good poet. He contributed " gospel verses," Bible *rímur*, and other devotional didactic poetry to Guðbrandur Þorláksson's *Vísnabók*, practically the whole first part of the book. Yet much of his poetry remains unpublished. In his youth he did not confine his output to the divine Muse, and at thirty he had a vision compelling him to recant his past. After that his poetry was devoted to the praise of God, thanksgivings, prayers, exhortations and advice. Like the last generation of Catholics he was drawn to the brighter side of Christianity: in his great output there is only one poem on Doomsday. Instead he has a beautiful poem on the Virgin Mary (*Maríuvísur*) deploring the neglect of her memory after the Reformation. To those who blame the country for the national decline, he retorts that it is a good land! As the father of a family, he loved to address his children and descendants, counting one hundred alive in a poem composed the last year of his life. His poetry is mild and serene, imbued with childlike simplicity and trust in God. His measures are mostly light and popular; he uses lullabies, *vikivakar*, and ballad refrains with telling effect.

Ólafur Einarsson

Ólafur Einarsson (1573–1651), son of the preceding, studied in Copenhagen and was headmaster of the Skálholt school before he became parson and dean at Kirkjubær in the East. Like his father he composed mostly religious poetry; his hymns were cast in the measures of the first hymnbooks, but with a vastly improved execution. Unlike his father, but like others of his day, he showed an increased concern and respect for the Devil. Like most, he looked back wistfully to the good old days and had harsh words to say about the trade monopoly and the sloth of his countrymen. He anticipated not only his son Stefán's satire of lazy farmhands and poor good-for-nothing crofters, but also his convivial poetry. Indeed the two, father and son, collaborated on the drinking song *Krúsar lögur*. He handed on to his descendants the poetic gift as well as his mother's proneness to nervous breakdown. In form, he appears to have reacted against the use of refrains in sacred poems, which his father had used with skill, but which had apparently been overdone by Ólafur's contemporaries.

Bjarni Jónsson skáldi

Bjarni Jónsson skáldi (*ca.* 1575–1655), of Húsafell in Borgarfjörður of the West, was one of the most original poets of his day. Though apparently a farmer, he left a good deal of religious poetry unusual in depth of feeling and sense of beauty. As a satirist, he took the same point of view as Ólafur Einarsson, but his satire was sharper, his wistful longing for the beauty of the Catholic churches more poignant (" Alda-söngur "). One would hardly have expected a farmer to be the first to introduce the playful paradoxes of the Renaissance (in France and Germany) derived from the classical *adynata*, called *Verkehrte Welt* in German, *öfugmæli* in Icelandic, but he actually set a fashion with his *öfugmælavísur*. Related in spirit is his " Lundúnar-kvæði," a mock-heroic praise of a small croft in his district (encomium *urbis*). He wrote *rímur* and had the honor of having one of his cycles continued by the greatest poet of the century, Hallgrímur Pétursson.

Hallgrímur Pétursson

We come now to the greatest poet of the seventeenth century and one of the greatest religious poets that Iceland has fostered: Hallgrímur Pétursson.

Hallgrímur Pétursson (1614–74) was born in or near Hólar, where he grew up with his father, a relative of Bishop Guðbrandur and sexton of the Cathedral. Under such favorable circumstances one would have expected a swift and smooth career for the young man, but if he ever entered the Cathedral school, he was apparently soon expelled for his sharp verses and his waggish tongue. Running away to Denmark, he became a blacksmith's apprentice in Copenhagen. According to legend, the future Bishop Brynjólfur Sveinsson came upon him in the black-smith's shop cursing vigorously in Icelandic. He put this wayward rela-tive of his in the famous *Frúar skóli* (Notre Dame) in Copenhagen; here Hallgrímur got a solid Latin-humanist education of almost four years (1632–36). He was still in the fourth class when fate—or the Devil—prepared for him a temptation and a fall which far outdistanced his youthful indiscretions.

In the summer of 1627 the peace-loving and defenceless survivors of the Vikings in Iceland were stunned by a raid of Algerian pirates on their shores. These " Turks " as the Icelanders called them, robbed, slew, and carried away for the slave market shiploads of Icelanders, among whom was a young married woman from Vestmannaeyjar by the name of Guðríður Símonardóttir. Nine years later this lady was ransomed for 200 *ríkisdalir*—a cow was then worth only four *rd*—and, with a number of her countrymen similarly situated, sent back to Denmark on the way to her native land. In Copenhagen, Hallgrímur Pétursson was entrusted with the task of refreshing the religion of these people, weeding out any chaff of Mohammedanism that still might linger in their minds. If the 22-year-old Hallgrímur succeeded in this, he also succeeded in succumbing to the exotic charms of the 38-year-old Guðríður. They had a child barely a year after her arrival in Copenhagen, and so Hallgrímur was guilty of adultery of the worst kind, since she was still, as far as they knew, a married woman. Fortunately for them, her husband had actually died, so that, home in Iceland, they had only to expiate for what amounted to a minor first offence of this kind. For a while (1637–44) Hallgrímur worked as a poor laborer and fisherman near Keflavík and soon he was made the parson at Hvalsnes. Then he was promoted to a much better living, Saurbær on Hvalfjörður, where he served as a fairly well-to-do parson for many years (1651–69). Then, having retired because of leprosy, he died blind at the nearby Ferstikla (1674).

Not counting the three *rímur* cycles of Hallgrímur, in which he showed great mastery of form, his secular poetry does not amount to one fourth of his voluminous production, and even so it was often permeated by his religiosity. But though he took a dark view of the world in general, we often find him yielding to a mellower and merrier mood. His praise of good food, beer, and tobacco was mockingly fulsome, his descriptions of rustic activities, like mowing hay or winding a " leg " of yarn, were extravagant burlesques. His thumbnail sketches of farmhands and neighbors were much gentler in their humor than similar poems by his colleague, Stefán Ólafsson. His satire could be sharp. In " Aldarháttur " (Ways of the Present World), it was humanistic and pagan, comparing the Golden Age of the Icelandic Commonwealth, with its military virtues and heroic deeds, to the present. Its leonine hexameter evoked the Renaissance spirit, its rich diction the skaldic style. Not only did Hallgrímur employ skaldic style and meters, but he was also considered, by scholars like Brynjólfur Sveinsson and Þormóður Torfason, one of the authorities of his age on Old Icelandic poetry. In some of his Christian didactic poems there are touches of *Hávamál*.

But chiefly Hallgrímur's satire was of the Christian kind, contrasting this evil world, ever worsening, and the brilliant picture of the happy world to come—for those who are not destined to go to the darker world after death. Naturally, there is much that was conventional in these descriptions, but one must not forget that Hallgrímur's was a dark age of poverty and depression with the poor either sunk in slothfulness or prone to boisterous ribaldry (like Hallgrímur's neighbors at Hvalsnes), while the rich were given to ostentation, pride and graft. Hallgrímur himself, though learned and not badly off, always identified himself with the poor common people. His censure of falseness, guile, bribery, and mockery has an authentic ring.

If Hallgrímur's satire fell short of Bjarni skáldi's fulminations, it was because of Hallgrímur's more positive nature, nowhere as evident as in his wise Christian counsel to young and old, timeless and classic in its simplicity and directness. Apart from his "Heilræðavísur" (Good Counsel) still on the lips of most Icelandic children, he composed a long row of hymns on related subjects. Otherwise his hymns dealt with the inconstancy and fickleness of this world and death; some were seasonal (New Year, summer, winter), others occasional (bridals, table, travel hymns) or prayers. His Bible hymns, like those of Einar Sigurðsson, were purely didactic. He also wrote some epitaphs and deeply-felt elegies and memorial poems, notably the beautiful and sensitive ones on his young daughter, Steinunn.

Hallgrímur's depth of spiritual feeling culminated in his Passion hymns (*Passíusálmar*). They were based on Martin Möller's *Soliloquia de Passione Jesu Christi* (1587), a famous German work of meditation and edification which became very popular in Iceland in Arngrímur the Learned's translation (Hólar, 1599). The *Soliloquia* represented a return, among the writers of prayer books in Germany, to the medieval mysticism of Augustin and Bernhard. The form of addressing the meditations to one's soul was adopted by Hallgrímur as was also the mechanism of quoting a bit of text, expounding it, and pondering on it in the course of each meditation or hymn. The story opens in hymn one with the Lord's entering the Garden of Gethsemane; it closes in hymn fifty with the guards posted by Pilate to watch the grave. And all along the thorny road Hallgrímur is ready with his Christian allegory and symbolism not only to point morals and draw consolation from the dread aspect of the crucified Lord, but also to submerge himself in Christ's Passion—indeed, to such an extent that it is often difficult to distinguish the suffering of the author from that which he so poignantly portrays. And he has done much more. He has made Christ a living symbol of suffering humanity—the suffering humans of the seventeenth century— whose only hope of escape from a cruel world as well as from a wrathful and righteous God was Christ's redemption, Christ's cross, hope of the heavenly Zion.

Closely related to the Passion Hymns was the great meditation "Um dauðans óvissan tíma " (On the Uncertain Hour of Death). And as the Passion Hymns—printed for the first time at Hólar in 1666 and for the sixtieth time in Reykjavík in 1947—became the favorite " God's Word " of generation after generation of Icelanders, so Hallgrímur's powerful dirge has been intoned over the ashes of most of his countrymen from its first appearance in 1660 up to the present day.

The largest collection of Hallgrímur's poetry, excluding the *rímur*, is *Sálmar og kvæði* (Hymns and Poems, I–II, 1887–90) by Grímur Thomsen and, including the *rímur*, *Hallgrímur Pétursson* (I–II, 1947) by Magnús Jónsson. Both include the Passion Hymns.

Stefán Ólafsson

At the side of Hallgrímur Pétursson we may place Stefán Ólafsson as, perhaps, the greatest secular poet of the seventeenth century.

Stefán Ólafsson (*ca.* 1620–88), son of the Rev. Ólafur Einarsson of Kirkjubær in the East, grew up there until he went to school at Skálholt (*ca.* 1638–41), after which he served as a secretary of Bishop Brynjólfur Sveinsson for a while. In Copenhagen (1643) while studying theology, he soon joined the learned humanist circle of Ole Worm, who became his preceptor and lost no time putting him to work translating *Völuspá* and *Snorra Edda* into Latin. The *Völuspá* translation was printed with the first edition of the poem by Resen in Copenhagen in 1665. Because of the assiduous correspondence of Ole Worm, the fame of the Old Icelandic literature had already reached Paris where Cardinal Mazarin, perhaps prompted by his minister in Denmark, in 1646 offered Stefán Ólafsson the office of a northern antiquarian to translate and edit Icelandic manuscripts. Bishop Brynjólfur advised against this, so that Stefán did not accept it, but, after finishing his studies in 1648, went back to Iceland. Here he soon got the parsonage of Vallanes in the vicinity of his father and his cousin, Bjarni Gissurarson, parson and poet at Þingmúli. In Vallanes, Stefán seems to have led as merry a life as was compatible with his dignity as country parson and dean, until he was forty. Then he was overtaken by the mental troubles inherited from his grandmother, as well as by other diseases that plagued him until his death in 1688.

Stefán Ólafsson loved drawing burlesque pictures of his servants and neighbors, at times in situations hardly printable. His juicy style was sometimes almost Rabelaisian, his figures twisted and contorted. His subjects were liable to have huge appetites, smearing themselves all over when eating, their bellies rumbling, their backsides noisy. " Sigurður scurra " with staccato Skeltonian block rimes is a good example of this type of poetry. Less grotesque and of a more genial humor, though still burlesque, are " Oddsbragur " (Ode on Oddur) and " Rönkufótsríma " (*Ríma* on Rönkufótur) about the two great anglers on Lagarfljót. Their piscatorial experiences on the treacherous river are described with an imagination worthy of Walt Disney. Burlesque, too, is the macaronic poem about the fat (*crassus*) sexton and his singing—Stefán Ólafsson obviously being well versed in music himself.

A sharper satiric sting is to be found in " Ómennskukvæði " (On the Sloth of the Age), the counterpart of Hallgrímur Pétursson's " Aldar-háttur," written in a variation of the leonine hexameter. It is not as brilliant as Hallgrímur's satire. Less general, more concrete, it is stocked with samples of the lamentable behavior of the never-do-wells. They love to spend the summer horseback-riding, visiting their neighbors and sporting their flashy clothes instead of working at haymaking. The poet would not mind letting them stew in their own juice when winter comes, but then, alas, they come applying for help to the more prudent farmers. Another " Ádeila " (Satire) has echoes from *Hávamál*. But how narrow, almost myopic, is the poet's satire is well illustrated by the fact that he devotes a long harangue to the deplorable attitude of his farmhands to work but only a short epigram, though a pointed one, to the " Danish devil," i. e., the merchant at Djúpivogur. In the " Ómennskukvæði," Stefán Ólafsson, like Hallgrímur, contrasts the present sloth with the active life in Old Iceland.

By and large the world must have seemed less reprehensible than ridiculous to Stefán Ólafsson. He was a gleeful observer of the manners of his maids, the plain folks riding to a bridal, the odd customs of an alien district (Hornafjörður). Besides, Stefán Ólafsson was genuinely devoted to the pleasures of a country gentleman : playing chess, smoking or snuffing the new tobacco, drinking beer and wine and, last but not least, riding his good horses. If we did not know that an older con-temporary of his father, the Rev. Ólafur Jónsson á Söndum, had com-posed *Gleður mig enn sá góði bjór* in praise of beer-drinking, and that his father had helped in composing his " Ölkvæði " (Beer Poem), we should have assumed that Stefán Ólafsson was the father of the genre. The same holds for his " tobacco poetry," but he does seem to have been the very first to compose " praise of horses," unless the honor goes to Jón Arason for his verse on Móalingur. As Stefán did translate a spirited description of a horse from Virgil's *Georgics* (III, 75–88), we suspect that this ancient poem may have had something to do with launching this type of poetry, so very popular, in Iceland. If so, it was immensely more successful than the pastoral, of which Stefán gives us an early and isolated specimen " Lúkidór og Krysillis," translated from the Danish—if correctly attributed to him.

In addition to some humorous comments on love and lovers as well as a slightly burlesque ballad, " Stássmeyjarkvæði" (Ballad on a Fair Lady) on a damsel in the throes of courtly love, Stefán Ólafsson wrote two genuine and beautiful love lyrics " Raunakvæði " (Lament—*Eg veit eina baugalínu*) and " Meyjarmissir " (Loss of a Maiden—*Björt mey og hrein*) which due to their haunting melodies are still on the lips of the common people. Like his father and grandfather, Stefán loved to give good rimed counsel to his children, but he also gave them the burlesque " Grýlu kvæði " (Poem on an Ogress), in ballad meter, which was to reinforce a genre as old as *Sturlunga saga* and still beloved or rather feared by Icelandic children.

In " Svanasöngur " (Swan Song—*Margt er manna bölið*), composed late by the bedridden poet, he refers to his loss of health when forty. Though he does not there recant his worldly poetry, we may surmise that he composed more of his many hymns and serious poetry after that crucial event in his life.

Stefán translated some hymns, among them some of Kingo's and the famous *Stabat mater dolorosa*, the meter of which he also used for humorous purposes, thereby starting a new and secular vogue for it in Iceland. He wrote Latin poetry, translated Aesop and Horace, and was by admiring countrymen dubbed the Horace of Iceland. He could with equal or more propriety have been called the Skelton of Iceland and, unlike the hapless English poet, he founded a prolific school of poets in the East of Iceland as he himself was the physical ancestor of many later poets. His humoristic approach survived in the East almost up to the present day.

Stefán Ólafsson combined mastery of the old meters—the staccato-cadenced *hneppt* and *runhent* (Skeltonian block-rimes) as well as of *rímur* —with experimentation in new forms: *vikivakar*, hymn and song forms, probably derived from contemporary poetry in Denmark and Germany. There was a great variety in the song forms; a good many were of intricate rime patterns and variegated diction, but some were simpler and more lyric in tone, notably the two beautiful love songs.

A small collection of Stefán Ólafsson's poetry was first published by the Icelandic Literary Society in 1823. A much fuller collection in two volumes, *Kvæði* (I-II, 1885–86) was published for the same society by Jón Þorkelsson (forni).

Bjarni Gissurarson

Bjarni Gissurarson í Þingmúla (1621–1712) was a grandson of Einar Sigurðsson, a cousin of Stefán Ólafsson, and a parson at Þingmúli in his vicinity; hence they were good friends and comrades in poetry. Like Stefán, too, he had studied at Skálholt and served as a secretary to Bishop Brynjólfur Sveinsson. He was a prolific poet and has left us three autograph collections of his poems, unfortunately not published, for he was an interesting poet. Bjarni composed many poems in the humoristic-realistic style of his cousin and one topsy-turvy poem about terrific and unnatural disasters heaping themselves upon an unsuspecting human being: "Hrakfallabálkur," an extremely popular poem. This poem was actually composed under the *Stabat mater* meter and because of its popularity there can be little doubt that it was in the main responsible for the secularization of that meter in Iceland. Jón Þorláksson learns directly from "Hrakfallabálkur." Humorous are also a "Grýluþula" and poems on the midwinter months, Þorri and Góa, both connected with their namesakes in "Hversu Noregur byggðisk" (*Flateyjarbók* I, 21–24), but here for the first time, like Grýla, personified realistically and humorously, and as such setting a pattern for imitation, first in the East and then all over Iceland. Bjarni was also capable of an unusually warm and deep feeling, as shown in his hymn to womanhood in which he compares the good wife to the life-giving and all-warming sun, not to speak of the extraordinarily ardent epistle which he, a septuagenarian, sends to an early love of his. In his patriotic poetry he follows the lead of his grandfather, boldly claiming Iceland to be better than the romantic India and giving his reasons: immunity to wars and the bounty of Icelandic nature. In this and in his rather unusual descriptions and praise of Icelandic nature he was really a forerunner of the enlightened hymnodist of Icelandic nature, Eggert Ólafsson.

Guðmundur Bergþórsson

Guðmundur Bergþórsson (1657–1705) was in many ways a most remarkable man and poet. A poor cripple, unable to walk and having use only of his left hand, he eked out a living by teaching. An omnivorous reader, he wrote on subjects shunned by lay and learned alike; his

"*Heimspekingaskóli*" (The School of the Philosophers) was a moralist potpourri of classical comments, probably translated from the Danish (or German). Yet he was not above lightly commenting on the fashionable headgear of the time (in *Skautaljóð*) causing thereby a poetical controversy. But he was at his best in more traditional themes, like his balladesque " Barbarossa kvæði," still a popular song, and in some of his 256 *rímur*, a number surpassing all earlier records. Most remarkable of these were *Rímur af Olgeiri danska* (i. e., Ogier the Dane, 1680) in sixty *rímur* with fifty-nine meters or 119 variations, if all are counted. To this he later added eight *Rímur af Otúel frækna* (i. e., Otuel the Brave) and twenty-four of Ferakut (Fierabras?), thus raising the " Matter of France " to a new pitch of popularity in Iceland. But while "*Heimspekingaskóli*" was printed in 1785, only one of the *rímur* was published during the nineteenth century and *Rímur af Olgeiri danska* not until 1947. The remainder of his *rímur* remain unpublished.

Jón Vídalín

Jón Þorkelsson Vídalín (1666–1720), born at Garðar near Reykjavík, a grandson of Arngrímur the Learned, was himself to become one of the most learned writers of the country. Having begun his study of Latin at seven and lost his father, who was one of the first learned physicians of Iceland, at eleven, the precocious boy had several hurdles to jump before he could absolve his examination in theology at the University of Copenhagen (1689). Even then, instead of taking holy orders, he tried his hand at soldiery and, like Hallgrímur Péturs-son, came near to being lost to the church. But after he entered the services of Bishop Þórður Þorláksson at Skálholt in 1691, the latter was impressed with his abilities to such an extent that he made him in rapid succession teacher, chaplain, and officialis, and finally appointed him his own successor. He succeeded to the see at the bishop's death in 1697, on which occasion the University gave him the title of Magister, forever after associated with him and his postil in the popular mind. As a bishop, Magister Jón soon became not only an active administrator but an influential churchman as well. As such he soon got into trouble with the arrogant secular leader, Oddur Sigurðsson; their feud lasted un-remittingly until the bishop's untimely death in 1720. Proud, quick to anger, and not always proof against the temptations of Bacchus, the bishop could not always avoid giving his wily and mean opponent an opportunity to strike home. But it seems doubtful whether his eloquent sermons would ever have become the masterpieces they are without his righteous indignation over conditions rampant in contemporary life.

Magister Jón wrote his postil near the climax of his fight with Oddur Sigurðsson. The first part was ready by 1715 and the whole published at Hólar, 1718–20 (*Húss-Postilla eður einfaldar Prédikanir yfir öll hátíða og sunnudaga guðspjöll árið um kring*). Vídalín has been shown to have relied chiefly on two theological works, one German-Latin, the huge *Harmonia Evangelica* by M. Chemnitz, P. Leyser, and J. Gerhard, the other English, *The Practice of Christian Graces, or the Whole Duty of Man* by R. Allestree. From the first he adopted the allegorical treatment and the abundance of learned commentary. From the latter he took a somewhat un-Lutheran (puritan-Calvinistic) point of view that man can save himself by knowing his faults and practicing the Christian virtues of repeated repentance and constant penitence. In this he differed materially from Hallgrímur Pétursson, whose penetrating and deep-felt meditations bordered on mysticism. Vídalín was no mystic but an angry orthodox moralist whose cold intellectual approach pointed the way toward the rationalisms of the eighteenth and nineteenth centuries rather than to the pietism then on the intellectual horizon in the Lutheran countries, soon to be preached by Ludwig Harboe in Iceland. Vídalín was happiest when he could crack his whip over the flagrant abuses of the age, the corrupt authorities, or the arch-enemy, Satan himself. That he did not spare himself is shown in his justly famous sermon on wrath, his own special weakness. His passionate nature and vivid phantasy revelled in the allegorizing and antithetical rhetoric of the time (baroque). His points were driven home with keen psychological sense and bloody irony no less than by imaginative paintings of the interior of hell. His style was sententious and shot through with proverbs, a trait endearing him to the common people. But in general he was far less of the people than Hallgrímur Pétursson had been, for he was a scholar with the ambition to write great literature to vie with the learned of his age; hence his Latin translations of Hallgrímur Pétursson's hymns, hence his own learned Latin poetry. Still, his clear eloquence, borne by his fierce indignation, could not but cast its spell on every reader and hearer, to such an extent that his postil came near to monopolizing the field of devotion far down into the nineteenth century (13th edition, 1838), and even now it retains much of its vigorous appeal (14th edition, 1945).

Páll Vídalín

Páll Jónsson Vídalín (1667–1727) was a grandson of Arngrímur the Learned and a great-grandson of Bishop Guðbrandur Þorláksson. A lawman (lögmaður) of the South and East of Iceland, he was an expert on law and wrote a learned commentary on the old law code. For years he collaborated with Árni Magnússon on an inventory of all real estate in Iceland (*Jarðabók Árna Magnússonar*), a work intended to be a reliable basis for future improvements—and taxation.

In his poetry he could play with difficult forms in a *háttalykill* (*clavis metrica*) to his beloved and in stately *vikivakar*, but the simple quatrain was his favorite. He used it in pointed epigrams on personalities or everyday events with such a skill that his countrymen compared him to Martial. In his day no one would excel him in dry wit and manly humor. He enjoyed translating Aesop's fables, but he also wrote hymns that have survived, for he was a God-fearing man. A collection of Vídalín's poetry was first made by Jón Þorkelsson (forni) in *Vísnakver* (1897).

Enlightenment (Neo-Classicism), 1750-1830

Foreign influence

During the eighteenth century, especially its second half, the scientific, liberalistic, and rationalistic spirit, ultimately derivable from Newton and Locke, Montesquieu and Voltaire, began to filter through to Iceland. Not only was magic condemned as a rank superstition, but the traditional orthodoxy was soon to conflict with the seemingly eternal laws of nature, a wide field for speculation and rationalization. Moreover, philosophers tended to extend the laws of nature to human affairs thinking that, by introducing scientific rationalistic methods, great improvements in human societies would follow. And, unlike the orthodox who, believing in original sin, were apt to take a pessimistic view of human nature, most of the new prophets believed in man's innate goodness, thinking—like Socrates—that what was really needed to establish a happy world was teaching everyone to know the truth and to act accordingly. Hence education-enlightenment became the watchword of the time.

The leaders

In Iceland the leaders of the movement were: the nationalistic poet and naturalist Eggert Ólafsson (1726–68), his friend the experimental agriculturist Björn Halldórsson, parson in Sauðlauksdalur (1724–94), the great statesman and social economist Jón Eiríksson (1728–87), who led the early movement from his high government offices in Copenhagen, the cosmopolitan Bishop Hannes Finnsson of Skálholt (1739–96), the popular editor, Prefect Magnús Ketilsson (1732–1803), and, finally, the cosmopolitan, rationalistic, and humanistic Chief Justice of Iceland, Magnús Stephensen (1762–1833) who led the movement to its rather bitter end.

When the leaders of the Enlightenment broke the two-century-old monopoly of "God's word" in Iceland, they did so with a flood of practical books and pamphlets on how to farm and fish to make a living in the country. These popular scientific works were, by the early leaders (notably Jón Eiríksson) deemed all important to raise the standard of living in the backward and calamity-stricken country, and they held sway throughout the period. Later two of the greatest tried to introduce the Enlightenment philosophy in works written to delight and instruct the common people: Hannes Finnsson in *Kvöldvökurnar* I–II (1796–97) and Magnús Stephensen in *Vinagleði* I (1797). Both were well written miscellanea using fables, fairy tales, maxims, dialogues, playlets, and essays on natural science, geography, anthropology, and history to drive home the gospel of Enlightenment, justifying the ways of God— often God in nature—to man. Most of these writings were probably translated, like the two *contes moraux* by Marmontel in *Vinagleði*.

Periodicals

The first literary societies and the first periodicals belonged to this period. The Invisible Society (1760) published *Konungsskuggsjá* in 1768. The new Press of Hrappsey got out the first periodical in Danish, *Islandske Maaneds Tidender* (1773–76), a monthly news published by Magnús Ketilsson. The next, a yearbook, was published by the Icelandic Society of Learned Arts (1779–96), guided by Jón Eiríksson and supplanted after his time by the Society of Enlightenment (1794–1827), led by Magnús Stephensen and publishing both a yearbook on current history, and, later, a monthly news sheet. Jón Eiríksson's aims were almost entirely utilitarian, while Magnús Stephensen would also gladly have given his countrymen refinement in taste and French esprit, though with scant success since he was a notoriously bad stylist. The Icelandic Literary Society was founded by the Danish linguist Rasmus Chr. Rask (1787–1832) in Reykjavík and Copenhagen in 1816 in order to preserve the Icelandic language and publish its literature, old and modern. Because of its nationalism this society was taken over by the coming Romanticists and still survives, its periodical *Skírnir* (1827——) being the oldest in Scandinavia. Growing interest in the Old Icelandic literature resulted in the foundation of the Society for Northern Antiquaries (1825) by C. C. Rafn (1795–1864); it published a series of *fornaldar* and kings' sagas.

Icelandic studies

Compared to the Renaissance, the period of Enlightenment was a time of great expanse and specialization in science, its crowning achievement being Eggert Ólafsson's and Bjarni Pálsson's monumental description of Iceland. But though popular science had the first claim on printing, yet the traditional interest in history and Icelandic studies remained strong, fostered as it was by the new Arnamagnaean Foundation (1760 ——).

Bishop Finnur Jónsson (1704–1789) of Skálholt was the son of Jón Halldórsson of Hítardalur, who had collected copious materials toward recording the church history of Iceland. Based on these, the bishop wrote *Historia ecclesiastica Islandiae*, published in four quarto volumes, 1772–78. He was aided by his son Hannes Finnsson, who also published Old Icelandic texts, wrote on social economy, and composed the popular educational book *Kvöldvökurnar*. Two stipendiaries of the Arnamagnean Foundation may be mentioned: Jón Ólafsson Grunnvíkingur (1705–79) had been Árni Magnússon's amanuensis, but was as superstitious and uncritical as his master was free from those blemishes. Yet, his memory saved part of *Heiðarvíga saga* from oblivion, and some of his collections, especially his huge dictionary of Icelandic, were valuable. Jón Ólafsson Svefneyingur (1731–1811), Eggert Ólafsson's brother, published the first modern treatise on Old Icelandic (Norse) poetry in 1786. Björn Halldórsson took time from his model farming to write an excellent Icelandic-Latin dictionary, published with Danish translations added by R. Chr. Rask in 1814. Hálfdan Einarsson (1732–85), headmaster of the Hólar School, wrote *Sciagraphia Historiae Literariae Islandicae* (1777), the first published literary history of Iceland, counting about 400 authors. The two historians Magnús Stephensen and Jón Jónsson Espólín (1769–1836) presented an interesting study in contrasts: the former used an allegorical, sentimental, Dano-German Enlightenment style in his *Eptirmæli 18. aldar* (1805–1806); the latter imitated the saga style in his monumental *Árbækur Íslands* (1821–55). Though less critical than Stephensen's work, it became a double pattern for nineteenth-century autodidact historians and for the nineteenth-century prose style. His nationalism endeared him to the coming Romanticists who published his work. Two professors at the University of Copenhagen still deserve mentioning: Grímur Jónsson Thorkelín (1752–1829), first editor of *Beowulf*, and Finnur Magnússon (1781–1847), grandson of Bishop Finnur Jónsson. Originally more interested in contemporary literature, he wrote on Ossian and composed poetry. He completed the edition of *Sæmundar Edda* (1787–1828) for the Arnamagnaean Foundation, translated the poems into Danish, and wrote on Eddic lore and mythology, comparing it with Persian and Sanscrit myths: a bold but premature attempt to do for Indo-European myths what Rask and Grimm had done for the Indo-European languages. He was also the greatest runic expert of his time.

Literature

Turning to the literature in a stricter sense we find the old genres of hymns, *rímur* and the lyric poetry continued, but supplemented by three genres in prose: the essay, the novel and the drama—in addition to the old romances and *lygi sögur*.

The Hymnbook of 1801, edited by Magnús Stephensen to replace the 200-year-old *Graduale* reflected his rationalism and his modern taste in music, but was otherwise undistinguished.

The *rímur* throve as perhaps never before in spite of Magnús Stephensen's savage attack on them and their tunes. Catering to public taste, the Press of Hrappsey printed several, among them three by Árni Böðvarsson (1713–77), the foremost *rímur* composer of his day and the first to have his work published in Iceland after the Bible *rímur* composers; at his death he had 221 cycles of *rímur* to his credit, not counting other verse of which his humorous "The Ships' Arrival" was the most popular. He may share that with Gunnlaugur Snorrason.

The new poetry of Enlightenment may be seen from two aspects: direct translations of the most celebrated poetical works of the time, and new native poetry composed according to the poetical theories of the time. We find the latter appearing first: in Eggert Ólafsson's modified neo-classic and didactic poetry: his bucolic poetry with patterns going back to classical antiquity (Virgil, Horace, Martial); his use of classical mythical names; his didactic dialogues; his use of allegory, unparalleled before, but imitated later in poetry and prose. Many of his poems were, like Pope's, annotated essays. His "imaginary country" satire (Swift, Holberg) and his great interest in nature (Haller, Rousseau) were both symptoms of the times, though only the latter was to become a powerful theme in all future poetry, reinforced in Scandinavia by Linné's botanical researches. Eggert Ólafsson's interest in skaldic verse and diction and archaic language was no doubt an inheritance of the Renaissance adulation of Old Northern Antiquities (Old Icelandic), to the study of which his brother, Jón Ólafsson Svefneyingur, was to devote his life, but this interest may also have been formed on analogy with the neo-classic admiration for classical antiquity. Though Eggert advised to keep the two mythological systems apart, he would occasionally mix them in the same poem. Most of Eggert's meters were traditional, among them an old hymn converted to the use of a drinking song (*Ó mín flaskan fríða*), but a few were new (e. g. the French Alexandrines).

The translations appeared later, mostly done by the great translator Jón Þorláksson, but also by others, among them Stephensen and Gröndal. They represented a transmission of cultural values unexampled since the Lutheran hymns, but repeated by the great translators of the nineteenth and twentieth centuries. Translated were the English Milton, Pope, and Thomson, the Norwegians Tullin and Wessel, the Danes Ewald and Baggesen, and the Germans Gellert and Klopstock. Some of this was second hand translation out of Danish and then usually in the Danish metrical form; otherwise the original meters were usually followed, except when replaced by the Eddic *fornyrðislag* which now served to translate not only the philosopher Pope and the nature hymnist Thomson, but also the great epics of Milton and Klopstock. These were, indeed, the first epics in the Beowulfian-Eddic *fornyrðislag* in Iceland; they would presumably have been enjoyed by Cædmon in England and the author of *Heliand* in Germany, had they arisen from their graves. The philosophic sweep of some of this poetry was found in no native contemporary poet, but, together with the popular educators' panegyrics of the starred heavens, may have inspired Björn Gunnlaugsson (1788–1876), mathematician and geographer, to write his remarkable philosophic poem *Njóla* (The Night, 1842).

It was no accident that the Norwegian Tullin, the first to be translated, was followed by Pope and Thomson, for he had been first to introduce the English free-thinking nature evangelists to Norway-Denmark—after which followed Danish translations of Pope, Young, and Milton. The Norwegians, Holberg, Tullin, Wessel, were more oriented toward England and France than the Danes, who were under stronger German influence. Their adulation of Klopstock was such that they invited him to live in Denmark (1751). Gellert's moralistic fables and tales were as popular in Denmark as they were with Jón Þorláksson. Of the Danish poets themselves, none was translated to the same extent as the " foreigners," perhaps because they were more easily accessible and understood. Wessel exerted considerable influence on his contemporary Sigurður Pétursson, Baggesen on the later Sigurður Breiðfjörð.

Toward the end, the Swedish Anacreon of the North, K. M. Bellman, began to exert his influence on Sigurður Pétursson.

When the essay abroad dominated not only prose but also poetry it was inevitable that it should spread to Iceland, even in prose form, favored by the rising periodicals. Since Magnús Stephensen was the editor of these, he had the chief opportunity to write essays, though his efforts even here were marred by his heavy Dano-German style. Still he succeeded in writing some spirited pieces: for example, his stirring panegyric to Enlightenment or his arraignment of slander, both in *Vinagleði*. Similar or better essays may be found in Hannes Finnsson's *Kvöldvökurnar*. Yet neither of these cosmopolitan writers can match the purity of the saga-like style found in the historical resumés of Jón Espólín's *Árbækur Íslands*.

Like the *rímur* the romantic *lygi sögur* flourished throughout the period, though occasionally admitting new and strange motifs from abroad. In 1756 a Swedish novel of the Robinson Crusoe type had been translated and published at Hólar. About 1770 this was imitated by Jón Bjarnason, parson at Ballará (1721–85), in his *Parmes saga Loðinbjarnar*, a cross between the *lygi sögur* and the new genre, with an Italian hero landing in Greenland. This was apparently the first novel written in Iceland, but not the only one of this period. Befitting an age of instruction determined to mix *utile dulci* we find Hannes Finnsson and Magnús Stephensen using fables (Aesop and others), sentimental moral tales, sometimes oriental, both in poetry (Gellert) and prose (Marmontel) to sugar-coat their pills. They were following the best patterns of the time, for did not Voltaire draw upon the *Arabian Nights* for the setting of his *Zadig*? But the enormous vogue of the *Arabian Nights* was soon to bear fruit in Iceland in the writings of the adventure story-teller Eiríkur Eiríksson Laxdal (1743–1816). He used the Arabian Night frame story technique to write a didactic utopia, called *Ólands saga* (History of Nonesuch Land) and filled with fairy tales, thus becoming a forerunner not only of the nineteenth-century novel (though no direct influence is visible) but also of the romantic collections of folk and fairy tales for their own sake, also typical of the nineteenth century. He also wrote *Ólafs saga Þórhallasonar*, based on similar materials, but more coherent and containing both nature descriptions and sketches from contemporary life.

Although lack of towns in Iceland explains the absence of the drama there, still one might have expected mystery plays at the two cathedrals or pageantry at their schools. There actually exists a mystery play (in translation) from about 1750, and the first dramatic stirrings seem connected with the Skálholt school. It was probably here that Snorri Björnsson (1710–1803), later parson of Húsafell, wrote his *Sperðill* (German: *Hanswurst*), perhaps during his long school days from 1724 to 1733, which about coincide with the time when L. Holberg, the greatest dramatist of the North, was writing his plays. And while the name *Hanswurst* belongs to a type of German play which Holberg fought, it looks as if *Sperðill* was not untouched by the Holbergian spirit: it is a satire on the vagabonds of the time, too numerous in an age of poverty. But this comedy was also, no doubt, connected with the buffoonery of the "Lord's Day" pageant (*Herradagur*), which apparently was an old tradition in the school and went with it to Reykjavík in the 1790's. Here the enlightened authorities at first looked with favor on the school comedies with the result that the bosom friends Geir Vídalín (1761–1823), later Bishop of Iceland, and the prefect Sigurður Pétursson (1759–1827), also a humorous poet, wrote their comedies *Brandur* and *Hrólfur*, respectively, for the students. *Hrólfur*, another variation on the *miles gloriosus* theme, written in the Molière-Holberg tradition, was soon followed by *Narfi*, in which Sigurður castigated the aping of Danish manners of his countrymen, as Wessel had the Francomania of his, and, above all, as Holberg had ridiculed the French foppishness in Denmark in his *Jean de France*. When Rask, shortly after, came to Iceland he found the application so apt that he actually adapted *Jean de France* to Icelandic conditions as a first skirmish in his campaign for the Icelandic language in Iceland.

Eggert Ólafsson

Eggert Ólafsson (1726–68) was a farmer's son of good stock, hailing from the West (Snæfellsnes). Having taken his bachelor's degree at the University of Copenhagen in 1748, he wrote a couple of treatises showing his interest in the natural history of Iceland as well as in Northern antiquities. This caused the Danish Academy of Sciences to recommend him, with Bjarni Pálsson, later Surgeon-General of Iceland, to travel all over the country collecting facts about its physical geography, its natural resources, and the life and customs of the inhabitants. They carried out this program during the years 1752–57, laying down their findings in the monumental *Reise igiennem Island* I–II, written by Eggert, first published in Danish in 1772, later in German, French, and

English (1805) translations. It was the first authoritative and comprehensive description of Iceland and its inhabitants. While writing this great work, Eggert spent his time partly in Iceland with his brother-in-law, the progressive and learned farmer-parson Björn Halldórsson in Sauðlauksdalur, partly in Copenhagen, where he is reputed to have led a faction of progressive nationalists among the Icelandic students, while a moderate and cosmopolitan party was led by the bishop's son Hannes Finnsson. The nationalists recommended return to the active life of the saga heroes as well as to the patterns of their language and poetry; hence Eggert Ólafsson's orthography and poetry were full of archaisms. Hannes Finnsson turned for guidance to contemporary Europe, neoclassic France and enlightened Germany. Actually Eggert Ólafsson was himself greatly indebted to Neo-Classicism and Enlightenment. By 1766 Eggert was back in Iceland (Sauðlauksdalur). He was then promised a high administrative office and could now marry his sweetheart (1767), which he did with aristocratic pomp and ceremony, composing many songs for the occasion. They had their honeymoon at his brother-in-law's in Sauðlauksdalur, but in May 1768, sailing for their new home in Snæfellsnes, they were lost at sea—a loss felt and mourned by the whole people.

Eggert Ólafsson expressed typical eighteenth-century ideas about poetry in the preface to his *Kvæði* (Poems, 1832). The art of poetry is the highest form of rhetoric, and, like the orator, the poet must move the human heart. To be a perfect poet three qualities are essential: facility in rime, high intellect, and good taste. Actually the poet was sadly lacking in the last of these qualities, according to our standards. He employed old and new meters, and his diction was often archaic. He sometimes used the fashionable paraphernalia of classical mythology; more often he substituted northern myths. Several of his poems were cast in allegorical form, at times in imitation of the pictorial art of the day. Most of his poems were didactic and moralizing, not a few satiric. The poems were often essays in rime and heavily annotated according to the custom of the time.

His fulsome praise of his monarch was to be expected in the age of absolute though enlightened monarchy; it was also in a way an expression of his patriotism. His patriotic poems were numerous and original in theme, though poor in execution. He was probably the first to personify Iceland as a woman in his allegorical form. This personification has survived in pictorial art and poetry (*Fjallkonan*, the Mountain

Lady). Imitating Holberg and Swift, he criticized his countrymen as *Sukkudokkar*, " hunters of butterflies," denizens of an imaginary country. He had only high praise for Icelandic nature, and, though he seldom neglected the economic aspect, he could eulogize the wilderness in the manner of the moderns (Albert Haller). Indeed he was the first nature poet in Iceland. He contrasted the pleasures of the city (Copenhagen) with the primitive life in Iceland, expressing his nostalgia for the latter.

In his best poem, *Búnaðarbálkur* (Poem on Farming), he describes the ideal thrifty, active, and imaginative farmer in a paradise of Icelandic nature, contrasting him with the all too common shiftless, ignorant, and superstitious peasant, a usual butt of satire before Eggert's day. The poem was dedicated to the poet's brother-in-law in whose image the ideal farmer was cast. This poem, the best of its kind in Icelandic literature, reflected the doctrines of the physiocrats and Rousseau's sentimental primitivism. It has never been matched, for Icelandic farmers have had a hard time idealizing their own life as such.

The wide vistas opened up to Eggert Ólafsson by the rationalistic philosophy of nature and Enlightenment gave him an abundance of fresh matter and a novel point of view. His utilitarianism was especially congenial to his contemporaries and immediate followers, while his nationalism endeared him to the Romanticists of the 1830's who belatedly published his poems. But in spite of his seemingly sound poetical theory, the quality of his work was so rarely sustained that his poetry is nearly unreadable today, except for its ideological content. His poetry was primarily secular, but shortly before his death he published a recantation admitting the shortsightedness of his natural philosophy and advocating a return to good Christian life—as if he knew that his end was not far off.

Jón Steingrímsson

Jón Steingrímsson (1728–91) wrote an autobiography which ranks with the travels of Jón Ólafsson Indíafari and the " Passion " of Jón Magnússon as the greatest prose work of that kind before the nineteenth century. He was born in Skagafjörður, studied there at Hólar, but became in 1760 a parson in the South, first in Mýrdalur, later (1778) at Kirkjubæjarklaustur in Síða. Here he lived through the terrific eruption near Skaftá, most dangerous in the history of the country, beginning on June 8, 1783. It sent a lava stream up to the very walls of the church, where he was busy exhorting his flock, emitted ashes and poisonous fumes so that most of the live-stock perished the first year, leaving the people to face stark famine the next. During the following years of suffering Jón fought hard for his people, even incurring the wrath of the rigid bureaucracy in his efforts for the distribution of relief. The autobiography was written partly to justify his actions at that time. It shows him as a God-fearing man of action, braving material and spiritual dangers alike with dogged persistence, even manly enjoyment. Like most of his fellow-churchmen of the time, he could only see the avenging hand of God in the plagues visited on his countrymen. But in spite of this pessimism, conditioned by the age, he had a sense of humor and told many a merry tale about himself and others. And what above all makes his book delightful reading is his sincerity, which often borders on the naive. Even this trait he has in common with Jón Ólafsson Indíafari, and, probably, most of the best autobiographers, notably Boswell, and the modern Icelandic Þórbergur Þórðarson. The autobiography was first published by the Historical Society, 1913–16, by Jón Þorkelsson (forni) ; a second edition was brought out in 1945 by his son, Guð- brandur Jónsson.

Benedikt Jónsson Gröndal

Benedikt Jónsson Gröndal (1762–1825) was born near Mývatn, studied classical literatures and modern belles lettres in Copenhagen, and became a judge (assessor) of the High Court in Reykjavík. He could turn a pointed epigram, though few of his verses have survived oblivion. His chief merit was to point the way for future translators of long poems, when he deliberately chose the simple *fornyrðislag* of the *Edda* instead of more difficult meters, native or foreign, to translate Pope's *Temple of Fame* (1789 or 1790) from the English. In so doing he may have been reacting against the skaldic archaisms of Eggert Ólafsson, though following him in the preference for the dialect of Northeast Ice- land, which, after all, was his own. He was right: barring the original meters, there was no medium more apt to render the pure thought of the originals. He was followed not only by Jón Þorláksson in *Paradise Lost* and *Messiah*, but also by his son-in-law Sveinbjörn Egilsson and his grandson Benedikt Gröndal in their versified translations of Homer. His poems, *Kvæði* (1833) were published after his death by his son-in-law.

Jón Þorláksson

Jón Þorláksson (1744–1819) was born in Selárdalur, Vestfirðir, the son of a parson. After studying at Skálholt he, too, became a parson who twice (1770 and 1773) forfeited his office for love affairs with a girl he was kept from marrying. After his rehabilitation he got a living at Bægisá in Eyjafjörður (1788) remaining there until his death. His weakness for the fair sex and his poverty never left him, but after sixty-one he became lame and sickly.

Jón Þorláksson was a prolific poet and a much greater master of form than Eggert Ólafsson. Though he could wield the old difficult meters, he cultivated the simpler measures, notably *fornyrðislag*. Much of his own poetry was of an occasional nature: humoristic comments on every-day events, good-natured banter with the girls or his children, a multitude of epitaphs and memorial poems, among which the ones on his own son and his friend Halldór Hjálmarsson are notable. Likewise he composed many hymns some of which still defend their place in the Icelandic hymnbook. If offended he could turn a pointed epigram. Only rarely was he provoked to satire and invective, as when the benevolent and anything but facile literary dictator, Magnús Stephensen, had taken liberty with his hymns in the hymnbook of Leirárgarðar (*Messusöngs og sálmabók*, 1801). There was hurling of invective on both sides, Jón Þorláksson of course the victor spiritually, if not materially. Yet, since Stephensen was his patron and he, himself, genuinely in favor of his strivings for enlightenment, he was fain to eat humble pie, end the controversy, and apologize.

Much more important than his own poetry were his translations. In them he tried what only Benedikt Gröndal (the Older) had attempted before in a small way: to bring some of the best in contemporary and recent poetry to the attention of his culturally isolated countrymen. His first books (1774 and 1783) contained translations from the poems of the Norwegian C. B. Tullin (1728–1765) whose nature poetry reflected J. Thomson's *The Seasons*. The translator points out the new note in contrast to Eddic and classical themes. Next came Pope's *Essay on Man* (1798) with its rationalistic philosophy. Then the poet launched his most ambitious undertaking: translating Milton's *Paradise Lost*. His friend, Halldór Hjálmarsson, co-rector at Hólar, had sent him a Danish version of Milton in 1791 and recommended his translation to the Society of Learned Arts (Lærdómslistafélag) which published the first book in 1793. But at the demise of the society (1796) only three books had appeared. In spite of these reversals the poet went on with his work, now aided by a German version, bringing it successfully to an end in 1805. Shortly after, encouraged by Magnús Stephensen, he undertook a translation of F. G. Klopstock's *Messiah*, an enormous task completed just before his death. He did not live to see the two great works published: *Paradísar missir* (1828), *Messías* (1834–38).

In the summer of 1814 the poet was visited by the Scottish agent of the British Bible Society, E. Henderson, who marveled at the indomitable spirit in so humble an abode. The poet, then working on Klopstock, "acknowledged the impossibility of his reaching the bold and adventurous heights of that poet so happily as he had done the flights of Milton. Alluding to his halting, he said it could not be a matter of surprise since Milton had used him for several years as his riding-horse and spurred him unmercifully through the celestial, chaotic, and infernal regions." Henderson considered his work to "rise superior to any other translation of Milton," rivaling or even surpassing the original itself. This is no doubt an instance of hyperbole, yet every critic has conceded that what Jón did to Milton by investing him in the Beowulfian-Eddic *fornyrðislag* was something extraordinarily fine. The effect on Icelandic poetical diction, nay, the very language itself was even more valuable, a thing to be especially grateful for at a time when the language was commonly maltreated by learned men, not least so the literary arbiter Magnús Stephensen. If Eggert Ólafsson was to contribute the valuable nationalist spirit to the coming Romanticists, Jón Þorláksson provided the very atmosphere in which they grew up and the soft, rich, and pliable form they could make use of. Bjarni Thorarensen's "Hail, thou great Milton of Iceland" was no empty greeting, but expressed the very great and general feeling of love and reverence for the aging poet laureate.

Sigurður Pétursson

Sigurður Pétursson (1759–1827) was born at Ketilsstaðir in the East, the son of a prefect, who took him as a boy of fifteen to Denmark to to be educated at Roskilde and Copenhagen. Here he studied first philology, later law. In 1789 he accepted a prefecture near Reykjavík where he could enjoy the companionship of his friend, later bishop, Geir Vídalín. Descended on the distaff side from Stefán Ólafsson, he was, like his ancestor, a merry fellow, until, at forty-two, his health failed.

Though a hardworking and brilliant student, Sigurður seems not to have despised the joys of the merry student life in Copenhagen, if one may judge by his Anacreontic songs, where the strains of Bellmann sound for the first time in Icelandic poetry. He was also attracted to the Norwegian Society and its chief exponent, J. H. Wessel (1742–85), whose humorous tale of *Stella* he later transposed into mock-heroic *rímur*. In Reykjavík, Sigurður Pétursson wrote two rollicking comedies for the Latin School: *Hrólfur*, or Gossip and Gullibility, a Molière-Holbergian variation on the *miles gloriosus* theme, and *Narfi*, or the Icelandic Fool with Danish Un-Manners, imitating Holberg's *Jean de France*, the Danish Fool of French Ill-Fashion. Though imitative, the comedy was a timely satire on the social conditions in Reykjavík, where the Icelandic rabble strove to imitate the "high-brow" Danish merchants. The theme recurred half a century later in Jón Thóroddsen's pioneer novel. But Sigurður Pétursson's playwriting was cut short, because the authorities, at the last *Herradagur*, January 28, 1799, when *Narfi* was shown, thought they smelt a revolutionary rat and forbade the show.

His works, poems and plays, *Ljóðmæli, Leikrit* were published after his death, 1844–46.

Jón Espólín

Jón Jónsson Espólín (1769–1836) was born at Espihóll, Eyjafjörður, the son of a prefect of scholarly tastes. Studying law at the University, Jón Espólín became prefect (1792) of several districts in succession, latest in Skagafjörður (1802–25). Like his relative, the poet Bjarni Thorarensen, he was a pious man, a severe judge, and nationalistic in a rationalistic, humanitarian, and cosmopolitan age.

His chief work, *Íslands árbækur í söguformi* (The Annals of Iceland in the form of History, 1262–1832, in twelve volumes, 1821–55), was not only a monument to his industry and learning, but also to his critical acumen. Written in the good old saga style, very different from the ordinary run of eighteenth-century prose, this great work obviously was in a position to exert considerable influence on the nineteenth-century language renaissance of Fjölnismenn, not least so, since one of the group, Konráð Gíslason, was the son of Espólín's secretary, right hand man, and imitator, Gísli Konráðsson. An attempted novel by Espólín was of little significance, but he may be called the father of a school of popular historians in the nineteenth century and after, foremost among whom was his just mentioned secretary, Gísli Konráðsson (1787–1877), author of a host of books of various descriptions, mostly unpublished.

Sveinbjörn Egilsson

Sveinbjörn Egilsson (1791–1852) was born at Innri-Njarðvík on Reykjanes, a farmer's son. He grew up in the stronghold of Enlightenment, the home of Magnús Stephensen at Viðey. Tutored at home, he studied theology at the University (1814–19), and became a teacher at the Latin school at Bessastaðir, which he and his fellow-teachers made famous (1819–46). After the school's removal to Reykjavík he became its headmaster (rector). Though an enthusiastic teacher of the Greek and Latin classics, he managed to arouse the interest of the students in their mother tongue by always insisting on immaculate Icelandic translations. He read his own prose versions of the classics to the students, but only two of these were published: Homer's *Odyssey* (1829–40) and the *Iliad* (1855). They represent the first artistic prose of the nineteenth century, fully emancipated from the heavy Danish-German element of the preceding centuries, unaffected in structure, but definitely colored by features of the original. They fully demonstrated the flexibility of the modern idiom for any conceivable use. They still retain their popularity as proved by the sumptuous edition of 1948–49.

Sveinbjörn Egilsson's astonishing linguistic renaissance was, no doubt, due to his prolonged preoccupation with Old Icelandic. He helped to edit *Sturlunga saga* (1817–20) and translated into Latin most of the *Fornmanna sögur* (1825–37) and *Snorra Edda* (1848–49). In so doing he gradually came to translate most of the skaldic poetry, deciding as early as 1824 to make a dictionary of it. This appeared after his death as *Lexicon Poeticum antiquae Linguae septentrionalis* (1854–60), the basis of all further research in the field. Sveinbjörn was also a poet of some note, leaving a volume of poetry and a partial translation of the *Odyssey* (completed by his son Gröndal) in *fornyrðislag*.

National Romanticism, 1830-1874

Foreign influence

The European tendencies ushering in the new Romanticism in Iceland were of two types: political and literary.

The political tendencies culminated in and spread from the French revolutions of 1789, 1830, and 1848. The first caused hardly a ripple in monarchistic Iceland; the second raised a romantic clamor for the rebirth of the Althing at Þingvellir; and during the third a deliberate realistic struggle was under way for an ever growing autonomy from Denmark. But throughout the period and, indeed, up to 1918, there was a never-flagging current of nationalism, so that the patriotic song of the nineteenth century (and after) more nearly took the place of the religious poetry of the age of orthodoxy, not to speak of the bucolic poetry of Enlightenment, to which—with Eggert Ólafsson's nationalistic emphasis—it was closely related.

The literary tendencies, which in Europe went under the name of Romanticism, sprang from diverse and scattered roots, but all had this in common: they were revolts against Neo-Classicism and Enlightenment, just as the French Revolution was a revolt against the enlightened French monarchy. Thus we see emotion take the place of reason, sentimentality replace the cold rules of etiquette, deep religious feeling oust the rationalistic free thinking. We find nature, idyllic or magnificent, pittoresque and awe-inspiring, preferred to the urban scene or the civilized scenery, just as simple country life, even the life of "noble" savages is preferred to civilized life. Herewith goes the lure of faraway romantic countries, interest in oriental tales (*The Arabian Nights*) and oriental gardens (China).

For the first time since the Renaissance, medieval life and art was preferred to the present, and not only the European Middle Ages with its knights, castles, and the Catholic Church (in which many Romanticists took a last refuge), but also Celtic and Northern (i. e., Icelandic) antiquities (*Ossian* and *Edda*; cf. P. H. Mallet). Even English poets (Gray) drew on the Northern antiquities, and in Germany they were fused with Tacitus to form the national romantic reconstruction of the "urgermanic" times (Gerstenberg and especially Grimm). Simple folk tales and folk songs were hailed and collected as sources of national values (Herder), while ballads and fairy tales were cultivated as art forms (H. C. Andersen) as peculiarly apt forms for the unbridled romantic phantasy. The ambitions of the early Romanticists were often titanic (*Prometheus, Faust*), their melancholy, when thwarted, a Byronic *Weltschmerz*. In general they yearned for the infinite and the absolute, preferring a quest to definite results. They sought variety of form or formlessness, their imagination was free, and their studied indifference—romantic irony—to their own work and to their readers superb.

In Germany the deep religious feeling of Klopstock's *Messiah* and the growing appreciation of Northern antiquities were a sign of the change. But the real leaders of the movement in Germany were Herder, Goethe, and Schiller, though the two last named, especially Goethe, later turned to a new classicism in their appreciation of the noble simplicity and quiet greatness of Greek art. Since Goethe and Schiller, especially the latter, became the favorites of the Romanticists in Iceland, and since these all went through a good schooling in Homer at the Latin School of Bessastaðir, it was perhaps natural that the Romantic movement in Iceland should be remarkably free from its excesses in Germany.

When Henrik Steffens in 1802 started to lecture on Romanticism in Copenhagen, there was among his hearers not only the Danish poet Oehlenschläger, but also the young Icelander Bjarni Thorarensen. Both became the first and in some respects the best romantic poets of their native lands. In Iceland Bjarni remained a solitary voice in the wilderness until joined by the young *Fjölnismenn* of the 1830's who, partly inspired by the late and embittered romantic poet Heine in Germany, undertook to spread the gospel of national Romanticism in Iceland.

The leaders

The leaders of Romanticism in Iceland were partly educators, partly politicians, and partly poets. Increased work in Icelandic (Old Norse) studies, the edition of the Eddas and the sagas, and growing admiration for them abroad, all combined to convince lay and learned alike of the great value of Icelandic as the classical language—the Latin—of the

North. Realizing this, the Latin School teachers at Bessastaðir in the twenties, notably Sveinbjörn Egilsson, forced their pupils to give immaculate Icelandic translations of the Latin and Greek classics, thus kindling in them love and admiration for their native tongue. The coming political and cultural leaders were all schooled by him and his colleagues.

The coming leaders were: the shortlived editor of *Ármann á Alþingi* (1829–32) Baldvin Einarsson (1801–33) and the editors of *Fjölnir* (1835–39, 1844–47) Tómas Sæmundsson (1807–41), Jónas Hallgrímsson (1807–45), Konráð Gíslason (1808–91), and Brynjólfur Pétursson (1810–51). Both Baldvin and Tómas were closer to the men of the Enlightenment in having the social, economic, and moral progress of their countrymen foremost at heart—and on an unusual tour of Europe (1832–34) Tómas gathered invaluable data of comparison on which to build his program of progress in Iceland. But they were also national romanticists in hailing the liberal ideas of 1830 and working for the rebirth of the Althing at Þingvellir, hoping to recreate its glorious past, conjured up in Jónas Hallgrímsson's beautiful and stirring program poem. Jónas, a naturalist and poet, contributed the arts and sciences to *Fjölnir*, writing among other things a scathing attack on *rímur* from a purely esthetic point of view. Konráð Gíslason wrote a brilliant essay on the Icelandic language and set about purifying it from two centuries of Dano-German dross and its baroque style. This campaign for the purification of the language set an epoch of linguistic nationalism which lasted unchallenged for nearly a century. It continued up to the modernist period of the twentieth century, and its strength still persists.

But the greatest leader in the fight for liberalism and Icelandic autonomy was Jón Sigurðsson (1811–79). He was not really a romantic like the Fjölnismenn but a hard-headed realist, as symbolized by the fact that he wanted the new Althing in Reykjavík and not at Þingvellir. And his efforts were crowned with success: not only did he get the new Althing established in Reykjavík in 1845, but in 1874 the Danish king visited Iceland and brought it its first partly autonomous constitution as a millenary anniversary present. Jón Sigurðsson was not only a great statesman who gathered poets and politicians alike to his liberalistic periodical *Ný Félagsrit* (1841–73), but as a president of the Icelandic Literary Society and as an active member of the Arnamagnaean Foundation and the Society for Northern Antiquaries, he was really the most influential leader of Icelandic (Old Norse) studies during his lifetime, he himself editing sagas, a *Diplomatarium Islandicum,* and a new periodical devoted to the history of Iceland and Icelandic literature.

In Iceland, Jón Sigurðsson's political struggle gave rise to journalism pro and con; the newspapers were at first usually weeklies, and mostly published in Reykjavík, though shortly after the middle of the century they began to appear also in Akureyri and, much later, in other provincial towns.

Icelandic studies

There was an accelerated tempo in Icelandic (Old Norse) studies during the 1820's owing to such men as Rask, Rafn, Finnur Magnússon, and Sveinbjörn Egilsson.

Of the Romantic period two great scholars have already been mentioned: Konráð Gíslason and Jón Sigurðsson. After *Fjölnir*'s demise, Konráð Gíslason succeeded Finnur Magnússon as a professor of Old Icelandic (Old Norse) at the University and buried himself in lexicographical, grammatical, and skaldic studies, so exact in method that they became models for the following Realists. Only in his eclectic edition of *Njála* did Konráð remain true to the romantic principle of beauty.

A new and entirely romantic type of studies was the collection of Icelandic folk tales and folklore for their own sake. This was taken up by Jón Árnason (1819–88) and Magnús Grímsson (1825–60), both in Reykjavík, on the pattern of Grimm's fairy tales.

The rector of the Latin School in Reykjavík, Jón Þorkelsson (1822–1904) was also a grammarian, a skaldic commentator, and lexicographer.

Eiríkur Jónsson (1822–99), lexicographer and editor, and Vilhjálmur Finsen (1823–92), justice of the Supreme Court and editor of *Grágás*, were both members of Jón Sigurðsson's circle in Copenhagen. So was, but to a lesser degree, Gísli Brynjúlfsson (1827–88), lecturer on Icelandic history and literature at the University and editor of the medieval romance *Tristrams saga.*

Two scholars, both friends of Jón Sigurðsson, were destined to lay the foundation of Icelandic studies in England: Guðbrandur Vigfússon (1827–89) and Eiríkur Magnússon (1833–1913). They became associated with Oxford and Cambridge respectively and perpetuated the rivalry of the two schools. Guðbrandur edited the monumental Old Icelandic-English dictionary, based on the collections of Cleasby (and Konráð Gíslason) in 1874. He also edited almost the entire body of

Old Icelandic poetry and prose in five huge collections, two of them in collaboration with York-Powell. Eiríkur translated a selection of Jón Árnason's Icelandic folk tales into English and collaborated with William Morris in translating the sagas into English.

Literary genres

In general it may be said that the literary genres of the preceding period survived, but with a great deal of different emphasis.

Since the romantic poets as a rule were genuinely religious in reaction to the rationalism of the Enlightenment, there are a number of excellent hymns dating from this period, especially when combined with the patriotic theme as in Matthías Jochumsson's great national anthem, 1874. He was the greatest hymn writer of the period. Of poets who specialized in hymn writing, the Rev. Helgi Hálfdanarson (1826–94) and the Rev. Valdimar Briem (1848–1930), later vice-bishop of Skálholt, were the most prolific and best. Related to the hymn writing was the philosophical poetry, first of its kind in Iceland, by Björn Gunnlaugsson (1788–1876) and Brynjólfur Jónsson frá Minnanúpi (1838–1914), but these men were better philosophers than poets.

Rímur flourished during the nineteenth century seemingly more than ever. Not only were the writers of this genre more numerous and more prolific than before—Magnús Magnússon (1763–1840), farmer and blacksmith, had 257 to his credit at death—but there were actually better poets than ever, counting such men as Sigurður Eiríksson Breiðfjörð (1798–1846) and Hjálmar Jónsson (Bólu-Hjálmar) (1796–1875) among their numbers. Moreover, it is generally agreed that Breiðfjörð's *Núma rímur* (a versified paraphrase of J. P. Florian's *Numa Pompilius*, 1835) were the best *rímur* of all time. Yet, when Jónas Hallgrímsson reviewed Breiðfjörð's *Rímur af Tristrani og Indíönu* in *Fjölnir* in 1837, he dealt the whole genre such a staggering blow that it never really recovered from it. It was the skaldic diction with its turgid baroque mannerism and meaningless tags that here clashed head on with the utmost in classical simplicity: Jónas Hallgrímsson's ideal of beauty. And, unfortunately for the *rímur*, it was not in theory only, for there was also Jónas's own ethereal poetry to shame the poetasters. Thus the *rímur*, immune to moral and utilitarian attacks, were tottering from a rapier thrust to their artistic heart. It did not really help matters that Helgi Sigurðsson (1815–88) was working on the most voluminous *háttalykill* of all time, demonstrating twenty basic meters with over two thousand variations (*Bragfræði íslenzkra rímna* [1888] 1891). Neither he nor others knew that the great variety of *rímur* meters had left their mark on some of the outstanding romantic poets of the North, among them, Oehlenschläger and Tegnér, and through them influenced world literature (Longfellow). It was left to the poets and scholars of the next period to revalue the *rímur* from a more sympathetic point of view. But then they could not be resuscitated because the public was becoming accustomed to new entertaining literature in the form of translated adventure, detective stories, and the new native novels.

The popular poetry of the Romantic period and after still decidedly made use of the *rímur* forms, though often coupled with Jónas Hallgrímsson's demands for classical perfection. Popular poets turned out occasional verse, on the weather, on their horses or dogs, congratulations to newly-weds, and condolences at death. Also humorous and sarcastic epigrams were composed that vied with Pope's couplets in pith and wit. The number of such poets was legion, but their great prophets were Bólu-Hjálmar and Páll Ólafsson.

The Romantic movement was essentially lyric, hence lyric poetry was both voluminous and variegated. The patriotism of the romantic poets was often tinged with religious fervor and most were, besides, devout Christians. The patriotic theme had three elements (all found in Eggert Ólafsson): admiration for the old heroic saga age with its manly virtues contrasted with present sloth; love of country, where Iceland was often contrasted with Denmark, and the simple country life with the demoralizing life of Copenhagen; and, finally, praise of the mother tongue. No one appreciated the educational values of the harsh country and its winter seasons as Bjarni Thorarensen, no one was as much at home in the heroic age as Grímur Thomsen with his ballads on figures from the sagas or from the Middle Ages. Both developed vigorous, manly styles. There was a growing body of topographical poetry singing the praises of certain districts and falling into two well defined types, though often mixed, one stressing the region's history and its saga heroes, the other simply a nature description. Bjarni Thorarensen always used the former approach; Jónas Hallgrímsson was the chief early exponent of the other, and naturally so, since he was a poet-naturalist like Eggert Ólafsson and tended to reflect his spirit. Being the greatest representative of unadulterated classic beauty among the Romanticists, he sometimes painted brilliant, often geologically correct, canvasses of his landscapes, sometimes placed himself in the midst of nature among familiar flowers and scenes, greeting them with the loving intimacy of a St. Francis. He could do the same with the birds, the farmer with his scythe, and the fisherman in his boat, and he was really the only one who succeeded in painting country life as attractive (which was Eggert Ólafsson's main concern). As Bjarni Thorarensen was the poet of rugged winter, Jónas was the songbird of summer. His comments on places that he visited were not like Eggert Ólafsson's but akin to those of Heine. All these nature themes were carried on and expanded by the later poets like Steingrímur Thorsteinsson and Matthías Jochumsson, the latter more akin to Bjarni and Gröndal, the former more an echo of Jónas. These later Romanticists were the first to sing of the waterfalls of Iceland, while already Eggert Ólafsson had made poetical commentaries on the volcanoes, the glaciers, and the geysers, thus enriching the poetical imagery of the Romanticists with these powerful contrasts.

The poetry in praise of the language ranges from Jónas Hallgrímsson's beautifully classical tribute *Ástkæra ilhýra málið* to Matthías Jochumsson's impassioned and profound hymn *Tungan geymir í tímans straumi,* cast fittingly in the venerable skaldic and Catholic *hrynhent-Liljulag.*

Very original love poetry was written by Bjarni Thorarensen and Jónas Hallgrímsson. Bjarni's was strangely ethereal and yet powerful with Eddic echoes, Jónas's was a classical expression of the sadness caused by lost love. Gísli Brynjúlfsson also wrote love laments, while Steingrímur Thorsteinsson, betrayed, hit back with a scathing denunciation.

Memorial poetry flourished as always, but was lifted to a rank of high poetry mainly by two of the romantic poets: Bjarni Thorarensen and Matthías Jochumsson. The former saw in his departed friends sturdy heroes, akin to the saga men and himself. The latter drew on such an enormous stock of human sympathy that he could lament the newborn babe as well as the great men of Iceland, past and present.

Of specifically romantic attitudes or themes, romantic irony was found in Jónas Hallgrímsson (from Heine) and Gröndal, the romantic melancholy (*Weltschmerz*) in Grímur, Gisli Brynjúlfsson, and Kristján Jónsson Fjallaskáld. In general Gröndal was the most fullfledged romanticist of the lot in spite of his familiarity with the classics and not uncommon use of classical myth paraphernalia, often for humorous purposes. He even turned Catholic, in romantic fashion, though more out of necessity than conviction. He had the romantic phantasy and cultivated it in a high-flown, florid style. His romantic irony appeared sometimes as indifference to his readers ("my task is composing, yours understanding"), partly as a reckless spurring of his Pegasus from the sublime heights of the starry heavens to the depths of low farce or parody, all in one poem. Indeed, his exuberant imagination, especially in his humorous poems, is his chief charm, though at his worst he may sink down to obscure twaddle. The wide range of his themes is also truly romantic: epic and *rímur* on the heroic *fornaldar* sagas, a dramatic poem on the twilight of the Gods, philosophic poems, poems on the titans Prometheus and Napoleon, a poem on the blue bird and golden eagle of Romanticism, mock heroics and mock idylls, poems on the infinite world and, finally, patriotic poems.

There is a parallelism between the early and late poets of Enlightenment and Romanticism in that the earlier poets translated little and the later a great deal, acting as cultural transmitters.

The earliest Romanticists (Bjarni and Jónas) translated some poems by Ossian, Schiller, Oehlenschläger, and Heine, which were obviously their favorites, though a few others were also represented (including Tegnér, Chamisso, and Goethe). The next generation (Gröndal, Grímur, Gísli Brynjúlfsson) discovered Goethe and the English poets, especially Byron, but also Shelley, Burns, Moore, even Shakespeare. But the greatest translators among the Romanticists were Steingrímur Thorsteinsson and Matthías Jochumsson, both almost outliving the following age of Realism. Both translated Shakespeare, Byron, Burns, Tennyson, Goethe, Schiller, Heine, Chamisso, Uhland, Tegnér, Topelius, Wergeland, and Björnson. To these Matthías added Shelley, Poe, Longfellow, Runeberg, Snoilsky, Fröding, Vinje, Ibsen, Lie, Grundtvig, Paludan-Müller, and Drachmann, thus joining hands, across Realism, with the great Neo-Romanticists of the North. This is not a complete but only a representative list.

Translations from the classics were done almost in inverse proportion to the above, mostly by the earlier Romanticists, especially Gröndal, who finished his father's translation of the *Odyssey* and did one of the *Iliad* himself, both in *fornyrðislag*, and Grímur Thomsen, who late in life did many translations from the ancient Greek classics.

The simple Eddic meters were much used by the early Romanticists, sometimes in pure form, sometimes in variations. Their impulse derived both from Jón Þorláksson and a contemporary edition of the *Edda*. They were used in original compositions, as Bjarni's memorial poems, and translations of epics (Gröndal: Homer) or even of shorter pieces.

Thus Gísli Brynjúlfsson translated Byron's *Ocean* into Egill Skalla-Grímsson's measures, recognizing the fundamental similarity of the two poets of the sea. The skaldic meters were also used, not least by a later romanticist like Matthías Jochumsson, who was a master of *dróttkvætt* and *hrynhent*.

Of classical meters some were transmitted by the transmitters, notably Grímur Thomsen who increasingly used the original meters. Bjarni Thorarensen translated a few lines of Ovid and Martial into wooden hexameters and pentameters, a measure which Jónas Hallgrímsson was to handle with perfection in his patriotic song *Ísland farsælda frón*. Toward the middle of the century Steingrímur Thorsteinsson, following the example of Goethe's *Hermann und Dorothea*, wrote the mock-heroic *Redd-Hannesar ríma* in the same meter; he was followed by Gröndal in his " Þingvallaferð " (1878), and Matthías' " Ferð upp í Fljótsdalshérað " (1900). Of other classical forms becoming popular may be mentioned Horace's *Integer vitae*.

To elucidate the origin of all the new romantic meters would lead too far, but here may be mentioned: the sonnet, the *terza rima*, and Heine's quatrain, all employed to perfection by Jónas Hallgrímsson, and Byron's *ottava rima* used by Gröndal in *Örvar-Oddsdrápa*.

The prose literature may be said to have started in earnest during the Romantic period, since the efforts of the previous periods since the Reformation were both scattered and remained unknown.

At the head of the prose genres may be placed the Icelandic folk tales, of which a few had already been written down by Árni Magnússon. Now, following Grimm, they were collected by Jón Árnason and his companion and published, a sample in 1852, the great collection (*Íslenzkar þjóðsögur og æfintýri*) in 1862–64. They were expected to reveal the hidden springs of nationality and they became right away important in two ways: as models of genuine rural prose style to be used in conjunction with the saga style, and as themes to be drawn upon by the coming novelists and especially the romantic dramatists.

Beautiful essays, some of them on literary criticism, were written by Jónas Hallgrímsson, Konráð Gíslason, Jón Sigurðsson, Guðbrandur Vigfússon, and others.

Art fairy tales (*Kunstmärchen*) and ironic sketches were written by Jónas Hallgrímsson and Jón Þorleifsson (1825–60). Short stories were written by Jónas, Jón Thoroddsen, and Páll Sigurðsson (1839–87). Jónas also wrote the mock-heroic " Gamanbréf."

The old chivalrous *lygi sögur* were still strong enough to produce their last and brilliant offspring, Gröndal's *Heljarslóðarorusta*, written in 1859. The new novel was now really born, under Scott's auspices, in Jón Thoroddsen's *Piltur og stúlka* (Lad and Lass, 1850), a romantic-realistic rural tale. Thoroddsen was followed by Jón Þorleifsson (1825–60), writing *Úr hversdagslífinu* (From Everyday Life), and Páll Sigurðsson (1839–87), writing *Aðalsteinn* (1879), both parsons and capable writers, though not up to Thoroddsen's standard. Finally, passing over a number of unsuccessful writers, two at least were quite popular, though hardly as good as the preceding: the carpenter Jón Jónsson Mýrdal (1825–99) with his *Mannamunur* (Different Men, 1872) and Mrs. Torfhildur Þorsteinsdóttir Hólm (1845–1918) with her many historical novels. She had the distinction not only to be the first woman novelist in Iceland but also to be the first to write on historical subjects, to wit, the seventeenth- and eighteenth-century bishops *Brynjólfur Sveinsson* (1882) and *Jón Vídalín* (1892–93). Torfhildur Hólm's career as a writer coincided with that of the Realists, whose philosophy and writings she shunned as immoral and was berated by them in turn. But her books were wholesome reading and were deservedly popular.

Finally, during the Romantic period the drama, connected with the Latin School in Reykjavík, then the only town of the country capable of raising an audience, came into its own. At first this scene was dominated by translations of the neo-classic humorists Molière and Holberg as well as of the romantic Danish playwrights, Hostrup (*Eventyr paa Fodrejsen*), Heiberg (*Elverhöj*), and others, while Shakespeare, though admired and later translated, was never acted. But soon native playwrights began to try their hand: first Matthías Jochumsson, who at Christmas (1861–62) wrote *Útilegumennirnir* based on an Icelandic folk tale, but perhaps influenced by Schiller's *Die Räuber*. Later he wrote a vaudeville, an historical pageant, and, finally, the historical play *Jón Arason* (1900) more in the Shakespearean than the fashionable Ibsenian manner. This was natural for Matthías as a translator of *Macbeth* (1874), *Hamlet, Othello*, and *Romeo and Juliet* (1887), and, as a matter of fact, he remained a romanticist throughout the period of Realism. The same was true of the other romantic playwright, Indriði Einarsson, though his debut play, *Nýjársnóttin*, came as late as 1871 and though he tried his hand at a realistic problem drama with *Skipið sekkur* (1902). Otherwise he wrote on folk tale themes or history in the manner of the Romanticists, notably *Dansinn í Hruna* (1921). After that he translated fourteen plays of Shakespeare.

Sigurður Breiðfjörð

Sigurður Eiríksson Breiðfjörð (1798–1846) was the foremost *rímur* poet of the nineteenth century with a strong lyric vein, which endeared him not only to the public but also to fastidious poets. Born of poor parents in Breiðifjörður of the West, he could not afford Latin School, but was sent to Copenhagen to learn a cooper's trade. In Denmark he learned to appreciate the poets of transition between Enlightenment and Romanticism, notably Baggesen. Back in Iceland (1818), he plied his trade in several places, married unhappily, became addicted to drink, but composed *rímur* and light poetry which won him many friends. In 1830 his friends sent him back to Copenhagen for a fresh start in life, which, however, failed. Instead, he became a cooper to the Royal Danish Merchant Company in Greenland, 1831–34. Here, in isolation, he wrote some of his best work, notably the celebrated *Núma rímur*, as well as a prose work on Greenland. Returning to Iceland, he had a brief reprieve of happiness with another wife before his death in misery in 1846.

Sigurður wrote over twenty-five cycles of *rímur*, of which fifteen were published, among them *Núma rímur* (1835, 1903, and 1937). The preface of *Núma rímur* shows that Sigurður had taken to heart the Enlightenment criticism of *rímur*, and that he really wanted to pour new wine into old bottles—and did so to some extent. Had he enjoyed the schooling and so acquired the taste of Jónas Hallgrímsson, he might have avoided the latter's vicious attack on his *Rímur af Tristrani og Indíönu* in *Fjölnir*, 1837. He could, to be sure, rest confident that the general public was on his side in the ensuing feud. Yet, being as much of a lyric poet as he was, he may deep down have felt the justification of this criticism. His collected poems, *Ljóðasafn* (I, 1951——), are being published.

Hjálmar Jónsson frá Bólu

Hjálmar Jónsson frá Bólu (Bólu-Hjálmar, 1796–1875), was born in Eyjafjörður but spent most of his miserable crofter's life in Skaga-fjörður, both districts of the North. He was happily married and had seven children, but his life was an unrelenting struggle against harsh nature and the callous indifference of more prosperous brethren. To be sure, his lot was no worse than that of many other fellow sufferers, but he was different, being endowed with a poet's sensitivity, the temper of a Viking, and Icelandic word artistry at its best. The result was a unique figure in Icelandic folk poetry. For Hjálmar was not only a strong realist in a romantic age, depicting Eggert Ólafsson's and Bjarni Thorarensen's glorious Mountain Queen (i. e. Iceland) as a pitiful old lady, nay, almost a bony hag, and yet with filial love, and he was not only a master of invective whose satire could vie with the strongest of the Reformation and Renaissance periods, but he was also a great master of poetic imagery of a sort that might have delighted Donne and the modern poets. Thus in his personal satires he almost always would follow his enemies beyond the grave. In spite of his poverty and lack of formal schooling, Hjálmar was a well-read man in Icelandic (even Danish) literature and had a small library of books and manuscripts. He collected genealogies and folklore and mastered all the old Icelandic meters as well as the *rímur* forms. He was also a wood carver of sorts. Altogether, he was among the greatest folk poets that Iceland has had. His *Ljóðmæli* (Poems) were first published in 1879 and again several times after that. His collected poems in two volumes came in 1915–19, his collected works, poems, *rímur* and prose, *Ritsafn* (I–V in 1949), were published by Finnur Sigmundsson.

Bjarni Thorarensen

Bjarni Vigfússon Thorarensen (1786–1841), the scion of a prominent family, son of a prefect, was born in Brautarholt near Reykjavík but grew up at Hlíðarendi in Fljótshlíð, the home of *Njála*'s most romantic hero, Gunnar. Tutored mostly at home, the brilliant and precocious boy entered the University at fifteen and completed his law study at twenty. After serving in government offices in Copenhagen, he became a deputy justice (1811) and justice of the Supreme Court in Reykjavík (1817). He held this office almost continually up to 1833, when he was made governor of North and East Iceland, residing in the North (Möðruvellir) to his death. In Reykjavík he also twice served as a temporary governor general of Iceland. This career bespeaks an unusually gifted man.

As a boy in the magnificent *Njála* country, Bjarni received lasting impressions of saga and nature, and learned how to make verse. In Copenhagen he listened to Henrik Steffens' lectures inaugurating Romanticism in Denmark. The pedestrian utilitarianism of the enlightened bourgeoisie was swept away by enthusiasm for geniality and mysticism. Oehlenschläger in Denmark, Schiller in Germany, both apostles of Romanticism, became Bjarni's favorites. The native Eddic poetry, in which Bjarni steeped himself, was a most potent influence, but he also learned from Jón Þorláksson (the use of *fornyrðislag*) and Eggert Ólafsson (the archaistic tendency). The stay in Copenhagen matured his poetry: in *Eldgamla Ísafold* (Ancient Iceland), due to become a cherished national song of Iceland, he sang his homesickness, contrasting the Danish flat lands with the magnificent mountains at home.

Back in Iceland Bjarni was sure to clash with the cosmopolitan, rationalistic, humanitarian, and pedestrian, yet great, leader of Enlightenment, Magnús Stephensen, the chairman of the Supreme Court. For Bjarni was the very opposite: nationalistic, orthodox, antihumanitarian, and genial. This naturally marked their co-labors, if not exactly collaboration, in the court, but found little expression in Bjarni's poetry. His antihumanitarianism and antiliberalism did not make for popularity in his time or after, but his conservative nationalism made him join hands with the young national-liberals, who in the eighteen-forties began to demand the resurrection of the Althing. And the high quality of his poetry, though small in amount, soon gave him undisputed sway in the literary world.

Already in Copenhagen Bjarni had seen his native land as a nurse of stern, manly virtues. This is nowhere better expressed than in *Þú nafnkunna landið* (You Renowned Land) where he considers the challenge of frost and fire, poverty and isolation, praying that the harsh country may forever protect its people from the softening and depraving influences of civilization—or else sink in the deep sea. A remarkable prayer by a man whose parents, though personally well off, had lived through the terrors and famine following the eruption near Skaftá. It was in keeping with his heroic spirit to write a eulogy of winter, in the garb of a splendid northern knight, locking earth in his iron embrace. This heroic spirit, born of Bjarni's familiarity with *Edda* and saga, also marked most of his nature poetry: he could not, for instance, praise his native Fljótshlíð without constant reference to the saga heroes. He could also personify his native district or his country as a lady, *Fjallkonan* (The Mountain Lady), a trait borrowed from neo-classic poetic inventory and first employed by Eggert Ólafsson. But Bjarni's use of this symbol may have had deeper personal meaning, for he was extremely attached to his mother and, through quirks of fate, was kept from marrying until he was thirty-four years of age. He had in his youth translated some fullblooded love poetry by Catullus and Ovid, his later love poetry was partly passionate, partly bantering verse on the rejected lover, but in his most original love poem "Sigrúnarljóð" inspired by Oehlenschläger and the *Edda*, he projects his love beyond earth and death into the ethereal interstellar spaces—a truly transcendental but by no means fully Platonic love poem.

That Bjarni should write good memorial poetry could be expected from his sincere and deep faith and his eye for heroic measures in man. But a genius only could have made his poems rank with Egill Skalla-Grímsson's "Sonatorrek" and Hallgrímur Pétursson's funeral dirge. He wrote them in different meters—one was cast in the German romantic ballad form—but his best were written in the simple Eddic *fornyrðislag*, sometimes mixed with *ljóðaháttur*. Justly famous are his memorial poems on Sæmundur Magnússon Hólm and Oddur Hjaltalín. The first-named was a man who, much like Bjarni himself, did not follow the beaten path and so earned the displeasure if not hatred of the mocking conformists. This crowd is depicted in bold imagery as a caravan moving to life's last stage, or a school of herring pursued by bigger and bigger fish into the jaws of the whale. The poem on the latter contains the often quoted warning to those who allow themselves to be carried downstream in life's current, not to blame the salmon running upstream and jumping the cascades.

Bjarni Thorarensen's poems, *Kvæði*, were first published in 1847, but a definitive edition in two volumes, *Ljóðmæli*, was first done by Jón Helgason in 1935.

Jónas Hallgrímsson

Jónas Hallgrímsson (1807–1845), descended from a family of poets, the son of Jón Þorláksson's chaplain, was born at Hraun in Öxnadalur (Eyjafjörður). He was nine when his father drowned, a loss that affected him deeply. At Bessastaðir (1823–29), guided by the remarkable teachers there, he became steeped in classics, ancient and Old Icelandic, and read a little Ossian. At the University (1832) he began with law, but soon turned to natural history (science) and literature, reading Schiller, Tieck, and especially Heine. With a group of schoolmates he started the periodical *Fjölnir* (1835–47) which brought forth his programmatic nationalistic-liberal poetry, translations from German romantic and liberal writers, and his scathing criticism of the old *rímur* poetry, from a strictly artistic point of view. What the review could not accomplish—to reform the taste for lyric poetry in Iceland—Jónas' own poetry amply did.

As a scientist Jónas began his explorations in Iceland in 1837. He continued his travels (1839–42) in spite of ill health, collecting a good

deal of material toward a geographical description of Iceland. He kept
working on this in Denmark until his premature death in 1845. His
friends devoted the last volume of *Fjölnir* (1847) to his unpublished
writings and brought out at the same time, a first edition of his *Ljóðmæli*
(Poems). His complete works, *Rit* (Works, 1929–37), were finally
published in five volumes by Matthías Þórðarson.

Romanticism in Germany and Denmark, the wave of liberalism caused
by the July revolution in 1830, and the nationalism in Eggert Ólafsson's
Poems (1832) all combined to mould Jónas. He himself contributed his
acute observation of nature, love of his land in its sunny moods, and a
keen—almost classical—sense of beauty. Drawing a glorious picture of
the ever beautiful land and contrasting the bustling life of the heroic saga
age and its Althing with the present lethargy and the ruins at Þingvellir,
he made " Ísland " into a ringing appeal to the slumbering people. The
resplendent summer nature, in beautiful word pictures attained by no
one before Jónas, was even more to the fore in the magnificent placid
" Gunnarshólmi " (Gunnar's Islet), describing a famous incident from
Njála, one of the very few passages in the sagas where a feeling for
nature is in evidence. The whole is cast in new Italian terzines of inter-
laced rime, concluding with two stanzas in *ottava rima*.

Unlike Bjarni, Jónas did not consistently see Iceland in connection
with the heroic saga age: on the contrary he most often saw it from a
naturalist's point of view. Thus " Skjaldbreiður " is nearly as good
geology as it is magnificent poetry, and no one but Jónas could have
elaborated on the vast vistas from the summit of Hekla as he did in the
poem celebrating the French scientist and explorer, Paul Gaimard. In
another type of nature poetry Jónas commented, in the manner of
Heine, on places visited by him; these poems are often short, pithy,
and personal. A third type of Jónas' nature poetry is represented by
Fífilbrekka gróin grund or " Dalvísur " (Valley Verses). This is
really a hymn, worthy of St. Francis, in praise of the most common
manifestations of Icelandic nature, the poet's bosom friends, realistically
observed and treated with loving care and piety. Related to this are his
poems on birds or animals: the " little golden plover," the " white
ptarmigan," and the " gray sparrow," though these poems are really
tragedies in miniature.

Valuing Eggert Ólafsson as highly as he did, it was natural for Jónas
to pay him tribute in an unusually elaborate and weighty poem " Huldu-
ljóð " (Ode to the Fairy). And he was trailing his master's footsteps,

when he drew the sensitive picture of the proud farmer at his haymaking ("Sláttuvísur") and the happy fisherman on the sea ("Formannsvísur"). The utilitarian spirit of the Enlightenment was here kept, but in an ennobled form.

The tragedy in Jónas' life—the loss of his father, the loss of a sweetheart to another man, his failing health and spirit—found expression in some poignantly beautiful poetry, like the exquisite and sad "Ferðalok" (Journey's End). But his friendship and conviviality gave the nation some of its most cherished festive songs, like "Vísur Íslendinga" (Verses for Icelanders—*Hvað er svo glatt*), the merry *Nú er vetur úr bæ* (Now is Winter Away), and the even merrier Bellmannian "Borðsálmur" (Table Hymn).

Like Jón Þorláksson and Bjarni Thorarensen, Jónas employed all the Old Icelandic meters, not least so the simpler ones. Of classical meters he used the hexameter and pentameter, of romantic meters the Italian terzines, the *ottava rima*, and the sonnet as well as the Spanish *redondilla*. From the German Romanticists he got several meters, notably the Heine quatrain. In translations he often adapted into *fornyrðislag*. His form excelled in classic simplicity, was limpid and musical, polished to a high degree. With him began a new era in Icelandic lyric form: Where Bjarni Thorarensen was rough, manly, and archaic, Jónas was polished, beautifully limpid, and modern in diction.

Jónas and his comrades loved to strike an "absurd comical" tone, usually quite burlesque, in their talk and private letters. It was a reflection of their romantic irony, their romantic revolt against their world. Some of Jónas' poetry is marked by this—poetry that he himself probably would not have published but is quite good *sui generis*.

Though the origins of the novel now can be traced to the Enlightenment period, it is still true that Jónas' short stories, sketches, and *Kunstmärchen* were the first published in Icelandic (*Fjölnir*, 1847).

"Grasaferð" (Gathering Iceland Moss), an idyl in bright summer landscape and limpid prose, was a worthy originator of the short story. Its motifs were popular with the coming playwrights.

Two fairy tales were imitated or adapted from H. C. Andersen's tales about animals or animated objects, one modeled on an unknown German romantic tale.

The few satirical skits are reminiscent of Heine, but "Gamanbréf til kunningja" (A Letter of Fun to Friends) was a highly amusing mock-heroic description of Queen Victoria's state visit to France in 1843. The style of this letter influenced Gröndal when he wrote his *Heljarslóð-arorusta*.

Jón Thoroddsen

Jón Þórðarson Thoroddsen (1818–68) has rightly been called the father of the modern Icelandic novel; there is no evidence that he knew anything of earlier attempts of the kind (Laxdal), except the short stories of Jónas Hallgrímsson. He was born at Reykhólar in Barða-strandarsýsla of the Northwest. Having studied with private tutors and at Bessastaðir Latin School (1837–40), he became a tutor at a parsonage in Eyjafjörður, was engaged to the parson's daughter, and had a child by her. Next year he went to Copenhagen to study law, but his fiancée had the mishap to meet another man and was given to him on the wrong assumption that Jón would have nothing to do with her. It is said that Jón's letter of reconciliation reached her just after the wedding. This was the bitter romance out of which Jón fashioned both of his love stories, and it definitely did not help his law studies, but may explain the gay abandon of his Bellmannian drinking songs from this period. In 1845 he was joined by another hapless lover, Gísli Bryn-júlfsson. The two collaborated on the liberal periodical *Norðurfari* (a sheaf of poems, *Snót* [1850] was done with another collaborator), and Gísli seems to have inspired his friend to read English literature, notably Scott. No doubt he also aided and abetted Thoroddsen's urge to write novels, and thus the first Icelandic novel, *Piltur og stúlka* (Lad and Lass) was written in 1848–49 and published in 1850, the year Jón Thoroddsen left for Iceland to become an acting prefect of his native district, Barðastrandarsýsla. Residing in Flatey on Breiðifjörður, he joined a circle of unusually alert and cultured men who had invited the most learned autodidact of the time, Gísli Konráðsson, pupil of Jón Espólín, and father of Konráð Gíslason, to stay with them and work on his many manuscripts. Jón realized that here was plenty of material if ever he was to buckle down to writing "a national epic" in Scott's sense. He made one abortive attempt to write it in Copenhagen in 1854, where he had returned to finish his law studies. But though he never finished the novel *Maður og kona* (Man and Wife), on which he worked inter-mittently from his return to Iceland until his death as a prefect of Borgarfjörður in 1868, it was really a great success amply fulfilling his fondest hopes.

Piltur og stúlka (Lad and Lass, 1850) is an idyl of a country boy and girl whose love is thwarted by complications, but finally are united. As characters, the lovers are too good to be really interesting; fortunately they are cast with others of a vastly different stamp, among which there is a country gossip and a niggardly farmer who both have become proverbial in Iceland. Likewise, idyllic shepherd scenes alternate with lively brawls at the fall round-ups of sheep, and, finally, we are introduced to the merry school life at Bessastaðir and to the half-Danish rabble in Reykjavík, already satirized by Sigurður Pétursson.

Maður og kona (Man and Wife, 1876) has a romantic plot and lovers that differ little from the earlier novel. But it has also a vast array of comic characters and much interesting folklore, which the author had had ample opportunity to observe during his long career as a magistrate. Belief in ghosts and magic had been endemic in the Northwest since the days of the plague-ridden parson Jón Magnússon. Here it is represented by an old bedridden crone. The heroic spirit of sagas and *rímur* has its representative in a giant farmer, old-fashioned and gullible, while that of the Bible is upheld by a much quoting deacon, who suffers inglorious defeat at the hands of the philistine farmer. The small society is ruled by a bland but avaricious and intriguing parson whose household is adorned by several odd characters including a half-witted fool.

Jón Thoroddsen's style was as fresh as his characters. Its basis was the ordinary rural talk and narrative, as represented in the folk tales and fairy tales, as well as the style of the sagas. Thoroddsen was, moreover, a master of parody and burlesque and could use for that purpose, not only the chancery and the sermon styles, but also the saga style and even Sveinbjörn Egilsson's Homeric style. His language was pure and rich.

Although Jón Thoroddsen is not known especially for his poems, his patriotic and nature songs have a lyric quality that recalls Jónas Hallgrímsson. They have remained very popular. Still his drinking songs and parodies are probably more original.

Jón Thoroddsen's poems (*Kvæði*) were first published in 1871, then in 1919. Steingrímur J. Þorsteinsson wrote an excellent study on the novelist, *Jón Thoroddsen og skáldsögur hans* (I-II, 1943), and published the prose works *Skáldsögur* (I-II, 1942).

Grímur Thomsen

Grímur Þorgrímsson Thomsen (1820–96) was born at Bessastaðir, the son of a jeweler and a business manager of the Latin School. At the

University in Copenhagen (1837) he studied esthetics, Hegelian philosophy, and modern European literatures, writing on contemporary
French poetry (1843) and Lord Byron (1845), a pioneer work in
Scandinavia that gained him not only an M. A. and Ph. D. but also a
very unusual stipend to travel through the capitals of Europe (1847).
His critical appreciation of H. C. Andersen, Runeberg, and Bjarni
Thorarensen was instrumental in establishing the reputation of these
poets in Denmark. Grímur Thomsen admired Fjölnismenn but kept
aloof from Jón Sigurðsson, associating more than any of his countrymen
with Pan-Scandinavian and Danish political leaders. These contacts
gained him entrance into the Danish foreign service, in which he
remained active until 1866. Resigning and returning to Iceland, he
bought Bessastaðir, married, and dwelt there as a gentleman farmer up
to his death.

Though Grímur contributed a poem to *Fjölnir* as early as 1844, his
first slim *Ljóðmæli* (Poems) did not appear until he was sixty (1880).
A second collection came in 1895; a second enlarged edition of the first
volume and *Rímur af Búa Andriðarsyni og Friði Dofradóttur* appeared
in 1906; a collected edition in two volumes was published in 1934.
Because of the late appearance of his poems and because of easily spotted
formal faults, his poetry was slow in gaining acceptance, not to say
popularity.

When Grímur began his career, Romanticism had lost its freshness
and the poet was enmeshed in disillusionment and the *Weltschmerz* of
Byronism. This line of thought is traceable from his first poem " Ólund "
(Spleen, 1844) to the complaints voiced by him on his birthday in 1862,
where he looks forward to a barren old age. He had crashed the golden
gates of high society, but the gains were not commensurable with the
efforts, judging by his masterful satire " Á Glæsivöllum " (At Glitter
Fields, 1865). But having made his escape, chilled to the very marrow,
he made a quick recovery in the more congenial atmosphere of his home
at Bessastaðir. Here he soon found himself re-creating the heroic past
of his nation, not in flashes like his predecessors, but in narrative form,
probably less indebted to the old ballad form than to the modern art
ballads of Schiller, Goethe, and Uhland. In these poems he revealed
himself as a dramatic storyteller and a master of character drawing:
his portraits of Halldór Snorrason and Hildigunnur lose nothing of their
pristine saga vigor. But though he preferably drew his figures from
Edda and saga, medieval story and legend, Germanic and Romance, were

also grist to his mill as shown by his gripping ballad on " Olifant."
Even historic figures, Icelandic and European, served him as models,
provided he found in them the sturdy, manly spirit of the heroic age.
His ballads were usually not long, but he could write cycles on saga
themes, longest of which was *Rímur af Búa*, . . . in several cantos, but
not cast in *rímur* meters despite the name.

As a romanticist Grímur was drawn to the mystic side of Icelandic
folklore, the ghost and the outlaw stories, as well as to the sterner aspects
of Icelandic nature, forming as it were a fitting frame for these stories
of horror. His poems on " Glámur," the ghost that Grettir fought, and
" Sprengisandur," an inland desert road haunted in the popular imagination by outlaws, are cases in point.

In his earlier days Grímur translated or paraphrased Ossian, Milton,
Byron, Runeberg, Oehlenschläger, La Fontaine, Schiller, and Goethe.
At times he would adapt rather than translate, as for example, in his
treatment of " Suomis sång " in " Landslag."

In his old age Grímur devoted himself to translating specimens from
the ancient Greek lyric poets and tragedians. Apparently he felt equally
at home among the ancients, as in his own Old Icelandic heroic age. He
filled a gap which the translations of the *Odyssey* and the *Iliad* had left
open, but his translations, though good, never won the popularity of
Homer in Iceland.

Grímur Thomsen did not have the facility of most Icelandic verse-
makers and could commit elementary metrical blunders. Instead few
were his equal as a master of style and diction, and this quality
endeared him to fastidious and discriminating readers. He always strove
for the *mot juste* and usually with success. And if he chose, he could
write poems of exquisite musical quality like " Endurminningin "
(Remembrance).

Still it was as the rough-hewn manly stylist that Grímur Thomsen
was at his best, a worthy representative of the heroic age with whose
figures he loved to converse and in the atmosphere of which he really
felt at home.

Benedikt Sveinbjarnarson Gröndal

Benedikt Sveinbjarnarson Gröndal (1826–1907) was born at Bessastaðir, the son of Sveinbjörn Egilsson, who taught him to love the
classics of his native country as well as those of Rome and Greece. In
Copenhagen (1846–50) his extensive studies in natural history, poetry,

and philosophy led to no academic degree, but after seven barren years in Reykjavík, he returned to Copenhagen (1857), where he this time met a Catholic missionary, Father Étienne de Djunkowsky, who took him to Kevelaer, Germany and converted him to Catholicism (1859). Shortly after, while leading a carefree life at the Catholic University of Louvain, Belgium, he wrote *Heljarslóðarorusta* (The Battle on Hell's Fields) on Napoleon III's victory at Solferino, January 25, 1859. In Copenhagen, after this Catholic interlude, he settled down to serious study of Old Icelandic philology (M. A., 1864), wrote on folklore and mythology, published the life and letters of his benefactor C. C. Rafn, and a key to his father's *Lexicon Poeticum*. Later he started a periodical of his own (*Gefn*, 1870–74), writing on politics, economics, philology, antiquities, Icelandic geography and natural science—not to forget the poetry. From 1874 to 1883 he served as a teacher at the Latin School in Reykjavík; after that, his long life was divided between drinking, study of nature, drawing, and writing. He published seven volumes of poetry, including his *Kvæðabók* (1900); a collected edition of his works has just been published (*Ritsafn* I–V, 1948–54, by Gils Guðmundsson).

One might have expected the ornithologist Benedikt Gröndal to have sung hymns to the birds of Iceland, but the "Gullörn og bláfugl" (Golden Eagle and Blue Bird) that he actually eulogized were not of this world, but denizens of that romantic land of fancy where Gröndal's soul loved to roam and gambol. Here, too, he found his lilies and roses, if he at all deigned to stroll the romantic meadow, but, as a matter of course, he much preferred mounting his winged Pegasus, soaring to a distant star, where he could watch the glistening show of aurora borealis and strum his golden harp as an accompaniment to the music of the spheres. In short, Gröndal was a fullblooded romanticist who, on the slightest provocation, would run riot, aided by his uncanny mastery of high-flown language, his paternal inheritance. At the best he shines in scintillating brilliance, a fiery comet among his dim planetary contemporaries; at his worst he sinks to mediocrity, and that, alas, altogether too often.

The poet was especially apt to fall into his grand romantic manner when writing on heroic Old Icelandic or Greek legends, e. g., *Örvar-Odds drápa* (1851), *Ragnarökkur* (Twilight of the Gods, 1868), and "Prometheus." Or, even more so, when offering to the Muse of philosophy, the poem "Hugfró" (Peace of Mind), inspired by Alexander Humboldt's *Kosmos*. This does not make easy reading in spite of the author's commentary. But Gröndal had simpler and more intimate strings on his lyre, which vibrated in his childhood memories " Æskan " (Youth), in his beautiful, patriotic " Vorvísa " (Spring Song, 1859), and in occasional nature-loving moods.

Still Gröndal was greatest as a humorist in verse and prose, the poetic epistles to his comic muse Mrs. Sigríður Einarsdóttir-Magnússon being of the best. On her birthday, March 17, 1855, he wrote to her a poem on a scroll twelve ells long, of one hundred stanzas in mock-heroic style featuring the Greek gods in the fashions of contemporary Reykjavík. Like Athena of old, Sigríður sprang from Zeus' head. Another letter written from within the monastery walls of Kevelaer, entitled " Gaman og alvara " (Gay and Grave), ranges from sublime fancies to deliberate nonsense; among other things it contains Poe's *Murders in the Rue Morgue* retold as a hymn parody. Comic too is the mock-heroic travelogue to Þingvellir (1878).

Gröndal's humoristic prose is even better than his poetry; here *Heljarslóðarorusta* (1861) stands supreme, written in sheer exuberance of spirit, a rollicking burlesque. In it modern history is cast in the form of medieval romance of chivalry: it is really the last *lygi saga* in Iceland, but unlike *Don Quixote*, it was not designed to criticize the genre, for Gröndal loved it, turning at least one cycle of *rímur* into a *lygi saga* (*Sagan af Andra jarli*), while he reversed the process with his favorite *Göngu-Hrólfs saga*. Though denying it, he was really influenced by the manner of Jónas Hallgrímsson's " Gamanbréf " when he wrote *Heljarslóðarorusta*. His more Rabelaisian satire *Þórðar saga Geirmundssonar* (1891) was not as good. Gröndal also wrote the Aristophanic farce *Gandreiðin* (The Witch Ride, 1866) as well as other playlets.

Finally, Gröndal wrote a great number of articles and essays on all the great variety of subjects that interested him. Not a few were fine instances of his whimsical wit and burlesque play and phantasy. Some were learned; others revealed his reactions to the changing winds of fashion. He was naturally opposed to the Realism of the eighties and he balked at Ibsen's use of the sagas. His letters and his autobiography *Dægradvöl* (Passing the Time, 1923) are marked by the same whimsical temperament, though the last-named can be more serious in tone when he himself is concerned.

Gröndal wielded, undoubtedly, the most versatile pen of his age. Oldest of the three great figures of the second half of the nineteenth century—Gröndal, Steingrímur, and Matthías—he first achieved fame and was, perhaps, the first to fade because of his romantic excesses, though he more than holds his own as a humorist. Apart from Homer's *Iliad* and *Odyssey* (translated, in part, with his father) in *fornyrðislag* and selections from the *Arabian Nights* in prose, he did little translating.

Gísli Brynjúlfsson

Gísli Brynjúlfsson (1827-1888) was born at Ketilsstaðir, Vellir in the East of Iceland, the son of a parson, descended from Einar Sigurðsson. In Copenhagen (1845) he was to study law but became attracted by Icelandic studies and European literature (Byron). Disappointment in love turned him into an ardent love poet and left him in a state of mind vacillating between Byronic despondency ("Faraldur") and Viking-like activism. The revolts of the masses in Paris, Ireland, and Hungary against the tyrants of 1848 fired his imagination not only to sing their praises in his poetry, but even to tell his countrymen all about it in the two volumes of *Norðurfari* (1848–49) which he published, together with his friend Jón Thoroddsen, another law student and hapless lover. This experience turned Gísli into a social democrat, first among his countrymen, and it may explain why he did not always see eye to eye with the more conservative Jón Sigurðsson, though other reasons are usually adduced, perhaps rightly. In 1874 he became a lecturer on Icelandic history and literature at the University, keeping that post until his death His *Ljóðmæli* (Poems, 1891) never gained much popularity in Iceland. His interesting and revealing *Dagbók í Höfn* (Diary in Copenhagen) was published in 1952.

Páll Ólafsson

Páll Ólafsson (1827–1905) was born in the East, the son of a parson; he had no formal education and lived mostly as a farmer and valued member of his community at Hallfreðarstaðir in the East. He was a romantic poet, an admirer of Jónas Hallgrímsson and the classical J. L. Runeberg; he also carried on the tradition of Bólu-Hjálmar and Sigurður Breiðfjörð but, perhaps, above all the school of humorous poetry in the East, going back to Stefán Ólafsson. His humorous epistles, unique in their art, belong to the same school. He was an unsurpassed master of the quatrain, but also used many other meters with equal ease. He sang of summer nature, praised his beloved wife (a rare theme with poets), his horses, and his strong "wine." His epigrams were unsurpassed for sarcasm and wit. In his poems, e. g., "Tíminn" (Time), he could turn similes from everyday life that would pass scrutiny from the modern metaphysical poets, though he has otherwise not the slightest trace of their baroque turbulence. Indeed, he was the greatest master of fluent form and as such emulated by Þorsteinn Erlingsson. His poems were published in two volumes (1899–1900) by his brother Jón Ólafsson (1850–1916), a poet, novelist, but above all a journalist. They were recently republished (1944) by his kinsman, the novelist Gunnar Gunnarsson.

Steingrímur Thorsteinsson

Steingrímur Bjarnason Thorsteinsson (1831–1913), born at Arnarstapi, Snæfellsnes, the son of a governor and a bishop's daughter, was early an avid reader and poet. Before leaving the Latin School in Reykjavík (1851) he had written a clever mock-heroic poem (*Redd-Hannesar ríma*) on rustic life in the classical measures of Goethe's *Hermann und Dorothea*. At the University (1851–63) he studied classical philology and read extensively in the modern European literatures, Scandinavian, German, English, and French. The years 1863–72 he spent in Copenhagen writing some of his finest patriotic poetry in support of Jón Sigurðsson's cause. In 1872 he returned to the Latin School in Reykjavík where he served first as a teacher then as a headmaster until his death at a ripe old age.

Steingrímur Thorsteinsson contributed his early poetry to *Ný Félagsrit* (1854) and the popular anthologies *Svava* (1860) and *Svanhvít* (1877). He edited the periodicals *Ný sumargjöf* (1859–65) and *Iðunn* (1884–89). His *Ljóðmæli* (Poems) came in four editions, 1881–1925. They were finally edited by his son Axel Thorsteinsson.

Steingrímur's lyric poetry, usually in good taste, sometimes distinguished, dealt with the themes of love, patriotism, and nature. Among his love lyrics there were many light poems depicting the happy lovers at play, e. g., " Draumur hjarðsveinsins " (The Shepherd's Dream), but his most deeply felt poem " Kveðja " (Farewell) was a bitter denunciation of the " fallen angel " who jilted him.

As a member of Jón Sigurðsson's national-liberalistic circle in Copenhagen, Steingrímur contributed many poems in praise of his country and many eloquent exhortations urging his countrymen to fight for national emancipation and political liberty. These poems, often stirring songs breathing the spirit of freedom and sincere love of country, did not miss their mark, nor did they fail to endear the poet to his countrymen. They continued the romantic line of referring now to the past, now to the nature of the country, but did not have Jónas Hallgrímsson's freshness of approach.

Already as a youth, the poet was captivated by Icelandic nature in various moods and many seasons. As a mature man he loved to make excursions to the scenic haunts of his native district or into the vast and little known uplands. In singing his experiences in the open, his moods ranged from the exhilaration of the glacier mountain scenery " Háfjöllin " (The High Mountains), to the deep melancholy ocean shore " Við hafið " (At the Ocean).

As a wise old man the poet grew less productive, more critical, and developed a sharp epigrammatic style.

In his translations Steingrímur was following the paths of Jón Þorláksson and Sveinbjörn Egilsson, aiming to enrich the native literature by foreign masterpieces in poetry and prose. Among these were: *The Arabian Nights*, Shakespeare's *King Lear*, Defoe's *Robinson Crusoe*, Tegnér's *Axel*, and H. C. Andersen's *Fairy Tales*. Here were also samples of the great lyric poets of the age: Ossian, Oehlenschläger, Wergeland, Björnson, Topelius, Tennyson, Byron, Burns, Petöfi, Chamisso, Heine, Goethe, and Schiller. The translations were usually made with taste, sometimes supreme skill. The title of *Kulturbringer* given the poet by the Austrian critic J. C. Poestion was thus amply justified.

With Benedikt Gröndal and Matthías Jochumsson our poet won popular acclaim as one of the three great national poets, *þjóðskáld*, of the second half of the nineteenth century. He was more classical than the other two, less genial and less romantic.

Matthías Jochumsson

Matthías Jochumsson (1835–1920) was born at Skógar in Þorskafjörður of the Northwest, of fine farmer stock. Too poor to aspire to a higher education, the twenty-two-year-old youth went to Copenhagen to become a merchant. Instead, he buried himself in the study of languages, the *Edda*, and classical and modern literatures under the friendly guidance of Steingrímur Thorsteinsson. Later some friends helped him to a more formal education, enabling him to graduate from the Latin School in 1863 and the School of Theology in 1865. After that he served as parson of various places, one of them the historic parsonage at Oddi, except for a period (1874–80) that he edited the newspaper *Þjóðólfur*, and the last twenty years of his life when he held a government grant in recognition of the fact that he was by common consent the poet laureate of the country. He edited another newspaper *Lýður* (1889–91) at Akureyri in the North. Here he lived over thirty years until his death at eighty-five immediately after his admiring countrymen had overwhelmed him with their loving esteem. Marrying three times, he lost two of his wives under circumstances that caused him great heartache. He was a great traveler, going abroad eleven times and making friends with significant men in many lands. He wrote spiritedly about his visits to America—the World Exposition in Chicago (1893)—and Denmark (1905).

Though Matthías wrote verse as a boy, it was with the play *Útilegu-mennirir* (The Outlaws, 1864, later called *Skugga-Sveinn*) that he won acclaim as a poet. It was significant as the first romantic play written in Iceland. Later he wrote a historical pageant, a vaudeville, and—his most ambitious undertaking in that genre—the historical play *Jón Arason* (1900) in the manner of Shakespeare, whose *Macbeth, Hamlet, Romeo and Juliet,* and *Othello* he already had turned into lively Icelandic. He was a great translator—even greater and more prolific than Steingrímur —and, in addition to a vast number of poems, he did Tegnér's *Frithiofs saga*, Byron's *Manfred*, and Ibsen's *Brand*.

His own lyric poems were first published in 1884, next in five volumes 1902–1906, a selection in 1915, and a complete one-volume edition (*Ljóðmæli*) in 1936. He wrote a romantic epic on *Grettis saga: Grettis ljóð* (1897), an excellent autobiography: *Sögukaflar af sjálfum mér* (1922), and a huge amount of personal letters, published after his death: *Bréf* (1935).

His own lyric poetry ranged from profound or exultant hymns to humorous, even hilarious, verse, from patriotic eulogies of Iceland and its scenic or historic districts to cosmopolitan praise of other lands. He lived two celebrations: a national one, the millenary of Iceland in 1874 and the turn of the century, 1900, celebrating both in odes, hymns, and pageantry. He outlived two generations and paid all prominent personalities, friends and family, his final respects in commemorative poems, individualized to an unusual degree. His fine memorial to Dr. Guð-brandur Vigfússon in Oxford was one of his outstanding commemorative poems.

The genius of Matthías Jochumsson was at once broad and profound. The essence of his personality was, no doubt, anchored in a deep mystic experience, described in " Leiðsla " (Ecstasy), from which he drew his inspiration. This gave him his optimistic trust in God and the love of his neighbor. But though secure, his religion was quite unconfessional and his searching spirit was in turn influenced by American Unitarianism, the "new" German theology and the Anglo-Saxon brand of theosophy and spiritualism. Abhorring the materialism and the atheism of the time, he sang the praise of God in some of the finest hymns of the Icelandic tongue, including the National Hymn, "Lofsöngur" (Hymn of Praise: Ó, Guð vors lands—God of our Land) of 1874. But though universally admired by the people, many of his unconventional hymns had to wait for the Icelandic hymnbook of 1945 to be admitted. Unlike most of his compatriots, he loved the nation more than the country and he was capable of voicing his distress and despair, nay, a scathing indictment, at nature's harshest treatment, e.g., in the famous poem "Hafísinn" (The Polar Ice), occasioned by its dread arrival in the spring of 1888. Similarly his indomitable spirit was excited to revolt against the overwhelming dread and dead force of Iceland's mightiest waterfall, Dettifoss. A child's tear, because alive, impressed him more.

Just as Matthías Jochumsson wrote fine obituary poetry, so he also excelled in commemorative poems on historical personages; his poems on Snorri Sturluson, Hallgrímur Pétursson, and Eggert Ólafsson being among the very best. They were marked by his ever ready sympathy and a fine sense for the dramatic representation, making them truly monumental. His command of the history, the literature, and the language of the country was phenomenal; he wielded skaldic and Eddic meters with equal ease as the modern measures of his translations, for example, of Shakespeare's blank verse. He wrote an inspired eulogy of the language in stately skaldic measures. The sagas and their personalities lived in him and, like Bjarni Thorarensen, he never sang the praise of a district without populating it with the heroes of old. Yet he was no blind admirer of the saga age; his sympathy with the suffering hero of the Christ type was probably more spontaneous.

Matthías enjoyed an everlasting buoyant spirit and fertile phantasy, somewhat reminiscent of Gröndal, of whom he had learned much as a young poet. But though he often was an inspired bard, he was seldom a consistently good artist. His poems were rarely without flashes of genius, but they could sink down to mediocrity in parts.

With Gröndal and Steingrímur Thorsteinsson, Matthías was considered one of the three great poets of the latter half of the nineteenth century. If his fame in the end eclipsed theirs it was not only because he lived longest, but because he was a man and poet of truly great proportions, worthy to carry on the double heritage of Iceland: the heathen spirit of Egill Skalla-Grímsson and the Christian one of Hallgrímur Pétursson.

Kristján Jónsson

Kristján Jónsson (1842–69) was born at Krossdalur in the North, a farmer's son, early orphaned and maltreated as a boy. Still he managed to read much, even foreign languages, and write poetry, a fact which gained him entrance to the Latin School in Reykjavík in 1864. But adversity had marked him: he had taken to drink, and disappointment in love broke his spirit. He left school in 1868 and died a year later at the age of twenty-six.

Admiring Gröndal's high-flown romantic diction, Kristján used it to advantage in his magnificent description of Dettifoss, a powerful waterfall which he was the first to put on the literary map. Like others he wrote patriotic poetry, and he could, at times, give free rein to his ebullient youthful spirit. But only on the surface. At heart he was sick with melancholy and this, naturally, became the characteristic note of his poetry: witness such poems as "Gröfin" (The Grave) and "Tárið" (The Tear). And if Gröndal taught him ebullience, his master in melancholy was no less a personage than Lord Byron himself.

The world-weariness and melancholy found ready resonance in and was heartily embraced by his poor and miserable countrymen. His poems, Ljóðmæli, were first published in 1872 by his schoolmate Jón Ólafsson, appearing after that in five editions, the last one in 1946.

Indriði Einarsson

Indriði Einarsson (1851–1939) was the first writer to devote himself exclusively to playwriting. A native of Skagafjörður, graduating from the Latin School in 1872, and from the University of Copenhagen as a political economist in 1877, he became an expert on statistics and economic affairs to the government of Iceland until he retired in 1918. He worked much for the temperance movement in Iceland and was closely associated with various dramatic undertakings in Reykjavík, being an active member of its Dramatic Society from 1897 and tireless in his efforts to establish a national theater, which, nevertheless, could not open until after his death. Out of his big family came some of the most distinguished actresses and actors in Iceland.

As an impressionable romantic youth, Indriði saw Matthías Jochums-son's *Útilegumennirnir* during his first winter at the Latin School. Six years later (1871) he wrote his first play, *Nýjársnóttin* (The New Year's Eve) for the school boys to produce. It was based on a fairy tale out of Jón Árnason's collection, a favorite practice of the romantic playwrights, partly in imitation of their Danish colleagues (cf. Heiberg's *Elverhöj*). *Nýjársnóttin* became very popular, especially in a revised version (1907) in which the fairy world was fashioned after Shakespeare's *Midsummer Night's Dream.* In his next play, *Hellismenn* (Cave Men, 1897) he drew on Jón Árnason's outlaw stories.

In Copenhagen (1872–77) Indriði came reluctantly under the sway of Realism and wrote, finally, one play in that manner: *Skipið sekkur* (The Ship Sinks, 1902). It was a problem play in the approved Ib-senian manner. Then, again emulating the Norwegians, he wrote the historical play *Sverð og bagall* (Sword and Crozier, 1899), the first of its kind in Iceland, based on an episode in *Sturlunga saga,* and, as the name indicates, depicting the struggle between heathen and Christian values. In this play Indriði succeeded even better than Ibsen and Björnson in striking the genuine saga tone.

Two more folk-tale plays were to follow, one mediocre, the other, *Dansinn í Hruna* (The Dance at Hruni, 1921), one of Indriði's best. The Devil has built the church at Hruni for the old priest, stipulating one of his two sons, who now has taken over his father's duties, as a reward. And so the son, to fulfil this destiny, dances in the church with the con-gregation on a Christmas eve until the church sinks. This, alone among Indriði's plays, is written in blank verse, to fit its Faustian theme.

After his retirement, Indriði wrote one more historical play and translated fourteen plays of Shakespeare in a form adapted to the scene; none of these have been printed. He also translated several Danish plays. He had the brilliant idea to tax the admission to the movies in order to build a national theater. The building of this had started before his death, but was not finished until after World War II, during which the British used the building as a warehouse.

Realism to Neo-Romanticism, 1874-1918

Historical background

In the struggle for national independence in Iceland the dates 1874 and 1918 are crucial. The first year marks the political and financial autonomy given Iceland on the millenary of the country's settlement, with pomp and ceremony at Þingvellir, August 2, 1874, by King Christian IX. The second year records full independence in personal union with Denmark, granted by King Christian X on December 1, 1918. The most important step on the road toward complete sovereignty was the establishment of home rule in Iceland in 1904.

Economically the seventies and eighties were hard years, bordering on famine, caused by volcanic eruptions (1875) and heavy polar ice drift (1881). During those hard years up to one fourth of the nation emigrated to North America, so that population growth stopped temporarily. But the tide turned during the nineties, owing mainly to improved methods of fishing, the old rowboats being replaced, first by big sailboats and, after the turn of the century, by motorboats and trawlers. This development started a drift of population from the country to the towns, the relation in 1900 being eighty to twenty per cent; in 1920, fifty-seven to forty-three per cent. The growth of the towns stopped emigration.

An optimistic belief in material and spiritual progress was very strong in the late nineties and the first decades of the twentieth century. True, World War I gave believers in human progress a jolt, but in Iceland it hardly affected people except those maturing in the twenties. It caused a war boom from which Iceland benefited moderately, directly and indirectly, since the Danes, gaining South-Jutland, were liberal enough to grant Iceland freedom.

Origin of Realism

Realism and Naturalism, born in the industrial centers of Europe, were made up of several strands. There was a belief in mechanical science, which had made industrialization possible. There was the Marxian theory of socialism (1867) motivated by the exploitation of the workers. English liberalism was still music to oppressed people. Darwin (1858) opened a vista of evolutionary progress, but dealt a blow to the authority of the Bible, also undermined by historical and textual criticism (Strauss). Science was the watchword of the Realists or the Naturalists in Paris, like Zola, who wanted literature itself to be scientific, "a slice of life." Since conditions of life were oppressive to the poor, pessimism always threatened. But the more optimistic spirits, or the more indignant, set themselves to improve the world by putting problems under debate in their writings.

The Danish defeat of 1864 had made the Danes ultranationalistic and archconservative, hostile alike to political and religious liberalism, to socialism, and to the new realistic literature. But the realistic ideas were introduced by Georg Brandes in his famous course of lectures: *The Chief Currents in Modern European Literature* (1871). This clarion call was soon heeded by the great Norwegian writers, Björnson, Ibsen, and Kielland, who quickly became popular in Iceland. Brandes's call was also heeded in Iceland, though in a land of isolated farms there was no room for urban socialism. But calls for better treatment of paupers and farmhands, as well as some way out for poor crofters, were timely enough, and so was political liberalism. But where the old Romanticists had been nationalists, the Realists set their hope in international progress of science to improve conditions even in Iceland. Perhaps most widespread of the realistic tendencies was anticlericalism and religious scepticism; it resulted in the "new theology" with less stress on hell toward the end of the century. Jón Helgason (1866–1942), later bishop, was its chief representative.

The Realists in Iceland

The first to raise the realist call in Iceland was the fiery nationalistic poet and journalist Jón Ólafsson (1850–1916), Páll Ólafsson's brother. He admired Brandes from a distance, translated Björnson and J. Stuart Mill (*On Liberty*, 1886), even wrote a realistic novelette. Usually, however, the beginnings of Realism are credited to *Verðandi* (1882), a yearbook published by students in Copenhagen who had heard Brandes and knew him. Of the four, Gestur Pálsson and Einar Hjörleifsson contributed short stories, Hannes Hafstein and Bertel E. Ó. Þorleifsson (1857–90) poems, but the last-named succumbed to the pessimism of the time and committed suicide. Hannes Hafstein, a virile fighter, was an admirer of the revolutionary Ibsen. Gestur Pálsson, following Kielland, was indignant at social injustice, hypocrisy, and man's ability to deceive himself morally. *Verðandi* was replaced by *Heimdallur* (1884) written by the same authors, carrying Brandes's life by Hannes Hafstein and translations from Björnson, J. P. Jacobsen, Drachmann, Kielland, Paul Heyse, and Turgenev. But now the leaders left Copenhagen: Gestur Pálsson (1882) for Iceland to take up journalism, Einar Hjörleifsson (1885) to do the same among his countrymen in Winnipeg, Canada, and Hannes Hafstein (1886) to take up politics in Iceland. In Iceland they were joined by Jónas Jónasson, writing drab short stories, but fought by the old romanticist Benedikt Gröndal and Páll Briem, who were scandalized at their antinationalistic point of view.

In the nineties, Realism continued to attract Icelandic writers in Copenhagen, at home, and in America. In Copenhagen, Þorsteinn Erlingsson contributed anticlerical and socialistic poetry to *Sunnanfari* (1891–1914) edited by the nationalistic Jón Þorkelsson (forni and others). In Iceland the farmers of Þingeyjarsýsla, educated by a brilliant local librarian, Benedikt Jónsson á Auðnum (1846–1939) studied not only the Norwegian authors and Strindberg, but also Carlyle, Herbert Spencer, Huxley, Darwin, Auguste Comte, Marx and Max Nordau. Hence the Þingeying authors, Þorgils Gjallandi (Jón Stefánsson), Guðmundur Friðjónsson, and Guðmundur Magnússon all began under realist auspices, though they all veered into Neo-Romanticism, especially the last two, since they lived longer. So, too, the regional authors of the district: Sigurður Jónsson, Jón Þorsteinsson, Indriði Þorkelsson, and others.

In Canada, Einar Hjörleifsson was soon joined by Gestur Pálsson, who died there a disillusioned man, but probably a convinced socialist. During the nineties the poets Stephan G. Stephansson and Kristinn Stefánsson (1856–1916) and the short story writer Gunnsteinn Eyjólfsson (1866–1910) all joined the Realist movement by writing social satires.

Progressive nationalism and idealism

Though the Realists were still gaining ground in the nineties, the oldest ones, Hannes Hafstein and Einar Hjörleifsson (Kvaran) were really changing into progressive nationalists and idealists, spurred by the optimism rampant in the world up to World War I. In Copenhagen national romanticism was represented by Jón Þorkelsson in his *Sunn-anfari*. Not only did he reveal the literary riches of the Icelandic late Middle Ages to the incredulous University, but he advocated a university in Iceland, a plea taken up in Reykjavík by Einar Benediktsson, who, curiously enough, became not only the most vociferous advocate of material progress in Iceland, especially the harnessing of waterpower by use of foreign capital, as well as a fervent nationalist, nay, even an imperialist, but also the first symbolist mystic in Iceland. Yet, it was the old realist Hannes Hafstein who as a Fabian progressive and as the first premier of Iceland (1904) was to break the country's isolation by introduction of the telegraph (1906).

The new University of Iceland opened in 1911, on June 17, the cente-nary of Jón Sigurðsson. Þorsteinn Gíslason was a poet and journalist close to Hafstein. Jón Trausti was a great believer in Einar Benedikts-son's progress and had the same Nietzschean tendencies to despise the crowd and parliamentarism. After 1900 Guðmundur Friðjónsson became more and more the conservative farmer, a lover of the soil, rustic virtues and the national heritage, but more and more suspicious of the towns and their foreign progressive "culture." Having returned from Canada a mellowed Christian reformer (1895), Einar Hjörleifsson (Kvaran) was really more concerned with spiritual than material progress, and having read F. W. H. Myers's *Human Personality and its Survival of Bodily Death* in 1904, he became a spiritualist. He was soon joined by Haraldur Níelsson, the ablest "new theologian" of the time, translator of the Bible, and though opposed by the positivist philosopher Ágúst H. Bjarnason and political enemies, they made great headway before the end of World War I.

Another occultism of Anglo-Saxon (ultimately Hindu) origin was theosophy; its message of universal brotherhood and reincarnation appealed to the same circles of intellectuals as spiritualism: old roman-tics like Matthías Jochumsson, an old realist like Jónas Jónasson, neo-romantics like Guðmundur Guðmundsson and Einar Benediktsson. After the war, spiritualism had not only its own organ published by Kvaran until his death (1938), but also won the support of *Eimreiðin* up to 1955. Theosophy was carried on by the essayist Jakob Kristinsson and the poet Grétar Ó. Fells. The philosopher Helgi Péturss[on] synthe-sized Icelandic nationalism, the idea of the superman, spiritualism, and theosophy into his "scientific" cosmology. Both spiritualism and theosophy were embraced and kept by Þórbergur Þórðarson in spite of his later Marxism. In the twenties, Kvaran's art and philosophy came in for criticism from a conservative nationalistic point of view by Nordal, Bjarni Jónsson frá Vogi, Árni Pálsson, also the rustic nationalistic group. The conservative nationalists, also critical of parliamentarism, produced the shortlived *Vaka* (1927–29).

Symbolism and decadence

Though it is obvious that the Icelanders got Realism through Brandes from France, it is equally obvious that the reaction against that Realism did not all stem from that origin, at least not directly and not over Denmark. Yet, the Danes were affected by French decadence and Symbolism so that they were in full revolt against Brandes already in the nineties, as described in an article in *Eimreiðin* (1898). But the first to preach the gospel of Symbolism in Iceland, so called because the artists favored symbols, images, allegory, and sought beauty, imagination, intuition, and God in nature, in short mysticism or religion, was Einar Benediktsson in his articles about literature, realistic and new, in *Dagskrá* (1897). He had himself been in Copenhagen in the early nineties; he was to become one of the chief representatives of symbolism in Iceland in his constant seeking of God in nature and the unity of mind and matter. In the late nineties three poets appeared, publishing their first books 1900–1905: Guðmundur Guðmundsson in Reykjavík and the two Þingeyings, Sigurjón Friðjónsson and Hulda (Unnur [Bjarklind] Benediktsdóttir, daughter of the librarian Benedikt á Auðnum). She ennobled the *þulur* (nursery rime) form, while he was the most facile versemaker of his day and a chief translator of neo-romantic verse (Scandinavian and foreign, e. g., P. Verlaine). Sigurjón was of a more philosophic bent; he derived his inspiration from the Norwegian periodical *Kringsjaa*. Worth mentioning, too, was the shortlived Jóhann G. Sigurðsson (died 1906) and the very fastidious but not very productive Sigurður Sigurðsson (debut 1906), devoted to his art, an admirer of Nietzsche, a hedonist and a bohemian—all attitudes that could be found not only in *fin de siècle* France, but also among the writers of the gay nineties in England and Scandinavia. One thing differentiated all the early Symbolists of Iceland—except Einar Benediktsson—from the progressive nationalists or idealists: they were interested not in politics but only in the quest for their ideal, their philosophy, and their art.

The Danish-Icelandic writers

All the attitudes of the early Symbolists, some of them intensified,

were found among the Danish-Icelandic writers, who, during the first
and second decade of the twentieth century, tried to make a living as
artists, denied them at home, by writing for a larger Scandinavian public.
The brilliant pioneer, Jóhann Sigurjónsson,, dramatist and lyric poet
(debut 1905) was followed by the poet Jónas Guðlaugsson (died 1916),
the dramatist Guðmundur Kamban, and the novelist Gunnar Gunnarsson.   These were followed in the twenties by the lesser writers Friðrik
Á. Brekkan and Tryggvi Sveinbjörnsson, the former a novelist and poet,
the latter a dramatist only.   Jóhann Sigurjónsson, especially, displayed
a great appetite for life, Nietzchean ambitions, and forceful emotions in
his works, combined with the faraway romantic Icelandic scene and
custom.   There was an increasing emphasis on love—both in Iceland
and Denmark—and Kamban made it the sole philosophy of his heroines,
but it was reserved for the authors of the twenties in Iceland to lift the
Victorian taboos in discussing love.   The war turned Kamban into a
social critic, Gunnar Gunnarsson, after an intermezzo of anxiety, into an
Icelandic national romanticist.

Literary genres

   Many of the literary genres of the Romantic movement were carried
into the realistic period though some with different emphasis.   There was
less interest in hymns because of the rationalist attitude.   The *rímur*,
though flourishing, were not generally approved by the Realists.   Verse
was now used for satire or description of the underprivileged (Gestur
Pálsson, Guðmundur Friðjónsson).   The realistic love poetry of Hannes
Hafstein had a new plastic quality, that of Þorsteinn Erlingsson, new fire.
Both wrote satires, the first urging revolt in Ibsen's terms, the latter
lampooning churchmen, even Christianity, as he saw it, in witty verse in
the vein of Byron's *Don Juan*.   This was probably one source of the
rather common narrative poetry of the period, cultivated also by Stephan
G. Stephansson in Canada.   Another source was probably *Frithiofs saga*,
especially among the neo-romanticists.

   In prose, apart from lectures and essays, the Realists cultivated
especially the short story (also the animal story), the novelette, and the
novel.   The Realists became, indeed, the chief novelists of the period,
though, when they got to novel writing (after 1900) most had become
more or less touched by the new progressive idealism or other new
tendencies.   Realistic drama was written by the old romanticist Indriði
Einarsson and by Einar H. Kvaran.

The new national romanticists, apart from carrying on the patriotic poetry inspired by the struggle for independence, for the first time not only gave the *rímur* their critical due as a valuable popular form but also demonstratively employed those tested meters in their own ambitious poetic efforts (Þorsteinn Erlingsson, Einar Benediktsson). Símon Bjarnarson Dalaskáld (1844–1916) was most prolific of the contemporary *rímur* poets, but Guðmundur Guðmundsson (skólaskáld) the most original in turning the form into a humorous political commentary in *Alþingis rímur* (1902). With this went interest in and respect for other traditional, nationalistic forms, notably *þulur* and, later, ballads (Gestur, pen name for Guðmundur Björnsson [1864–1937]). The great discoverer of the late Middle Ages, Jón Þorkelsson (pen name Fornólfur), went back to his beloved period for matters and meters, notably that of *Ljómur*.

Those influenced by Symbolism and related neo-romantic tendencies, wrote primarily verse. There was the highly ornate philosophical poetry of Einar Benediktsson, the simpler philosophical strains of Sigurjón Friðjónsson, the highly variegated light songs of Guðmundur Guðmundsson, the personal lyric of Hulda, the fastidious bohemian verse of Sigurður Sigurðsson, the toweringly ambitious lyric of Jónas Guðlaugsson, and the lyrical gems, sparkling and profound, of Jóhann Sigurjónsson. Less and less these men used art for propaganda, more and more for revealing their innermost feelings. Here also belong the romantic drama and the romantic novels of the Dano-Icelandic writers.

Among the neo-romantics Guðmundur Guðmundsson and Gestur were the most prolific translators of verse.

Icelandic studies

Though one would expect the romantic line to be followed without a break in studies of the national literature and language, one may notice a certain influence of realistic fashions. For one thing: practically all the scholars were anticlerical and antisuperstitious. New stress on a scientific approach in philology was realistic. Out of it came a phonetic approach to orthography and language, Björn M. Ólsen (1850–1919); diplomatic editions and higher criticism in philology, Finnur Jónsson (1858–1934); interest in material culture, Valtýr Guðmundsson (1860–1928), Jón Jónsson [Aðils] (1869–1920); and the great geographer and cultural historian Þorvaldur Thoroddsen (1855–1921). Definitely realistic was the idea of placing the Eddic poems in Iceland (B. M.

Ólsen) or Norway (Finnur Jónsson), though Ólsen might be blamed for national romanticism in so doing. Future research showed that Ólsen's view of the sagas was more realistic than that of Finnur Jónsson.

Definitely national romantic was Dr. Jón Þorkelsson's (forni, 1859–1924) interest in the literature after 1400, including *rímur*, starting with *Om Digtningen på Island i det 15. og 16. Århundrede* (1888), and Ólafur Davíðsson's studies in Icelandic riddles, sports and pastimes, *vikivakar* (dances), rigmaroles and nursery rimes (*þulur*): *Íslenzkar gátur, skemtanir, vikivakar og þulur* (1887–1903) as well as collections of folk tales and studies in magic.

The spirit of progress combined with national romanticism to produce results of lasting value. The sagas were edited in a popular edition (1891–1902). The Icelandic Literary Society moved its Copenhagen branch to Reykjavík, merging its *Tímarit*, devoted to Icelandic studies, with a new semipopular magazine *Skírnir* (1905———). A Historical Society was founded to publish post-Reformation sources. Many collectors of folk tales were active, but publication had to wait for the twenties, since which time it has never ceased. Most important was the founding of the new University of Iceland, 1911, with Björn M. Ólsen as rector and professor of Icelandic language and literature, Jón Jónsson Aðils, teacher of the history of Iceland. Two professors of philosophy, Guðmundur Finnbogason and Ágúst H. Bjarnason (1875–1951), became important transmitters of culture and enrichers of the language. The latter wrote a series of popular books on the history of religion, culture, and philosophy down through the ages, first published in 1905–15, and completely revised during the forties.

Outside of Iceland, Icelandic studies were represented in Copenhagen by Finnur Jónsson (1887–1928), professor of Old Icelandic, and Valtýr Guðmundsson (1890–1928), professor of Modern Icelandic, also the historian Bogi Th. Melsteð (1860–1929) and the librarian Sigfús Blöndal (1874–1950) who, with his wife Björg Þorláksdóttir, was engaged in the writing of a monumental Icelandic-Danish dictionary, published with the aid of Jón Ófeigsson (1881–1938) 1920-24.

In America, Halldór Hermannsson (1878–1958) became in 1905 the Curator of the Willard Fiske Icelandic Collection at Cornell University, later a professor of Scandinavian languages and literatures at the university. With his catalogues of the collection in 1914, 1927, and 1943, as well as his periodical *Islandica* (1908–1945; 1958) he established himself as the greatest bibliographer of Iceland after Árni Magnússon.

Gestur Pálsson

Gestur Pálsson (1852–1891) was born in Reykhólasveit of the Northwest, the son of a book-loving farmer. He was to study theology in Copenhagen (1875) but was instead attracted to the modern literature, while a disappointment in love started him on the road to drink and dissipation. He was one of the chief contributors to *Verðandi* in 1882. Back in Reykjavík (1882–90) he became a government clerk and newspaperman, as such airing his realist ideas on education (against the classics) and on the romantic literature of his countrymen, which he felt overvalued the saga tradition and held no hope for the future. Chafing under the petty life in a small town—which he exposed in a brilliant lecture, 1888—he left Reykjavík for Winnipeg, Canada, which, however, on closer inspection he found equally unbearable and would have left but for his premature death in 1891.

Gestur Pálsson made his debut with some rather mediocre poems (1874), but he was the most brilliant prose writer in *Verðandi* to which he contributed his first short story " Kærleiksheimilið " (Home of Charity), a bitter satire on the brazen hypocrisy and tyranny of masters, maltreatment of paupers, and spineless moral weakness—all occurring on a " model " country farmstead. In Reykjavík, Gestur Pálsson wrote several short stories, among them " Hans Vöggur " (1883), the life of a water-carrier in Reykjavík, " Skjóni " (1884), one of the earliest animal stories in Iceland, and the tragic " Sagan af Sigurði formanni " (Story of Skipper S., 1887), in which the main character, because of his superstition, caused his brother's death. In *Þrjár sögur* (Three Stories, 1888) the two last rank with the author's best: " Tilhugalíf " (Engagement) was an acid satire on " benevolent society " in the small town, Reykjavík, while " Vordraumur " (Spring Dream) depicted a spirited lady, an ardent hedonist and lover of nature and animals, rather than of humankind—just like her creator, the author.

Apart from Brandes, Gestur Pálsson was influenced by Turgenev and, especially, Alexander Kielland. Both Kielland and Gestur were masters of satire and irony, both hated those in power, whether monarchs or demagogues, both lavished their sympathies on the underdog. Gestur did not have any illusions about democracy; he was a socialist before his time.

The most complete edition of Gestur Pálsson's works, *Ritsafn* (1927) was introduced by his friend Einar H. Kvaran.

Jón Stefánsson

Jón Stefánsson (pen name Þorgils Gjallandi, 1851–1915) was born, lived, and died as a farmer in the beautiful district on Lake Mývatn in the North. Here he was introduced to the sagas in the home of his uncle and to Scandinavian realist writers of the eighties (notably Norwegian) through the library of Benedikt Jónsson at Auðnir, another friend. He was forty when his revolutionary spirit, long pent up, at last found outlet in the short stories of *Ofan úr sveitum* (From the Countryside, 1892). Like other Realists he revolted against the conventions of the church and the hypocrisy of the clergy and public opinion. He was first of the prose writers to describe love as an irresistible natural force. He was to do all this much better in his chief work *Upp við fossa* (By the Waterfalls, 1902), really the first good novel since Thoroddsen's days. His treatment here of the love theme made an epoch in Iceland for psychological insight and intensity of emotion and was considered by many to be indelicate, if not indecent. It was a tragic story of incestuous love between a parson's daughter and his illegitimate son, stopped by the parson's revelation of the truth. But, unlike what he had done in his earlier stories, he treats the parson here with almost as great a sympathy and understanding as his unfortunate children. In this respect his realism has mellowed: he is more interested now in the fates of his heroes than in changing the conventions.

Like most Realists, Þorgils Gjallandi wrote a number of animal stories, about his dogs, sheep, cows, and horses. But unlike his colleagues, he was less tempted to see them as sufferers at the hands of their cruel owners than as heroes in their own right. Unforgettable is his story of the young mare who braves glacier rivers and rough lava fields to get back to her stud and her foal, but breaks a leg and is frozen to death in the wilderness. In it we have the heroic ideal of the sagas combined with the uncompromising individualism of the Realists.

Þorgils Gjallandi's style was as virile as his manly characters, but humor was rare in his prose. The sentences could become clipped and abrupt when charged with subdued but heavy feeling. And like the saga writers he could leave things unsaid—to be read between the lines.

His collected works, *Ritsafn* in four volumes, followed by a detailed life, were published in 1945 by Arnór Sigurjónsson.

Jónas Jónasson

Jónas Jónasson (1856–1918) was born in Eyjafjörður, educated in

Reykjavík. He served as a parson in the South (1883–85) and as a teacher at Akureyri, Eyjafjörður (1908–18) and in his literary work he combined the vocations of preacher and scholar. He welcomed *Verð-andi* and wrote himself a number of short stories mirroring the culture of his parishioners in the South, drawing a far from flattering picture of local bullies, hypocritical robbers of widows, shysters and chiselers of tithe—or political windbags and lazy good-for-nothings.

His historical novelettes were influenced by the popular saga style of Jón Espólín and Gísli Konráðsson. His only long novel was a failure. He lacked the brilliant wit and the indignation of Gestur Pálsson, but he could be mean and sarcastic. There was often a dry matter-of-factness about his stories. The scholar in him made him a closer student of local color and custom than some of his colleagues, and he wrote an excellent and unique work on Icelandic folklore and folkways after the Reformation: *Íslenzkir þjóðhættir* (1934). He also served as an editor of a periodical for popular edification and education.

His collected works in three volumes, *Rit Jónasar Jónassonar frá Hrafnagili*, were published by his sons, 1947–1949.

Jón Svensson

Jón Stefán Sveinsson (1857–1944) was born at Möðruvellir in Eyja-fjörður, the son of a book-loving clerk and a pious mother. When he was growing up, the lure of America was just beginning to be felt in Iceland, and one of his brothers went there. The fate that awaited Jón was, however, much more exceptional: he was offered an education in France by the young Catholic mission in Iceland, hoping perhaps to see him return to his native country as a propagandist of the only true faith. Jón left Iceland as a boy of twelve in 1870, but returned only to visit. He became a fine Jesuit scholar, devoted to his new mother church, and an excellent teacher, spending about a quarter of a century at a Catholic school in Denmark. During this time he never could forget Iceland; he visited it once (1894) and wrote many articles about his experiences and the Old Icelandic literature, of which he translated *Gunnlaugs saga* into German.

In 1912 Jón fell seriously ill and spent the next two years as a convalescent at Exaten, Holland. Here he wrote the book *Nonni* (1913) in German, the book which was to establish his fame as a writer for youth. It was followed by *Nonni und Manni* (1914), *Sonnentage* (1915), *Die Stadt am Meer* (1922), *Abenteuer auf den Inseln* (1927), and *Auf Skipalón* (1928). This series of Nonni books recounting the good boy's experiences in his native Eyjafjörður, in the romantic city of Copenhagen, and on the beautiful Danish Islands, was interrupted by another travel book *Die Feuerinsel im Nordmeer* (1933) telling about the author's triumphal tour to the millenary celebration of the Alþing in 1930, but it was brought to a close with *Nonni erzählt* in 1936.

The books had an instant appeal in all Catholic lands in western Europe and were translated into a number of languages, including the author's native tongue (1922———). One effect was that the author became one of the most popular lecturers on Iceland, not only in Catholic western Europe, but also in America, and even in Japan, both of which countries he visited on a world tour 1936–38 after which he returned to his old haunts. He died in Cologne, Germany, in 1944.

As a celebrated writer for youth Jón Svensson was compared to H. C. Andersen and Mark Twain, but his art was totally different. He told his own experiences with quiet simplicity and reverend piety, as truthfully as he could manage. Yet he had an eye for adventure and an uncanny ability to shroud his faraway land in a romantic haze. Even more extraordinary was his knack of turning seemingly prosaic everyday experience into something really interesting. His style was quiet, limpid, and clear. He was really a romanticist.

Þorsteinn Erlingsson

Þorsteinn Erlingsson (1858–1914) was born of well-to-do parents at Stóramörk under Eyjafjöll and grew up in the Njála countryside. Here he was discovered by two of the leading poets of Iceland, Steingrímur and Matthías, who brought him to Reykjavík and persuaded the third outstanding poet, Gröndal, to tutor him for the Latin School. In 1883 he went to Copenhagen to study law, but soon turned to Icelandic studies (Old Norse) and literary pursuits, though his life in Copenhagen, until he went home in 1896, was a struggle with poverty and ill health. Back in Iceland he first became an editor of provincial journals, but finally settled in Reykjavík, where he eked out a meager living by teaching, but was nevertheless very happy with his second wife (1900–1914).

There was a streak of romanticism in Þorsteinn which kept him a lifelong friend of Gröndal and especially of Steingrímur. He shared their admiration for the Iceland of old—unlike the cosmopolitan Hannes Hafstein, who ridiculed the excessive romantic nationalism. Like Steingrímur he was attracted by " the beautiful soft and mellow " (Nordal) and he wrote fervent love and nature lyrics. He loved nature in its summer garb, and he expressed his sympathy with birds and beasts not only in poems but also in exquisite animal tales in the form of oriental stories. He was deeply interested in Icelandic folk poetry and polished the quatrain of Sigurður Breiðfjörð and Páll Ólafsson to a new perfection. He brought the same perfectionism to bear on the form of all his poetry. But Þorsteinn was not only a romanticist but also one of the greatest among the Realists—a revolter, though almost against his own will. Like others he hailed Brandes as a leader, but he owed his development no doubt primarily to the fact that he was living in Copenhagen at a time when a jealous and harsh regime was keeping the poor citizens in abject poverty bordering on slavery. This turned him into a social democrat a generation before socialism found any reception in Iceland, a violent revolter against state, church, and especially the fundamentalist God, presumably omnipotent, whose harsh treatment of the world he could never put up with and whose injustices he never would countenance. The wonder was that he should cling so tenaciously to this old belief. His nationalistic revolt against the Danes was similarly deep-rooted and radical. It began with the celebrated poem on Rask's centenary November 24, 1887, which brought him an official rebuke and probably shortened his days at the University. After that he began to contribute poems, first to *Sunnanfari*, later to *Eimreiðin*, but his first collection, *Þyrnar* (Thorns) came in 1897. A second, slightly enlarged edition came in 1905, but the two posthumous editions of 1918 and 1943 were edited and furnished with introductions by Sigurður Nordal. *Þyrnar* contained not only the romantic poems on love, nature, "auld lang syne," and the harsh radical poems on the fate of the gods, destitution and wealth, but also poems in a lighter satirical vein which Þorsteinn had learned from Byron, his favorite poet next to Goethe. In this light vein he wrote some of his best satires such as " Eden," " Jörundur," about a shortlived rebel king of Iceland, and " Eiðurinn " (The Oath), describing the love story of Ragnheiður Brynjólfsdóttir in Skálholt (later celebrated in a great novel by Kamban). He also began composing the history of Fjalla-Eyvindur (about the same time made into a famous play by Jóhann Sigurjónsson). Of his later poetry, " Við fossinn " (At the Waterfall) is very notable for in it he takes a romantic stand against the progressive's dream of utilizing the waterfalls for industry; a dream cherished by many of the progressives around and after the turn of the century, but by no one like Einar Benediktsson whom Þorsteinn hated for this and perhaps also for his tough form—the very opposite of his own pure and simple perfection.

Einar Kvaran

Einar Hjörleifsson Kvaran (1859–1938), was the son of a parson, hailing from Stefán Ólafsson's parsonage in the East, but grew up in Skagafjörður and Vatnsdalur of the North. Graduating in 1881 from the Latin School, he went to Copenhagen to study political economy but deviated into literature, the burning questions, and the high life of the day. His contribution to *Verðandi* was rather shocking, describing the ups and downs of student life. Instead of returning to Iceland, he went to Winnipeg, Canada (1885) there to join a colony of his countrymen. Here he helped to found the two weeklies, *Heimskringla* (The Globe, 1886——) and *Lögberg* (The Tribune, 1888——), serving as an editor of the latter until 1895 when he went home to Iceland for good. In Winnipeg he lost one family and founded another. He also exchanged the reforming zeal of the Realists with the gospel of brotherly love and forgiveness. He wrote his first successful short story *Vonir* (Hopes, 1890), hailed as a masterpiece by Brandes, and composed some poems of subdued melancholy. In one of them he asked the question " Is there anything on the other side [of the grave] ?" which was to occupy his mind the rest of his life.

In Iceland Einar became a journalist (1896–1906) taking an active part not only in the political struggle for independence, but also concerning himself with education, the temperance movement, and the theater. Most of all he was interested in spiritualism, having been converted in 1904 by reading F. W. H. Myers's *Human Personality and its Survival of Bodily Death*. With his friend, the enthusiastic minister and professor of theology, Haraldur Níelsson, he organized a " Society of Psychic Research," wrote and lectured to spread the gospel, finally becoming an editor of their organ *Morgunn* (Morning, 1920–38). For Kvaran, conversion to spiritualism was a logical development from his previous scepticism, for only by what he considered to be positive proof could be regained his belief in life after death.

After his success with *Vonir* Kvaran wrote a number of short stories published in three collections (1901–13), most of them mirroring rural life from his youth. A few of the earlier ones were still critical of the home tyrants, like Gestur Pálsson's stories had been, but above all they were sympathetic to the sufferers: the orphans, a seduced maid, an old woman losing her son to America. He preached no revolt but Christian charity, forgiveness, and self-denial. He could even doubt whether a just cause was worth fighting for. Some of these stories rank with Kvaran's best work, not least so the crisp, impressionistic "Þurkur," (Dry Spell, 1905) ; others might be a bit too sentimental.

Having quit journalism, Kvaran could tackle more ambitious literary undertakings, novels and plays. He began with a double novel, *Ofurefli-Gull* (Overwhelming Odds—Gold, 1908-11) depicting for the first time the bourgeoisie of contemporary Reykjavík under the impact of the ideas of the "new theology," seemingly harmless, but odious to the old and sinister rulers of the town, though these villains were not allowed to go unconverted to the liberal new gospel of love—an almost invariable treatment of Kvaran's villains. The novels were written with persuasion, though some of the characters tended to be a little shadowy apart from their ideology. Two plays followed : one historical the other laid in contemporary Reykjavík, the latter advising wives to forgive their husbands' peccadilloes.

With the novel *Sálin vaknar* (The Soul Awakens, 1916) a new period was inaugurated in Kvaran's authorship, comprising all of his later works : three novels, two plays, and one volume of short stories. They were all marked by two things : a spiritualistic outlook and an optimistic emphasis on success and happiness in life. The belief in success and progress was already implicit in "Anderson" (1913), a short story of an American-Icelander who was to bring modern civilization to the country, and these optimistic heroes marched on in Kvaran's books until the series was brought to an end with *Gæfumaður* (The Fortunate Man, 1933), hero of his last novel. Yet the heroes always tended to be anaemic in comparison with the villains. The saving graces of woman were always emphasized.

Kvaran wrote a simple direct and strictly selective style, glittering in his descriptions of nature, spiced with dry humor, and glowing with the warm humor of his profound intellect. He lacked variety, virility, and the pathos of strong emotions. His psychological analysis often revealed traces of William James's theories of the subconscious.

Kvaran's liberalistic humanitarianism, optimism, and spiritualism exerted an enormous influence during his lifetime but did not go unchallenged. In the twenties Nordal challenged his outlook as cheap and demoralizing, causing a celebrated literary controversy. His spiritualism was even more viciously attacked in the thirties by H. K. Laxness who by then had become the apostle of the younger generation.

His collected works, *Ritsafn* in six volumes, were published by his friend Jakob Jóh. Smári in 1944.

Jón Þorkelsson

Jón Þorkelsson (pen name Fornólfur, nickname forni, 1859–1924) was born at Ásar, Skaftártunga in the South, the scion of prominent families. At the University in Copenhagen he studied Icelandic history and literature, writing a notable thesis *Om Digtningen på Island i det 15. og 16. Århundrede* (On the Poetry in Iceland during the fifteenth and sixteenth centuries, 1888), a pioneer work in the field. The following years were filled with research, but in 1898 he returned to Reykjavík, soon becoming the director of the National Archives, a position he held until his death. He was a prolific editor and scholar, a founder and president of the Icelandic Historical Society (1902———). He wrote many historical, biographical, and literary works.

In Copenhagen he edited *Sunnanfari* (1891–97), an important publication open to the poetry of young authors. It was anticlerical as the Realists had been, but progressive nationalistic where they had been socialistic and cosmopolitan. It was, in other words, neo-romantic and it published the first poetry of Einar Benediktsson, the greatest of that group. If Jón Þorkelsson published an occasional poem of his own in these early days he did not think much of it. Later he was to become attracted to themes from his own research, and these he published, under the pseudonym Fornólfur, from time to time, and finally in book form, *Vísnakver Fornólfs* (Fornólfur's Quire of Verse, 1923). In an engaging preface, he tells of his ambition as a youth to turn his "finds" into poetry, but instead his life has been spent in salvaging the flotsam on the shores of the great ocean of time, and practically no time is left to turn it into art. Like other great workers he often reverts to the flying time, and how little he can accomplish; likewise, though not often, to the dwindling fires of his youth. He is attracted primarily to the great men of the church and state in the later Middle Ages, like Björn Guðnason í Ögri opposing Bishop Stefán in 1517, or the two last Catholic bishops Ögmundur and Jón Arason, at the hour of their betrayal and execution. Then he composes a love poem in praise of Ólöf Loftsdóttir, the greatest lady of her time in Iceland, using as his spokesman her court poet Svartur. But the greatest poem in the collection is "Vísur

Kvæða-Önnu," the life of a vagrant poetess who was branded as a thief, but had the good luck that she could, during a famine, lend to Þingeyrar monastery six hundredweight of butter, and thus gain the monks' prayers. Almost all the poems are cast in the new meters from the later Middle Ages, e. g., the *Ljómur* meter, a marvelously fitting form for the subject matter.

Hannes Hafstein

Hannes Pétursson Hafstein (1861-1922) was born at Möðruvellir in the North, the son of a governor. Unusually precocious, he graduated at nineteen (1880) from Latin School in Reykjavík and at twenty-five (1886) from the Law School at the University of Copenhagen. A brilliant career lay ahead: he was to reap the fruit of a fresh victory in Iceland's struggle for autonomy, becoming the first premier of the country, 1904-1909, and again 1912-1914. As such he had the chance to guide his country on its first steps toward political and economic independence and, by introducing the telegraph and telephone, break its age-long isolation. Some of this progress he had already dreamed of during his student days in Copenhagen when, as a member of the *Verðandi* group, he sounded the clarion call of realism and progress in the feature poem " Stormur " (1882), praising the purging and bracing powers of the tempest.

He was indeed the most gifted poet of the group, virile and spirited in life, love, and poetry alike. His social radicalism in those days is obvious from his portrait of Georg Brandes in *Heimdallur* (1884), his translation of Ibsen's poem " Til min ven revolutionstaleren " as well as from his own declaration that he wants to cut away and weed out all the unhealthy growth in his nation. But equally old was his fervent love of country, beautifully expressed as early as 1880 in " Ástarjátning " (Declaration of Love), more often mixed, later on, with constructive programs for progress or dream visions of the future than with the former satire. In Iceland his travels gave rise to spirited travel and nature poetry in which the poet again could voice his masculine admiration for the bracing storms or stop to paint a raging river or a waterfall in their wild power—in a fittingly grand style. He is also a friend of the clear summer weather. Since fate made him a political leader he had less time or inclination for poetry, although there are three great poems written in this period from the leader's point of view. In one, " Landsýn " (Land Seen), he has a vision of coming storms clashing over the isolated island; in another one, perhaps his greatest—" Í hafís-num" (In the Polar Ice)—he paints the picture of an intrepid skipper caught in the ice, walking on top of an iceberg and guiding his ship out of the ice, but remaining there himself. In his early love poetry Hannes struck a new realistic note in description of his sweethearts. Yet as in the case of Ibsen, his wife was the only great love of his life, and having lost her (1913) he lamented her in beautiful poetic fragments. A popular and convivial student, he left a number of poems in the *Wein, Weib, und Gesang* tradition. He translated fragments of Ibsen's *Brand*, a few poems by Björnson, J. P. Jacobsen, Goethe, Drachmann, but chiefly a number of Heine's poems. A sheaf of his poems was published in 1893, and a collected edition *Ljóðmæli* (Poems) in 1916 which was enlarged in 1925. The 1916 edition was reprinted in 1951.

Einar Benediktsson

Einar Benediktsson (1864–1940) was born at Elliðavatn near Reykja-vík and there grew up with his parents until they were separated in 1872. His mother was a poet, his father a judge of the Supreme Court, later prefect in Þingeyjarsýsla (1874–1897). The father was, after Jón Sigurðsson, the greatest leader of the movement for Icelandic inde-pendence, and the boy followed him, though he loved his mother more, attributing his poetic vein to her inheritance. He studied law in Copen-hagen at a leisurely pace (1884–1892) but also immersed himself in the cultural and literary currents of the time. In his Latin School days he had imitated Egill Skalla-Grímsson, in Copenhagen he read and admired Browning and started translating Ibsen's *Peer Gynt*, although it was not published, as *Pétur Gautur*, until 1901 (in a bibliophile edition, the first in Iceland). Einar Benediktsson did not join the Brandes realists (who were too socialistic and cosmopolitan for his taste). Instead he con-tributed his first poetry to the intensely nationalist *Sunnanfari* (1891–——). Back in Iceland he started *Dagskrá* (1896–98), for a while the first Icelandic daily, to fight for his ideals: national independence, a university in Iceland, improved fisheries (trawlers), and improved trade. In *Dagskrá* he was still a socialist by persuasion though not at heart; after the turn of the century, following Brandes, he had no doubt justified the rugged individualism of capitalism with the philosophy of Nietzsche. At the same time he realized that only a flood of the world's capital could change Iceland. After a short career as a prefect, he therefore devoted the most active years of his life (1907–22) and his great ingenuity and personal charm to win European capitalists for his industrial plans in Iceland. If he did not succeed, he at least could live in cultural centers of Europe, and in a style denied most of his fellow countrymen since the days of Egill Skalla-Grímsson.

During the twenties he lost most of his money and during the greater part of the thirties he was inactive as a poet, living in seclusion on the farm Herdísarvík, south of Reykjavík. He published five volumes of poetry; *Sögur og kvæði* (Stories and Poems, 1897), *Hafblik* (Calm Water, 1906), *Hrannir* (Waves, 1913), *Vogar* (Billows, 1921), and *Hvammar* (Grass Hollows, 1930). Selections from his prose, *Laust mál* (I–II, 1952) with a full life of the poet were published by Steingrímur J. Þorsteinsson.

Though Einar Benediktson's early poetry, like the symbolic " Skútahraun," was to some extent socialistic, he soon turned from the sordidness of Realism to the new French gospel of Symbolism, which he himself advocated in his articles on Icelandic literature in *Dagskrá* (1897). It was to replace the base direction of Realism with lofty aspirations for beauty, stars, eternity, and God. The new poets were to plant their feet in reality but train their eyes on the stars. They were to seek " soul in nature," and, if this be interpreted " spirit in matter," we get the two strands which enervate most of Einar's poetry, for, like many of his contemporaries, e. g., Strindberg and A. Einstein, he had the mystic's drive not only to deify and unify the world, but also to identify himself with it at every turn in his poetry, as Hallgrímur Pétursson identified himself with Jesus. He was a keen observer and could give fine impressionistic sketches both in poetry and prose, but one of the prose sketches, " Gullský," (Golden Cloud) stands out as a first report of his mystic experience.

This pantheist mysticism is an ever growing element in Einar Benediktson's poetry, from the early " Norðurljós " (Aurora Borealis) to " Elivogar " and " Hnattasund " (Global Channels) among his last. One finds it not only in the cosmological poems like " Jörð " (Earth) and the chaotic " Ymir," but also in nature poems like " Í Slútnesi " (In Slútnes) and " Dettifoss," where he speaks not only of harnessing the water power but also the nervous power of the brain—both from the same infinite source of divine energy. There were moments when he could feel that he had wasted his poetic powers in this titanic quest for the ever elusive ultimate and absolute—for example, " Gamalt lag " (Old Melody)— but he kept stubbornly on. He even tried to clarify his pantheistic views in three prose essays in *Eimreiðin*: "Alhygð" (Pantheism, 1926), "Gáta geymsins" (The Riddle of the Universe, 1926), and "Sjón-hverfing tímans" (The Illusion of Time, 1930), but these are not always much clearer than his poems on the subject.

Already in his first book the poet had given splendid impressions of places he had visited, e. g., "Ásbyrgi." Two journeys, one to Italy, summer 1903, the other from Reykjavík to Mývatn, Dettifoss, and Hljóðaklettar, summer 1904, released a flood of this kind of poetry, though usually with the added mystical element. In Italy, with the classics in the back of his mind, he describes an evening in Rome, a storm on Lake Trasimenus, the Cathedral of Milan, and Venice. The modern metropoles are depicted in Paris, London, and a sketch of Fifth Avenue, New York. A glimpse of the modern machine age we get from the shipyard in Newcastle-on-Tyne, an immersion in music from the concert in Queens Hall, London. With all these foreign and cosmopoli-tan themes Einar Benediktsson, Viking-like, enriched the hoard of native Icelandic poetry, and set the pattern for future writers, though none of them matched him as a globe-trotter, except Laxness.

But however cosmopolitan Einar Benediktsson now seemed to be—and he had spurned that outlook in the Realists—he was even more a con-firmed Icelandic nationalist politically and culturally. He was not only an admirer of the saga, Egill, and Snorri, but also of the lowly popular *rímur*, hence his selected edition of Sigurður Breiðfjörð, and hence his own "Ólafs ríma Grænlendings" (1913) in the most difficult meter of *sléttubönd*. As to the language, he early concluded not only that it de-served to be kept pure, but also that it was the most perfect instrument of thought on earth; never at a loss for a word—his own poetry goes far to prove this contention. His dreams and aspirations, as set forth in "Væringjar" (Varangians), for the future of Icelandic poets and intel-lectuals, were correspondingly high-flown. Two elements of Einar Bene-diktsson's Icelandic nationalism were not shared by most of his com-patriots: his views that Iceland, as Thule ("Sóley"), had an Irish pre-history, and his interest in, if not imperialistic designs on, Greenland, Iceland's old colony (cf. "Ólafs ríma Grænlendings"). But this last-named desire was part of his high-flown ideas about Iceland's brilliant future, which, toward the end, approached more and more megalomaniac dreams—yet, which of the great powers would *not* have claimed Green-land after having found it and had a colony there for five centuries?

It remains to show to what extent Einar Benediktsson's poetry was marked by his belief in the technical progress of his country, and his truly titanic efforts to raise foreign capital to harness water power, exploit mines, and further trade. His programmatic poems of progress all date from around the turn of the century, before he had plunged himself into active salesmanship. They are "Aldamót" (Turn of the Century), "Minni Íslands" (Iceland's Toast, 1901), "Haugaeldur" (Mound Fires), and "Dettifoss." But one searches in vain in all his poetry for any sign of, not to say a celebration of, his financial successes. On the other hand there are two unusually personal poems, "Pundið" (The Talent) and "Einræður Starkaðar" (Starkaður's Monologue) which bespeak a deeply anguished conscience over lost life. His "speculations" were, of course, perfectly legitimate from a businessman's point of view, and it is doubtful whether he regretted them as such, though all of them failed, partly owing to his countrymen's resistance, fearing exploitation of foreign capital, a factor Einar could not predict when he was forming his companies. But the time- and spirit-consuming conviviality of his companions, though Einar excelled in that too, was something which he regretted more and more, for writing poetry was the one occupation which Einar Benediktsson felt worthy of himself.

As an inheritor of skaldic verse and *rímur*, Einar Benediktsson wrote in a grand ornate style usually in stanzas of long lines, sometimes of his own invention. "Útsær" (The Ocean) is a fine and typical example of his art. He was master of contrasts, and fond of mirroring macrocosmos in microcosmos. A good deal of his poetry may be defined as a tough and persistent double-fugue on two motifs: the world and myself. His aristocratic respect for his art was such that in all his extensive poetry he hardly ever struck a false formal note, still less did he allow himself the use of his artistic gift but for the loftiest aims. In this perfectionism he differed from both Matthías and Stephan G. Stephansson, whose muses were often liable to nod; he did not quite enjoy Matthías' lofty inspiration and childlike faith, nor Stephan G. Stephansson's firmness of character. But otherwise he towers, titan-like, over all his contemporaries.

Þorsteinn Gíslason

Þorsteinn Gíslason (1867–1938) was born in Eyjafjörður but grew up in Fljótsdalshérað in the East. At the University in Copenhagen he wanted to specialize in Modern Icelandic literature but was turned down on the ground that there was no such thing. In Iceland he became one of the ablest journalists of the country (especially *Lögrétta*) and performed a valuable service in introducing foreign literature to the country in reviews and surveys of books. He also translated Scott, Björnson, Ibsen and Fröding (even Shelley), but his own poetry, occasional (for official celebrations) or humorous, was rather mediocre. Yet he wrote a few good nature lyrics. He was really a progressive nationalist, played and active part in the politics of his day, and wrote their history from his own point of view.

Sigurjón Friðjónsson

Sigurjón Friðjónsson (1867–1950) was born in Aðaldalur and grew up at Sandur in Þingeyjarsýsla, the brother of the more prolific poet and writer Guðmundur Friðjónsson. With little schooling he became a farmer in his home district. While his brother was attracted to Realism, he was attracted to the neo-romantic Symbolism, with which he became acquainted through the Norwegian periodical *Kringsjaa*. While his brother was a master of the ornate style, he cultivated the simple lyric in poetry and prose, singing of growth, love, spring, and summer. Like Hulda he wrote *þulur*. Though he had long been contributing poems to periodicals, his collections came late: *Ljóðmæli* (Poems, 1928), *Heyrði eg í hamrinum* I-III (I Heard from the Cliff, 1939–44), and *Barnið á götunni* (The Child in the Street, 1943). The poems that he wrote in his seventies and eighties testify to an unusually fertile Indian summer. His mystic union with nature is often in evidence. He did some good translations, among them poetry of Joh. Jörgensen and E. Axel Karlfeldt. One of his sons, Arnór Sigurjónsson, became a historian, another one, Bragi Sigurjónsson, a poet.

Guðmundur Friðjónsson

Guðmundur Friðjónsson (1869–1944), a farmer's son, born in Aðaldalur in the North, himself became a hard-working farmer at Sandur in the same district, raising twelve children—two of them promising poets: Þóroddur and Heiðrekur. But unlike Bólu-Hjálmar, who never left his district, Guðmundur Friðjónsson had two years of high school and traveled frequently as a lecturer all over Iceland. Nevertheless, he always had the somewhat narrow point of view of the farmer, but compensated for it with the acuteness with which he observed what fell within his vision. Guðmundur lived through the famine years of the 1880's as a sickly boy in his teens, and for a long time his health was such that he thought he would die young. But his marriage made a man of him and gave his poetry wings. He wrote five volumes of poetry, the chief ones being: *Úr heimahögum* (From Native Haunts, 1902), *Kvæði* (Poems, 1925), *Kveðlingar* (Ditties, 1929) and *Utan af víðavangi* (From Far Afield, 1942). He wrote one novel, *Ólöf í Ási* (1907), ten collections of short stories (1898–1938), and four volumes of essays, in addition to a great number of poems, essays, and articles in periodicals and newspapers. Collected works, *Ritsafn* I-VII, came in 1955–56, his life by his son Þóroddur, in 1950.

Guðmundur started as a realist with attacks upon church, clergy, and conventions. His novel about a loveless marriage was not only a pleading for increased personal freedom, it was also at the time daring in its treatment of the sexual theme, though both Þorgils Gjallandi and, later, Jón Trausti were to exceed him in this—and all three seem Victorian to us now.

In his short stories Guðmundur Friðjónsson praised the substantial virtues of the farmers—their industry, prudence and patience—but frowned upon things that threatened their existence: high taxes to church and state, the rising towns with their attraction for the country people. He took an adverse view of the so-called culture to be had in the towns, the new popular school system (1907), the increased demands of a rising standard of living. He demanded financial independence of individuals as well as of the state, admired men of action and substance, and did not want political independence for the nation before it was financially solvent. Socially he was a conservative: against co-operatives and socialism in turn, not to speak of communism. With the years he became more and more a national romantic.

Both in his poetry and prose Guðmundur Friðjónsson described the passive Christian hero with predilection and sympathy, an early example being " Ekkjan við ána " (The Widow at the River). This is rather remarkable in view of his admiration of the saga heroes, of which he also has examples among his epitaphs of men of substance. Striking and odd characters were also his favorite topics.

Fettered as he was to the soil and at the mercy of subarctic nature's cruel whims, he could hit back at her, or God's, cruelty with hard fists. On the other hand, the situation could nurse his longing for the romantic far away, even America, though he forswore that escape when he married. Often this romantic longing merged with his religious feeling into mysticism.

Guðmundur Friðjónsson wrote a number of flawless short stories and even when not perfect, their value was always enhanced by his rich and ornate personal style. His poems were marked by the same rich style: in general, they were in the skaldic style tradition; their polyphony of thought and metaphor may remind one of Bach. It was a style which had the wholehearted approval of Einar Benediktsson, and was admired by Guðmundur Finnbogason and Sigurður Nordal.

Helgi Péturss[on]

Helgi Péturss[on] (1872–1949) was born in Reykjavík, the son of a policeman; his mother was a scion of poets and scholars. Having studied natural history and geography in Copenhagen (1891–97), he joined an expedition to Greenland. As a result of loss of sleep on the boat, he suffered a temporary nervous breakdown, from which he probably never recovered completely, though he lived (in Reykjavík) to a ripe old age.

He wrote an important dissertation on Icelandic geology, claiming that the wide-spread palagonite was not a volcanic but a glacial formation (1905). He wrote essays on evolutionary theory, his impressions of nature, and on the Icelandic poets and the Icelandic language. To him Icelandic was the classic language of the North, superior to the " corrupted " sister languages. He felt that real Icelandic culture had never recovered from the introduction of Christianity. He was also favorably impressed by what he had heard of Nietszche.

By 1912 he thought he had made some epoch-making discoveries regarding the nature of sleep and dreams, which, as a sufferer of insomnia, he had pondered. He concluded (1) that in sleep the person is charged with extraneous vitality, (2) that dreams are induced into the dreamer's mind by another person, and (3) this inducer of dreams is usually a being on another planet.

On these " observations " he based the philosophy laid down in *Nýall I* (1919), so called " because it is the first book of a new epoch "—with five more volumes following under slightly variant names.

In the light of this bio-radiation or bio-induction in sleep, a medium's trance and the inspirations of prophets fell readily into pattern, but the so-called " other world " was in reality life on other planets. With many contemporaneous philosophers Helgi Péturss shared the idea of an original source of energy irradiating matter or chaos. But he felt that evolution from this original *primum mobile* was not necessarily good

(di-exelixis), but also could be bad (dys-exelixis); the first development resulting in planetary paradises, the other in infernos. The infernos
could only be saved by coming to an understanding of their plight and
by interplanetary appeal to the better worlds.

Because of World War I, Helgi Péturss was in little doubt that our
planet was an inferno that needed quick action to be saved. As a discoverer of the new cosmic principle of bio-radiation, he was in even less
doubt that *he* was the Saviour, provided his words were heeded. His
synthesis of science, religion, and occultism paralleled the international-
istic spiritualism of E. H. Kvaran, but differed in being super-national-
istic, making the Icelanders the chosen people since they produced Helgi
Péturss, the intellectual saviour of the world.

This dream of Iceland's intellectual greatness was shared, though in
somewhat less concrete form, by the greatest poet of the period, Einar
Benediktsson, also a mystic.

Guðmundur Magnússon

Guðmundur Magnússon (pen name Jón Trausti, 1873–1918) was
born in extreme poverty on the northernmost tip of Iceland, Rif, Melrak-
kaslétta, on the Arctic. Losing his father at five, he lived with foster
parents and his mother through the tough famine years of the eighties
until at sixteen he was left to shift for himself as best he could. Having
devoured whatever books came his way, among them the sagas, he decided at twenty to learn the trade of printing. Starting at Seyðisfjörður
in the East he followed his trade to Reykjavík, Copenhagen (1896–98),
and back to Reykjavík, where he lived as a printer until his death by
the Spanish influenza in 1918. But he was far from confined to his trade,
having many outside interests. In 1896 he traveled as a guide to an
archeologist through the North of Iceland, and had ever after a weakness
for travel and mountaineering. He took a tour of Europe, visiting
Germany, Switzerland, and England in 1903. As a printer in Copenhagen he studied stagecraft and became instructor and stage manager
for the Reykjavík Dramatic Society. He was also a good draftsman
and illustrated some of his poems.

But above all he was a writer. He started with two volumes of
poetry (1899 and 1903), the first of small account, the latter, *Íslands-
vísur*, containing some tender nature lyrics and progressive patriotic
songs. His poems show that though he was touched by the realist revolt
against church, clergy, and popular conventions, he was primarily a

progressive idealist, believing with Einar Benediktsson and Einar
Kvaran in the material and spiritual progress of his country. He wrote
a historical play (1903) which was a success only insofar as it brought
him a government grant for his educational trip to Europe. As the
reviews had not been flattering, Guðmundur decided to fool his critics
by publishing his next books under the pseudonym Jón Trausti. The
novel *Halla* (1906), a signal success, was followed in rapid tempo by
Leysing (Spring Floods, 1907), and *Heiðarbýlið* (The Mountain Cot,
in four volumes, 1908–11) as a continuation of *Halla*. *Halla-Heiðar-
býlið*, laid in the sixties and seventies, ending with the great frost-winter
of 1881–82, described the hard life of the isolated mountain cotters in
northeast Iceland. The heroine, a healthy country girl seduced by an
irresponsible young parson, fled to the mountain cot to be alone with her
secret. Here she lost not only her love child but also another child and
her husband before she left with two children for the budding village of
the trading place. Here also she was the butt of the malicious country
gossip and a generous partner in the often sordid interplay of characters
of the countryside. It is obvious already here that Jón Trausti loves
the sturdy rugged individualists. It is even clearer in *Leysing,* a social
novel describing the fight between the last representative of the old
Danish monopoly trader and the rising co-operatives, laid in the village
to which Halla had repaired from her mountain cot. One would have
expected the progressive Jón Trausti to have sided with the new co-
operative: instead his sympathies—just like Hamsun's—are with the
old trader who has tried his best to reform the rotten practices of loan-
trading, heritage of the monopoly, but without success. His observation of the fumbling, often plainly immoral methods of the rising democracy in church and state turned Jón Trausti into a conservative,
writing *Borgir* (Castles, 1909) against the free church movement, and
Bessi gamli (1918) against the rising socialism of the twenties. Though
Jón Trausti hardly knew Nietzsche, he thus ranked himself with the
antidemocratic writers of the North, notably the Dane Jacob Knudsen.
After *Borgir,* Jón Trausti turned to historical subjects, writing first
Sögur frá Skaftáreldi (Stories from the Eruption near Skaftá, 1912–13),
based on Jón Steingrímsson's autobiography as well as his own recol-
lections of the famine of 1881–82. More romantic were the four tales of
Góðir stofnar (Good Stock, 1914–15), laid in the fourteenth and sixteenth centuries, with their saga-like women characters. *Tvær gamlar
sögur* (Two Old Tales, 1916) were not really historical though one was

laid in the Reformation period, the other in the early seventeenth century. It may be said that Jón Trausti brought his writing to a close with
Bessi gamli (1918). He had also written one more insignificant (folk
tale) play and two volumes of short stories that contain some of the
finest samples of his art, like " Á fjörunni " (The Watchman, 1909).
His poems, *Kvæðabók*, were posthumously edited in 1922; his complete
works, *Ritsafn*, reprinted 1939–46.

Jón Trausti was a moralist, an accomplished storyteller, but he lacked
literary style.

Guðmundur Finnbogason

Guðmundur Finnbogason (1873–1944) was born in Ljósavatnsskarð,
Þingeyjarsýsla, of farmer parents. He studied psychology and philosophy
with Harald Höffding at the University of Copenhagen (1896–1901).
His first tasks were to draw up a modern school system for Iceland, and
to start *Skírnir*, the old periodical of the Icelandic Literary Society, on
a new career as a literary magazine in Iceland. Next, he got a scholarship to give lectures on psychology, using them for his thesis *Den
sympatiske Forstaaelse* (French: *L'intelligence sympathique*, 1913).
After serving as a teacher of psychology at the University of Iceland
(1916–24), he was made a librarian of the National Library, Reykjavík,
serving up to 1944.

Guðmundur wrote a dozen books and innumerable essays, some of
them collected in *Huganir* (Essays, 1943). He also was a good speaker;
his speeches were collected in *Mannfagnaður* (Good Cheer, 1937).

To begin with, Guðmundur Finnbogason was a typical progressive
idealist trying to inform and improve his people. He changed the Latin
School to a Gymnasium of Modern Languages. He introduced William
James, McDougall, Bergson. After 1916 he wrote on applied psychology, reading, mowing, drying fish, and—during the depression—
how to improve democracy.

But after 1916 Guðmundur Finnbogason became more and more of a
national romanticist, interested in the national character. Had the harsh
country improved the race by natural selection? That was the view of
E. Huntington's *The Character of Races*. But there were more facets to
the problem: the sagas and the skaldic art, customs, sport, pastimes,
not to forget the language. Finally the essays were synthesized in
Íslendingar (Icelanders, 1933), one of his greatest works.

To improve the language, along the nationalistic puristic lines laid down by Fjölnismenn, without disfiguring it with foreign loan words, was Guðmundur's intent. He was an active coiner of new words, both as a translator of various subjects, as an author using the technical vocabulary of psychology, as a law-giver on family names (1913), and as a member of an informal academy for coining words for tradesmen, sailors, merchants, and engineers. He subscribed heartily to Einar Benediktsson's poetic dictum that Icelandic is never at a loss for a word and, like Einar, he proved it. The law on names, especially family names, was designed to give those who adopted one, according to international custom, a choice of more Icelandic sounding names (like Kvaran, Kamban, Kjaran); but the family-name custom was ably attacked by several men, notably Bjarni Jónsson frá Vogi, who in 1925 succeeded in prohibiting it by law.

Intellectual curiosity was one of Guðmundur Finnbogason's chief charms; he wrote in a vigorous and lucid style.

Guðmundur Guðmundsson

Guðmundur Guðmundsson (1874–1919) was born in the Njála-country, Rangárvallasýsla in the South, the son of a poor verse-making farmer. After graduating from the Latin School (1897), where he gained the lasting designation " School Poet," he was to study medicine, but was diverted to literature. As a journalist in Ísafjörður (1906–1909) he married a girl who remained a lasting inspiration to his work. After 1913 they lived in Reykjavík until his premature death.

He was a prolific poet, publishing seven collections during his lifetime: *Ljóðmæli* (Poems, 1900), *Guðbjörg í Dal* (1902), *Strengleikar* (Melodies, 1903), *Gígjan* (The Fiddle, 1906), *Friður á jörðu* (Peace on Earth, 1911), *Ljósaskipti* (Twilight, 1913), and *Ljóð og kvæði* (Songs and Poems, 1917), while a volume of translations was published in 1924, and a collected edition, *Ljóðasafn* (three volumes), in 1934.

" He was a sensitive soul, deeply religious by nature and with strong mystic leanings; it was therefore natural that the Neo-Romanticism and Symbolism of the nineties should appeal to him." (R. Beck). His revolt against Realism was seen in his early emotional and lyrical prose pieces.

He was, indeed, to develop into the greatest songbird among the Icelandic poets and the greatest master of the lyrical form: his facility of playing with rime was phenomenal. The musical quality of his verse was indicated by titles like *Strengleikar* (Melodies) and *Gígjan* (The

Fiddle). Among his themes love looms large, not only the saddened or tragic love of youth but also the love of his wife, home, and hearth. Not a few of these poems, though highly lyrical, were cast in a narrative or fable form; some of them celebrated heroes and heroines from *Njála*. In nature poetry he continued the line of Jónas Hallgrímsson, but nature and love elements were often combined. As a great idealist, he hated practical politics, but celebrated the introduction of Christianity in Iceland, sang " Peace on Earth " (*Friður á jörðu*, 1911; 2nd ed. 1913) in an inspired oratorium text, and joined the theosophists in their quest for brotherhood on earth and in their expecting the advent of a new great Master. He also fought for the political independence of Iceland and for temperance.

He was a competent linguist and read Baudelaire and Verlaine, the archpriests of Symbolism, in the original. In his translations he went unusually far afield, including poets of Slavonic, Hungarian, and Romance origin.

Sigfús Blöndal

Sigfús Benedikt Bjarnason Blöndal (1874–1950), hailing from Húnavatnssýsla, studied classical philology and English at the University of Copenhagen and worked first as a librarian at the Royal Library, later as a lecturer on Icelandic in the University.

He was a prolific writer and editor, but his greatest work was the Icelandic-Danish dictionary, *Íslenzk-dönsk Orðabók* (1920–1924), a monumental work, and of great importance to later writers (Laxness, Ól. Jóh. Sigurðsson). The work on the dictionary was shared by his wife, Björg Þorláksdóttir, also a poet and playwright, and Jón Ófeigsson, a teacher. Two of his editions, the life of *Jón Ólafsson Indíafari* (1908–1909) and *Píslarsaga Jóns Magnússonar* (1914) proved to set important patterns for future experimenters in style, like Þórbergur Þórðarson.

Blöndal wrote many essays on Icelandic literature, among them one on the continuity in the literature. He was also a neo-romantic poet publishing two volumes of poetry, *Drotningin í Algeirsborg* (The Queen of Algiers, 1917), and *Sunnan yfir sæ* (From the South over the Ocean, 1949). " The Queen " is a narrative poem relating the romantic fate of an Icelandic girl in exile, robbed by the Algerian pirates in 1627. The volume also contains " The Last Voyage of Jón Indíafari," which is a classic in its simplicity. Blöndal was a prolific translator from many languages, notably English (Tennyson, Shelley) and Greek (Theocritus,

Aristophanes, Sophocles, Euripides [*The Baccantes*], Sappho, Anacreon). He was also an amateur musician and composed many of his poems to be accompanied by the guitar. His last work was a history of the Varangians (1954), published after his death.

Theódór Friðriksson

Theódór Friðriksson (1876–1948) was born in Flatey, an island off the north coast, the son of a fisherman. He himself eked out a meager living for his family as crofter, shark-fisher, and a migratory fisherman commuting between the great fishing centers Vestmannaeyjar in the South, Siglufjörður in the North, his home being in Húsavík in the North. But after 1930 he stayed mostly in Reykjavík and devoted himself more and more to his lifelong interest: writing.

He started with a collection of short stories, *Utan frá sjó* (From the Sea, 1908), echoing the realism of Gestur Pálsson and Jónas Jónasson, but interesting because here, for the first time, the poor village fisherman appeared in Icelandic literature. It looked as if here was a man who would do for this typical member of the Icelandic society what Guðmundur Friðjónsson had done for the farmer. He did remain true to this subject matter, writing among other things the novel *Útlagar* (Outlaws, 1922), about the shark-fishermen, on which he later wrote an informative work: *Hákarlalegur og hákarlamenn* (1933). In the late twenties and the thirties he wrote some books about village workers rising against their capitalistic exploiters, e. g. *Líf og blóð* (Life and Blood, 1928). These were interesting precisely because they were written not by the intellectual leaders, but by a laborer of the crowd. But, to be truthful, Theodór Friðriksson never became a class-conscious writer in the communist sense; he remained the individualist he had been born; his was not an orderly world but the motley kaleidoscopic crowd of the fishing centers, observed and described with impressionistic fidelity. This is especially true of his last and greatest work, the autobiography *Í verum* (In the Fishing Places, 1941). The continuation, *Ofan jarðar og neðan* (Above and Below Earth, 1944), was the history of the British-American occupation from the author's working man's point of view.

Sigurður Jónsson

Sigurður Jónsson (1878–1949), son of one of the best local poets of Þingeyjarsýsla, Jón Hinriksson (1829–1921), was born in Eyjafjörður but grew up and spent his manhood as a farmer in the beautiful district of Mývatnssveit, which he celebrated in a splendid and heartfelt poem, " Blessuð sértu, sveitin mín " (Blessed Be You, My Home District), a poem so popular that it attained the distinction of becoming the national song of rural Iceland. Love of the soil, not too common in Iceland, was characteristic of much of his poetry, published in three volumes, one of which bore the title of the above poem. He was a friend and neighbor of Jón Stefánsson (Þorgils Gjallandi) and paid him a worthy tribute at his death.

Sigurður Sigurðsson

Sigurður Sigurðsson (frá Arnarholti, 1879–1939) was born in Copenhagen, the son of an Icelandic teacher and a Danish girl. He grew up in the home of Dr. Björn M. Ólsen, teacher, later headmaster of the Latin School in Reykjavík. For a long time he lived as a well-to-do pharmacologist in Vestmannaeyjar but spent his last years as a poor man in Reykjavík.

Sigurður made his debut in collaboration with Jónas Guðlaugsson with a little book called *Tvístirnið* (The Twin Stars, 1906), containing patriotic poetry, nature lyrics, love poetry, and miscellaneous lyrics and songs. Later he published *Ljóð* (Poems, in three editions 1912, 1924, 1933). He was obviously a lyric poet of note, of fiery temperament, deep personality, and impeccable taste. He could endow his poetic descriptions with an unusual plastic quality. He was an admirer of Nietzsche, and had the decadent's appetite for life in any form, cf. " Í dag " (To-day), a poem symbolic of his changing fortunes. Unfortunately he did not write much more nor anything that would quite live up to his earliest poetry—whether due to cares of this world or his own perfectionism. His last poems *Síðustu ljóðmæli* (1939, published after his death by Sigurður Nordal) left something to be desired in polish, but testified to his old poetic powers.

Unnur Benediktsdóttir Bjarklind

Unnur Benediktsdóttir Bjarklind (pen name Hulda, 1881–1946) was born and brought up in a home which in many ways was the fountainhead of Þingeying culture in the nineties and after; she was the daughter of Benedikt Jónsson á Auðnum, librarian of the district library unique in rural Iceland at the time. Here she received an excellent home education, including foreign languages, so that she could read not only

Scandinavian, but also English and German, even French, masters in the original. Of the Icelandic heritage she was especially devoted to the folk and fairy tales, as well as to the folk poetry in *Íslenzkar gátur, skemtanir, vikivakar og þulur, 1887–1903.* Of the poets she loved Eggert Ólafsson for his rural poetry and Benedikt Gröndal for his lyrical quality and romantic spirit.

She was only twenty when she began to contribute poems to periodicals, but she had the good luck to be discovered by two of the leading poets of the day, Einar Benediktsson and Þorsteinn Erlingsson (1905), and hailed as a star of the neo-romantic movement partly because of her pure lyric vein, partly because of her deft imitation of the folk poetry, notably the *þulur*: rhapsodies and nursery rimes. This revival and refinement of the *þulur* was indeed a lasting contribution, imitated by many after her (Theódóra Thoroddsen, Sigurður Nordal).

Though a busy housewife and often of delicate health, Hulda turned out numerous volumes of poetry and prose. Her first volume of poems, *Kvæði,* appeared in 1909, her seventh and last, posthumously in 1951. In them is " the fragrance of flowers and birch woods, sunny spring and summer, and the murmur of bubbling brooks " (R. Beck). Of individual poems, " Helga Bárðardóttir " a veiled self-portrayal, " Kross-saumur " (Cross-stitch), and the memorial to her father deserve to be singled out. She also won a prize for a poem written to celebrate the establishment of the Icelandic Republic on June 17, 1944.

After contributing fairy tales to *Sumargjöf* in 1905 she wrote more than ten volumes of prose—the first *Æskuástir* (Youthful Loves, 1915–19) in two volumes, the last, *Í ættlandi mínu* (In my Native Land, 1945), just before her death—but some remained unpublished. She wrote short romantic love stories, sketches, fairy tales, humorous short stories, and a two-volume novel, *Dalafólk* (People of the Valleys, 1936–39), written in reaction to Laxness' *Sjálfstætt fólk,* describing life on the good old manorlike paternalistic farmsteads. Her picture may be slightly idealized; nevertheless, it no doubt mirrors life as lived in the cultured homes of Þingeyjarsýsla as well as the ideals that sprang up in that fertile soil.

Jóhann Gunnar Sigurðsson

Jóhann Gunnar Sigurðsson (1882–1906) was born on Snæfellsnes in the West and died prematurely as a young student of theology in Reykjavík. He was considered to be a genius by his schoolmates and his

Kvæði og sögur (Poems and Stories, 1909) show that he was a spiritual brother of Guðmundur Guðmundsson and Hulda, in other words, one of the pioneers of Neo-Romanticism in Iceland.

Jóhann Sigurjónsson

Jóhann Sigurjónsson (1880–1919) was born at Laxamýri in the North, of well-to-do parents and literary forbears. After graduating from the Latin School in Reykjavík (1899) he was to study veterinary science in Copenhagen, but burned his bridges and turned to literature instead. He joined the Scandinavian (Norwegian) bohemia in Copenhagen with some of his fellow countrymen who adored Brandes and studied Nietzsche. He himself wanted to emulate the three great dramatists of the North, but to do so he understood that he had to write in a common Scandinavian medium. So he published his plays in Danish although he wrote them both in Danish and Icelandic, thereby starting an innovation—followed by some—in Icelandic literature which was considerably criticized by many of his countrymen, and not without reason. Still, if he wanted to devote himself to his art exclusively, this was the only road open to him, and after a fashion he succeeded. After a couple of interesting dramatic failures (*Dr. Rung* and the *Hraun Farm*) he made a smash hit with *Fjalla-Eyvindur* (Danish: *Bjærg-Ejvind og hans Hustru*, 1911). Georg Brandes hailed it as the best book of the year, and it went on a triumphal tour of Scandinavian theaters, but its success in Europe was considerably dampened by World War I. In the play he combines the hunger of his bohemian existence with romantic folk tale, folkways, and nature motifs from Iceland, testing the tempestuous love of a spirited woman against hunger in the Icelandic winter mountains. The woman's somber strength of character struck the critics (Brandes) as saga-like. The intense emotions were new in Icelandic literature, and so was the lyrical and symbolic style, but in taking his matter from a folk tale, he was following the pattern set by Matthías and Indriði.

From a folk tale, too, was *Galdra-Loftur* (Danish: *Önsket*, The Wish, 1915), a Faust-like legend about a student at the Cathedral School at Hólar, in the early eighteenth century, who sold his soul to the Devil for power. It is, indeed, a play about the Nietzschean will to power, prophetic of the ambitious postwar dictators. Loftur stands between the seduced maid, whom he wishes to kill, and who commits suicide, and the bishop's daughter; he himself perishes during the conjuration scene in the cathedral.

These two plays show Jóhann Sigurjónsson at his best. He wrote one, *Lögneren* (The Liar, 1917), on a theme from *Njáls saga*, but with less success. The evil hero had the ambitions of Dr. Rung and Galdra-Loftur, no doubt a trait borrowed from the author himself; indeed, his venturing to improve on the great *Njáls saga* told volumes of this ambition—no one had had the temerity to do so before.

His next play, *Elsa*, was to be on a modern subject, but he died before it was published, from a galloping pulmonary tuberculosis.

Though Jóhann Sigurjónsson was primarily a playwright, he wrote some perfect lyric poems in simple meters, some even in free verse. They are few, but rank with the very best of the period. His collected works, *Rit*, were published in two volumes, 1940–42.

Jónas Guðlaugsson

Jónas Guðlaugsson (1887–1916) was born at Staðarhraun in the West, the son of a parson-poet who passed his talent on to two sons. Already in the Latin School (1902–1905) he shocked some of his staid fellow-students by his ambition to become a great poet, but his first efforts—*Vorblóm* (Spring Flowers, 1905), *Tvístirnið* (Twin Stars, 1906, in collaboration with Sigurður Sigurðsson, *q. v.*), and especially *Dagsbrún* (Dawn, 1909)—seemed to show that there was a talented lyric poet behind the ambition.

Despairing of success in Iceland which, as he says in one poem, could at most afford a few flowers on his grave, he went to Norway (1908–1909, 1910) and Denmark (1911–16) where he eked out a meager living by journalism, as he had done after he left school in Iceland. He joined the bohemian circle of Jóhann Sigurjónsson, and was just beginning a new life as a married man when death snatched him away at Skagen, Jutland.

But in the short span of his life Jónas Guðlaugsson did prove that he was a lyric poet of rank, with his three collections *Sange fra Nordhavet* (Songs from the Northern Ocean, 1911), *Viddernes Poesi* (Wilderness Poetry, 1912), and *Sange fra de blaa Bjærge* (Songs from the Blue Mountains, 1914). He also wrote two novels: *Solrun og hendes Bejlere* (Solrun and her Suitors, 1913), and *Monika* (1914), as well as a volume of short stories, *Bredefjordsfolk* (The People of Breiðifjörður, 1915), but though these neo-romantic tales from his native district are not uninteresting in their picturesqueness and mysticism, he will probably longest be remembered for his poems. They are emotional expressions of his longing abroad—a nostalgia for his home, its mountains, and the northern seas. His soaring ambitions for himself and his homeland found expression in many a poem and many a symbol. One of his love poems won fame for its unusual imagery ("The Church on the Mountain"), which seemingly was to inspire Gunnar Gunnarsson's naming of his greatest novel.

Guðmundur Kamban

Guðmundur Jónsson Kamban (1888–1945) was born in the vicinity of Reykjavík, but grew up partly in the Northwest. At the Gymnasium in Reykjavík (graduating in 1910) he came under the influence of Einar H. Kvaran. But though he actually wrote his first book at a spiritualistic séance, it was Kvaran's humanitarian, cosmopolitan, and progressive thought which made a lasting impression on him and turned him into a neo-realist. In Copenhagen (1910) Kamban studied philosophy, literature, aesthetics, playwriting and elocution, and came under the spell of Jóhann Sigurjónsson, writing two romantic plays in that mood: *Hadda-Padda* (1914) and *Kongeglimen* (Wrestling before the King, 1915). Brandes was greatly impressed by *Hadda-Padda*: "Such profound and exquisite womanhood, such inflexible masculine will, have hardly ever been combined on the stage before." The heroines, the romantic symbolism, the lyric style, and the picturesque Icelandic background were traits that Kamban had in common with Jóhann Sigurjónsson, but he substituted modern Reykjavík society for Sigurjónsson's folk-tale outlaws.

A stay in New York (1915–17), after which he returned to Copenhagen, turned Kamban into a social critic with interests in penology. The hero of *Marmor* (Marble, 1918), a judge, concludes that criminal law and punishment should be abolished. He is tolerated as long as he confines himself to theory, but when he buckles down to cases, society sends him to an insane asylum, though after a century it erects him a monument. *Ragnar Finnsson* (1922) was a novel about an intelligent and sensitive man who, by American prison life, is turned into a dangerous criminal. Both works look at crime and punishment from the same point of view. In *Vi Mordere* (We Murderers, 1920), Kamban's best, he once more exonerated a criminal, who in exasperation killed the real offender, his flighty and thriftless wife. It was the first in a series of plays on marriage, in which he partly, but not quite, changed his old Victorian attitudes toward the modern laxness of the twenties. *De*

Arabiske Telte (The Arabian Tents, 1921) illustrated this clash in a home with three generations, but Kamban's attitude seemed neutral; it was only in a later (1939) revised form that he obviously sided with the old generation. Two more books, the play *Örkenens Stjerner* (The Stars of the Desert, 1925) and the film novelette *Det Sovende Hus* (House in Sleep, 1925), also dealt with marriage, while *Sendiherrann frá Júpíter* (The Ambassador from Jupiter, 1927), which according to Kamban was a time and spaceless criticism of Western culture after the war, advocated Tolstoy's and Gandhi's passive resistance. It was Kamban's most comprehensive satire—and his worst play, hence unsuccessful on the stage in Copenhagen.

After having spoken his mind to the Western world, Kamban turned to seventeenth-century Iceland and wrote the monumental work *Skálholt* (I–IV) about Bishop Brynjólfur Sveinsson, his rebelling daughter Ragnheiður, and her lover Daði Halldórsson. The pious annals of the time record her public oath forswearing all intercourse with Daði, yet forty weeks later she gave birth to his son. Kamban assumes that she gave herself to Daði immediately after the oath in defiance of her stern father. Indeed, he sees in both the same inflexible, stubborn saga-character of the sort that could not be bent, only broken. And broken Ragnheiður was, not by her father's command but by the consumption that killed her.

Ragnheiður has been compared to Kristin Lavransdatter, but there is this difference: the latter, in spite of her sinning, has the conscience of her age; Ragnheiður's conscience, like a twentieth-century woman's, is her love only. In *30th Generation* (1933) Kamban returns to the Reykjavík of the present, pointing with pride to its modernity in outlook and morals. His last novel, *Jeg ser et stort skönt Land* (I see a Wondrous Land, 1936), was a successful attempt to retell the Greenland and Vinland sagas with modern psychological motivation. His last plays were *Komplekser* (1941) and *Grandezza* (1941), the first a satire on the disturbing effects of Freudian complexes upon marriages, the latter a hilarious satire on sensational journalism.

With exception of the years 1927–29 spent in Reykjavík, Kamban lived mostly in Denmark, working for the theaters in Copenhagen. As the jobs were not very remunerative, he tried to get positions in theaters in England and Germany. In Germany his books sold better, hence he could stay in Berlin while writing his Greenland-Vinland book, which he dedicated to the Nordic spirit. But when World War II broke out, his connections in Germany were interpreted, wrongly, as Nazi sympathies, and at the end of the war he was shot by Danish patriots, the innocent victim of rumor and patriotic zeal.

Gunnar Gunnarsson

Gunnar Gunnarsson (1889———) was born at Valþjófsstaður in Fljóts-dalur in the East, and came of a long line of parsons and farmers. At eighteen, the boy cut loose from his farm moorings and went to Denmark, determined to become a writer. There a little schooling at the well-known folk school at Askov awaited him, but chiefly toil and trouble, even hunger, on his road to writing. Success came in Copenhagen in 1912 with the first part of *Af Borgslægtens Historie* (From the Annals of the Borg Family), a romantic modern family saga. He lived in or near Copenhagen up to his fiftieth anniversary (1939), when he returned to Iceland, settling at Skriðuklaustur in Fljótsdalur, in the immediate vicinity of his birthplace. After ten years, made difficult by World War II, he moved to Reykjavík (1949) to live there.

Gunnar Gunnarsson has nearly forty volumes to his credit, not counting contributions to periodicals. Though primarily a novelist, he also published poems, short stories, plays, essays, and speeches and did much translating. Of his nine volumes of short stories we can only mention the novelette *Advent* (1937) which as *The Good Shepherd* (1940) became a best-seller in America.

Gunnarsson's first large novel, *Af Borgslægtens Historie* (four volumes, 1912–14), was written under auspicious stars: prewar peace idealism, his budding love, and his increasing nostalgia for the Icelandic home he had left. It was a re-creation of this home in a romantic distance, a family saga of the Icelandic countryside with heroes and villains, one of whom turned a legendary saint, reminiscent of Selma Lagerlöf's saints. Interesting, brisk story-telling, adept character-drawing, dramatic contrasts, and above all the romantic Icelandic distance turned this first work into a constant best-seller in Scandinavia, and to some extent elsewhere in Europe; it was even translated into English as *Guest the One-Eyed* (1920), and it was the first Icelandic work to be turned into a movie.

World War I cut the ground from under Gunnarsson's idealistic optimism and forced him to come to grips with problems of existence: how to keep one's faith—in God, in the meaning of life, in humanity— in the face of the onslaughts of blind fate or evil chance. About this he wrote a series of somber problem novels and plays, 1915–20, most important of which was the close-knit *Salige er de enfoldige* (Blessed Are the Poor in Spirit, 1920), called in the English translation *Seven Days' Darkness* (1930), because it takes place during one week in Reykjavík (1918) darkened by the Spanish influenza on the one hand and Katla's volcanic eruption on the other. It is also a spiritual duel between a humanitarian doctor and a cynic, and it is the humanitarian who at the end of the week is taken to an insane asylum. In the plays, equally drab, there were marks of Strindberg and the expressionistic drama.

After the threatening storm clouds of the problem novels the sky is clear again in the subsequent novels of the past, some autobiographical, others historical. It looks as if the author won serenity by focusing upon his own history and that of his nation, with a new faith in his race. The great autobiographical novel *Kirken paa Bjerget* (The Church on the Mountain, 1923–28) re-creates in five volumes the author's experiences from infancy to manhood. *Leg med Straa* (Playing with Straw) brings the boyhood memories from Fljótsdalur, *Skibe paa Himlen* (Ships in the Sky) the family's moving to Vopnafjörður and the mother's death there, *Natten og Drömmen* (The Night and the Dream) describes the growing pains of the adolescent and his decision to go to Denmark, *Den uerfarne Rejsende* (The Inexperienced Traveler) his reactions to the new world, and *Hugleik den Haardtsejlende* his hardening and maturing to a successful writer in Copenhagen. Compared with the romantic family saga, these are realistic memories with an amazingly rich gallery of persons described with humor and gusto. The book is literally alive and not only with people and animals but also with rivers, lakes, mountains; nay, the very stones speak from this intensely personal work.

Having finished the autobiography, Gunnarsson resumed work on a series of novels based upon Icelandic history, the first of which, *Edbrödre* (Sworn Brothers) had appeared in 1918, dealing with the first settlers, and was followed by *Jörð* (Earth, 1933), *Hvide-Krist* (White Christ, 1934), and the play *Rævepelsene* (The Foxes, 1930), a dramatized version of *Bandamanna saga*. *Graamand* (Grey Man, 1936) was taken from *Sturlunga*. *Jón Arason* (1930) was the story of the last Catholic bishop in Iceland. *Svartfugl* (Black Gull, 1929) was an eighteenth-century crime story. Finally there was the highly original *Vikivaki* (1932) with its playful mixture of historical themes and the present.

Back in Iceland Gunnarsson wrote *Heiðaharmur* (The Heath's Sorrow, 1940) about the fighting crofters of the northeast uplands in the last quarter of the nineteenth century, and his book, *Sálumessa* (Mass for Souls, 1952), is a continuation of that. These books are closely related both to the histories and the autobiographies. But his last, the novelette *Brimhenda* (Sonata on the Sea, 1954), is set in a fishing village of the south coast.

Friðrik Á. Brekkan

Friðrik Ásmundsson Brekkan (1888 ——) was born in Miðfjörður in the West, and as a child had his imagination kindled by the sagas. Like Gunnar Gunnarsson he went to Denmark (1910) and Askov, where he read much and published his first novel. During the twenties he published in Danish one collection ·of short stories (1923), one of poetry (1926), and one historical novel on a saga theme: *Ulveungenes Broder* (Brother Wulfing, 1924). It is *Njála*'s Bróðir in the battle of Clontarf. Returning to Iceland (1928), Brekkan became a journalist and teacher in Akureyri and Reykjavík. Since World War II he has been an archivist in the National Museum of Iceland.

Back home he published two more collections of short stories (1928–1942) and two historical novels, *Maður frá Brimarhólmi* (A Man from Brimarhólmur, 1943), about a returned convict from the first half of the nineteenth century, and *Drottningarkyn* (Queen Kin, 1947), about Hallgerður langbrók and her henchman Þjóstólfur, both of *Njáls saga*. Þjóstólfur is here made to be her lover.

Brekkan's historical novels are all well written and make entertaining reading.

Tradition and Revolt Between the World Wars, 1918-1940

Historical background

Though Iceland reached the goal of her national romantic strivings after World War I, the effect was not one of national unity, but rather a dispersal of interests fostered by different political groups. One might have thought that the ancient and still numerous farmers (57 per cent of the population) might have started to rule the country. Instead, there was first a conservative party governed by the numerically few but comparatively wealthy and powerful fish producers and merchants of the towns, while the town workers were just beginning to feel themselves as a social class apart from the others. In the twenties Jónas Jónsson frá Hriflu, a Þingeying, one of the ablest journalists of the country, succeeded with the help of youth leagues and co-operatives to organize the farmers into a party that could take over the government, though only with the help of a labor party which was to grow stronger during the great depression of the thirties. There was a great national romantic celebration of the millenary of the Althing in 1930, after which the depression set in with full force and with it the rise of a new leftist party, the Communists. Though smaller than the labor party, they were more vocal, enjoying the leadership of the keenest intellectuals of the day, hence exerting strong influence on young writers. By 1940 only 30 per cent of the population remained as farmers; the rest was in the towns—in industry (21 per cent), fisheries (16 per cent), communications (9 per cent), commerce (7 per cent), or government service (6 per cent).

Direct influence of World War I upon the writings of the period 1914–30 was apparently slight. It helped Einar Benediktsson's speculations, but hardly his poetry; the speculations scandalized Einar H.

Kvaran. Yet, the shock was registered in Gunnarsson's problem novels, perhaps also in the pervasive anxiety of the young lyric poets immediately after 1918, unless this anxiety is rather derivable from the romantic *Weltschmerz* as described by Þórbergur Þórðarson, fashionable among the budding poets already before the war. But this brooding grew to a culmination in Laxness' *Vefarinn mikli* (1927). The opposite extreme, an abandonment to the temptation of worldly joys and worldly experience, noticeable in Nordal's " Hel," Davíð Stefánsson's new poetry, and Kristmann Guðmundsson's novels, may also have been a kind of war psychosis, though it is paralleled in the gay nineties in other lands.

Traditional literary tendencies

During the twenties and thirties the traditions of the preceding neoromantic period were carried forward or intensified by some of the poets or writers, while others broke completely with them, usually turning socialist in thought, sometimes revolutionary in style.

Of the traditionalists there were at least three groups. There was first the group of progressive idealists led by Einar H. Kvaran. The pure poet Jakob J. Smári was close to it, likewise Einar's son, Ragnar Kvaran, a critic, and the young Axel Thorsteinsson, a novelist; while Elínborg Lárusdóttir, a very prolific and popular novelist, joined the group in the thirties.

A second group was that of conservative nationalists. Already during the war some, like Bjarni Jónsson frá Vogi and Árni Pálsson, had reacted against the cosmopolitan culture of Kvaran (e. g., family names) as well as the foreign exploitation of Icelandic waterfalls. During the twenties and after, Guðmundur Finnbogason and Sigurður Nordal strove for a deeper analysis of the national character, stressed the continuum of the literary tradition (*rímur*), and put a new emphasis on rustic cultural values. Nordal found Kvaran's spiritualistic art faded, but held up as patterns of the rustic culture Guðmundur Friðjónsson, the poetesses Theódóra Thoroddsen (1863-1953) and Ólína and Herdís Andrésdóttir (twins: 1858–1935, 1858–1939), but above all the Canadian giant Stephan G. Stephansson. Three more women could be added: Ólöf Sigurðardóttir á Hlöðum (1857–1933), poetess; Kristín Sigfússdóttir (1876–1953), playwright; and Hulda. Some of the young poets were partly attracted to this group: Hagalín, Davíð Stefánsson, Jón Magnússon, and Jóhannes úr Kötlum. During the thirties Guðmundur Ingi Kristjánsson (1907 ——) became the farming poet *par excellence,* a new Eggert Ólafsson. Several of these writers, as well as professional collectors like Sigfús Sigfússon (1855–1935), were interested in folk poetry, folk tales, and folklore; others, like Björn O. Björnsson, in topographical-historical studies (1930——).

Two poets—Jakob Thorarensen and Örn Arnarson (Magnús Stefánsson)—were both nationalistic in outlook but more realistic than the above group; Örn was also nearer to the socialists.

The watchword of the third group was: live fully and give free expression to your feelings whether sadness or joy, hate or love, seriousness or humor. These individualist poets, revolting against the Victorian prudery of the nineteenth century and shying instinctively from the intellectual poetry of Einar Benediktsson, were later branded as bourgeois by the socialist writers. They often were admirers of the *fin de siècle* poetry of France, England, and Scandinavia. Thus Nordal had studied Walter Pater before he drew Álfur á Vindhæli (1919), the first typical character of this sort, sketched in purple lyrical prose. The individualistic point of view was intensified in Laxness' *Vefarinn mikli* (1927), and varied in Kristmann Guðmundsson's novels—while the short stories of Þórir Bergsson (Þorsteinn Jónsson) and Davíð Þorvaldsson (1901–1932) are much more subdued psychological studies. The leading poets of the group, Stefán frá Hvítadal and Davíð Stefánsson, were followed by the melancholy romantics Sigurður Grímsson (1896——) Jóhann Jónsson, Magnús Ásgeirsson, and Tómas Guðmundsson. Richard Beck, Guðmundur Frímann (1903——), Kjartan Gíslason frá Mosfelli (1902——), Vilhjálmur Guðmundsson frá Skáholti (1907——), and Guðfinna Jónsdóttir frá Hömrum (1899–1946) were all related to this group. Likewise to some extent the great poet Jón Helgason, who did not publish his serious poetry until 1939. Since Kristján Albertsson (1897——) was the first to proclaim the greatness of *Vefarinn mikli,* he may be considered the critic of this group, though he was probably more closely connected with Kvaran's and Kamban's cosmopolitanism.

Revolters in style and thought

The fourth group comprises those who revolted in style and thought. There were only two revolters in style, both connected with the literary coterie of Unuhús; in fact, Þórbergur Þórðarson's life had actually been saved by the kindly Maecenas Erlendur Guðmundsson, master of Unuhús, when Þórbergur was a starving youngster just before World War I. During the war, Þórbergur had reacted against the romantic erotic effusions of his fellow poets, parodying them and filling stately skaldic meters with futuristic nonsense. In 1924 he published *Bréf til Láru* to preach his newfound socialism, where the form proved even more important than the message, for he did here precisely what Shaw had done for the English of the nineties: introduced the gentle art of shocking. He broke several taboos, showed no delicacy in praising himself, but also no lack of humor whether dealing with himself or others. When he chose he was a master of classical prose, but he had no scruples against admitting foreign words or involved constructions of the German-Danish baroque time (*ca.* 1600–1800) for grotesque or burlesque effect. Here was then the first real breach against the purist style which had reigned supreme since *Fjölnir*. Halldór Guðjónsson (Kiljan Laxness), the younger of the two style renovators, had been thrown into the maelstrom of postwar Europe (notably Germany) with Marx, Nietzsche, and Freud as beacons on the shore, but Strindberg and Johannes Jörgensen at the tiller. For a while he reached a safe haven in a Catholic monastery in Luxembourg, whence he sent home surrealistic poetry and gathered material for the great autobiographical novel recording his mental development, " a witch-brew of ideas presented in a stylistic furioso " (Peter Hallberg), *Vefarinn mikli frá Kasmír* (1927). I have long thought that this work was marked by the chaos of German Expressionism; at any rate it has the abandon advocated by André Breton, the master of French Surrealism. It created a sensation in Iceland and was hailed by Kristján Albertsson as the epoch-making work it really was. In the future, Laxness was always in the vanguard of the stylistic development, but he was followed in the thirties by the much older Kamban who tried to write seventeenth-century style in a period novel, and by the younger Hagalín, who tried to fuse certain characteristics of old folks' talk in Vestfirðir and Magister Jón Vídalín's preaching into a new style.

Turning now from style to thought, we can say that the Catholic Church made one more convert: Stefán frá Hvítadal. Otherwise the trend among all was to socialism, which now for the first time had natural soil among the poor workers of the towns. In many ways the attitude of the new writers resembled that of the Realists of the eighties: they wrote social satires in the hope of improving the world. And as far as they grounded their satire in native conditions, they might be called neo-realists, though insofar as they built their hopes on the Russian Utopia, they might be charged with Romanticism.

In Denmark Kamban wrote dramas critical of Western culture up to 1927. In Iceland the budding socialism was criticized by Jón Trausti (1918) and advocated with moderation by Hagalín (1927). But the first to proclaim socialism in a fierce attack on the present order was Sigurjón Jónsson (1888——) in a two-volume novel (1922–24), which, though genuinely indignant, had the bad luck to be overshadowed by Þórbergur Þórðarson's brilliant *Bréf til Láru* (1924). With *Alþýðubókin* (1929) Laxness, just back from Upton Sinclair's California, joined the socialist bandwagon and was followed by Gunnar Benediktsson, one of the best critics of the cause.

During the thirties—the depression—Sigurður Einarsson opened the decade with his programmatic *Hammer and Sickle* (1930), while some old and almost all young writers rallied to the banner of Kristinn E. Andrésson (1901——) and his periodical *Rauðir pennar* (1935–1938). The first convert, the national romantic poet Jóhannes úr Kötlum (1932), was followed by the novelists Gunnar M(agnússon) Magnúss (1898——), Stefán Jónsson (1905——), Sigurður Benediktsson Gröndal (1903——), Halldór Stefánsson, Ólafur Jóhann Sigurðsson, and Guðmundur Daníelsson, who soon broke away from the group. There followed the poets Guðmundur Böðvarsson, farmer; Steinn Steinarr (Aðalsteinn Kristmundsson), bohemian; and Jón (Jónsson) úr Vör, poor villager, who all have remained more or less faithful to the socialist gospel, though the two last-named, especially Steinn Steinarr, turned to a new experimental formalism and intensified introspection during the forties. Not leftist, though starting in the thirties, were the novelists Elínborg Lárusdóttir (1891——), Þórunn Magnúsdóttir, and Sigurður Helgason. Snorri Hjartarson wrote a novel in Norwegian (1934) ; he was to become one of the finest poets of the forties.

Icelandic studies

In the interwar period, Icelandic studies were represented in Reykjavík by Sigurður Nordal, professor of literature (1918–1945) ; Alexander Jóhannesson (1888——), professor of language (1915–58), a prolific historian of language and an etymologist; Páll Eggert Ólason (1883–1949), professor of history (1921–29), a prolific bibliographer (catalogue of the manuscript collections of the National Library, 1918–1937), author of fundamental studies on the Reformation period and the nineteenth century (Jón Sigurðsson), history of Iceland in the sixteenth and seventeenth centuries, and an Icelandic biographical lexicon; Barði Guðmundsson (1900–57), professor of history (1930–31) and archivist, a brilliant but erratic scholar; Árni Pálsson (1878–1952) professor of history (1931–43), more celebrated as a wit and essayist than as a scholar.

Of scholars not connected with the University the great schoolman Sigurður Guðmundsson (1878–1949), headmaster of the school at Akureyri, wrote many penetrating studies of Icelandic literary figures, old and modern. Guðbrandur Jónsson (1888–1953), son of Jón Þorkelsson (forni), specialized in Catholic studies, wrote an antiquarian description of the Cathedral at Hólar and a life of the last Catholic bishop, Dr. Helgi P. Briem (1902——) wrote on Iceland's Independence 1809.

Here the editors of *Íslenzk fornrit* (1933——) under the leadership of Sigurður Nordal may fittingly be mentioned. Nordal started the series with *Egils saga* in 1933. Björn Karel Þórólfsson (1892——) had written a monumental study of *rímur* before 1600 and had done some editing in Copenhagen; he edited *Vestfirðinga sögur*. Einar Ól. Sveinsson (1899——) had written on fairy tales (*Märchenvarianten*) and a literary study on *Njála* (1933) and was to write a monumental study of the Sturlung Age (1940); he edited *Laxdœla, Njála* (1954) and others. Guðni Jónsson was a prolific writer on several matters; he edited *Grettis saga* and others. Björn Sigfússon (1905——) edited *Ljósvetninga saga* and others. Bjarni Aðalbjarnarson (1908–1953) wrote a fundamental work on the kings' sagas (1936) and edited *Heimskringla* (1941——).

In Scandinavia, Icelandic studies were represented by Jón Helgason (1899——), first professor of Old Icelandic in Oslo (1926–27), then in Copenhagen (1929——), also a curator of the Arnamagnaean Collection and a prolific and painstaking editor; Sigfús Blöndal (1874–1950) taught Modern Icelandic (1931–46). Jakob Benediktsson (1907——), a classical scholar, edited Icelandic Renaissance Latin writings, collaborated on an Old Icelandic dictionary sponsored by the Arnamagnaean Foundation, and became after World War II editor-in-chief of a modern Icelandic dictionary sponsored by the University of Iceland in Reykjavík.

In America Stefán Einarsson (1897——) began teaching Old Icelandic at The Johns Hopkins University in 1927 and has since then published books on Icelandic language and literature, especially of the modern period. Richard Beck (1897——) began teaching Icelandic at the University of North Dakota in 1929, and has since then been an extremely prolific writer and lecturer on Modern Icelandic literature and literary figures, and also an editor of several American-Icelandic poets.

Sigurður Eggerz

Sigurður Pétursson Eggerz (1875–1945), was born in Hrútafjörður
in the Northwest, of a family of parsons and lawyers, and studied law in
Copenhagen (1895–1903), where he joined Jóhann Sigurjónsson's circle.
In Iceland his political career took him to the highest position in the land,
and prevented his writing until his sixties.

He published *Sýnir* (Visions, 1934), essays, short stories, speeches
and poems, all in a strong lyric vein, similar to the prose poem. His
plays, *Það logar yfir jöklinum* (Fire over the Glacier, 1937) and *Lík-
kistusmiðurinn* (The Coffin Maker, 1938), are dramas of great ideals
and tempestuous passions, akin to but surpassing in fervor the romantic
Danish-Icelandic plays. A third play, *Pála* (1942), was more subdued
in tone. In these plays there is an expressionistic tendency to suppress
individualizing detail and exaggerate the emotions that make his dramas
unusual in Icelandic literature, though Gunnarsson's *Dyret med glorien*
(The Animal with the Halo, 1922) is of a similar cast.

Magnús Stefánsson

Magnús Stefánsson (pen name Örn Arnarsson, 1884–1942) was
born near Langanes in the Northeast, of poor parents in a time of near
famine. Toward the end of his life in a hospital in Hafnarfjörður, in
one of his finest poems, he paid a sensitive and beautiful tribute to his
mother guiding his first steps of life. The Icelandic home (*baðstofa*)
recital of *rímur* and sagas staked out his road as a poet; that road led
him through a high school and a teachers' college (Reykjavík, 1909)
and, finally, through a self-imposed course in foreign languages and
literatures (Scandinavian, English, and German). Yet, except for one
year, which he did not enjoy, he did not become a teacher but alternated
clerical work in winter with manual work (fishing, road-building) in
summer. His youthful love, "Ásrún," was to become a bittersweet
memory only, for he remained a bachelor with not a little of the vagabond
in him: traveling on foot all over his native land, collecting stones, plants,
and impressions for memorable poems.

His ambition to become a poet was coupled with an unusually keen
self-criticism. It was not until 1920 that he published a few poems in
Eimreiðin, but their success was such that he was moved to publish his
Illgresi (Weeds) in 1924, a slim volume. After his death, it was published (1942) with additions and a sketch of his life by Bjarni Aðalbjarnarson. The poems remain uniformly of a high quality.

Considering his origins and life it was small wonder that the poet should turn to satire of the existing order in revolt against an inhuman God and malevolent, hypocritical, and superficial men. Yet his instrument was more often irony and whimsicality than direct satire. He was too complete a man himself to see only one side of life, and he found not a few heroes worthy of his praise. So the thoroughly Icelandic "Sheriff Sigurður," embodiment of the saga-spirit, so the famous fisherman type, "Stjáni blái," and so, finally, the berserk sailor-politician Oddur sterki, in whose honor the poet composed a rollicking cycle of *rímur* (1938).

There are more good poems about sailors, sailing, and the sea, like the poem "Hrafnistumenn," the official song of the Icelandic seamen.

As befits a satirist he has also left many biting epigrams; but in general his outlook mellowed with the years and with his poetical success.

Þorsteinn Jónsson

Þorsteinn Jónsson (pen name Þórir Bergsson, 1885——) was born in Hvammur, Norðurárdalur, in the West, the son of a clergyman, who gave his son a solid home education. Poor health compelled him to take a position as a clerk, first in a post office, later in a bank in Reykjavík. As early as 1912 he published a short story, but his first collection, *Sögur* (Stories) came in 1939. It was followed by a novel, *Vegir og vegleysur* (Ways and No Ways, 1941), *Nýjar sögur* (New Stories, 1944), a volume of poems (1947), more short stories, *Hinn gamli Adam* (The Old Adam, 1947), and the novel *Hvítsandar* (White Sands, 1949).

Þorsteinn Jónsson is always a competent short story writer and some of his stories are excellent. His lack of political bias and his interest in character studies, as well as in his art, range him squarely with the neoromanticists. He does not have the humor of Jakob Thorarensen or the social satire of Halldór Stefánsson. In some of his fiction (e. g., the first novel) there are echoes of Hamsun, lover of nature and admirer of women, but Þorsteinn Jónsson lacks Hamsun's humor and is quieter in tone.

Though character development or description is his main interest, he can also describe situations and moods; cf. the horror story "Í Gilja-reitum." His post-World War II stories differ in no way from his earlier production, and they have no nationalistic bias, though they describe inevitable incidents.

Jakob Thorarensen

Jakob Jakobsson Thorarensen (1886——) was born in Húnavatns-sýsla of a family of poets (Bjarni Thorarensen) and scholars. He grew up in Hrútafjörður and Reykjarfjörður, Strandir, and was early formed by that harsh and rugged nature to a stern manliness. One of his grandfathers told him stories of the brave shark fishermen he was to celebrate in a memorable poem, the other one became his pattern as a man of action and strong personality. As a youth Jakob Thorarensen worked on a farm or, sometimes, as a fisherman; but when he was nineteen he went to Reykjavík, where for a long time he plied his trade as a carpenter or house-builder. Within a short time he had a home and a good and growing private library in which he could improve his unschooled but intellectually curious mind. But though he gradually gained the use of foreign languages and traveled to Scandinavia (cf. his poem " Sogn ") he was primarily influenced by the native literary tradition within which his kinsman Bjarni Thorarensen and Grímur Thomsen matched his manliness, while Einar Benediktsson may have inspired his philosophical approach.

Jakob Thorarensen was a prolific author who published more than a dozen volumes. He made his debut with *Snæljós* (Snow Blink, 1914), a collection of poems which was followed by three others before the series was broken by *Fleygar stundir* (Winged Hours, 1929), the first of four volumes of short stories. His collected works, entitled *Svalt og bjart* (Cool and Bright), were published in 1946. Since then one more volume of poems and two of short stories have appeared. Jakob Thorarensen was an intellectual rather than a lyric poet.

Whether he wrote poetry or prose Jakob Thorarensen was a realist, a lover of a rugged landscape, clear and cool northern skies and, in general, the sterner side of Icelandic nature. He admired strong and flawless characters whether of the saga age or of the present. Conversely, he had no use for laggards or braggarts, whiners or hypocrites. He would portray his characters in short but deft narrative sketches, often with friendly humor, yet not infrequently with biting irony. But in spite of his satirical bent he was not a socialist, like his fellow-realist Magnús Stefánsson (Örn Arnarson), being apparently too much of an individualist for that. As a philosopher he was in general resigned to life as it came, but was not always averse to kicking against fate and God, when he felt in the mood.

His short stories were among the best written at the time, marked by the same deftness in character drawing, the same keen eye for life's multifarious, yet everyday, problems, the same humor and irony, as the poems.

Sigurður Nordal

Sigurður Jóhannesson Nordal (1886——) was born and brought up in Vatnsdalur in the North, of a stock of poets and scholars; he studied Icelandic philology at the University of Copenhagen, writing a thesis on the sources of Snorri's *Ólafs saga helga* (1914). After an interval in Germany and Oxford, where he studied psychology and philosophy, he returned to Iceland to lecture on these subjects and take over the chair of Old Icelandic Literature at the University of Iceland (1918). This he kept in one way or another until, in 1951, he became the Minister of Iceland in Denmark. His works on *Snorri Sturluson* (1920) and *Völuspá* (1923) at once revealed his stature—W. P. Ker compared his essays with those of Saint-Beuve—and made him a popular lecturer in Scandinavia, even in America, where he held the Charles Eliot Norton professorship of poetry at Harvard 1931–32. Later, universities of Scandinavia and Great Britain, among them Oxford, vied with each other in giving him honorary degrees.

Though Nordal's thesis was strictly philological, he was no dry-as-dust scholar: indeed, he had already buried himself in the literature of the *fin de siècle* (Pater, Maeterlinck, Baudelaire) and composed poetry both in verse and prose. His exquisite prose poem "Hel" (The Goddess of Death) in *Fornar ástir* (Old Loves, 1919) was not only unique in Icelandic literature, but made the book the best of the year. It is the study of a Don Juan, Álfur frá Vindhæli, who like a butterfly flits from flower to flower, savoring all the sensation of the world without ever wanting to shoulder the responsibilities of life. After death Nordal gives him amnesia and turns him over to his first love, who, like Solveig in *Peer Gynt,* always had treasured him in memory. Here is the same appetite for life and hedonism which are characteristic of the great lyric poets of the twenties, notably Davið Stefánsson. That they were a self-portrait of the young Nordal was obvious, and equally obviously they represented a phase in his life or dreams which he wanted to renounce—to a degree—when he became a scholar. Yet, only to a degree! He treated the same problem, posed by many choices or one, facing every individual, in his lectures on "Centripetal and Centrifugal Personality" (1918), advocating the Golden Mean, a synthesis of the two. As to his own work, he vowed that from now on he would not publish anything where his scholarship and his poetic vision were not integrated to the best of his ability. This sounded like and was meant to be a challenge to Finnur Jónsson's narrow philological point of view.

His brilliant book on *Snorri Sturluson* (1920) was the first sample of this synthesis, showing Snorri as a writer and chieftain, a tragic bi-polarity in his life, and sketching the development of the sagas as a function of two great interests: truth seeking and entertainment. The introduction to *Völuspá* made this difficult Eddic classic speak directly to a modern audience. Great influence on contemporary writers was exerted by his essay on the continuity in Icelandic Literature in *Íslenzk lestrarbók 1400–1900* (Icelandic Anthology, 1924). In this he emphasized the role of the *rímur* as a conserver of language, poetic diction, and metrical practices (the old Germanic alliterative verse), and saw the history of Icelandic literature as a fruitful struggle between foreign influence and national inheritance. This nationalistic stand involved him in literary controversy during the late twenties when he took a stand for the farm culture of Þingeyjarsýsla but against the weak spiritualistic-humanitarian attitudes of Einar H. Kvaran and frowned on the contemporary " fads of Europe," represented by Laxness' Catholic *Vefarinn mikli*. Neither did he trust the radical socialists, but fortunately for him, some of them, notably the youth leader and critic Kristinn Andrésson (1901——), carried on his nationalism in the thirties and forties. In the thirties Nordal and his disciples, notably Einar Ólafur Sveinsson, were busy at work on the new literary edition of the sagas: *Íslenzk fornrit*. Nordal published *Egils saga* (1933) and a few others, besides being the leader of the whole enterprise (there are now thirteen volumes; *Njáls saga* has been published by Einar Ólafur Sveinsson). In these editions, in general following Bédier's methods, he tried to lay the foundation of a new criticism of the sagas, as they have been preserved to us. Though not denying the importance of oral tradition, he sees the sagas mostly as written works, products of real authors, not scribes, and he demonstrates their place in the development after the kings' sagas, mostly during the thirteenth century, the Sturlung Age. A survey of these views is found in his " Sagalitteraturen " in *Nordisk Kultur*, 1953.

Already as a young man abroad, notably in Oxford, Nordal was prodded by the inferiority complex of a member of a small nation to make clear to himself what, if anything, in the cultural tradition of this isolated and insignificant people was worth telling about abroad and devoting a lifetime of work to at home. He soon came to the conclusion that not only the Eddas and the sagas had intrinsic value, but also the way this old literature had become, so to speak, the very bread on which the people as a whole had survived during long centuries of famine and depressions, up to the rebirth in the nineteenth century. With this in mind he wrote his Harvard lectures, and in the late thirties he resumed the work, planning to write a three-volume book *Íslenzk menning* (Icelandic Culture) for the literary society Mál og Menning. Actually the first volume, appearing in 1942, exceeded even the fondest hopes of his admirers. It was an epoch-making study of Icelandic culture and its institutions from the beginning up to the thirteenth century. As by-products of his studies, Nordal wrote a number of essays on the leading Icelandic poets, like Egill Skalla-Grímsson, Grímur Thomsen, Þorsteinn Erlingsson, Stephan G. Stephansson, and others. These essays were collected in *Áfangar I–II* (Stages, 1943–44), while *Líf og dauði* (Life and Death, 1940) are philosophical radio talks, and *Uppstigning* (Resurrection, 1946) is a Pirandellian play of revolt against the confines of a small town.

Stefán Sigurðsson frá Hvítadal

Stefán Sigurðsson frá Hvítadal (1887–1933) was born at Hólmavík in the Northwest, but grew up on farms, one of them Hvítadalur in the same vicinity. An attempt to learn the printer's trade failed because of ill health which dogged him all his life. The years 1912–16 were spent in Norway, working, sight-seeing, and suffering in a sanatorium. Back in his home district he married and had a large family, but died prematurely. When in Reykjavík he was a member of the Unuhús coterie.

His first poems *Söngvar förumannsins* (The Wanderer's Song, 1918, second edition 1919) struck a new note in Icelandic poetry and became a literary event. In Norway he had learned much of Ibsen, Per Sivle and especially Wildenvey; he had adapted their verse forms to suit his own personal expression, after which they became the rage of young poets in Iceland. His poetry was perhaps more personal than any heard before in Iceland. In it he poured out his love to the fair sex, his love of nature, summer, and spring in strains that were doubly poignant because one could always sense the threat of ever-impending death. Naturally sorrow and sad laments find their place in the poems, too, but rejoicing of youth, and praise of life are really dominant, for the poet was a man at heart. Few could express the perhaps somewhat reckless but perfectly natural aspirations of youth as he did in " Hjarta-rím " (Heart Rime). But however reckless and worldly the young lover could be—as testified by some of his love poems or his praise of women—there was in him also a deep strain of spirituality which rang out the church bells in " Aðfangadagskvöld jóla 1912 " (Christmas Eve), brilliant in form and profound in feeling.

With this first book Stefán rose to undreamed heights in the firmament of Icelandic poets. In his second book, *Óður einyrkjans* (The Song of the Lone Cotter, 1921), he had already passed the zenith, although the book in general is fine. He has now become an earthbound tiller of the soil and makes a genuine effort to fuse poetry and his work, but cannot avoid clashing with the earlier dreamer and wanderer. The old themes are still there, but lack the first freshness; to compensate he turns to folklore and fairy tales.

It was the religious note which was to grow to the exclusion of most other things in his future poetry. Like Laxness, another member of the Unuhús coterie, Stefán frá Hvítadal became a Catholic in 1923, though his friend, Þórbergur Þórðarson, always doubted the sincerity of his conversion. His next work was *Heilög kirkja* (Holy Church, 1924), a sonorous *hrynhenda*, a praise poem, in the tradition of *Lilja*. Of his next book, *Helsingjar* (Geese, 1927), he devoted about half to Catholic religious poetry, while the rest was on traditional worldly subjects, the two outstanding poems being in praise of women and poets. *Anno Domini 1930* was occasioned by the millenary of the Althing; it was posthumously published (1933). A collected edition of his poems (*Ljóðmæli*) with an introduction by the poet Tómas Guðmundsson was published in 1945.

Sigurjón Jónsson

Sigurjón Jónsson (1888——) was born in Reykjavík, but grew up in extreme poverty in Húsavík of the North. After a short schooling he became a bank clerk in Reykjavík. Here he met the writers of the Unuhús coterie, and, like others of that group, developed from a romantic idealist and theosophist into a socialist and satirical writer. Though by no means the best of that group, he had the distinction of being the first. Having started with some highly romantic fairy tales and poems, which gained him a parody by Þórbergur Þórðarson, Sigurjón unleashed his biting satire on Reykjavík during and after World War I in *Silkikjólar og vaðmálsbuxur* (Silk Gowns and Homespun Pants, 1922) and *Glæsi-*

mennska (Dandyism, 1924). After that Sigurjón lapsed into silence, not broken until his retirement from the bank. Then—after 1945—he came back with epigrams, short stories and fairy tales, some of which contained his best writing, also a revised edition of *Silkikjólar*, and some mediocre plays. But most surprising of the late works was *Ingvildur Fögurkinn* (1951–52), based on *Svarfdœla saga*, written in a very individualistic way, with saga style, modern style, lyric passages, verse and fairy tale style all mixed. This would seem to be an inauspicious undertaking, but somehow the author manages to succeed, and the work compares favorably with other sagas in modern garb, if one excepts Laxness' *Gerpla*. And, due to his theosophist background, he interprets Old Icelandic sorcery better than most other imitators of the sagas. Two more "sagas" from his pen are *Gaukur Trandilsson* (1953) and *Helga Bárðardóttir* (1955).

Jakob J. Smári

Jakob Jóhannesson Smári (1889——) was born at Sauðafell in Miðdalir in the West, the son of a parson who was a philologist of note and of a verse-making family. He studied Old Icelandic philology at the University of Copenhagen (M.A. 1914), and later became a teacher of Icelandic language and literature in the Gymnasium of Reykjavík. He wrote textbooks on grammar (notably syntax), essays on cultural and literary subjects, and was a busy reviewer of books.

Smári published three volumes of poetry: *Kaldavermsl* (1920), *Handan storms og strauma* (Beyond Storms and Currents, 1936), and *Undir sól að sjá* (Looking toward Sunset, 1939), the titles all significant of his poetic tendency. The first means a spring that runs cool in summer, warm in winter, a symbol of his deep and steadily flowing poetic vein. For Smári is always a personal lyric poet *par excellence*, whether he writes love poems or descriptions of nature—usually in its quieter and mellower moods—nay, even when he describes the most bitter winter. He is in reality a mystic who readily identifies himself not only with fellow-humans and animals, but also with the whole of nature and any facet of it. Fundamentally this is the attitude of the Symbolists and Neo-Romanticists, and Einar Benediktsson is another fine example, but the difference between him and Smári is that between the raging waterfall and the smooth-flowing spring or the quiet pond that mirrors eternity in its waters. Besides, Einar Benediktsson is more intellectual, Smári more personal. Smári is a great master of form and likes to employ the sonnet, but also many other meters, not all of them simple, though his form is almost always smooth and flawless. His familiarity with oriental wisdom (theosophy) and spiritualism has visibly enhanced his search for eternal values, but though he acknowledges his indebtedness to socialism (acquired in Denmark), the poems that testify to this are very few. His poetry is all beyond the storms and stresses of this world, for he is no fighter but a dreamer, a dreamer to whom the glorious Icelandic sunsets become the gates of eternity.

Þórbergur Þórðarson

Þórbergur Þórðarson (1889——) was born in Suðursveit, a remote district in the Southeast. As a farm boy he desired to become a sailor; the sailor aspired to learning and, though he found no favor in elementary schools, he was fortunate enough to be able to study Icelandic language and literature at the University of Reykjavík (1913–18), and to ease his bohemian hunger at the hospitable table of Erlendur Guðmundsson of Unuhús (1913). This house was frequented by many poetic aspirants, among them Þórbergur's friend Stefán frá Hvítadal, who already was finding a perfect voice for the emotions of the time in erotic, melancholy, but simple strains. Þórbergur, originally an admirer and imitator of Einar Benediktsson, was converted to the simple lyric, but reacted with parodies both to his first mentor's skaldic style and to his present friends' erotic effusions. Specimens of his futuristic, Heinesque poetry were published as early as 1914 and 1915, but united and expanded in *Hvítir hrafnar* (White Ravens, 1922), the title a parody of Davíð Stefánsson's *Svartar fjaðrir* (Black Feathers).

In 1917 Þórbergur Þórðarson buried himself in the study of oriental philosophy, theosophy and spiritualism, practicing *yoga* with considerable success. He described this rebirth in " Ljós úr austri " (Ex oriente lux, 1919), the first in a row of brilliant personal essays. Sincerely attracted by the theosophic ideal of brotherhood of men, he was soon disillusioned, when he felt that they did nothing to attain it, and so he turned to the study of socialism. This study bore an unexpectedly fine fruit in his next book: *Bréf til Láru* (Letter to Laura, 1924).

The book was intended to be a manifesto of socialism, and it contained sharp attacks on the existing order, not least the Protestant and the Catholic churches, as well as theosophists and spiritualists—for hypocrisy and easy-going life—for the author had no quarrel with Christ's teachings, nor did he doubt the existence of life after death. This matter was embedded in a picturesque frame of personal essays and sketches, anecdotes, and tales quite often autobiographical, aways humorous, frequently at his own expense. And it was written in a brilliant style, paradoxical and shocking to the Victorian code of decency and common sense. These qualities made it a milestone in the development of literature and prose style, paving the way for Laxness, Kamban and Hagalín to leave the puristic classical style behind.

The *Letter* involved Þórbergur in a fierce controversy with the representatives of church and capital, during which he wrote perhaps his most brilliant essay, " Eldvígslan " (Initiation by Fire, 1925), in answer to a letter of Kristján Albertsson, the best young capitalistic critic at the time. No less brilliant was the autobiographical " Lifandi kristindómur og ég " (Living Christianity and I, 1929).

As a university student, Þórbergur Þórðarson seemed predestined to become a student of national culture, and so he did, though he debunked the farm culture in *Letter to Laura*. He collected dialectal words and folk tales, published in *Gráskinna* 1928–36. Both were as fit exercises for his scientific meticulousness as they were appealing to his almost gullible mysticism.

From theosophical brotherhood and socialism there was only a step to internationalism and Esperanto, which he embraced in 1925. He taught it, wrote it, and espoused its cause in *Alþjóðamál og málleysur* (International Language and Lesser Tongues, 1933). In 1934 Þórbergur Þórðarson visited Russia and wrote about it the ironical *Rauða hættan* (The Red Scare, 1935). At the same time he wrote a newspaper column against the Nazis which earned him a fine from the Supreme Court, at Hitler's request.

The unusually loud personal note present in all Þórbergur Þórðarson's work first prompted him to publish a sheaf of letters (1933) and finally resulted in a resolve to write his autobiography, unlike Gunnarsson, with names unchanged and with the fullest exercise of truthfulness he could master. It appeared as *Íslenzkur aðall* (Icelandic Nobility, 1938) and *Ofvitinn* I-II (The All-Too-Wise *or* The Eccentric, 1940–41), covering the period 1909–1913, from the time he left the fishing smack until he entered the gates of Unuhús. Though realistically written and claiming to tell nothing but the truth, it is no less a highly imaginative novel. It is full of eccentric personalities, odd happenings, and comic scenes. It is not only the story of the diffident lover, romantic dreamer, the sarcastic cynic, and the fumbling philosopher, Þórbergur Þórðarson himself, but also a canvas of the age on which move budding celebrities like the poet Stefán frá Hvítadal and the future royal secretary Tryggvi Sveinbjörnsson, beside a host of minor figures, all intensely alive.

Having written that much about himself, he paused to write two spiritistic books, but after that he assumed the role of Boswell to write the memoirs of an old parson in six volumes, *Æfisaga Árna Þórarinssonar* I–IV (1945–50). Wagging tongues said that here the fastest liar in Iceland had met the most gullible scribe, but, however that may be, the work is as unique in Icelandic literature as Boswell's *Dr. Johnson* is in English, and there is no doubt that the scribe attempts to transfer his author—stories, tall tales, miracles, prejudices, superstitions, and personal style—with the utmost fidelity to the pages of the book. That he has succeeded in this is unquestioned.

From the exciting octogenarian, Þórbergur turned his keen observation to the life of a baby, a niece in the family born in 1943, to which he has devoted two volumes called *Sálmurinn um blómið* (The Hymn about the Flower, 1954–1955), a fascinating book written from the point of view of the child—with baby-talk and all.

Gunnar Benediktsson

Gunnar Benediktsson (1892———) was born in Austur-Skaftafells-sýsla, of farmer and parson stock. He served as a pastor in Saurbær, Eyjafjörður, 1920–31, but then resigned and turned socialist, living in Reykjavík, Eyrarbakki, and, at present, Hveragerði, the artist colony.

Gunnar Benediktsson wrote several novels and one play, to expose the rotten social order of his time, but most of them lack the spark of living art. Having more intellectual powers than imagination, he is at his best in his lectures and essays. He is not only the keenest intellect among the socialists, but one of the outstanding essayists of the country. His *Æfisaga Jesú frá Nazaret* (Life of Jesus, 1930) interpreted Jesus as a revolutionary leader. His essays were published in the collections *Sýn mér trú þína af verkunum* (Show Me Your Faith by Your Deeds, 1936), *Skilningstré góðs og ills* (The Tree of Knowledge of Good and Evil, 1939), *Sóknin mikla, um Finnagaldur* (The Great Attack; about Finn Sorcery, 1940), and *Hinn gamli Adam í oss* (Old Adam in Us, 1944). His last works are *Saga þín er saga vor* (Your History is Our History, 1952), a history of Iceland during and after World War II, and *Ísland hefur jarl* (Iceland Has an Earl, 1954), interesting comments on the Sturlung Age.

These essays contain the best history of ideas in Iceland during the first third of the century, fine profiles of contemporaries and associates, literary criticism and reactions to world events—all from the Marxist point of view. The style is classical and ironical, but lacks the whimsicality of Þórbergur Þórðarson and the capricious conceits of H. K. Laxness.

Halldór Stefánsson

Halldór Stefánsson (1892——) was born in the East and grew up in Eskifjörður, the son of a local postmaster. As a bank clerk in Reykjavík he published his first short story in 1921, and his first collection of short stories, *Í fáum dráttum* (In Few Strokes, 1930), was partly written during a vacation in Berlin. Four more volumes followed, all containing short stories, excepting *Innan sviga* (Within Parentheses, 1945), a short novel. A last volume (1950) also contained some short plays.

Halldór Stefánsson was interested in three things: the fate of the underprivileged and poor, peculiar and psychologically interesting individuals, and methods of short story telling. Because of his first interest he belongs with the socialistic group of writers, though this tendency is by no means always present. In reality he is more interested in the individual than in his society. The last preoccupation has turned him into one of the most decided experimentalists in short story writing. His stories have usually a characteristic firm structure. This firmness also extends to his style, which is often humorous and ironic, sometimes punning. Of his short stories, " Death on the Third Floor," the punning " Réttur " (" Right " = " Course of Food ") and " Dream for Sale " may be mentioned. The last-named describes the impact of World War II on an Icelandic character, while " England Expects Every Man to Do His Duty " tells the story of an English private in Iceland. But " Hernaðarsaga blinda mannsins " (The Blind Man's Warfare) is a masterpiece, perhaps his best.

Davíð Stefánsson

Davíð Stefánsson (1895——) was born at Fagriskógur, Eyjafjörður, in the North, his father a farmer and member of the Althing, his mother a sister of Ólafur Davíðsson, the prolific folklorist. He first went to school at Akureyri, but his studies were interrupted by ill health so that he did not graduate from the Gymnasium in Reykjavík until 1919. He made a great many journeys abroad. He was for a long time a librarian in Akureyri (1925–52) and was, besides, a lover and collector of books, as some of his poems show.

Davíð Stefánsson was to become the chief romantic poet of the twenties (and thirties), a most popular poet of his time and the most prolific one. He was to achieve what the early neo-romantics like Hulda and Guðmundur Guðmundsson had striven for—a complete realization of the personal lyric poetry giving an uninhibited expression to his changing moods of love and hate, hope and despair, exultation and sadness. Though many of his contemporaries had striven for the same full scale of emotional poetry and would readily imitate him, only Stefán Sigurðsson frá Hvítadal had acquired the new tone before him, and his poetry remained more limited in form and themes. But both he and Davíð Stefánsson avoided the essentially skaldic forms of Einar Benediktsson and turned to the simpler forms of foreign and native poetry, Davíð Stefánsson to the folk-song (ballad) forms that he had learned from the great collection of his uncle Ólafur Davíðsson (*Íslenzkar gátur, skemtanir, vikivakar, og þulur*, 1887–1903) at his mother's knee.

Davíð Stefánsson was not quite unknown when he published *Svartar fjaðrir* (Black Feathers, 1919), but it was a resounding success, admired by young and old alike; by the first for the fiery emotions, by the latter for the ennobled folk-song forms. It won him a stipend to see Italy, celebrated in many poems of his next collection, *Kvæði* (Poems, 1922). There followed *Kveðjur* (Greetings, 1924) and *Ný kvæði* (New Poems, 1929), all four united in a collected edition, 1930. In the thirties there appeared *Í byggðum* (Among Human Habitations, 1933) and *Að norðan* (From the North, 1936), then after a longer pause *Ný kvæðabók* (New Poems, 1947), his last one. No doubt, his very best work is to be found in these poems, though not all of them could be of equal worth.

Love poetry, sensual or spiritual, exulting or sad, native or Italian, naturally predominates in the earlier volumes, which also contain most of the folklore and folk song themes, even these shifting from light or humorous to ominous and threatening moods and horror stories, like the exotic " Abba-Labba-Lá." Often there is " a deep undercurrent of heartache and sadness " (R. Beck) as in the lullaby to his mother " Mamma ætlar að sofna " (Mother is Going to Sleep). In others, inescapable destiny is lamented in symbolic poems like " Krummi " (The Raven), while pioneers like " Myndhöggvarinn " (The Sculptor) often receive his praise. His travels inspire poems imbued with longing for the faraway romantic countries (*útþrá*) and his nostalgia for home, as well as descriptions of sights seen. Thus his first train ride is turned into a symbol of the course of life. After 1924 a note of social satire is increasingly heard, and he may have gone to Russia to take a look at that land of promise (before 1929), but without being much impressed except, perhaps, by the vodka. He does write the famous eulogy on " Konan sem kyndir ofninn minn " (The Woman Who Keeps my Stove Burning), and in the volume dating from the depression year of 1933 his reformatory zeal against capitalism and Church is at its greatest, though never toeing the communist line. At home he lamented the flight of the farmer to the cities and the growing bureaucracy. His last volume of poems (1947) contains his reactions to the war at home and abroad, showing his hatred of planned totalitarianism and his admiration for Norway—also his disillusion at the quick rearmament.

It is impossible to trace all his themes, but something must be said of his humorous and whimsical tales in verse, of which " My John's Soul " is justly famous and has furthermore inspired him to write his best play, the equally delightfully humorous and whimsical *Gullna hliðið* (The Golden Gate, 1941). As early as 1926 Davíð Stefánsson had written an unsuccessful play, but *The Golden Gate* was eminently successful not only in Reykjavík but in Oslo and Edinburgh as well. After that he wrote *Vopn Guðanna* (The Weapons of the Gods, 1944) on the oriental tale of Josaphat and Barlaam and *Landið gleymda* (The Forgotten Land, 1953) about the Greenland missionary, Hans Egede. Almost as popular as *The Golden Gate* was his historical-realistic symbolic novel, *Sólon Islandus* (I–II, 1940), the story of an Icelandic vagabond of the nineteenth century. It is a truly Icelandic tragedy, the life of an ambitious, artistic dreamer with no means to realize his ambition, or to develop his talents which might have borne fruit in a bigger nation. Thus elucidated, Sólon becomes a significant figure in Icelandic fiction, comparable to the Norwegian Peer Gynt.

Jón Magnússon

Jón Magnússon (1896–1944) was born in Borgarfjörður of poor parents, but grew up with his mother in the historic Þingvallasveit. For many years he lived in Reykjavík as a cooper ; later he became the owner of a furniture store. He was self-educated and a great book lover.

In spite of hard work, his mind was always occupied with poetry, and he wrote five volumes of it before his premature death. He started with

Bláskógar (Blue Forests, 1925), inspired by ardent love for his home, the beautiful Þingvallasveit, and he ended with *Jörðin græn* (Green Earth, 1945), a symbolic tribute to the Icelandic mother earth. Jón was an unusually warm personality, as the glint in his eyes would tell, and his warm heart burned with a quiet flame in all his poetry, whether he dealt with the blessed green earth, the flocks of sheep and the playing spring lambs (*Hjarðir*, Flocks, 1929), or with his fellow-countrymen— from orphans, who he felt were his special brothers and sisters, to his favorite poets. Yet, there was one breed of man whom he singled out for special treatment; indeed, he wrote a whole book in honor of one of them, *Björn á Reyðarfelli* (1938). These were the men who, resisting the flood tide of movement from the country to the town, had clung to the upland farms and given their lives to keep them as human habitations in spite of hard natural conditions and the tendency of their children to forsake this heritage for a less rigorous existence. When a man like that died, Iceland's stature had been lowered one man's length, as the poet remarked about one of these cotters. Jón saw in their faithful struggle and in their unrelenting manhood a symbol of the thousand-year-old struggle for survival of the nation itself and the chief hope for its future. In this he joined hands with most of the national-romanticists of the twenties, Guðmundur Friðjónsson, Nordal, his brother-in-law Davíð Stefánsson, and others. For though Jón lived in Reykjavík, his roots remained in Þingvallasveit.

Jóhann Jónsson

Jóhann Jónsson (1896–1932), born in Snæfellsnes in the West, died prematurely in Leipzig, Germany, after studying at the Gymnasium in Reykjavík and the Universities of Leipzig and Berlin.

At school in Reykjavík (1917–20) he made a great impression on his fellow-poets as being the most gifted of the group, and the few poems that survive from that period sustain fully that judgment. To be sure, he shared his fellow-poets' gloomy, sad mood, but in his case it had a genuine, personal cause, since he was ill and partly crippled. His experiment in free verse was better than anything attempted in that genre at the time; witness his poems: " Hvað er klukkan . . . ? " (What time is it. . . ?), " Ljóð " (Poem), and " Söknuður " (Sorrow). Jóhann composed " Sorrow " when his fatal tuberculosis knocked on the door for the second time. It is thus, in a way, a death poem, a poignant lament over his irrevocably lost poetry and life.

His *Kvæði og ritgerðir* (Poems and Essays, 1952) were published by his friend and fellow-poet Halldór Kiljan Laxness.

Sigurður Einarsson

Sigurður Einarsson (1898———) was born in Fljótshlíð—the Njála country—of good farm stock with interest in literature, but grew up in Vestmannaeyjar as a fisherman. He graduated in theology from the University of Iceland in 1926 and had after that a chequered and colorful career as a parson, educator, politician, radio commentator, lecturer, essayist, and professor of theology. At present he is pastor at Holt undir Eyjafjöllum.

He published three volumes of poetry: *Hamar og sigð* (Hammer and Sickle, 1930), as the name indicates, exclusively socialistic poems; *Yndi unaðsstunda* (Hours of Bliss, 1952) and *Undir stjörnum og sól* (Under Stars and Sun, 1953). Though the first volume is frankly propaganda, the poems are not without literary merit, notably the beautiful " Sordavala." The second volume contains love poetry and manly comments like " Hann er kaldur með köflum " (It Is Quite Often Cold), also interesting thumbnail sketches of his friends and fellow-poets Halldór Kiljan Laxness and Tómas Guðmundsson. His most notable essays are found in *Líðandi stund* (Passing Hour, 1938). He has also written books on education, modern orthodox theology, and personal history from a cultural point of view.

Finally Sigurður has written the play *Fyrir kóngsins mekt* (By the Power of the King, 1954), dealing with the oath-taking at Kópavogur, July 28, 1662, when the Icelanders by threat of weapons lost the last vestiges of their freedom to the Danish monarch. It is a fine play in verse—with modern overtones.

Guðmundur G. Hagalín

Guðmundur Gíslason Hagalín (1898———) was born in Arnarfjörður in the Northwest of a stubborn race fostered by the barren country and the wild though productive sea. At home he alternated fishing and reading; in Reykjavík he entered the Gymnasium (1917) only to decide against study. Instead he took up journalism for the conservatives in the East (Seyðisfjörður, 1920–23), but soon turned socialistic. After traveling and lecturing in Norway (1924–27), he was appointed a librarian in Ísafjörður, a position he kept until 1946 when he moved to Reykjavík to devote himself to writing. In Ísafjörður he was also active in all kinds of municipal and political tasks.

Hagalín is a prolific author, having to his credit fourteen volumes of short stories, eight novels, three biographies, his own autobiography in four volumes so far, a play and a volume of essays, though many remain unpublished. His collected works (*Ritsafn*, 1948——) are being published.

Hagalín got his start in the melancholy lyric period at the end of World War I, his first stories showing interest in strange, warped personalities, his (only) poems having a melancholy folk-tale tinge. But he soon found his field in short stories and novels describing the life of the fishermen of his native Vestfirðir with broad humor and gusto. He wrote "Hefndir" (Vengeance, 1923) under the influence of the sagas and Nietzsche, but the main early influence was that of Hamsun, resulting in a romantic-nationalistic primitivism, seen in his first novel (1924)—where the new generation is found vitiated when compared with the old—as well as in the dramatic sagalike novelette " Þáttur af Neshólabræðrum " (The Tale of the Brothers at Neshólar, 1925). In 1927 Hagalín professed socialism with his *Brennumenn* (Firebrands) and has since remained a social democrat, but his heart was with the rugged individualists of the old order, as his primitivistic folk of " Mannleg náttúra " (Human Nature, 1929) show. During the thirties Hagalín, like Kamban and Laxness, gave up the classical puristic style of his early works (perhaps to some extent inspired by Faulkner) for one more earthy and smelling of the sea. In this rough and robust dialect, assumed in order to depict the primitive character, as he saw it close to the soil, he wrote several short stories and the novels *Kristrún í Hamravík* (1933) and *Sturla í Vogum* (two volumes, 1938). The first pictures an old woman in an isolated cottage facing the Arctic, a poor widow, yet perfectly content and self-contained, a master of her small world, fearing neither God nor man. The latter describes a farmer, rugged, individualistic, in his development toward a social consciousness that finds outlet in practical co-operation with his fellow men. During the thirties Hagalín also wrote two excellent adventurous biographies : of a shark-fisherman and a skipper. These, first of their kind, were soon imitated.

During and after World War II Hagalín wrote, apart from a lot of short stories, *Blítt lætur veröldin* (The Lure of the World, 1943), a description of an adolescent in development; *Konungurinn á Kálfsskinni* (The King at Kálfsskinn, 1945) ; and *Móðir Ísland* (Mother Iceland, 1945). The first is an ambitious novel in the Kristrún í Hamravík style, depicting fascism in miniature in an old folks' home in Ísafjörður. *Mother Iceland* describes war conditions in Reykjavík and its demoralizing effects. The style and tenor of these two books have been much criticized, not only by the leftist critics whom Hagalín attacked in his essays *Gróður og sandfok* (Growth and Sand Storms, 1943), but also by others.

Hagalín is now writing his autobiography, of which four volumes have appeared to date: *Ég veit ekki betur* (I Know No Better, 1951); *Sjö voru sólir á lofti* (Seven Suns Aloft, 1952); *Ilmur liðinna daga* (Perfume of Days Bygone, 1953); and *Hér er kominn Hoffinn* (Here Hoffinn is Come, 1954), full of facts, life and humor.

Jóhannes Jónasson úr Kötlum

Jóhannes Jónasson úr Kötlum (pen name Anonymus, 1899———) was born in Dalir in the West—the country of *Laxdœla saga*—of poor cotters. He became a teacher (1921), first at home, later in Reykjavík, but has for many years devoted himself to literary pursuits and lives now in Hveragerði.

As a youth he was a fervent national-romantic member of the Youth League, a patriotic and progressive organization, but the depression of the thirties converted him into an ardent socialist, and so he has remained, in spite of his romantic attachment to the soil. He has been a very prolific writer: by 1951 he had published eight volumes of poetry and three novels, not counting juvenile books. His collected poems, *Ljóðasafn*, appeared in 1949.

The two first volumes of his poetry, *Bí, bí og blaka* (Sleep, Baby, Sleep, 1926) and *Álftirnar kvaka* (The Swans Are Singing, 1929) were mostly traditional and romantic in theme, containing not only love, nature lyrics, and folk songs, but also another " Háttalykill " (Clavis Poetica). But the poem " Ef ég segði þér allt " (If I Told You All) shows his social consciousness awakening to the misery and oppression around him.

And though he next was to vie with Einar Benediktsson and Davíð Stefánsson in eulogizing the millenary of the Althing, his next books, *Ég læt sem ég sofi* (I Pretend Sleeping, 1932) and *Samt mun ég vaka* (Yet I Will Stay Awake, 1935) mark his complete conversion to communism. In his satires of the bankrupt capitalistic world and his preaching of the new social gospel, his style gains in force but loses in lyric quality. The first volume contains the realistic-humorous yet sympathetic portrayal of his father (" Karl faðir minn "), a fine poem; in the second appears the poem " Frelsi " (Freedom), which was featured in the first volume of *Rauðir pennar* (Red Pens, 1935), of which periodical he was one of the founders. One of the poems berates the horrors of the Nazis. Others are in the old lyric and personal strain, like " Lind fyrir vestan " (A Fountain in the West).

In *Hrímhvíta móðir* (Rime White Mother, 1937) he surveys the history of his beloved country from a socialistic point of view. Here is a beautiful lyric in honor of Jónas Hallgrímsson, but the poet succeeds best in the poem " Þegnar þagnarinnar " (Thanes of Silence), a tribute to the nameless common man in Iceland. *Hart er í heimi* (Woe Is in the World, 1939) is largely devoted to the disturbing antidemocratic signs of war, but also contains a love-hymn to the soil: " Ástarkvæði til moldarinnar "—and the heroic saga of an Icelandic horse, " Stjörnufákur " (Star Steed) that comes to a tragic end in an English coal mine.

During and just after World War II he published two collections of poems: *Eilífðar smáblóm* (Eternity's Flower, 1940) and *Sól tér sortna* (Sun Turns Black, 1945). Both contain poems reflecting his attitudes toward the warring parties, especially his sympathy with Norway and Denmark; also his distrust of England. Both, notably the first, are rich in lyrics, personal or in praise of his beloved soil. The latter contains important autobiographical poems in several of which he gives himself an ironical whipping for having lost his voice as a poet just when he had gotten a house and the nation had given him a poet's stipend. He does not feel at ease after the political victory of the Communists; he feels that he himself should have fought with his hands rather than through his poetry.

But if he lacked a cause to fight for, he found one when the Americans began their attempts to get bases in Iceland. As early as 1934 the poet made an unsuccessful attempt to write a novel. The next, *Verndarenglarnir* (The Protecting Angels, 1943), his reaction against the English occupation, suffered perhaps from its very actuality, but the trilogy *Dauðsmannsey* (Dead Man's Island, 1949), *Siglingin mikla* (The Great Voyage, 1950), and *Frelsisálfan* (The Continent of Liberty, 1952), about famine-stricken Icelanders of the 1880's and their voyage to the promised land of America shows that he is really also a good novelist.

In the fifties Jóhannes úr Kötlum first published two volumes of poetry, *Sóleyjarkvæði* (Sun Island Poems, 1952) and *Hlið hins himneska friðar* (The Portals of Heavenly Peace, 1953), both in his old manner, patriotic and pacifist. But after two years he broke the silence with *Sjödægra* (Seven Days' Mountain, 1955), poetry in an entirely new key, less tendentious but of a more exquisite lyric beauty than he had ever before achieved. At the same time he revealed that he was the "Anonymus" who in 1948 had done *Annarlegar tungur* (Strange Tongues), translations in imitative non-alliterative meters, including names like Edith Sitwell, T. S. Eliot, Carl Sandburg, E. E. Cummings, and Walt Whitman. Obviously his experimentation had borne fruit in his own poetry.

Jón Helgason

Jón Helgason (1899——) was born in Borgarfjörður in the West; he studied old Icelandic philology at the University of Copenhagen and wrote a thesis on Jón Ólafsson (amanuensis of Árni Magnússon) for the University of Iceland in 1926. After that he first became a professor of Icelandic language and literature at the University of Oslo, Norway, then (1927) the librarian of the Arnamagnaean Collection in Copenhagen and (1929)—after Finnur Jónsson—professor of Old Icelandic language and literature at the University of Copenhagen. Like his predecessor, Jón Helgason was especially active as an editor of the manuscript treasures of the Arnamagnaean Collection. But he has also written a literary history of the Old Norse-Icelandic literature: *Norrön litteraturhistorie* (1934) and *Norges og Islands digtning* (The Poetry of Norway and Iceland, in *Nordisk Kultur*, 1953) besides many other things.

A perfectionist as scholar and editor, Jón Helgason's task often was to weed out uncritical theories and assumptions, rather than to advance theories of his own. As a poet, his perfectionist attitude early made him into a sharp-tongued satirist, though often his humor could be more genial, and student-like, not infrequently cast in parodies of form from the different periods of Icelandic literature, all of which he commanded with equal ease. That he wrote serious poetry as well no one knew until he published *Úr landsuðri* (From the South East, 1939, 2nd enlarged edition 1948), revealing himself as one of the great lyric poets of the present. In his early days in the Arnamagnaean Collection there were moments when the poet could feel life calling and tempting him with something greener than the dust of the library, cf. "Lestin brunar . . ." (The Train Rushes . . .). Mostly, however, it is devotion to his work, to his beloved collection, and to the far-away homeland which finds eloquent expression in his poetry, though nowhere more magnificently than in his great poem " Í Árnasafni " (In the Arnamagnaean Collection). Here he dwells, half-dreaming, contrasting the street noises outside with the " swift and perpetual flow of the ages " inside the walls. His eyes roam over the volumes, records of thousands, the strong heathen classics and the meek Christian spirituals. He sees the authors stepping out of their works and watching him write—all animated by that strange urge for study and writing which also drives him on. Time will come when all that he has left for posterity " will be found on a few yellowed pages." Destruction and time trumpet their threatening *memento mori,* not only for him who is now alive, but also for his beloved ward, the dead-yet-living collection:

> Letters must fade and the finest of bindings go rotten;
> Fame won today will so soon be completely forgotten.
> Gordian knots we may tie which old Time then will sever;
> Tombstones will crumble, inscriptions will vanish forever.
> (Mrs. Mekkin Perkins' translation)

In view of the significance of the Arnamagnaean Collection for Icelandic culture and of the nation's love for its treasures, nowhere more poignantly expressed than in Jón Helgason's poem, it is no wonder that the Icelanders are trying hard to get it back home.

Jón Helgason writes anguished poetry about the flight of time and the mutability of all things; he laments his exile and writes strong poems about the harsh but fascinating face of Icelandic nature—which, like the giant of Lómagnúpur, summons everyone of her sons in a cold and deep voice, back home.

Magnús Ásgeirsson

Magnús Ásgeirsson (1901–1955) was born at Reykir in Borgarfjörður in the West. He studied Icelandic philology at the University in Reykjavík, and was for a long time a clerk and journalist, during World War II a co-editor of *Helgafell* and a librarian in Hafnarfjörður.

Magnús Ásgeirsson was the greatest translator of his generation, publishing six volumes of translations, *Þýdd ljóð,* 1928–41. From these a book of selections was published in 1946, introduced by Snorri Hjartarson, and this was followed by a seventh volume of translations *Meðan sprengjurnar falla* (While the Bombs Fall, 1945). He has translated hundreds of poems by more than one hundred authors, mostly of Scandinavia, particularly of Sweden. Next in order are poets of the United

States, Germany, and England. His favorites are Gustaf Fröding, Hjalmar Gullberg, Karin Boye of Sweden, Nordahl Grieg of Norway, who spent some time in Iceland during World War II, and Edgar Lee Masters and Carl Sandburg of the United States.

Magnús Ásgeirsson's selections testify to his socialistic outlook but show little interest in modernistic form. T. S. Eliot is conspicuously absent. Yet, by his inclusion of the Swede Artur Lundkvist as well as Edgar Lee Masters and Carl Sandburg, he has given young Icelandic poets a taste of modernism which did not fail to have an effect (e. g., Jón úr Vör).

Magnús Ásgeirsson's last work was an anthology of young poets, *Ljóð ungra skálda 1944–54* (1954) by twenty authors, with a brief introduction. He died in the summer of 1955.

Tómas Guðmundsson

Tómas Guðmundsson (1901——) was born at Efri-Brú, Grímsnes, in the South on the great and beautiful river Sog. Graduating from the University of Reykjavík as a lawyer, he practised for a while and was then for many years employed in the State Office of Statistics (1928–1943). He was a co-editor of *Helgafell* (1943–46, 1954), a literary periodical of note, and has for many years been connected with musical comedy in Reykjavík.

Tómas belonged to a generation that burst out in plaintive romantic lyric immediately after World War I, he himself being one of sixteen college poets whom he later celebrated in verse. He was perhaps the purest representative of the group in the dreamily romantic and highly polished verses that he published in *Við sundin blá* (At the Blue Sounds, 1924). But the times were not opportune for dreams, and the poet's voice was silenced for years. When he found his voice again in *Fagra veröld* (Fair World, 1933), his interest had shifted from the romantic future to the romantic past, the memories of his beloved college days, described now with wistful sadness, now with whimsical humor. His sense of beauty was the same, but he found beauty now more often in the familiar haunts and everyday occurrences, though the far away had not altogether lost its lure. Witness the gem " Japanskt ljóð " (Japanese Poem). He now sang the beauty of Reykjavík, first among Icelandic poets, echoing the dreams and heartaches of its youth, mirroring its tranquil summer nights, the splendor of its sky, but also its bustling activity, the ships in the harbor, and, at times, the humorous straits of its dignified citizens. What was most important: his form and diction had gained a newborn perfect, almost colloquial simplicity, not unlike that won by Jónas Hallgrímsson nearly a century ago.

These poems were hailed with enthusiasm, three editions being called for in two years. The grateful city sent its eulogist on a tour of the Mediterranean countries, the romantic splendors of which inspired a good many of the poems in *Stjörnur vorsins* (Stars of Spring, 1940), though most of them continued the old themes on wine and women, so surprisingly alike in Sudan and Grímsnes. There were student songs, bits of whimsical autobiography, and humorous—often slightly irreverent—remarks about God and his good, if not quite perfect, world. And there was still the ability, if not quite as potent as of old, to dream Aladdin-like of wonderful romantic palaces, and retain the dream, at least in the poet's mind, a wonderful instance being the much admired and purely lyric " Þjóðvísa " (Folk song).

Tómas Guðmundsson's *Fljótið helga* (The Holy River, 1950) was written during and after World War II and unmistakably so, though the poet, mastering both feeling and form, succeeded in talking in a dignified, subdued tone about the burning outrage of the time. For though, like his friend on the river, the beautiful and self-centered phalarope philosopher, the poet would much rather turn his sensitive eyes and ears from the ominous din of war, life pays him an urgent visit ("Heimsókn"), and he can ignore neither the cries of his Scandinavian brethren nor the menace to personal freedom, his most prized heritage, whether stemming from black shirts or red (cf. " Að Áshildarmýri "). To this extent, then, the cataclysm tore him from his ivory tower; otherwise he remained the same, brooding increasingly on the sad mutability of beauty and youth, the brooding like a heavy ground swell under the rippling surface of his brilliant wit or whimsicality or his polished placid form. *Fljúgandi blóm* (Flying Flowers, 1952) is a selection from Tómas Guðmundsson's poetry; a collected edition, *Ljóðasafn*, appeared in 1953.

Davíð Þorvaldsson

Davíð Þorvaldsson (1901–32) was born at Akureyri in the North, the son of a merchant. He studied literature at the Sorbonne in Paris, but in 1929 was compelled to go home sick with tuberculosis, which shortly after caused his untimely death.

Like Jóhann Gunnar Sigurðsson and Jóhann Jónsson, Davíð was

highly regarded by his schoolmates and his short stories, collected in
Björn formaður . . . (Björn the Foreman. . . , 1929) and *Kalviðir*
(Withered Branches, 1930) were very promising, though not great.
His descriptions of the less fortunate and the sick were excellent, and he
wielded a keen psychological analysis.

Halldór Kiljan Laxness

Halldór Guðjónsson Kiljan Laxness (1902——) was born in Reykjavík but brought up at Laxnes, a farm in the neighborhood. His parents
were farmers. Of the younger generation of Icelandic writers, he was
the greatest and most consistently modernistic. Like no one else, he
represented the youthful urban population of Reykjavík, cut loose from
its thousand-year-old-farm moorings, searching vigorously for a new
mode of living among the possibilities of the post-World War I world.
He received his first impulse in the lyric and national-romantic atmosphere of the early 1920's, publishing his book (1919) under Hamsun's
influence, when seventeen, but he soon plunged himself into introspection, philosophy, and religion, following the example of Johannes Jörgensen, Strindberg, and Sigrid Undset.

As a youth he steeped himself in Expressionism in Germany, in
Catholicism in a monastery in Luxembourg, and in Surrealism in France
(1924–26), after which he went to Iceland, Canada, and California
(1927–30) to fortify himself in a communism which since then has
served him as a leading hypothesis, not shaken by several visits to Russia.
He returned to Iceland in 1930 and wrote his books there, or wherever
his travels might take him, for he is a confirmed globe-trotter. He has
lived, since World War II, in Gljúfrasteinn, Mosfellssveit.

Halldór Kiljan Laxness is a very prolific author; he has now, not
counting translations (Gunnarsson, Hemingway, Voltaire), over thirty
books to his credit: seventeen volumes of novels, nine volumes of essays,
three of short stories, three plays, and one volume of poetry.

From his Catholic period date *Undir Helgahnúk* (Under the Holy
Mountain, 1924) and *Vefarinn mikli frá Kasmir* (The Great Weaver
from Casmir, 1927). The latter book looms as a milestone of a new age
in the Icelandic novel; it was expressionistic and autobiographical, a
true picture of the turmoil in the author's mind, written in a style marked
by free and uninhibited eloquence. In it he reduced the ideal of the
Church, as he understood it, *ad absurdum*. Having returned to Iceland
from California, where he tried to write for the films, he aired his

socialistic views in a book of brilliant burlesque and satirical essays, *Alþýðubókin* (The Book of the People, 1929), one of a long series in which he discussed his many travel impressions (Russia, western Europe, South America), unburdened himself of socialistic satire and propaganda, and wrote of the literature and the arts, essays of prime importance to an understanding of his own art.

His only contribution to poetry was the modernistic burlesque lyrics in *Kvæðakver* (Poems, 1930), but though quite unpretentious from the poet's point of view they, too, made an impression, though they were little imitated. He wrote two plays and several short stories, some of them truly distinguished, but his greatest contribution was his novels. Before and including *Vefarinn* they had been very much self-centered; after that the themes were taken from the life of his small nation, present or past, but written from his cosmopolitan point of view and endowed with universal significance. During the thirties he wrote three novels of many volumes each, all dealing with the present. The first, *Þú vínviður hreini* (1931) and *Fuglinn í fjörunni* (1932; English translation of both, *Salka Valka*, 1936), treated the small fishing village; the next, *Sjálfstætt fólk* (two volumes, 1934–35; English translation: *Independent People*, 1946), was about the poor farmer; and the third, *Ljós heimsins* (The Light of the World, four volumes, 1937–40), was about the poet of the people. These novels were conceived on a grand scale, the poor but energetic village girl and the independent cottage farmer emerging at the same time as heroes of monumental stature, individuals and symbols of their class. The poet, though anything but a hero, being the lowly subject and scapegoat of a cruel world, was no less grandly conceived as a symbol of the crucified spirit, forever rising in beauty as the light of this world.

To understand *Sjálfstætt fólk* one should read " Dagleið á fjöllum " (Day's Journey in the Mountains), which gives the theme *in nuce*, while Laxness' essay on the *Passíu-sálmar* of Hallgrímur Pétursson throws essential light not only on the hero of *Ljós heimsins*, Ólafur Ljósvíkingur, but also on the early eighteenth-century milieu in *Íslandsklukkan*. During the forties Laxness, with one exception, wrote novels about the past, first the three-volume novel *Íslandsklukkan* (Iceland's Bell, 1943), *Hið ljósa man* (The Bright Maid, 1944), *Eldur í Kaupinhafn* (Fire in Copenhagen, 1946), about Árni Magnússon and his times, and finally *Gerpla* (Heroica, 1952) about the Old Icelandic heroes (*garpar*) of

Fóstbrœðra saga. The early eighteenth-century novel tells how the Old Icelandic heroic spirit of freedom is conserved through an oppressive age by the combined efforts of the doggedly stubborn common man (Jón Hreggviðsson) and the enlightened and unselfish collector of the old manuscripts, Arnas Magnaeus. In *Gerpla* Laxness is back in the world of the heroic spirit, but instead of extolling it he shows its natural limits in comparison with Christianity and Eskimo culture, and turns the heroes, Þorgeir Hávarsson and Þormóður Kolbrúnarskáld, into deeply tragic, quixotic figures. This " saga " is written in a surprisingly real saga-style, just as *Íslandsklukkan* partly imitates the early eighteenth-century baroque. The only modern book of the forties was *Atómstöðin* (The Atom Station, 1948), describing the terrible demoralizing effects of the World War II boom in Iceland and written in protest against granting the Americans air bases in 1946. It was followed by a play, *Silfurtunglið* (The Silver Moon, 1954), on the same theme.

In his novels on contemporary themes, Laxness created a new style, alternately lyrical and rationalistic, sympathetic and cynical, full of storms and stresses, that contrasted vividly with the classic puristic style of his predecessors and contemporaries. He also gave a perfect illusion of eighteenth-century and saga styles in his historical novels. He has been increasingly concerned with the architecture of his novels, admitting even fantastic elements if they suited his purpose, banning realistic details if they did not. By his standards, the novel should be a self-contained unit of its own. The strict formalism of his last novels contrasts vividly with the expressionistic abandon of *Vefarinn.* A fierce social criticism runs through all his novels, though less overt in the historical novels, and always subordinated to artistic demands. This satire has alienated readers at home and abroad, but all have been compelled to admire the brilliance of his style, his vigorous symbolism, the high poetic quality of his lyric vein, and the art with which he fuses characters and scenery into one vast panorama of intensified reality.

In his youth, while writing *Vefarinn,* he suffered from the inferiority complex of a small national, torn between love of his country and the lure of cosmopolitanism, but his historical novels, especially his modern saga, show to what extent he has now embraced the traditions of his native land, the land of *Edda* and saga. It was a significant gesture, when he emphasized this debt in his speech to the Swedish king, when receiving the Nobel prize for literature on December 10, 1955.

Kristmann Guðmundsson

Kristmann Guðmundsson (1902——) was born in Þverfell in Borgarfjörður in the West. His mother came of a family deeply rooted in the
soil, his father was a temperamental rover. His youth was marred by
lack of parental care, yet he grew up to be a healthy boy whose optimism
and enterprising nature nothing could curb. Having been a jack of all
trades, even a poet and a publisher of a periodical, he finally decided
(1924) to go to Norway and become a writer. Two years later his
debut book of short stories, *Islandsk Kjærlighet* (Icelandic Loves, 1926)
was an immediate success. Since then he has written fifteen volumes of
novels and a great many short stories, some published in *Ritsafn* I
(1952; VIII, 1954). His books have been more widely translated than
those of any other Icelandic author (over thirty languages). He was
seven times married: his first wife was a Norwegian, his last Icelandic.
He lived in Oslo and Copenhagen up to 1938, when he returned to live
in Reykjavík; since World War II he has lived in Hveragerði.

Kristmann Guðmundsson is a master of the modern romance. As no
other Icelandic novelist he understands the psychology of love, especially
young love, and describes it with an abandon which recalls Davíð
Stefánsson's love lyrics, and a realism which nevertheless strikes one
as ethereally romantic. In him the spiritual and physical aspects of love
unite in harmony without the bad conscience that troubled the pre-World
War I writers, like Kamban, who had to fight a struggle of emancipation
from the ideology of Victorian love. Kristmann has somewhere told of
his first love: a young girl he met at sixteen and knew for a short time
only, but whose torch he carried forever after. He told a charming
idyl like that in his debut book, expanded it in *Den blå kyst* (The Blue
Coast, 1931), and varied it in *Den förste vår* (The First Spring, 1933).
Hvite netter (White Nights, 1934) describes the irresistible force that
draws the poet from civilization back to the white nights of his youth
and a childhood love, but also his disillusion. *Ármann og Vildís* (1928)
may reveal the author's first disillusion in marriage, while *Félagi kona*
(Comrade Wife, 1947) is a sort of a witch's sabbath describing the
deterioration of sex morality during World War II. In spite of all
disillusion its moral is still: live and love to the fullest extent of your
power. Next to love, character interests Kristmann most of all. This is
evident in his family sagas: *Brudekjolen* (1927, English: *The Bridal
Gown*, 1931); *Livets Morgen* (1929, English: *Morning of Life*, 1936);
Sigmar (1930); *Börn jarðar* (Children of Earth, 1935); and *Nátt-*

tröllið glottir (The Night Troll Grins, 1943). Of these, the *Morning of Life* is perhaps best, incarnating once more, in the protagonists, the heroic ideal of the sagas. The sequel, *Sigmar*, was intended to show the shift from capitalism to socialism, but only the play of personalities, not ideologies, came through. *Nátttröllið glottir* shows some of the author's reactions on his return to Iceland.

He wrote three historical novels, two before, one after World War II: *Det Hellige Fjell* (The Holy Fell, 1932), describing the old Norse and Irish settlement of Snæfellsnes (where he grew up); *Gyðjan og uxinn* (1937-38, English: *Winged Citadel*, 1940), a historical romance from pre-Greek Crete, full of allusions to modern psychoanalysis and pre-World War II politics—also considerably autobiographical. His last historical romance, *Þokan rauða* I–II (The Red Fog, 1950-52) deals with the author of *Völuspá*, the son of a Norse father and Irish mother, born in Breiðifjörður when Christianity is dawning on Iceland, and introduced to the ancient mysteries in Ireland and Greece. After that he takes an active part in the heroic enterprises of his homeland, but remains also a seer and a dreamer. *Völuspá* comes to him in a burst of inspiration on a quiet Icelandic summer morning. This book, like some of the author's later works, shows that he is turning more and more to the mystic wellsprings of life. Moreover, it reveals influence both from Irish matter and Nordal's *Íslenzk menning*. In 1955 the author published the novelette *Harmleikurinn á Austurbæ* (The Tragedy at Austurbær), laid in Norway; a volume of poetry, *Kristmannskver*; and the first volume of a history of world literature.

Guðmundur Frímann

Guðmundur Frímannsson Frímann (1903——) was born in Húnavatnssýsla (in Langidalur) of farmers, studied art with Einar Jónsson the sculptor, but abandoned it as a career. After that he lived as a tradesman in Akureyri with art and writing as his hobby.

He made his debut with *Náttsólir* (Night Suns, 1922), following it with *Úlfablóð* (Wolf Blood, 1933), under the pseudonym Álfur frá Klettastíu. But it is with his last two books that he really made his mark: *Störin syngur* (The Sedge Sings, 1937) and *Svört verða sólskin* (Sun Will Darken, 1951). Here are nostalgic memories from the home of his youth, anguish and despair as in the beautiful poem " Blóm " (Flowers) about the lily-like falling snowflakes, but not unrelieved by hope of summer. Finally there are character sketches and memorials, among them one on his mother, another on a luckless vagabond fellow-poet—both reflecting profound emotions.

Lárus Sigurbjörnsson

Lárus Sigurbjörnsson (1903———) was the son of an orthodox minister in Reykjavík and his wife, an authoress, and member of the Althing. He was to study at the University of Copenhagen, but turned to journalism and wrote short stories, published in 1925. In Reykjavík, he took an active part in theatrical activities at the Gymnasium and in the Dramatic Society, translating a number of plays and writing a few on his own account: *Þrír þættir* (Three One-Acters, 1930) in the suggestive way of Arthur Schnitzler. But he has been even more active as a theatrical critic and historian, has published a bibliography on the subject, and is writing the history of the theater in Iceland. He was also, for a while, an archivist of the recently opened (1950) National Theater in Iceland.

Guðmundur Böðvarsson

Guðmundur Böðvarsson (1904———) was born at Kirkjuból in Borgarfjörður in the West, and lives there still, a self-educated farmer. Yet, in spite of his days' labor and his evenings' weariness, he produced, between 1936 and 1952, five volumes of poetry, the first named *Kyssti mig sól* (The Sun Kissed Me), the last *Kristallinn í hylnum* (The Crystal in the Pool). He is no Guðmundur Ingi eulogizing his land—though his land may be of the best in Iceland. Neither is he a Guðmundur Friðjónsson in revolt against harsh nature, singing his passive and active heroes a myopic praise—though one does find the farmer's love of sun and spring and summer, and fertile fields; *cf.* the title of his first book. Actually he is more like Stephan G. Stephansson in outlook, if not in the tone of his poetry. Like Stephan he is a radical who echoes the romantic hopes and doubts of socialism in his poetry, though he feels he neither can nor does fight for it as he should. His anguish finds expression in the poem about the tired navigators who, finally, found no land (1936), his sympathy with the revolting Spaniards in " Spánskt kvæði frá 17. öld " (A Spanish Poem from the Seventeenth Century) and in the powerful symbolic war poems " Vísurnar við hverfisteininn árið 1936 " (The Verses at the Whetstone, 1936) and "Smiðjuljóð" (The Poem of the Forge). In the same way he follows the fortunes of World War II and his country's independence in 1944 and after, in dignified strains, full of striking, often original, symbolism, perhaps as an interested spectator, but never a man of the ivory tower. He is deeply anxious about the new American garrison in the country. In 1950 he wrote an introduction to a collection of poems by an older fellow-poet from his home region: *Stolnar stundir* (Stolen Hours, 1950) by Halldór Helgason (1874——) who resembles him in outlook, both farmers, tillers of the soil.

Guðmundur Ingi Kristjánsson

Guðmundur Ingi Kristjánsson (1907——) was born at Kirkjuból in Önundarfjörður in the Northwest, the son of a farmer; he took over his father's farm and lives there. He received inspiration from a folk school, the co-operative movement, and the Icelandic Youth League, all fanning his idealistic love of the soil. He wrote two volumes of poetry, *Sólstafir* (Sunbeams, 1938) and *Sólbráð* (Sun Thaw, 1945), on themes from rural life and work, in continuation of Eggert Ólafsson's bucolic poetry but actually inspired by the Danish rural poet Jeppe Aakjær. Guðmundur Ingi Kristjánsson is practically the only poet-farmer who can sing of his soil, his sheep and cows, his hay and his work with genuine feeling, and if his simple form at times is not perfect, there is compensation in the sincere depth of expression.

Bjarni M. Gíslason

Bjarni M. Gíslason (1908——) was born in Tálknafjörður in the Northwest. A poor fisherman and sailor, he published a volume of promising poems in 1933 and went, after that, to Denmark, where he studied at Askov and came under the influence of the Danish critic Jörgen Bukdahl, on whom he wrote an essay in 1949. In Danish Bjarni M. Gíslason published one more volume of poetry " in a pleasant, lyric strain, with the poet's native Iceland as a recurrent theme." (R. Beck) After World War II came *De gyldne Tavl* (The Golden Tablets I–III, 1944–5), a novel indicating the author's spiritual origin from two sources: Christianity and the sagas. His essays and lectures on Icelandic literature and culture were published in three volumes—one of them on Iceland during the Anglo-Saxon occupation. His studies of literature were finally crystallized in *Islands Litteratur efter Sagatiden ca. 1400–1948*, a spirited, if not always quite reliable, synthesis which attempts to show the merging of the two forces, the native tradition and Christianity. In the modern period Bjarni M. Gíslason takes a definitely anti-communistic stand, seemingly as a Christian social demo-

crat and a Danish "Folk High School" man. In 1946 he wrote a
sketch of Iceland during World War II and in 1954 a spirited plea
for the return of the manuscripts of the Arnamagnaean Collection to
Iceland (2nd ed. 1955).

Aðalsteinn Kristmundsson

Aðalsteinn Kristmundsson (pen name Steinn Steinarr, 1908–1958)
was born in Vestfirðir, but grew up in Dalir, the country of Stefán frá
Hvítadal and Jóhannes úr Kötlum. He came to Reykjavík, a crippled
youth, at the height of the depression, to strive and starve. Nothing
seemed more natural for him than to join the Communists and the group
around *Rauðir pennar*. His first book, *Rauður loginn brann* (Red
Burned the Flame, 1934), was dedicated to his comrades and espoused
their cause in simple lyrics of a deep personal note. Yet, there were signs
already in this first book of his that he was beginning to doubt the
communistic gospel as well as anything else (*cf.* "Veruleiki," Reality),
and in the following book, *Ljóð* (Poems, 1937), he enthroned his own
doubt and fell prey to speculations about himself and this world. But
that second book also testified to his increased preoccupation with form;
seemingly he had taken notice of at least some of the modernists abroad.
Most of his poems were short, the diction simple, the form strict,
designed to give a single idea a brilliant form. Among the finest poems
one may mention "Sement," "Marmari" (Marble), "Verdun," "Vor"
(Spring), and "Ekkert" (Nothing), an epitome of his nihilism. The
same intellectual pessimism reigned in *Spor í sandi* (Tracks in the Sand,
1940), the title itself programmatic. Even here the poet excelled in
expressing feelings of frustration, misery, and *vanitas vanitatum*. One
must, indeed, go back to the seventeenth century and Hallgrímur Pétursson to match his interpretation of mutability and nothingness in "Ljóð"
(Poem). But in spite of this dark despair, the poet was increasingly
aware of his worth as an artist, feeling that he, even with his lame hand,
had been able to roll a rock out of humanity's path to intelligence; *cf.*
"Chaplinvísan 1939." As to his form, he usually strove to clothe a
far-fetched, even metaphysical, thought in as narrow confines of form as
possible, and frequently so that the main thought or point was reached
only through devious paths, throwing, when reached, a sudden glow of
illumination over the poem.

The theme of *vanitas vanitatum* ran with undiminished force through
Ferð án fyrirheits (Journey without Promise, 1942), but here the poet's

form had reached perfection. Though the poet here might slap his fellow countrymen or the " Imperium Britannicum " with felling irony, most of the poems were philosophical or metaphysical. Instances are " Til hinna dauðu " (To the Dead) and the famous " Í draumi sérhvers manns er fall hans falið " (In Every Man's Dream Lurks his Fall). There were also some abstract poems, like " Utan hringsins " (Outside the Ring) ; this genre was to increase in frequency after World War II.

After the war Steinn Steinarr traveled in Scandinavia, England, and France, probably reinforcing the impulses he had already received from modernists like Carl Sandburg, Artur Lundkvist, and the *fyrtitalister* in Sweden. He also learned from modern abstract painters to use geometrical forms in his poetry—a cone, a cube, a triangle—as well as colors. This abstractness marks his last cycle of poems: *Tíminn og vatnið* (The Time and the Water, 1948), which carried Archibald MacLeish's motto: " A poem should not mean, but be." A selection from his poems *100 kvæði* (100 Poems, 1949) with some additional new ones was published in 1949, a full collection, *Ferð án fyrirheits*, in 1956. The poet died May 25, 1956.

Guðmundur Daníelsson

Guðmundur Daníelsson (1910——) was born in the rich southern lowlands, the son of a well-to-do farmer. He became a teacher (1934) and has practised that profession together with his writing.

After an indifferent sheaf of poems (1933) he made his debut with *Bræðurnir í Grashaga* (The Brothers of Grashagi, 1935), a broad and rich epic of the southern lowlands in rain and shine, peopled with robust characters, headstrong men and voluptuous women. A sympathy with the underdog and a somewhat Laxnessian style seemed to indicate a leftist writer, but the continuation, *Ilmur daganna* (The Perfume of the Days, 1936) turned out to be a genuine re-creation of the author's youth, with no such tendency, mirroring only the author's genuine love of life, especially love life and its varied manifestations.

The same was true of the next two books, *Gegnum lystigarðinn* (Through the Amusement Park, 1938), expressing the author's healthy reaction to the rootless towns, and *Á bökkum Bolafljóts* (On the Banks of Bullock River, 1940), another broad epic of the South, this time built on a grandmother's tales about his ancestors. Next he wrote a trilogy, *Af jörðu ertu kominn* (From Earth) consisting of *Eldur* (Fire, 1941), *Sandur* (Sand, 1942) and *Landið handan landsins* (The Land beyond the Land, 1944), partly based on observations he had made as a teacher

in Húnavatnssýsla, partly on material from his own South, especially
the spirited fight against the encroaching desert sands at Rangárvellir.
The composition was perhaps influenced by William Faulkner. Like all
his books this is full of memorable characters, like the pastor Gylfi in
Eldur and the poet Rögnvaldur of *Landið*, like the author himself a Don
Juan and a relentless romantic seeker of the land beyond the everyday,
the romantic Utopia. Two collections of short stories (1944 and 1955),
a play, which was an angry reaction to his countrymen's dancing around
the war golden calf (1946), and another sheaf of poems, *Kveðið á glugga*
(Sung at the Window, 1946), marked only a pause in the production
of his novels. Of these he wrote two more, *Mannspilin og ásinn* (The
Face Cards and the Ace, 1948) and *Í fjallskugganum* (In the Shade of
the Mountain, 1950), both dealing with strong characters whose unruly
love trips them in their ruling passion: one hero's desire for the fertile
soil, the other's for his mountain kingdom. A third novel, *Musteri óttans*
(Temple of Fear, 1953), deals with blackmail and fear, while his last
novel, *Blindingsleikur* (Blind Man's Bluff, 1955) tells a symbolic story
of aspirations out of the mists. It is one of his best, if not his best.

Finally, Guðmundur Daníelsson has written two travel books, one,
Á langferðaleiðum (On Long Voyage, 1948), describing his tour of
America in the summer of 1945, the other, *Sumar í Suðurlöndum*
(Summer in the South, 1950), describing a tour of Europe, notably
France and Italy, in 1948–49. His tour of America seems to have made
him a friend of the Anglo-Saxon world. Like Davíð Stefánsson and
Kristmann Guðmundsson, Guðmundur Daníelsson is a hedonist who
receives with eager hands whatever life has to offer him, but who has
a streak of primitivism in him which makes him at times wilder than
any of his contemporaries, though his strong primitive characters may
remind one of Hagalín's heroes. He is also an accomplished story-teller.

Ólafur Jóhann Sigurðsson

Ólafur Jóhann Sigurðsson (1918——), the son of a farmer, was born
on Álftanes near Reykjavík but brought up in beautiful but poverty-
stricken Grafningur. Intent upon becoming a writer, the boy left home
at fifteen (1933) and eked out a meager living in Reykjavík by writing
juvenile stories, until he could publish his first novel, *Skuggarnir af
bænum* (The Shadows of the Farm, 1936), his own story in Laxness's
style, but with a tender individual quality which made it a notable first
book. This was during the worst depression years; he starved and

joined the radical circle of *Rauðir pennar* (1935). He told of this frustrated life in *Liggur vegurinn þangað?* (Does the Road Lead There?, 1940), written in Copenhagen (1936–7) in Hemingway's terse, hard style. Back home he lived again from hand to mouth, but managed to write a number of short stories, far from radical, though most of them were studies of the underprivileged or miserable; they were marked by an unusually careful workmanship and an uncanny insight into and ability to convey delicate shifts in moods of mind and nature. The boom of World War II improved his lot; he even managed a visit to Columbia University (1943–44), where he studied with Manuel Komroff, but seemingly with small effect on his writing. Just before, he had written his most ambitious work, the novel *Fjallið og draumurinn* (The Mount and the Dream, 1944), revealing in spots a lyric style in nature descriptions unsurpassed in beauty and richness. It was in reality a story of his old home region, the banks of the beautiful and beloved Sog, and of its people in weal and woe, purified through the distance of time, a book somewhat similar to Gunnar Gunnarsson's *The Church on the Mountain*. Its gallery of characters was marked by the fact that not only the heroes and heroines but also the most insignificant persons were treated with the same loving care. The continuation of this novel came as *Vorköld jörð* (Spring Cool Earth, 1951). After the war he wrote two collections of short stories, a couple of which were published in *The American Scandinavian Review*. One of them " The Padlock," is an excellent specimen of his quiet, unobtrusive art of the mood. This same mastery of mood is also shown in the novelette *Litbrigði jarðarinnar* (Earth Changing Color, 1947), the story of a youthful love, where the somber fall turns into green summer in the mind of the sixteen year old boy, and *vice versa*, according to the blazing or dying of the flame of love in his heart. In his handling of the subtle moods, Ólafur Jóhann Sigurðsson sometimes reminds one of Katherine Mansfield or the Russian A. P. Chekhov.

Ólafur Jóhann Sigurðsson wrote *Nokkrar vísur um veðrið og fleira* (Some Verses about the Weather . . . , 1952) ; these verses are marked by a quiet lyrical note akin to his lyric prose style. In 1955 two more books appeared: a volume of short stories, *Á vegamótum* (At Crossroads) and the first part of a long novel, *Gangvirkið* (The Clockwork). In spite of outward calm, these books show the people at sharp crossroads and demonstrate what effect the war had on the human clockwork subjected to its stresses.

After World War II, 1940-1956

Historical background

Unlike the first, the second World War had an immediate and incalculable effect upon Iceland and its literature.

This was owing to the Anglo-Saxon occupation of the country, first by the British (1940), then by the Americans (1941), the first breaking the neutrality of the country, the latter coming by invitation. The Icelanders, though neutral, sympathized with the allies and thanked God for being occupied by them rather than by the Germans or the Russians. They also were glad to contribute their mite toward the liberation of oppressed people, not least so their fellow-Scandinavians in Finland, Norway, and Denmark. As to their own safety and future there were facts not so reassuring, particularly the ratio during the war years between native and foreigner. There were probably two natives to one foreigner for the whole country but perhaps the reverse in Reykjavík, where one-third of the country's inhabitants were concentrated around the British military airport. As the Anglo-Saxons had money not only to buy all exportable produce but also to employ everyone, it is understandable that the country was thrown into a moral and economic turmoil the like of which it had never experienced. Before the war it was an austere, backward country, sunk in debt; after the war it was a country with a high standard of living and the simple life, which had characterized the nation as a whole, had inevitably succumbed to the processes of economic development. During the war bank accounts grew large in England and America, but there was an inflation which before the end of the decade had evened the score in foreign banks.

Important steps taken, even for the literature, during the decade were the proclamation of a Republic in Iceland on June 17, 1944 and the establishment of an American military air base in that country. The proclamation cut the last political ties with Denmark under a general national rejoicing marred only by the realization of the fact that the old sister nation was still smarting under the heel of Hitler. Poets and writers joined in the jubilation and the nation was united as rarely before. But storm clouds and discord were not far off. Though the Americans, like the English, had promised to leave the country after the war (1945), they proved loath to leave the airport in Keflavík and proposed to rent it for 99 years. The Icelanders objected but gave the Americans the right to operate it as civilians for a few years (1946). But having joined the United Nations and the Atlantic Pact (1949)—with the proviso, however, of harboring no troops in peace time—the Icelanders, out of fear of Russia and no doubt in consideration of American business and money, reluctantly admitted an American garrison to Keflavík (1951). Though approved by the three democratic parties and the majority of the Althing, this whole development was not only opposed by the Communists (who might have welcomed a Russian garrison!) but also deplored by many loyal Icelandic nationalists who feared continued demoralization, perhaps even ultimate denationalization resulting from a protracted stay of a big foreign garrison in the country.

This has given a growing nationalist tinge to the youngest poets, even those who are not Communists. Some of them are also strongly pacifist, an attitude not too hard to understand in the members of an old neutral country. They feel that it is neither logical nor reasonable that the East and the West should prefer threatening each other, or actually destroying each other with atom bombs, rather than getting together and composing their differences at the conference table. In this the youth may be underestimating the Communist threat to freedom, but it is not forgotten by the older men (Kristján Albertsson, Tómas Guðmundsson, and Gunnar Gunnarsson) who are staunch supporters of the West.

Boom in books

The war boom released a veritable flood in publications. There were many editions in the Old Icelandic field, ranging from solid works to editions de luxe. Most important was a new popular edition designated to include *all* the old genres: Eddas, sagas, historical sagas, bishops' lives, mythical-heroic sagas (*fornaldar sögur*), romances of chivalry (*riddara sögur*), and fantastic adventure stories (*lygi sögur*). A Rímnafélag, a society to publish *rímur* after 1600, was started, and Sir William A. Craigie compiled his monumental *Sýnisbók íslenzkra rímna* (three volumes, 1952).

In the modern field old classics out of print and popular authors were published in collected editions, and writers could not satisfy the demands of the publishers some of whom, notably the Mæcenas Ragnar Jónsson, paid so well that the writers for the first time could live by their pen, even build themselves houses. Publications of folkloristic literature, historico-topographical writings, memoirs, and biographical works of reference went on apace. Two literary societies, the communistic-nationalistic Mál og Menning and the co-operative and state-sponsored Menningarsjóður og Þjóðvinafélagið, were reorganized so as to publish not only periodicals but also translations of foreign masterpieces, mostly novels. In 1955 a third society of this kind, Almenna bókafélagið, was founded by anticommunistic lovers of Western democracy. The large and splendid literary periodical *Helgafell* (1942–46, 54——) was typical of the period. While *Ritlist og myndlist, Líf og list, Menn og menntir,* and *Vaki* were more ephemeral, they were all, like *Birtingur* (1953——), mouthpieces of young writers and artists. Unfortunately there was, too, a growing number of trashy (sex, crime) periodicals, patterned on Anglo-Saxon models.

Translations from the English went on at a quickened pace: Hemingway, A. Huxley, D. H. Lawrence, W. S. Maugham, Steinbeck, Erskine Caldwell, Sinclair Lewis, Saroyan, and many of the older generations.

Special war themes

Of special war themes one may mention fulminations against totalitarianism, black and red (Hagalín, Davíð, Tómas), protestations in defense of personal freedom and freedom of opinion, admiration for the heroism of Finland, Norway, and Denmark, often contrasted with the Icelandic fool's paradise. The demoralization of the occupation period (*ástandið*) is described in novels by Jóhannes úr Kötlum, Hagalín, Guðmundur Daníelsson (a play), Kristmann Guðmundsson, Þórunn Magnússdóttir, Jón Björnsson, and, later, Ólafur Jóhann Sigurðsson, but nowhere as dramatically as in Halldór Kiljan Laxness' *Atómstöðin* (1948). Allowing for his communistic point of view, there can be little doubt that the picture he draws of postwar society in Reykjavík, completely torn from its moorings by the avalanche of foreign gold, once more proving the *Hávamál-Sólarljóð* adage " Margr verðr af aurum api " (Gold turns many a man into a fool), was only too true. Of these authors only Jóhannes, Þórunn, Ólafur Jóhann, and Laxness were communistic, while the others were definitely anticommunistic, some having written essays in that vein (Gunnarsson and Hagalín) and all uniting their efforts for personal freedom in Almenna bókafélagið, 1955.

Other tendencies

By making them well-to-do the war boom took the wind out of the leftists' sails in various ways. Some felt very uneasy about it, like Jóhannes úr Kötlum, until they could rally to the nationalist cause.

Laxness devoted most of the decade to writing historical novels, steeping himself in sagas until he could produce his heroic tragedy, *Gerpla*, from a pacifist point of view, but in unmistakable saga style. Others, not leftists, were also busy writing sagas, though not attempting the saga style, except to some extent Sigurjón Jónsson in his three sagas. Brekkan's novel on *Njála's* evil genius, Hallgerður langbrók, was a love story, while Kristmann Guðmundsson's novel on *Völuspá's* author was a story describing inspiration and Irish and Greek mysteries. This was not the only Irish influence noticeable during the decade.

In his historical novels Laxness occupied himself more and more with form: every detail should be integrated with the whole; if it does, it does not matter whether it is realistic or fantastic. Þórbergur Þórðarson, Ólafur Jóh. Sigurðsson, Ási úr Bæ, Agnar Þórðarson, and Indriði G. Þorsteinsson all experimented with style.

In poetry Steinn Steinarr led the experimentation in abstract style, while Jón úr Vör wrote free verse without alliteration and rime, a form frowned upon by traditionalists who pointed out that nothing like it had been seen in Iceland since the Reformation hymns of inglorious memory. Free verse to imitate the original meters was employed by Anonymus (who of all people turned out to be Jóhannes úr Kötlum), translator of T. S. Eliot and other modern or primitivist poets. But Snorri Hjartarson experimented with (consonant) assonances and inrimes as no one else, keeping the alliteration. Some of the younger poets like Jón Jóhannesson and Einar Bragi Sigurðsson even attempted to match Tómas Guðmundsson's polish in style.

In spite of the rejoicing of 1944, a spirit of frustration—though not perhaps quite the despair of T. S. Eliot and Sartre—seemed to animate some of the younger poets, following in the footsteps of Steinn Steinarr, apostle of nihilistic despair. The term *atómskáld*, " atom poet " (coined by Laxness in *Atómstöðin* ?) was used to designate, among the younger poets, either those who employed untraditional free verse, or those—especially Hannes Sigfússon and Sigfús Daðason—who resorted to darker metaphors or irrational conceits in their poetic diction. Elías Mar and others tried to combine the old and the new. He is usually quite clear.

The mood of the atom poets is probably nowhere better formulated than in Sigfús Daðason's passage: " I do not ask for peace of soul, placed as I am in the midst between heaven and hell, new and old, East and West, between difficult and easy things, between what I have to do myself and what others, now gone, have done for me; no, that would be asking too much. But I pray that I might be given relief from the emptiness of soul, the indifference and numbness which does not see the light, does not feel the water, sense the earth, and I ask that I be given surcease from such a day as now has passed towards evening, over an empty April sky." Related feelings are the pathological suffering of Jóhann Pétursson and the T. S. Eliot-like loneliness of Thor Vilhjálmsson.

After all this fumbling frustration it is really heartening to see the rising nationalism and love of country in poets like the brothers Þóroddur and Heiðrekur Guðmundsson as well as in those of the patriotic anthology *Svo frjáls vertu móðir* (As Free Be You Mother, 1954) from the last decade, published on the tenth anniversary of the Republic. Still, several of these poems lack the direct approach so common in the (anti-Danish) patriotic poetry of the preceding century. Just as *Gerpla* clothes her satire in historical symbolism, so some of this poetry is allusive or parabolic rather than outspoken. Is this an influence from the Nazi occupation of Norway and Denmark or fear of America? Or are the writers following in Kafka's footsteps?

Poets, novelists, and playwrights after 1940

It is convenient to list here the poets, novelists, and playwrights—most but not all of them young—making their debut after 1940, though some of them have been mentioned before. All are promising writers, though it is, of course, difficult to predict their future.

In the forties appeared: the humorist Kristinn Pétursson (1914——) ; the prolific traditional Kristján Einarsson frá Djúpalæk (1916——) ; the romantic Þorsteinn Valdimarsson (1918——) ; the tradition-loving sons of Guðmundur Friðjónsson á Sandi, Þóroddur (1906——) and Heiðrekur (1910——). The new composer of *rímur* Sveinbjörn Beinteinsson (1924——) was hailed as a renewer of that old art by no less an authority than Sir William A. Craigie. Ingólfur Kristjánsson (1919———) and the philosophical Gunnar Dal (pen name for Halldór Sigurðsson, 1924——) were both traditional and romantic.

The atom poets belong mainly to the fifties, though Stefán Hörður Grímsson (1920——) and Hannes Sigfússon (1922——), both daring in imagery, started in 1946 and 1949. They were followed by Thor Vilhjálmsson (1925——) Sigfús Daðason (1928——), and Jón Óskar (1921——), all students of postwar Paris and deeply influenced by French or Romance literatures (Sartre, Paul Eluard, Camus, and the Spanish-American Pablo Neruda) in form and matter, especially the first two. Einar Bragi (Sigurðsson) (1921——) and Elías Mar (1924———) stood with one foot in the old tradition, while the older poets Jón Jóhannesson (1904——) and Ólafur Jóhann Sigurðsson (1918——) had both feet planted in it. Mainly traditional, too, is the youngest, Hannes Pétursson (1931——) who looks like a major poet.

An anthology of the poets, *Ljóð ungra skálda* 1944–54 was published by Magnús Ásgeirsson in 1954, his last work. By that time the revolters against rime and alliteration were already in the majority.

Some of the novelists were rooted in the old farm culture: the retired housewife Guðrún Árnadóttir frá Lundi (1887——) and Jón Björnsson (1907——), returned from Denmark, where he had made his debut in the thirties. Both were prolific, she writing romantically about farmer heroes within her long memory, he novels on historical or present-day themes. Oddný Guðmundsdóttir (1908——) also wrote farm life stories. Þórleifur Bjarnason (1908——) and Jón Thorarensen (1902——) both wrote romantically about life in old fishing stations, the first in Vestfirðir, the second on Reykjanes; both were, besides, busy collectors of folklore. Two men growing up in poverty and want in fishing villages wrote about their experiences: Vilhjálmur S. Vilhjálmsson (1903——) of Eyrarbakki, a history of the workers' movement there, and Óskar Aðalsteinn Guðjónsson (1919——) of Ísafjörður about the depression there. Jóhann J. E. Kúld (1902——) described his dangerous sailor's life during the war, while Ástgeir Ólafsson (pen name Ási í Bæ, 1914——) wrote a hardboiled story of a fisherman's life in Vestmannaeyjar, and Guðmundur J. Gíslason (1925——) described one summer of herring fishing in Siglufjörður. Of others may still be mentioned: the prolific girls' novelist Ragnheiður Jónsdóttir (1895——); the artistic short story writer Svanhildur Þorsteinsdóttir (Þorsteinn Erlingsson's daughter, 1904——) ; the humoristic short story writer Kristján Bender (1915——) ; the pathological Jóhann Pétursson (1918—) ; Stefán Júlíusson (pen name Sveinn Auðunn Sveinsson, 1915——), whose first novel gave a student's impression of the United States, the only one of the many students who went to America during the war to attempt that, hence rather interesting for Americans. Thor Vilhjálmsson (1925——) did not do the same for France, though his sketches and prose poems were saturated with Sartre's Paris atmosphere.

Most promising novelists of the youngest generation are Agnar Þórðarson (1917——) and Elías Mar (1924——) both born and brought up in Reykjavík. Elías has written several novels and short stories as well as some poetry; his story about a misguided youth in Reykjavík stands out among his writings. Agnar has several unpublished plays and two novels to his credit; the novels are written with psychological insight and quite mature workmanship. The first describes high life in Reykjavík, the second a Hamlet-like figure who attempts a revolt against the general demoralization. Promising, too, seem the most recent to make their appearance, Hannes Sigfússon, also a poet, and Indriði G. Þorsteinsson.

Two Icelanders made their debut with novels in Denmark during the war, Þorsteinn Stefánsson (1912——), whose novel about a fjord in the East of Iceland won him the H. C. Andersen medal for 1943, and the poet and lecturer Bjarni M. Gíslason with a philosophical novel in the spirit of Grundtvig and the Danish " Folk High Schools."

During the forties the best plays written were *Gullna hliðið* by Davíð Stefánsson and *Uppstigning* by Sigurður Nordal, his first play. Other notable plays were Halldór K. Laxness' *Snæfríður Íslandssól* (1950) and *Jón Arason* by Tryggvi Sveinbjörnsson (published in *Modern Scandinavian Plays*, 1954, by The American-Scandinavian Foundation), both given at the opening of the National Theater in 1950.

One would have expected that this opening of the National Theater, as well as the demand of the State Broadcasting (since 1930) for short plays would serve as a stimulus to younger playwrights. Actually there have been a number of playlets written though not usually published. Yet the only promising playwright to appear was Jakob Jónsson with his *Sex leikrit* (1948).

Icelandic studies—1940 and after

At the University in Reykjavík Einar Ól. Sveinsson, having just published his book on the Sturlung Age (1940), succeeded Nordal as a professor of the Old Icelandic literature (1945), while Steingrímur J. Þorsteinsson (1911———) took over the Modern Icelandic literature (1945). Having written the most profound book of the decade, *Íslenzk menning* (I, 1942), Nordal remained a professor without teaching duties until in 1951 he was made Minister of Iceland in Copenhagen. Björn Guðfinnsson (1905–50) joined the faculty as a professor of the modern language in 1941; he wrote a monumental study of the dialects. He was succeeded by Halldór Halldórsson (1911———). In 1945 Jón Jóhannesson (1909–57), co-editor of *Sturlunga saga* (1949), was made a second professor of history, while Þorkell Jóhannesson (1895———) in 1944 had succeeded Árni Pálsson as first professor of the subject. Of the large *Saga Íslendinga* Þorkell covered the period 1750–1830 while Jónas Jónsson, the erstwhile premier and political leader, wrote of the period 1830–74. After the war Jakob Benediktsson was made the editor of a modern Icelandic dictionary (1550———) sponsored by the University. Not connected with the University were four communistic intellectuals, the historians Einar Olgeirsson and Björn Þorsteinsson who wrote about the Old Icelandic Commonwealth, Kristinn E. Andrésson, covering the literary history 1918–1948, and Gunnar Benediktsson who wrote partly about the Sturlungs, partly the history of the country 1940–49. Gunnar M. Magnúss wrote a factual and somewhat annalistic history of the war in Iceland from a more objective point of view.

In America Kristján Karlsson (1922———) succeeded Halldór Hermannsson as a curator at Cornell in 1948 and was in turn succeeded by Jóhann Hannesson (1919———), a promising scholar, in 1952, while Finnbogi Guðmundsson (1924———) took over the newly established chair of Icelandic literature and language at the University of Manitoba, Winnipeg, Canada.

Þóroddur Guðmundsson

Þóroddur Guðmundsson (1904———) was born at Sandur in the North, son of the poet-farmer Guðmundur Friðjónsson. He attended rural schools and teachers colleges in Iceland, Norway, Denmark, and Sweden and has been a teacher, since 1948, in Hafnarfjörður. He wrote *Skýjadans* (Cloud Dance, 1943), short stories, *Villiflug* (Wild Flight, 1946), *Anganþeyr* (Fragrant Thaw, 1952), and *Sefafjöll* (Summits of the

Spirit, 1954), poems filled with a quiet pathos for traditional values and nostalgia for the country and his old home. Obviously he carries on the heritage of his father though he does not imitate his form. Even better than his short stories and poems is the biography of his father: *Guðmundur Friðjónsson* (1950), really a great work, where the obvious filial piety does not interfere with the author's frankness and sense of justice. The picture he draws of the crowded farm—there were twelve children—is unforgettable.

To an increasing extent, Þóroddur Guðmundsson's volumes of poetry carried translations from English (Scotch and Irish) poetry. This interest resulted in a visit to these countries, described in *Úr Vesturvegi* (From the British Isles, 1953), by which he was deeply impressed.

Jakob Jónsson

Jakob Jónsson (1904———) was born at Hof, Álftafjörður, and grew up in the village of Djúpivogur in the East. The son of a parson, he in turn became a parson at Djúpivogur, Wynyard, Saskatchewan, Canada (1938–39) and Reykjavík. He wrote his first play for his congregation at Wynyard. His two first plays, especially *Öldur* (Waves) were idyls from his home village. *Tyrkja-Gudda*, the most ambitious one and perhaps his best, deals with the famous Hallgrímur Pétursson's notorious wife, a returned slave from Algiers. *Hamarinn* (The Hammer) castigates the demoralization during and after World War II. Of his short radio plays, *Barrabas* was the best. These and other plays, published as *Sex leikrit* (Six Plays, 1948), make Jakob Jónsson one of the more promising of the younger playwrights, the only one to specialize in that genre.

Apart from the plays, Jakob has also published *Í kirkju og utan* (In and Outside of Church, 1949), a collection of essays and speeches in which he opposed the Atlantic Pact and advocated continuation of Iceland's neutral status.

Snorri Hjartarson

Snorri Hjartarson (1906———) was born in Borgarfjörður in the West of well-to-do parents who would have put him through the Gymnasium in Reykjavík but for his poor health. He started early to write poetry, but gave it up for a spell while studying art (expressionistic painting) in Copenhagen and Oslo. In Norway he wrote the novel *Höit flyver ravnen* (High Soars the Raven, 1934) about an artist's dilemma between love and work. Shortly afterwards he returned to Iceland (1936). After some lean years he got a job at the Public Library in Reykjavík, becoming its chief librarian in 1943. A year later he published his *Kvæði* (Poems, 1944), all written during World War II, 1940–44. It was a remarkable debut book, more significant than any other since Laxness' *Kvæðakver*. There was hardly a trace of the war in it; it was an intensely personal hymn of praise to his motherland, a moving confession of his joy at being back home, and exultation over the fact that he had at last found himself in his poetry, confident about his future course. This is clear from many passages in his poetry, but most magnificently expressed in the final poem, "Það kallar þrá" (Yearning Calls), explaining his yearning back to the mountain of his childhood, whose spirits summon him to "work and duty, / Defiant: Trust the everlasting rocks / Dwell by the anvil: blacksmith, metal, fire / And forge in truth unbreaking / If not a sword, then golden odes on shields!" (Magnús Á. Árnason's translation.)

Though there is some free verse, many poems are cast in traditional forms—at first sight. On closer inspection one finds experimentation in them: unexpected rimes, lots of inrimes and assonances, even consonant assonances used instead of rimes. This technique—reminding one of an earlier Snorri's *Háttatal*—is brilliantly employed in the leading poem of the collection: "Í Úlfdölum" (In Wolf Dales): "Það gisti óður / minn eyðiskóg / er ófætt vor / bjó í kvistum," with *gisti: kvistum, óður: eyði-, skóg: bjó* riming or assonating. This is verbal music of harmony and dissonance, but Snorri is no less a verbal painter than a musician, as his scale of color-adjectives shows. This persistent modulation of music and color makes the poems often not easy to read, but enhances their artistic value.

Snorri's second book, *Á Gnitaheiði* (On Gnitaheiði, 1952) is marked by the same formal qualities, though here are more very short, simple poems than in the first book. But whereas the first book was also a hymn to the Icelandic newborn independence, 1944, this book registers the poet's sorrow and fears at seeing Iceland quickly being sucked into the maelstrom of international power politics—in poems like "Marz 1949," "Í garðinum" (In the Garden), "Hamlet," and others.

Jón Björnsson

Jón Björnsson (1907——) was born in Holt in Síða in the South, a farmer's son. He studied in "folk high schools" in Norway (1929) and Denmark (Askov, 1930) and lived in Copenhagen 1933–45. After World War II he returned to Reykjavík, and has lived there since.

During the thirties Jón Björnsson wrote a great number of short stories for popular magazines and newspapers in Denmark. In the period 1942–54 he wrote eight novels, the two first, *Jordens Magt* (The Earth's Power, 1942) and *Slægtens Ære* (Family Honor, 1944), in honor of rural life in Iceland. He came back to that subject in *Dagur fagur prýðir veröld alla* (Beauteous Day Brightens the Whole World, 1950), dealing with the flight of the farmers to the towns aggravated by World War II. *Búddamyndin* (The Buddha Idol, 1948) describes an individualistic townsman who gets crushed between the millstones of society: the political parties. The rest of his novels are historical: *Kongens Ven* (The King's Friend, 1946) deals with the fifteenth-century robber-bishop Jón Gerreksson, drowned like a dog by the provoked Icelanders; *Valtýr á grænni treyju* (Valtýr in the Green Coat, 1951) treats of an eighteenth-century judicial murder, while *Eldraunin* (The Fiery Test, 1952) deals with the age of witchcraft, with overtones from modern absolutisms and witch-hunting. *Bergljót* (1954) is a seventeenth-century novel ending with the country's subjection to the absolute monarch in 1662, also with modern overtones.

Jón Jónsson úr Vör

Jón (Jónsson) úr Vör (1917——) was born in Patreksfjörður in the Northwest of poor parents. He grew up during the worst depression, but won independence during the last war boom and lives now in Fossvogur near Reykjavík. He made his debut with an interesting poem on a summer day in his village in *Rauðir pennar* 1935. His first book *Ég ber að dyrum* (I Knock at the Door, 1937) and *Stund milli stríða* (A Moment between Wars, 1942) seemed not very significant, but with *Þorpið* (The Village, 1946, 2nd ed. 1956), he reverted to the village of his birth, describing it in free verse not unlike Edgar Lee Masters' *Spoon River Anthology*, though not influenced by it but by Swedish leftist poets whose acquaintance the poet had first made in Magnús Ásgeirsson's translations. The free verse form was, from now on, his special medium. The description of the half-starving fishing village and its humble figures was realistic, but not bitter; on the contrary, the poet, having left it behind, could recreate it from his memory with something like a romantic nostalgia for disappeared youth. It haunted him as bygone Reykjavík haunted Tómas Guðmundsson, and by the same token he was able to invest it with a strange tranquil beauty in spite of its ugliness. The style was quiet and unobtrusive, matching the humble themes. The poet has published two more books: *Með hljóðstaf* (With Alliteration, 1951), where his two first volumes are partly reprinted, and *Með örvalausum boga* (With an Arrow-less Bow, 1951). These books contain impressions of his life in Reykjavík during the war, impressions from a visit to Scandinavia, and continuation of old themes. His poetry is endowed with the same quiet perfection as before, but the youthful enthusiasm of his first poems is now exchanged for a sceptical pessimism: he does not believe that the poor will ever inherit the land.

American-Icelandic Writers

Introduction

Following in the footsteps of their Scandinavian brethren, the Icelanders began emigrating to America *en masse* during the seventies and eighties, driven by volcanic eruptions (1875), hard years, and restiveness from foreign rule.

A few pioneers had left as early as 1855 for the promised land of Utah, and in 1863 for the " coffee fields " of Brazil. But the bulk went in the seventies to the Midwest of the United States or Canada, settling partly in Minnesota and North Dakota, partly in Manitoba, both in the booming city of Winnipeg and in Nýja Ísland, " New Iceland," on the west shore of Lake Winnipeg, where the settlers were at once greeted by " hell and high water."

Still, here they founded an Icelandic community (1877–87), unpacked their books, and founded their first newspaper, *Framfari* (The Progressive, 1877–80). And here arose at once their spiritual leaders the Lutheran parsons, the shortlived, fundamentalist and saintly Páll Þorláksson (1849–1882) of North Dakota, the towering orthodox ecclesiastical leader Jón Bjarnason (1845–1914), often considered greatest of them all, the liberal " new theologian " Friðrik J. Bergmann (1858–1918), and the Unitarian Rögnvaldur Pétursson (1877–1940). All were at the same time apostles and upholders of Icelandic nationality, but had they been given the choice between heaven and Iceland, it is likely that the first two would have chosen heaven, but the last-named Iceland.

Besides the churches, several other organizations did much to further intellectual activities or keep alive the Icelandic traditions. So reading circles and temperance societies were active in many places; the latter did much to stimulate acting and playwriting. The Icelandic Culture Society, founded by Stephan G. Stephansson and others in North Dakota in 1888, deserves mention because of its illustrious founder (of whom more will be said later). It was patterned on Professor Felix Adler's Ethical Culture Societies. A similar, even more ambitious society was founded about the same time in Winnipeg, where about 1903 there also arose an Icelandic verse-makers' club. But most important was the still active Þjóðræknisfélag Íslendinga í Vesturheimi (The Icelandic National League in America), founded in 1919 and flourishing under the energetic leadership of Rögnvaldur Pétursson (to 1940) and Richard Beck (1897——), professor of Scandinavian languages and literatures at the University of North Dakota. The latter—in countless speeches, lectures, and articles in newspapers and periodicals, Icelandic, English, and Norwegian—has done more than any other to spread the gospel of Icelandic culture among his compatriots and the natives of America. A very limited selection from his writings was published as Ættland og erfðir (Native Land and Inheritance, 1950). Beck was also a facile poet in the national-romantic tradition, as his Icelandic volume Ljóðmál (1929) and his English Sheaf of Verses (1945) show.

Among the many periodicals the weekly newspapers Heimskringla (The Globe, 1886——) and Lögberg (The Tribune, 1888——) are most important. They are now the oldest newspapers published in Icelandic. Of the church journals, Sameiningin (Unity, 1886——), organ of the Evangelical Lutheran Church (Rev. Jón Bjarnason), is the oldest and most important upholder of orthodoxy. Breiðablik (Broad View, 1906–14) launched the "new theology" of Friðrik J. Bergmann, Heimir (1904–14) the Unitarianism of Rögnvaldur Pétursson; this does not complete the count.

Tímarit Þjóðræknisfélags Íslendinga (1919——) is devoted to the cultural heritage, publishing poems, short stories, essays and articles on literary figures, all of national importance. Editors have been Rögnvaldur Pétursson, until his death in 1940, and after that Gísli Jónsson.

Almanak Ólafs S. Thorgeirssonar (1895–1955) has, since 1899, included contributions toward the history of the various settlements in style with and inspired by the old Landnáma. After Thorgeirsson's death (1864–1937) R. Beck served as editor until the periodical's demise.

Some periodicals were designed to delight rather than educate; these cannot be mentioned here.

Stephan G. Stephansson

Stephan G. Stephansson (Stefán Guðmundarson, 1853–1927) was born at Kirkjuhóll in Skagafjörður in the North, the son of poor crofters, but related to the Gröndal family. After eking out a meager existence in several crofts in the North, the family left Iceland, when Stephan was twenty (1873), for Wisconsin. Next, the family settled at Gardar, North Dakota (1880), and for the third and last time near Markerville, Alberta, Canada. Here Stephan raised a large family, took an active part in local affairs, and, at night, composed his many volumes of poetry. Here he died, "a white-haired veteran of seventy-four" (Watson Kirkconnell) with no worldly honors but recognized as one of the greatest poets and personalities of his race.

Stephan early (1873) started contributing poems to newspapers, but he made his debut with *Úti á víðavangi* (Out in the Open, 1894), and then published *Á ferð og flugi* (En Route, 1900). Then came *Andvökur* (Wakeful Nights, I–III, 1909–10; IV–V, 1923; VI, 1938), containing the bulk of his poetry. To this were added *Kolbeinslag* (The Lay of Kolbeinn, 1914), about a seventeenth-century *kraftaskáld* who tested his poetic mettle against the Devil; *Heimleiðis* (Homeward Bound, 1917), occasioned by his trip to Iceland as a guest of the nation; *Vígslóði* (The War Trail, 1920), his pacifistic answer to World War I. His newspaper articles in prose were printed in *Vestan um haf* (1930), an anthology of American-Icelandic poetry and prose. Other articles and letters were printed in *Bréf og ritgerðir* (1938–48).

The homeland, though distant, never relinquished its hold on the poet. He celebrated the districts where he grew up, Skagafjörður and Bárðardalur, in magnificent poems and took his stand in the poetic controversy on waterfalls with "Fossaföll." His countrymen used to meet once a year celebrating "Icelanders' Day," to fortify their memories of their homeland with speeches and poems; Stephan G. contributed many, but no one as beautiful as *Þótt þú langförull legðir* (Though You Longfarer Travelled), a song which long has taken its place in the repertoire of singing Icelanders with the most valued patriotic poems. It is of course no wonder that such a song should come from one exiled, for as the Icelandic proverb says: "No one knows what he has had, until he has lost it."

In "Útlegðin" (The Exile) the poet states that the foster-mother, the new land, could not quite replace "his mother." Nevertheless, he has sung about the new land in so many and variegated poems that Watson Kirkconnell declares: " No other Canadian poet in any language presents a comparable picture of Western Canada." Fortunately for him the Rocky Mountains in the distance reminded him somewhat of his rocky home-land, hence one of his earlier poems is devoted to them. But the longer he stayed the more he grew to love the landscape: the hills, the hardy spruce woods, the lakes, the rivers, the brooks; the challenging Alberta winters and the mild and bright summers—these, also, to some extent reminding him of home. Here he learned to love and distinguish the many kinds of trees. Here he also produced from memory perfect word-pictures of the flat prairies he had left behind.

Though Stephan had to forego formal schooling in Iceland, he had as a boy read and largely learned not only the Bible, but also the Eddas and sagas, so it was no empty phrase when he said in " Ástavísur til Íslands " (Love Verses to Iceland) : " Your Golden Age and sagas they dwell in my heart." Like Bjarni and Grímur he was an ardent admirer of the heroic spirit of the sagas as we meet it in figures like Grettir and his brother Illugi (" Illugadrápa "), the farmer of Hergilsey in Gísla saga—though, significantly, both Illugi and the farmer could be Christian heroes because of their self-sacrifice. The poet never retired to his golden saga age as an escape, but drew on its figures as symbols and patterns for the present generation.

Conversely, he found in the present generation many worthy of his praise and love, as his many memorials show, for though he always had his feelings under control, he was deeply touched by the passing of friends. Among his closest was Helgi Stefánsson, brother of Jón Stefáns-son (Þorgils Gjallandi), and all agree that the portrait he painted of him was also a true self-portrait. He could also commemorate a stranger like André Courmont who, like Morris, had been bewitched by the sagas. Naturally the poems about his mother and his two sons, especially Gestur, who had been electrocuted by a live wire, show deepest into his feelings, but they are far from sentimental. Stephan wrote no love poetry, except one poem to a little curly-headed girl of six whom he had met and befriended in Wisconsin thirty years before.

But " Kurlý " is not a loving portrait only. It gives also a glimpse of the fertile checkered prairie where the roads are free, while the farm gates may display the very un-Icelandic " no trespassing." A fuller picture of the prairie life is drawn in the narrative poem Á ferð og flugi (the form borrowed from Þorsteinn Erlingsson), and it is no flattering picture of a mining town, ruined by greedy speculators, ready to starve, in spite of two churches, one drugstore selling liquor, and a dancehall—ideal soil for violence, drunkenness, harlotry, and hypocrisy. The poet's anticapitalistic and anticlerical stand is clear here, as is also his compassion with human outcasts, and that not only in capitalistic America, but also in his homeland; cf. " Jón hrak." Stephan was in no doubt about his socialist views, yet, as an individualist farmer and as an intellectual aristocrat, he realized that he was not one of the crowd; cf. " Jafningjarnir " (The Peers). And farmer though he was, he had a wide cosmopolitan outlook which, guided by his humanitarian conscience, frequently took offense at world, even British, events, like the Boer War. But at no time was his voice raised louder in revolt than in *Vígslóði*, describing the horrors of World War I and condemning leaders on both sides in general for sending youth to the slaughterhouse, and his compatriots in specific for joining the army. Naturally, this did not help his popularity in Canada for a while.

Like Þ. Erlingsson, Stephan soon reacted against the orthodox Christianity of his time and turned atheist. But he was no enemy of the Master from Nazareth, and sympathized with more liberal views like the " new theology " sponsored by his friend (though former antagonist) Friðrik J. Bergmann, and even more so with the Unitarianism of his friend and literary executor Rögnvaldur Pétursson.

Since Stephan was an idealist and a thinker he often had to strain style and form, rather than not to say what he wanted, having no time to polish. As to form, he was really in the skaldic *rímur* tradition of ornate style, hence his variety of verse forms and his unbelievably rich diction. Yet he did not lack the light lyric touch, as some of his best poems show, e. g., " Kvöld " (Evening) and " Við verkalok " (At Close of Day). With Matthías and Einar Benediktsson he was one of the greatest Icelandic poets of his time, and the greatest character of the three. Watson Kirkconnell calls him the leading poet of Canada; F. S. Cawley believes him to have been the finest poet of the Western world.

Kristinn Stefánsson

Kristinn Stefánsson (1856–1916) was born in Skagafjörður, emigrated in 1873, and lived after 1881 in Winnipeg as a carpenter. He made his debut with *Vestan hafs* (West of the Ocean, 1900), but his best poems are found in *Út um vötn og velli* (From Lake and Prairie, 1916). Like Stephan G. Stephansson he was a radical socially and in church matters, as several of his satirical poems testify, but he also loved to describe and contemplate nature, notably in its spring and summer garb. But though he described the Canadian scene and paid tribute to his land of adoption, he was firmly rooted in Iceland memories and Icelandic literary tradition, Steingrímur Thorsteinsson and Þorsteinn Erlingsson being his favorites.

Þorbjörn Bjarnason

Þorbjörn Bjarnason (pen name Þorskabítur, 1859–1933) was born in Kjós in the South, emigrated to Winnipeg in 1893, and went in 1897 to North Dakota, where he lived as a manual laborer until his death

Nokkur ljóðmæli (A Handful of Poems, 1914) shows the poet to be a socialist in politics and radical in matters of church, though his poem on the " Sermon on the Mount " shows his love for the teachings of Jesus. Otherwise his poems were devoted to memories of his beloved homeland; the splendors of Borgarfjörður, where he grew up, and the poetry of his masters: Steingrímur Thorsteinsson, Þorsteinn Erlingsson and Bólu-Hjálmar.

Kristján Níels Júlíus Jónsson

Kristján Níels Júlíus Jónsson (pen name K. N. or Káinn, 1860–1936) was born of poetic stock in Akureyri in the North, emigrated to Winnipeg in 1878, lived a few years in Minnesota, but spent most of his life in the Icelandic settlement in North Dakota, as a farmhand or cowherd. His intimate knowledge of farm life gave him innumerable themes for humorous and droll remarks; his knowledge of Icelandic poetry, not least of the popular masters, and his direct contact with American humor molded him into the humorist; he was without peer not only among his compatriots in America but also in Iceland.

Accustomed to throw out a verse on any occasion when the fancy struck him, he did not at first pay much attention to his products, and his first collection, *Kviðlingar* (Ditties, 1920), was more in the nature of an appetizer than a full course of his poetry. Fortunately the energetic and poetry-loving R. Beck made another collection while the poet was still alive, though it did not come out until after his death: *Kviðlingar og kvæði* (Ditties and Poems, 1945), with introduction by the editor and the Rev. Haraldur Sigmar, K. N.'s pastor and lifelong friend.

To quote Beck: " K. N.'s sparkling and infectious humor consists primarily in an original and versatile play on words. He had an uncanny ability to cast new light on things, not least through brilliant use of

anticlimax and the unexpected ending. Local individuals and happenings are largely the targets of his humor, although he occasionally goes
farther afield. Generally, his whimsical humorous sallies are good
natured, arousing laughter rather than leaving a lasting sting, and pleas-
ing by their unfailing linguistic skill; but sometimes his swift rapier
thrusts are biting in their sarcasm. His fondness for Bacchus was well
known and is reflected in many of his verses; Prohibition was a thorn
in his side."

K. N. revealed the same anticlerical attitude as Stephan G. Stephansson and shared his sympathy for the down-and-out; he himself was never
very far removed from their lot.

Just as he was a master of the pun, so he also wielded the parody with
great glee; witness his murderous take-off of Jónas Hallgrímsson's
"Gunnarshólmi." Quoth Jónas about Gunnar á Hlíðarendi's refusal to
go into exile (Njála):

> Því Gunnar vildi heldur bíða hel
>   en horfinn vera fósturjarðarströndum.
> For Gunnar would much rather suffer death
>   than leave behind his mother-country's shores.

But K. N. turns this into a story of Gunnar the American-Icelander,
with these significant changes:

> Því Gunnar vildi heldur go to hell
>   en heima vera á fósturjarðarströndum.
> For Gunnar would much rather " go to hell "
>   than stay at home on mother-country's shores.

Knowing the lot of the earliest emigrants, K. N. knew very well that he
was here speaking the literal truth.

Jónas A. Sigurðsson

Jónas Ari Sigurðsson (1865–1933) was born in Húnavatnssýsla in
the North into a cultural milieu, and emigrated in 1887 to North Dakota.
He studied theology at a Lutheran seminary in Chicago, graduating in
1893. After that he served as a parson of conservative Lutheran Icelandic
congregations in North Dakota and Canada. His poems *Ljóðmæli* were
published after his death in 1946, edited by R. Beck.

As a man of religion, he composed and translated a number of hymns
and sacred or philosophical poems. His memorial poems also bear this
stamp. He could describe nature, both Canadian and Icelandic; *cf.* the
sweeping " Mt. Rainier." Yet, perhaps, his deepest inspiration was drawn

from the spirit of the Eddas and sagas, his country's history and folkways, and from the everflowing fountain of the native language. This made him an untiring preacher of Icelandic nationalism, not only in his poetry, but also as a leader of the Icelandic National League in America. It was therefore no accident that the American Icelanders entrusted him with poetic greetings at the millenary celebration of the Althing in 1930.

Gunnsteinn Eyjólfsson

Gunnstein Eyjólfsson (1866–1910) was born in Fljótsdalshérað in the East, fled from the volcanic ashes, and emigrated in 1876 to " New Iceland," Keewatin, Canada, where he lived as farmer and merchant. A self-made, talented man, he composed music and short stories in the realistic fashion.

His boiling indignation at hypocritical church people in Winnipeg finds expression in *Elenóra* (1894), the story of a country girl's degeneration in the town. His chapters on Jón á Strympu, a " New Icelandic " Dolittle, are of a more genial humor, though sarcastic enough. His complete works, entitled *Jón á Strympu*, were published in 1952 by Gísli Jónsson, poet and publisher in Winnipeg.

Jóhann Magnús Bjarnason

Jóhann Magnús Bjarnason (1866–1945) was born in Fljótsdalshérað in the East, fled from the volcanic ashes in 1875 to Halifax County, Nova Scotia, thence in 1882 to Winnipeg. He spent most of his life teaching children in the Icelandic settlements in Manitoba and North Dakota, but died in Elfros, Saskatchewan.

Jóhann Magnús Bjarnason was early an avid reader of Icelandic sagas, fairy tales, poetry, and *rímur*, but also of Homer and English literature from Chaucer to Dickens, though Robert Louis Stevenson was his favorite in mature years. His earliest work, *Sögur og kvæði* (Stories and Poems, 1892) and *Ljóðmæli* (Lyric Poems, 1898) showed that he was somewhat under the influence of the realists Gestur Pálsson, Einar Hjörleifsson (Kvaran) and last but not least, Stephan G. Stephansson. But as soon as he found that people were hurt by his satire, he dropped it altogether and turned to romance in realistic disguise. Yet, his first work after this had at least a realistic foundation, for it was an autobiographical novel, *Eiríkur Hansson* (1899–1903), describing his adolescence in Nova Scotia. It had a family likeness to his beloved *David Copperfield* in characters, mannerisms, and sentimentality. In his next book, *Brasilíufararnir I–II* (The Brazil Immigrants, 1905–1908), the romance was in full flower. There were marvellous adventures in store for the four fictitious Icelanders in that southern land of romance. A good deal of the second volume of *Brasilíufararnir* was episodic, almost a self-contained short adventure.

This, too, was the nature of most of his later short stories, published in *Vornætur á Elgsheiðum* (Spring Night on Elk Moors, 1910), from Nova Scotia, and *Haustkvöld við hafið* (Autumnal Nights by the Ocean, 1928) from the west coast. The motif is always the lone Icelander abroad, in various situations but always the same in character: noble, conscientious, proud of his old country and traditions. And the author was careful not to localize his stories on the unromantic prairie. There is only one exception: *Í Rauðárdalnum* (1913–22), a mystery story laid in Old Winnipeg. His heroes were strictly ideal heroes in spite of their apparent realism; they were created to raise the spirits of his inferiority-complex-ridden countrymen. Small wonder that the author also wrote a number of fairy tales, of which *Karl litli, saga frá Draumamörk* (Little Charles, a Story from Dream Forest [1918] 1935) was a sort of potpourri. J. M. Bjarnason's books had an engaging simplicity about them which made them as popular as Nonni's books. The secret was the man behind the books: one of his friends described him truly in these words: "He was a good man, good friend, good teacher, good poet."

As a romance writer he was practically unique among his fellow-Icelandic writers, who, since Brandes, had forsworn the form. His *Ritsafn* I–IV was published (1942–50).

Sigurður Júlíus Jóhannesson

Sigurður Júlíus Jóhannesson (1868–1956) was born in Ölfus in the South, but grew up in Borgarfjörður. He worked his way through the Latin School in Reykjavík before he went to America in 1899, where he completed his medical studies in Chicago in 1907. After that he served as a country doctor among his countrymen in Canada, since 1920 in Winnipeg. If the doctor's career was an outlet for Dr. Jóhannesson's all-embracing sympathy for suffering humanity, so was his journalism. As an editor of *Dagskrá* (1898–99), *Lögberg* (1914–1917), and *Voröld* (1918–21) he stood for socialism and pacifism right in the teeth of his countrymen's conscription propaganda for World War I, one of the main supporters of Stephan G. Stephansson's views. In his poems

Sögur og kvæði (Stories and Poems, 1900–1903), *Kvistir* (Twigs, 1910), and the selected *Ljóð* (1950) he was the same intrepid knight errant of humanitarian causes—temperance, socialism, pacifism—whether in compassionate sympathy with the miserable, angry denunciations of the oppressors or in stating the philosophy of his humanitarian endeavor.

Gísli Jónsson

Gísli Jónsson (1876——) was born in Jökuldalsheiði in the East, went to school at Möðruvellir, and emigrated to Winnipeg in 1903, where he lived by the printer's trade with Guðrún H. Finnsdóttir, the short story writer. He collaborated with the Unitarian Reverend Rögnvaldur Pétursson in founding the periodicals *Heimir* (Unitarian) and *Tímarit Þjóðræknisfélags Íslendinga í Vesturheimi* (the organ of the Icelandic National League, 1919——), and succeeded Pétursson as an editor of it in 1940. He also helped to publish the poems of several of his compatriots. His first volume of poems, *Farfuglar* (Birds of Passage, 1919), revealed not only his radical views in church matters, his immigrant's feelings of rootlessness, symbolized by the birds of passage and, to some extent, by his long outlaw narrative poem, but also showed him to be a master of lyric expression and musical form. This is especially clear in his translations of German songs, or in poems composed to fit the music of a master, for Gísli Jónsson was a tenor as well as a poet, and fond of the German and Scandinavian composers. His poem " Móðurmálið " (The Mother Tongue) was in turn set to music by his friend, the Icelandic composer Sveinbjörn Sveinbjörnsson. On his eightieth birthday the poet sent another volume of poems *Fardagar* (Moving Days, 1956) to his friends, his final greetings.

Guttormur J. Guttormsson

Guttormur Jónsson Guttormsson (1878——) is the only one of the American-Icelandic writers to be born in Canada, at Icelandic River (now Riverton), " New Iceland," of parents who escaped from volcanic ashes in the East to succumb to the plagues and hardships of pioneer life. After a youth of reading, toil, and trouble, Guttormur J. Guttormsson succeeded in obtaining his parents' farm (1911) on the edge of the Canadian wilderness, and has lived there ever since, the father of a large family. His life thus in many ways paralleled that of Stephan G. Stephansson and with similar results for his poetry.

He wrote four volumes of poems: *Jón Austfirðingur* (1909), *Bónda-*

dóttir (The Farmer's Daughter, 1920), *Gaman og alvara* (Jest and Earnest, 1930) and *Hunangsflugur* (Bumble Bees, 1944) ; one of short plays, *Tíu leikrit* (Ten Plays, 1930). His poems were collected in a one-volume edition, *Kvæðasafn*, in Iceland in 1947.

Naturally, Guttormur's first poems deal with his memories of the pioneers and their hard life; among these poems " Sandy Bar," describing their graveyard, is outstanding and established his fame as a poet, while a description of an Indian festival records his contact with the neighboring redskins. These first poems showed how steeped he was in the native Icelandic tradition, surprisingly so for one born in America. But he was no less well versed in Anglo-Saxon and, to some extent, European literature. And though he approved the humanitarian-socialistic ideals of Stephan G. Stephansson, as evidenced by anticapitalistic satires like " Bölvun lögmálsins " (The Curse of the Law), he soon discarded the realistic method for the approach of Symbolism learned from Maeterlinck, William Blake, and Poe. Symbolism is found in the poem " Býflugnaræktin " (The Care of the Bees), in which the poet " uses a familiar episode of bee-keeping to adumbrate the spiritual tragedy of his own life " (Watson Kirkconnell). Symbolism is also the hallmark of the semi-mystical plays, where, for instance, the " Ring," in which a lost person walks in the forest, stands for the circle of life. Allegory and dialectic pseudo-rationalism also dominate many of his plays; some are moral, others social or artistic satires, others deal with the great themes of life and death. The motif of a unity seen under dual aspect is also frequent in these plays; thus love and hate, youth and age, life and death, likewise the dual personality exemplified in " Þekktu sjálfan þig " (Know Yourself). An Icelandic theater critic, Lárus Sigurbjörnsson, considered Guttormur to be the best expressionist playwright in Icelandic. Guttormur is quite often a humorist, both in his plays, his poems, and his essays. Like most of his compatriots, he is deeply loyal both to Canada and to Iceland.

He is a master of various metrical forms, from skaldic verse, heavy hexameters, and intricate *rímur* forms to the lightest and most musical meters.

Þorsteinn Þ. Þorsteinsson

Þorsteinn Þ. Þorsteinsson (1879–1955) was born in Svarfaðardalur of literary-minded parents. In 1901 he went to America, settling in Winnipeg as a tradesman. He remained there except for the years

1907–1908, which he spent in Vancouver, B. C., and 1920–21, 1933–37, which he spent in Iceland.

He published two volumes of poetry, *Þættir* (Strains, 1918) and *Heimhugi* (Home Thoughts, 1921), and two literary periodicals, of which *Saga* (1925–30) was notable, containing many of his poems, short stories and sketches. In his poems he experimented with forms, e. g. the sonnet (his *sónháttur*) ; this was true also of his impressionistic prose sketches. Like Þorsteinn Erlingsson and Stephan G. Stephansson he was a radical and wrote social satires, yet he was a loyal Canadian and true to his Icelandic heritage, not least so to its manly heroic spirit.

In his short stories he described the Icelandic immigrant with humor and sympathy, delighted like Jóhann M. Bjarnason in telling about his bravery, and had obviously little use for mothers who told their children to turn the other cheek instead of striking back, Viking-like. His origin in realistic Iceland of the nineties is obvious in his hostile attitude toward the orthodox church.

In Iceland Þ. Þ. Þorsteinsson wrote two remarkable historical works : *Vestmenn, Landnám Íslendinga í Vesturheimi* (Westmen, the Settling of Icelanders in America, 1935) and *Æfintýrið frá Íslandi til Brasilíu* (The Adventure from Iceland to Brazil, 1937–38). On the strength of these excellent works he was commissioned to write a full history of the American-Icelandic settlements, *Saga Íslendinga í Vesturheimi* (1940–1945), but he completed only three volumes of it. The work was completed in two more volumes written by Dr. Tryggvi J. Oleson, professor of history at the University of Manitoba (1951–1953).

Einar Páll Jónsson

Einar Páll Jónsson (1880——) was born in Jökuldalsheiði, a half-brother of Gísli Jónsson. He went to the Latin School in Reykjavík, emigrated to Winnipeg in 1913, and has been an editor of the weekly *Lögberg* since 1917. He was, like his brother, musically inclined and liberal in church allegiance. He wrote two volumes of poetry, *Öræfaljóð* (Songs of the Wilderness, 1915) and *Sólheimar* (Sunny Worlds, 1944).

E. P. Jónsson is an idealist akin in attitude and spirit to the great symbolists of the homeland, Einar Benediktsson, Einar Jónsson (the sculptor) and Matthías Jochumsson, all of whom he celebrates in his poems. His deep love of Iceland finds expression in many poems, *e. g.* " Móðir í austri " (Mother in the East) and the beautiful poem on Jökuldalur, revisited in 1946, as well as in his burning zeal to fight for and keep the Icelandic heritage in the new country.

Páll Bjarnason

Páll Bjarnason (1882——) was born at Mountain, N. D., the only one of the American-Icelandic writers to be born in the United States. His parents hailed from the North and East of Iceland. At twenty-four years of age he went to Canada, homesteading near Wynyard, Saskatchewan. Since 1933 he has lived in Vancouver, B. C. Páll wrote two volumes of poems, *Fleygar* (Wedges, 1953) and *Odes and Echoes* (1954). About half of the first volume are translations into Icelandic, most of the second volume are translations from the Icelandic.

Most of the original poems in Icelandic or English date from the depression years when " ' God is in heaven ' And things are far from right," as the poet tells us. His indignant reaction may not be great poetry though genuine enough. His translations show that he used great poetry as an escape from the evil times. His translations from the Icelandic are most remarkable for the fact that he has attempted to transpose the Icelandic form (alliteration, inrime, assonance) intact into English. This is no easy matter, but I believe that he has often been successful and not least so when most was at stake as in translations of great poems by Stephan G. Stephansson and Einar Benediktsson, both masters of the ornate skaldic form.

Jakobína Johnson

Jakobína Sigurbjörnsdóttir Johnson (1883——) was born in Þingeyjarsýsla of the North, the daughter of the poet Sigurbjörn Jóhannsson (1839–1903), who took his family to Argyle, Manitoba, in 1889. At first a school teacher, she married Ísak Jónsson, brother of the poets Einar Páll and Gísli Jónsson. They moved to Seattle, where she raised a large family and was active in cultural and social affairs, a good speaker on Iceland and other subjects. In 1935 she was invited by the Icelandic Youth League to revisit her homeland.

Like her sister-in-law Guðrún Finnsdóttir, she early began publishing in American-Icelandic periodicals, but her first selection of poems published was *Kertaljós* (Candle Light, 1939), a volume which won acclaim at once for its rare lyric quality and pure beauty, which were to mark her poetry from now on, whether she composed it herself or translated it. Her next collection was *Sá ég svani* (I Saw Swans, 1942), poems for children. Apart from this she translated a number of Icelandic poems in R. Beck's *Icelandic Lyrics* (1930) and *Ice-*

landic Poems and Stories (1943), as well as Martin S. Allwood's *20th Century Scandinavian Poetry* (1950) and three plays: *Lénharður fógeti*, by E. H. Kvaran, *Galdra-Loftur*, by Jóhann Sigurjónsson, and *Nýjársnóttin*, by Indriði Einarsson.

As already stated, pure limpid language and lyric quality mark all of Jakobína Johnson's poetry; she is really a songbird, and it is only natural that she should sing of birds. Children are another favorite theme, not only in the second volume which is marked " for children," but also in her first; her mother's heart is also often occupied with the home and the hearth. She is thoroughly American and proud of it (*cf.* her use of the adjective *amerísk* about her friend Sylvia) ; she is content and happy, and does not brood about the immigrant's lot as did her sister-in-law Guðrún H. Finnsdóttir. Yet the manly figures of the sagas have a romantic lure for her, Icelandic place-names string themselves into beads of pearls, and the tempo of the *vikivaki* tempts her. No wonder that she likes to go back to Iceland and send her friends there.

Guðrún Helga Finnsdóttir

Guðrún Helga Finnsdóttir (1884–1946) was born of a family of poets in Skriðdalur of the East. She went to Winnipeg in 1904 as the wife of the printer and poet Gísli Jónsson. They had a good-sized family and took an active part in the social life of their compatriots. Having raised her family, she began writing short stories for newspapers and the *Tímarit Þjóðræknisfélags Íslendinga* in Winnipeg, edited first by a friend, later by her husband.

Her stories were published in *Hillingalönd* (Enchanted Lands, 1938) and in *Dagshríðar spor* (Tracks of Day's Struggle, 1946), and some of her essays and talks in *Ferðalok* (Journey's End, 1950), a memorial volume published after her death by her husband.

Her stories deal with the American scene, from the point of view of the immigrant still rooted in the old country. She is loyal to her new home, but cannot help seeing the uneven bargain of the immigrant, who for the new land gives himself, body and soul, and his children for a thousand generations. This inexorable fate is always at the back of her mind. But there is a lot more to these stories than that. She despises hypocrisy and in church matters prefers Unitarianism to orthodoxy. She knows how split her countrymen were in the face of World

War I and how united they were against Hitler's totalitarianism during World War II.

In some of her latest stories, e. g., " Frá kynslóð til kynslóðar " (From Generation to Generation), she voices her heartfelt belief in the heritage of the race, a heritage passed from parent to child, whether the parties approve of it or not. She gives examples of how the Icelandic-Nordic heritage still can assert itself in people who would not have regretted abandoning it long ago. Thus the authoress, in spite of all, tries to save her dearest native values.

Bibliography

Old Icelandic Literature

Jón Þorkelsson. *Om Digtningen på Island i det 15. og 16. Århundrede*, Köbenhavn, 1888.

Finnur Jónsson. *Den oldnorske og oldislandske litteraturs historie*, I-III, Köbenhavn, 1894–1902, 2nd ed., 1920–24.

Eugen Mogk. *Geschichte der norwegischen-isländischen Literatur*, Strassburg, 2nd ed., 1904 (*Grundriss der germanischen Philologie*).

William Paton Ker. *Epic and Romance*, London, 1897, 2nd ed., 1908.

Fredrik Paasche. *Kristendom og kvad*, Kristiania, 1914.

Bertha S. Phillpotts. *The Elder Edda and Ancient Scandinavian Drama*, Cambridge, 1920.

Henry G. Leach. *Angevin Britain and Scandinavia*, Cambridge, Mass., 1921.

Gustav Neckel. *Die altnordische Literatur*, Leipzig, 1923.

Andreas Heusler. *Die altgermanische Dichtung*, Potsdam, 1924, 2nd ed., 1941.

Fredrik Paasche. *Norges og Islands litteratur indtil utgangen av middelalderen*, Kristiania, 1924.

Erik Noreen. *Den norsk-isländska poesien*, Stockholm, 1926.

Knut Liestöl. *The Origin of the Icelandic Family Sagas*, Oslo, 1930 (Instituttet for sammenlignende kulturforskning).

Halvdan Koht. *The Old Norse Sagas*, New York, 1931.

Bertha S. Phillpotts. *Edda and Saga*, New York, 1931 (*Home University Library*).

H. Munro and N. (Kershaw) Chadwick. *The Growth of Literature*, I-III, Cambridge, 1932–40.

Margaret Schlauch. *Romance in Iceland*, New York, 1934.

Björn K. Þórólfsson. *Rímur fyrir 1600*, Kaupmannahöfn, 1934 (*Safn fræðafélagsins*).

Jón Helgason. *Norrön litteraturhistorie*, Köbenhavn, 1934.

Jan de Vries. *Altnordische Literaturgeschichte*, I-II, Berlin, 1941–42 (*Grundriss der germanischen Philologie*).

Sigurður Nordal. *Íslenzk menning* I, Reykjavík, 1942.

Lee M. Hollander. *The Skalds*, New York, 1945.

Sigurður Nordal and Jón Helgason. *Litteratur-historie*, B, Norge og Island, Stockholm, 1953 (*Nordisk Kultur*).

G. Turville-Petre. *Origins of Icelandic Literature*, Oxford, 1953.

Origins, Culture

Bogi Th. Melsteð. "Ferðir, siglingar og samgöngur milli Íslands og annara landa á dögum þjóðveldisins," *Safn til sögu Íslands*, Kaupmannahöfn og Reykjavík, 1912–14.

Guðmundur Hanneson. *Körpermasse und Körperproportionen der Isländer,* Reykjavík, 1925 (*Árbók Háskóla Íslands*).

A. W. Brögger. *Den norske bosetning på Shetland,* Oslo, 1930.

Þorkell Jóhannesson. *Die Stellung der freien Arbeiter in Island bis zur Mitte des 16. Jahrhunderts,* Reykjavík, 1933.

Jón Steffenssen. "Uppruni Íslendinga," *Samtíð og saga,* Reykjavík, 1946.

Einar Olgeirsson. *Ættasamfélag og ríkisvald í þjóðveldi Íslendinga,* Reykjavík, 1954.

Helmut Arntz. *Handbuch der Runenkunde,* Halle, Saale, 1944.

Eddic Poetry

Eduard Sievers. *Altgermanische Metrik,* Halle, 1893.

Andreas Heusler. *Deutsche Versgeschichte,* Berlin, 1925 (*Grundriss der germanischen Philologie*).

Edwin Jessen. "Über die Eddalieder," *Zeitschrift für deutsche Philologie,* 1871.

Sophus Bugge. *Studier over de nordiske Gude- og Heltesagns Oprindelse,* I, Christiania, 1881–89.

Karl Müllenhoff. *Deutsche Altertumskunde,* V, Berlin, 1883–91.

Björn M. Ólsen. "Hvar eru Eddukvæðin til orðin?" *Tímarit hins íslenzka Bókmenntafélags,* Reykjavík, 1894.

Andreas Heusler. "Heimat und Alter der eddischen Gedichte," *Archiv für das Studium der neueren Sprachen und Literaturen,* 1906.

Henrik Ussing. *Om det indbyrdes Forhold mellem Heltekvadene i ældre Edda,* Köbenhavn, 1910.

Gudmund Schütte. "Nibelungsagnet," *Edda,* 1917.

Sigurður Nordal, editor. *Völuspá,* Reykjavík, 1922–23 (*Árbók Háskóla Íslands*), 2nd printing in 8vo, 1952.

Hugo Pipping. "Eddastudier" I–IV, *Studier i nordisk filologi,* Helsingfors, 1925–30.

Birger Nermann. *The Poetic Edda in the Light of Archaeology,* Coventry, 1931 (Viking Society for Northern Research).

Wolfgang Mohr. "Entstehungsgeschichte und Heimat der jüngeren Eddalieder südgermanischen Stoffes," *Zeitschrift für deutsches Altertum,* 1938–39.

Hans Kuhn. "Westgermanisches in der altnordischen Verskunst," *Beiträge zur Geschichte der deutschen Sprache und Literatur,* 1939.

Barði Guðmundsson. "Uppruni íslenzkrar skáldmenntar," *Helgafell,* Reykjavík, 1942–44.

Fritz Askeberg. *Norden och kontinenten i gammal tid.* Uppsala, 1944.

Axel Olrik. "Om Ragnarok," *Aarböger for nordisk Oldkyndighed,* 1902.

James G. Frazer. *The Golden Bough,* I–XII, London, 1911–15. In the abridged one volume edition, New York, 1922 (and later editions), chapter LXI is entitled "The Myth of Balder," and chapter LXV "Balder and the Mistletoe."

Gustav Neckel. *Die Überlieferung vom Gotte Balder,* Dortmund, 1920.

Franz Rolf Schröder. *Germanentum und Hellenismus,* Heidelberg, 1924.

Magnus Olsen. "Trollruner," *Edda,* 1916.

Magnus Olsen. "Fra Eddaforskningen. Grímnismál og den höiere tekstkritikk," *Arkiv för nordisk filologi,* 1933. Both articles in *Norröne Studier,* Oslo, 1938.

Dag Strömbäck. *Sejd,* Uppsala, 1935.

Karl Bruhn. "Mysteriös utbildning och undervisning i Norden under hedna tiden," *Festskrift tillägnad B. Rud Hall,* Stockholm, 1946.

Stefán Einarsson. "Alternate Recital by Twos in *Widsíþ* (?), *Sturlunga*, and *Kalevala*," *Arv*, 1951.

Hans Kuhn. "Heldensage vor und ausserhalb der Dichtung," *Edda, Skalden, Saga*. Festschrift . . . Felix Genzmer, Heidelberg, 1952.

Didrik Arup Seip. "Har nordmenn skrevet opp Edda-diktningen?" *Maal og Minne*, 1951. Also: "On the Original of the Codex Regius of the Elder Edda," *Studies in Honor of A. M. Sturtevant*, Lawrence, Kansas, 1952.

Hans Kuhn. "Die norwegischen Spuren in der Lieder Edda," *Acta Philologica Scandinavica*, 1952.

Skaldic Poetry

Sophus Bugge. *Bidrag til den ældste Skaldedigtnings Historie*, Christiania, 1894.

Rudolf Meissner. *Die Kenningar der Skalden*, Bonn, 1921.

Jan de Vries. *De skaldenkenningen mit mytologischen inhoud*, Haarlem, 1934.

Jan de Vries. "Een skald onder de troubadours," *Verslagen en Mededelingen der Kon. Vlaamschen Academie*, 1938–39.

Ove Moberg. "Den fornnordiska skaldedikningens uppkomst," *Acta Philologica Scandinavica*, 1943.

Åke Ohlmarks. "Till frågan om den fornnordiska skaldediktningens ursprung," *Arkiv för nordisk filologi*, 1943.

Jón Helgason and Anne Holtsmark. *Háttalykill enn forni*, Köbenhavn, 1941 (*Bibliotheca Arnamagnaeana*).

Einar Ól. Sveinsson. "Dróttkvæða þáttur," *Skírnir*, Reykjavík, 1947.

Hallvard Lie, "Skaldestil-Studier," *Maal og Minne*, 1952.

Stefán Einarsson. "The Origin of Egill Skallagrímsson's *Runhenda*," *Scandinavica et Fenno-Ugrica. Studier tillägnade Björn Collinder*, Stockholm, 1954.

Poetry of the Later Middle Ages: Sacred and Secular

Eiríkr Magnússon, editor and translator. *Lilja* (*The Lily*), London, 1870.

Guðbrandur Jónsson, editor. *Lilja*, Reykjavík, 1933. 2nd ed. 1951.

Einar Ól. Sveinsson. "Íslenzk sálmaþýðing (Heilags anda vísur)" *Skírnir*, Reykjavík, 1942.

Gunnar Finnbogason. "Var bróðir Eysteinn í Þykkvabæ höfundur Lilju?" *A góðu dægri. Afmæliskveðja til S. Nordals*, Reykjavík, 1951.

Stefán Einarsson. "Icelandic Popular Poetry of the Middle Ages," *Philologica. The Malone Anniversary Studies*, Baltimore, 1949, and *Skírnir*, Reykjavík, 1949.

Björn K. Þórólfsson. "Dróttkvætt og rímur," *Skírnir*, Reykjavík, 1950.

Stefán Einarsson. "Íslenzk helgikvæði á miðöldum," *Tímarit Þjóðræknisfélags Íslendinga*, Winnipeg, 1954 (contains bad printer's errors).

The Sagas

Björn M. Ólsen. *Om den saakaldte Sturlunga Prolog*, Christiania, 1910 (*Christiania Videnskabs-Selskabs Forhandlinger*).

Andreas Heusler. *Die Anfänge der isländischen Saga*, Berlin, 1913 (*Abhandlungen der kgl. preuss. Akademie der Wissenschaften*).

Sigurður Nordal. *Snorri Sturluson*, Reykjavík, 1920.

Halldór Hermannsson, editor and translator. *Íslendingabók*, Ithaca, N. Y., 1930 (*Islandica*).

Pétur Sigurðsson. "Um Íslendinga sögu Sturlu Þórðarsonar," *Safn til sögu Íslands*, Reykjavík, 1933–35.

Einar Ól. Sveinsson. *Sagnaritun Oddaverja*, Reykjavík, 1937 (*Studia Islandica*).

Björn M. Ólsen. "Um Íslendingasögur," *Safn til sögu Íslands*, Reykjavík, 1937–39.

Sigurður Nordal. *Sturla Þórðarson og Grettis saga*, Reykjavík, 1938 (*Studia Islandica*).

Sigurður Nordal. *Hrafnkatla*, Reykjavík, 1940 (*Studia Islandica*).

Jón Jóhannesson. *Gerðir Landnámabókar*, Reykjavík, 1941.

Sigurður Nordal. "Snorri Sturluson. Nokkrar hugleiðingar á 700 ára ártíð hans" (A supplement to *Snorri Sturluson* 1920), *Skírnir*, Reyjavík, 1941.

Sven B. F. Jansson. *Sagorna om Vinland*, Stockholm, 1945 (*Kungl. Vitterhets Historie och Antikvitets Akademiens Handlingar*).

Barði Guðmundsson. "Stefnt að höfundi Njálu," *Andvari*, Reykjavík, 1950.

Barði Guðmundsson. *Gerfinöfn í Ölkofraþætti*, Reykjavík, 1951.

Lárus Blöndal. "Grýla (i. e. Sverris saga)," *Á góðu dægri. Afmæliskveðja til Sigurðar Nordals*, Reykjavík, 1951.

Jón Jóhannesson. "Tímatal Gerlands í íslenzkum ritum frá þjóðveldisöld," *Skírnir*, Reykjavík, 1952.

Modern Icelandic Literature

J. C. Poestion. *Isländische Dichter der Neuzeit*, Leipzig, 1897.

Halldór Hermannsson. *Icelandic Books of the Sixteenth Century*, Ithaca, N. Y., 1916 (*Islandica*).

Halldór Hermannsson. *The Periodic Literature of Iceland . . . to 1874*, Ithaca, N. Y., 1918 (*Islandica*).

Páll E. Ólason. *Menn og menntir siðskiftaaldar* I–IV (especially IV), Reykjavík, 1919–26.

Arne Möller. *Hallgrímur Péturssons Passionssalmer*, Köbenhavn, 1922.

Magnús Jónsson. *Hallgrímur Pétursson*, Reykjavík, 1947.

Halldór Hermannsson. *Eggert Ólafsson*, Ithaca, N. Y., 1925 (*Islandica*).

Arne Möller. *Jón Vídalín og hans Postil*, Odense, 1929.

Páll E. Ólason. *Saga Íslendinga, IV Sextánda öld*, Reykjavík, 1944.

———. *Saga Íslendinga, V Seytjánda öld*, Reykjavík, 1942.

———. og Þorkell Jóhannesson, *Saga Íslendinga, VI Tímabilið 1701–70*, Reykjavík, 1943.

Þorkell Jóhannesson. *Saga Íslendinga, VII Tímabilið 1770–1830*, Reykjavík, 1950.

Jónas Jónsson. *Saga Íslendinga, VIII Tímabilið 1830–1874*, Reykjavík, 1955.

Stefán Einarsson. *History of Icelandic Prose Writers 1800–1940*, Ithaca, N. Y., 1948 (*Islandica*).

———. *Skáldaþing*, Reykjavík, 1948.

Richard Beck. *History of Icelandic Poets 1800–1940*, Ithaca, N. Y., 1950 (*Islandica*).

Kristinn E. Andrésson. *Íslenzkar nútímabókmenntir 1918–1948*, Reykjavík, 1949.

Bjarni M. Gíslason. *Islands Litteratur efter Sagatiden, ca. 1400–1948*, Köbenhavn, 1949.

Stefán Einarsson. "Halldór Kiljan Laxness Nóbelsverðlaunahöfundur," *Tímarit Þjóðræknisfélags Íslendinga*, Winnipeg, Man., 1956.

Peter Hallberg. *Den store vävaren*, Stockholm, 1954.

Editions

Sophus Bugge; *Norrœn fornkvæði . . . Sæmundar Edda*, Christiania, 1867.

B. Sijmons and Hugo Gering. *Die Lieder der Edda*, I–III, Halle, 1906–31 (*Germanistische Handbibliothek*).

Gustav Neckel. *Edda*, Heidelberg, 1914 (*Germanische Bibliothek*).
Gudbrand Vigfusson and F. York Powell. *Corpus Poeticum Boreale*, I–II, Oxford, 1883.
Finnur Jónsson. *Den norsk-islandske Skjaldedigtning*, IAB–IIAB, Köbenhavn, 1912–15.
Ernst A. Kock. *Den norsk-isländska skaldediktningen*, I–II, Lund, 1946–49.
Einar Munksgaard. *Corpus Codicum Islandicorum Medii Ævi*, I–XX, Köbenhavn, 1930–55 (facsimile edition of manuscripts).
Jón Helgason. *Manuscripta Islandica* I–II, Köbenhavn, 1955–56 (in continuation of the preceding).
Sigurður Nordal. *Íslenzk fornrit*, Reykjavík, 1933–54 (13 vols., best edition).
Guðni Jónsson (and others). *Íslendingasagnaútgáfan*, Reykjavík, 1946–50 (34 vols. containing: *Íslendingasögur, Sturlunga saga, Byskupa sögur, Annálar, Snorra* and *Sæmundar Eddur, Riddara sögur, Fornaldar sögur, Karlamagnúss saga, Þiðriks saga*; more to come).
Guðbrand Vigfusson and F. York Powell. *Origines Islandicae*, I–II, Oxford, 1905 (sagas in original and translation).
Gudbrand Vigfusson. *Sturlunga Saga*, I–II, Oxford, 1878.
Kristian Kaalund. *Sturlunga saga*, I–II, Köbenhavn, 1906–11.
Jón Jóhannesson (and others). *Sturlunga saga*, I–II, Reykjavík, 1946.
Guðbrandur Vigfússon. *Biskupa sögur*, I–II, Kaupmannahöfn, 1858–78.
Jón Helgason. *Byskupa sögur*, I hefte, Köbenhavn, 1938 (incomplete).
Jón Þorkelsson. *Kvæðasafn frá miðöldum*, Reykjavík, 1922–27.
Jón Helgason. *Íslenzk miðaldakvæði*, I–II, Köbenhavn, 1936–38 (incomplete).
Svend Grundtvig og Jón Sigurðsson. *Íslenzk fornkvæði*, Köbenhavn, 1835–38, 1885.
Ólafur Briem. *Fornir dansar*, Reykjavík, 1946.
Jón Árnason. *Íslenzkar þjóðsögur og æfintýri*, I–II, Leipzig, 1862–64; 2nd ed. Reykjavík 1925–39; 3rd ed. *ibid.* 1954.
Jón Árnason and Ólafur Davíðsson. *Íslenskar gátur, skemtanir, vikivakar og þulur*, Kaupmannahöfn, 1887–1903.

Anthologies

Sigurður Nordal. *Íslenzk lestrarbók 1400–1900*, Reykjavík, 1924.
———. *Íslenzk lestrarbók 1750–1930*, Reykjavík, 1930; 3rd ed. 1942.
Sigurður Nordal, Guðrún P. Helgadóttir og Jón Jóhannesson, *Sýnisbók íslenzkra bókmennta til miðrar átjándu aldar*, Reykjavík, 1953.
Einar Ól. Sveinsson, Páll E. Ólason, Snorri Hjartarson, Arnór Sigurjónsson og Tómas Guðmundsson. *Íslands þúsund ár*, I–III, Reykjavík, 1947.
Sir William A. Craigie. *Sýnisbók íslenzkra rímna (Specimens of the Icelandic Metrical Romances*, I–III), London, 1952.

TRANSLATIONS

Anthologies of Old Icelandic Literature

A Pageant of Old Scandinavia. Ed. by Henry Goddard Leach, New York (ASF), 1946.
Old Norse Poems. The most important Non-Skaldic Verse. Tr. by Lee M. Hollander, New York, 1936.
The Skalds. A Selection by Lee M. Hollander, New York (ASF), 1945.

The Eddas

The Poetic Edda. Tr. by Henry Adams Bellows, New York (ASF), 1923.
The Poetic Edda. Tr. by Lee M. Hollander, Austin, Texas, 1928.
The Prose Edda. Tr. by Arthur G. Brodeur, New York (ASF), 1916.
The Prose Edda. Tr. by Jean I. Young. Introd. by Sigurður Nordal, Cambridge, 1954.

Sacred Poetry

Lilja (The Lily), by Eysteinn Ásgrímsson. Ed. and tr. by Eiríkr Magnússon, London, 1870.
Icelandic Meditations on the Passion. Selections from the Passion-Hymns of Hallgrím Pétursson. Tr. by Charles V. Pilcher, New York, 1923.

The Sagas: Collections

The Saga Library. Tr. by William Morris and Eiríkr Magnússon, I–VI, London, 1891–1905. Contains *Hávarðar saga, Bandamanna saga, Hœnsa-Þóris saga, Eyrbyggja saga, Heiðarvíga saga, Heimskringla.*
Origines Islandicae. Ed. and tr. by Gudbrand Vigfusson and F. York Powell, I–II, Oxford, 1905. Contains *Landnámabók, Íslendingabók, Kristni saga, Hungrvaka, Þorláks saga biskups, Páls saga biskups, Jóns saga biskups, Hœnsa-Þóris saga, Harðar saga, Eyrbyggja saga, Laxdœla saga, Gísla saga, Hávarðar saga, Vatnsdœla saga, Kormáks saga, Ljósvetninga saga, Víga-Glúms saga, Hrafnkels saga, Droplaugarsona saga, Eiríks saga rauða, (= Grœnlendinga saga), Þorfinns saga karlsefnis (= Eiríks saga rauða), Flóamanna saga, Fóstbrœðra saga, Grœnlendinga þáttr.*
The Saga of the Volsungs and the Saga of Ragnar Lodbrok. Tr. by Margaret Schlauch, New York (ASF), 1930.
Four Icelandic Sagas. Tr. by Gwyn Jones, New York (ASF), 1935. Contains *Hrafnkels saga, Þorsteins saga hvíta, Vápnfirðinga saga, Kjalnesinga saga.*
Voyages to Vinland. Tr. by Einar Haugen, New York, 1942. Contains *Eiríks saga rauða* (alias *Þorfinns saga karlsefnis*), *Grœnlendinga saga* (alias *Eiríks saga rauða*), *Grœnlendinga þáttr.*
The Sagas of Kormák and the Sworn Brothers. Tr. by Lee M. Hollander, New York (ASF), 1949.
Three Icelandic Sagas. Tr. by M. H. Scargill and Margaret Schlauch, New York (ASF), 1950. Contains *Gunnlaugs saga* (Scargill), *Bandamanna saga, Droplaugarsona saga* (Schlauch).

Individual Sagas

Heimskringla. Tr. by Samuel Laing, London (1951) (*Everyman's L.* 2 Vols.).
Heimskringla. Tr. (from the Norwegian) by Erling Monsen and A. H. Smith, Cambridge, 1932 (illustrated with maps).
The Saga of Grettir the Strong. Tr. by George A. Hight, London (1914) (*Everyman's L.* 699).
The Laxdœla saga. Tr. by Thorstein Veblen, New York, 1925.
Egil's Saga. Tr. by E. R. Eddison, Cambridge, 1930.
The Saga of Gísli Son of Sour. Tr. by Ralph B. Allen, New York, 1936.
The Vatnsdalers' Saga. Tr. by Gwyn Jones, New York (ASF), 1944.

The Story of Burnt Njal. Tr. by George W. Dasent, London (1949) (*Everyman's L.* 558 or 426).

Njál's Saga. Tr. by Carl F. Bayerschmidt and Lee M. Hollander, New York (ASF), 1955.

The Saga of the Jómsvíkings. Tr. by Lee M. Hollander, Austin, Texas, 1955.

The Life of Gudmund the Good Bishop of Holar. Tr. by G. Turville-Petre and E. S. Olszewska, Coventry, 1942 (The Viking Society for Northern Research).

The Saga of Hrafn Sveinbjarnarson. Tr. by Anne Tjomsland, Ithaca N. Y., 1951 (*Islandica*).

Full bibliographies of the Eddas, the Sagas of the Icelanders, the Kings' Sagas, and the Mythical-Heroic Sagas are found in *Islandica* from 1908 onwards, by Halldór Hermannsson and Jóhann S. Hannesson.

Anthologies of Modern Icelandic Literature

Icelandic Lyrics. Originals and Translations. Ed. Richard Beck, Reykjavík, 1930.

The North American Book of Icelandic Verse. Tr. by Watson Kirkconnell, New York, 1930.

Icelandic Poems and Stories. Ed. Richard Beck, New York (ASF), 1943.

20th Century Scandinavian Poetry. 1900–1950. Ed. by Martin S. Allwood, Mullsjö 1950 (the part on Iceland by Stefán Einarsson).

Odes and Echoes. By Paul Bjarnason, Vancouver, Canada, 1954 (notable translations in original meters).

Modern Poetry

Einar Benediktsson. *Harp of the North.* Transl. by Frederick T. Wood, Charlottesville, Va., 1955.

Modern Prose

Icelandic Legends. Collected by Jón Árnason. Tr. by George E. T. Powell and Eiríkr Magnússon, I-II, London, 1864–1866.

Modern Novels

Jón Svensson. *Nonni and Manni,* Dublin, 1929.

Guðmundur Kamban. *The Virgin of Skalholt.* Tr. by Evelyn Ramsden, Boston, 1935.

———. *I see a Wondrous Land,* New York, 1938.

Gunnar Gunnarsson. *Guest the One-Eyed,* London (1920).

———. *The Sworn Brothers,* London (1920).

———. *Seven Days' Darkness.* Tr. by Roberts Tapley, New York, 1930.

———. *The Night and the Dream.* Tr. by Evelyn Ramsden, Indianapolis, 1938.

———. *Ships in the Sky.* Tr. by Evelyn Ramsden, Indianapolis, 1938.

———. *The Good Shepherd.* Tr. by Kenneth C. Kaufman, Indianapolis, 1940.

Kristmann Guðmundsson. *The Bridal Gown.* Tr. by O. F. Theis, New York, 1931.

———. *Morning of Life.* Tr. by Elizabeth Sprigge and Claude Napier, New York, 1936.

———. *Winged Citadel.* Tr. by Barrows Mussey, New York, 1940.

Halldór (Kiljan) Laxness. *Salka-Valka.* Tr. by F. H. Lyons, Boston, 1936.

———. *Independent People.* Tr. by J. A. Thompson, New York, 1946.

Modern Plays

Jóhann Sigurjónsson. *Modern Icelandic Plays*. Eyvind of the Hills. The Hraun Farm. Tr. by Henninge Krohn Schanche, New York (ASF), 1916.

————. *Loftur: A Play*. Tr. by Jean Young and Eleanor Arkwright, Reading, 1939.

Guðmundur Kamban. *Hadda-Padda. A Drama*. Tr. by Sadie Luise Peller, Foreword by Georg Brandes, New York, 1917.

Tryggvi Sveinbjörnsson. *Bishop Jón Arason*. Tr. by Lee M. Hollander in *Modern Scandinavian Plays*, New York (ASF), 1954.

On Pronunciation

A few hints about the pronunciation of Icelandic names may not be out of order. They are all stressed on the *first* syllable, but unstressed syllables are never as weak as in English and vowels retain their quality in them.

Most of the vowels sound like English vowels: *a* as in f*a*ther; *á* as in c*o*w; *i*, *y* as in s*i*t; *í*, *ý* as in mach*i*ne; *o* as in l*a*w; *ó* as in n*o*te; *ú* as in sch*oo*l; *æ* (*œ*) as in *i*ce; *ei*, *ey* as in *ei*ght. *U* is slightly similar to German M*ü*tter, *ö* as in German h*ö*ren, and *au* as in French f*eui*lle.

Icelandic consonants are often quite different from their English counterparts. Thus *fn* is pronounced *bn*, *ll* pronounced *dl* after vowels and between vowels: *Höfn* (höbn), *Hafnir*; *Höll* (hödl) *Hallir*. Similarly *Sveinn* (sveidn). At the end of words *bn*, *dn*, *dl* are completely voiceless.

H is a strong breath (rough breathing, Greek *spiritus asper*) not only as in English before vowels and semivowels: *how*, *hue*, *what* (cp. Icelandic *hár*, *hjör*, *hvatur*) but also before the consonants *l*, *n*, *r*: *Hlíð*, *Hnöttur*, *Hrafn*. The *hl* is similar to Welsh *Ll* in *Lloyd*.

J has always the sound of *y* in *y*es, even in *Björn*. *K* is pronounced before *n* in *Knútur*. *R* is trilled as in Scottish. *Z* and *s* are both as in *s*un, never as in ea*s*y. The Old English letters *ð* and *þ* are preserved only in Icelandic; *þ* is like *th* in *th*in; *ð* like *th* in brea*th*e.

But it is impossible to give an idea of Icelandic pronunciation in a few short paragraphs. Those who are interested can be referred to my *Icelandic: Grammar, Texts, Glossary*, Baltimore, The Johns Hopkins Press, 1956; to be had from the publishers, Baltimore 18, Md., U. S. A.

This is an index of historical and fictitious persons, Icelandic place names, titles of books (works) in Italics, titles of stories, poems, and articles hyphenated, a list of first lines in Italics (or hyphenated) marked with an asterisk. Literary topics and folklore motifs are also well indexed here.

Icelandic personal names are mostly made up of a given name and a patronymic: Snorri Sturluson (son of Sturla), Guðrún Finnsdóttir (daughter of Finnur), but there are a few family names: Sigurður (Jóhannesson) Nordal. In Iceland the given (first) name is always used in address and reference, never the patronymic (Jóhannesson) but sometimes the family name (Nordal).

In non-Icelandic bibliographies this custom is usually respected up to 1500: Snorri Sturluson, but Finnsdóttir, Guðrún, Jóhannesson, Sigurður or Nordal, Sigurður. In this index all persons are listed Icelandic fashion under the given name: Sigurður Jóhannesson Nordal, but after 1550 there is a reference from the patronymic or the family name to the given name: Jóhannesson or Nordal. *See* Sigurður.

Old Icelandic spellings and forms are used in this book up to 1550, after that modern Icelandic orthography and forms. Most conspicuous is the ending *-r* which becomes *-ur*, the small words *at, ok, ek* becoming *að, og, eg* or *ég*. Other differences are seen in *Álptafjörðr, bœr, Eyrr, Gizurr, Loptr, Mária* becoming *Álftafjörður, bær, Eyri, Gissur, Loftur, María*. A complete normalization along these lines, is, however, not attained.

A few errors in capitalization and accents have been corrected in the index. On p. 52 "edition" of *Eyrbyggja* should read "translation," on p. 72 "*versus*" Lucifer, "*verus*" L., on p. 79 *Officium* "Thorlacii," O. "Thorlaci" and on p. 163 "Tróju" saga should read "Trójumanna" saga.

Index

Spencer, Herbert, 251
Sperðill (Ger. *Hanswurst*), 212
Spezar-þáttr, 145, 149
Spielmannslied, 20
" spirit in matter," 267
spiritualism, 246, 252, 262, 263, 273, 283, 302, 304, 352
spiritualistic, 281, 289, 298
spjör (spear), 53
Spoon River Anthology, 338
Spor í sandi (Tracks in the Sand), 324
sports, and pastimes, 256
spott (slander, lampoon), 38, 85. *See also* lampoon
" Sprengisandur," 239
*Stabat mater dolorosa, 80, 81, 188, 201. *See also* meter
Staðarbakki, 173
Staðarhóll, 110
Staðarhóls-Páll. *See* Páll Jónsson
Staðarhraun, 282
stafhent, 87
stage craft, 273
stallari (Marshal), 62
standard of living, 207
stanza: *40–41*, 42, 92; artificial, 52; asymmetrical, 80; complexity of, 187; dance, 92; form, 88; four-line, 86; half (*helmingr*) 50; introductory, 89, 92; quatrain, 85; riming, 188; sequence, 80; symmetrical, 80; three-line, 86–87; three-part form, 80; two-line, 86, 87; variation of sentences in, 66; whole, 50
Starkaðr the Old, 51, 160. *Cf. Saxo* and *Heimskringla*
" Stássmeyjarkvæði " (Ballad on a Fair Lady), 201
State Broadcasting, 334
State Office of Statistics, 315
statuary, 190
stay-at-homes, 169
stef (refrain), 52, 59, 92. *See also stef-stofn, viðlag*
Stefán Einarsson, 293
Stefán frá Hvítadal. *See* Stefán Sigurðsson frá Hvítadal
Stefán Hörður Grímsson, 333
Stefán [Jónsson], bishop of Skálholt, 264
Stefán Jónsson, novelist, 292
Stefán Júlíusson (pen name: Sveinn Auðunn Sveinsson), 334
Stefán Ólafsson, 52, 80, 185, 186, 188, 189, 190, 191, 192, 194, 195, 197, *199–202*, 217, 242, 262
Stefán (Sigurðsson) frá Hvítadal, 290, 291, *299–300*, 302, 304, 306, 324
Stefánsson. *See* Davíð, Halldór, Helgi, Jón, Kristinn, Magnús, Sigurður, Þorsteinn
Steffens, Henrik, 221, 231
Steffensen, Jón, 5
stef-stofn (refrain-stem), 92, 187. *See also stef, viðlag*

Steinbeck, John E., 330
Steingerðr, 60
Steingrímsson. *See* Jón
Steingrímur (Bjarnason) Thorsteinsson, 226, 227, 228, 241, *243–44*, 245, 246, 260, 345
Steingrímur J. Þorsteinsson, 237, 267, 335
Steinn Steinarr. *See* Aðalsteinn Kristmundsson
" Steins-biblía," 173
Steinunn, daughter of Hallgrímur Pétursson, 188, 198
Steinunn Finnsdóttir í Höfnum, 188
Stella, 218
Stephan G. Stephansson (Stefán Guðmundarson), 251, 254, 269, 289, 299, 322, 340, *342–44*, 346, 347, 348, 349, 350, 351, 352
Stephansson. *See* Gestur, Stephan G.
Stephensen. *See* Magnús
stepmothers, 165, 166, 167
Stevenson, Robert Louis, 347
Stiklarstaðr, 63
stinginess, 160
" Stjáni blái " (poem on a fisherman hero), 295
Stjórn, 171
" Stjörnufákur " (Star Steed), 312
Stjörnu-Oddi, 97
Stjörnur vorsins (Stars of Spring), 316
Stolnar stundir (Stolen Hours), 323
Stóramörk, 260
storms, magic, 166
" Stormur," 265
story: adventure, 129, 225; animal, 235, 254, 257, 258, 261; best short, 137–38; crime, 286; detective, 225; fishing, 333; ghost, 149, 157; horror, 239, 295, 306; love, 146, 236; lying, 129; mock-adventure, 191; mystery, 348; oriental, 261, 307; outlaw, 142, 239, 248; troll, 149, 157. *See also lygi sögur*, skaldic
storytellers, 126, 158
Strandir, 296
Strauss, David Friedrich, 250
Strengleikar (Marie de France's Breton Lays), 162
Strengleikar (Melodies), by Guðmundur Guðmundsson, 276
stress, 48, 86, 175
Strindberg, J. A., 193, 251, 267, 286, 291, 317
Strjúgur, 185
Strömbäck, Dag, 25
stuðlafall, 86, 87, 88
*Stuðlafalls þó stofna gjöri eg rímu, 87
stuðlar (staves, props), 40, 48, 50
stúfar (masculine endings), 66
Stund milli stríða (A Moment between Wars), 338
Sturla í Vogum, 310
Sturla Sighvatsson, 144, 155
Sturla Þórðarson, 64, 108, 109, 112, *120–21*, 138, 149, 154, 155, 156, 158